The Fundamentals of Adverti   HWBI

The Voice of British Advertisers

Published in association with the ISBA.

The Incorporated Society of British Advertisers (ISBA) represents £6.5 billion of marketing communications spend and is the single body, within the UK, to represent advertisers' interests across all marketing communications disciplines. Founded almost 100 years ago, ISBA's fundamental remit is vigorously to promote and protect the interests of British advertisers. By acting as their 'voice', ISBA influences Government, the media, agencies, consultants, suppliers and other bodies in the marketing communications industry to help create and sustain an environment that maximizes the effectiveness of its members' marketing activities.

The Fundamentals of Advertising

Second Edition

John Wilmshurst, MA, FCAM, FCInstM

and

Adrian Mackay, BSc (Hons), DipM, MCIM, MBA

OXFORD AUCKLAND BOSTON JOHANNESBURG MELBOURNE NEW DELHI

Butterworth-Heinemann
Linacre House, Jordan Hill, Oxford OX2 8DP
225 Wildwood Avenue, Woburn, MA 01801-2041
A division of Reed Educational and Professional Publishing Ltd

 A member of the Reed Elsevier plc group

First published 1985
Reprinted 1986, 1988, 1990, 1991, 1992, 1993, 1995, 1997, 1998
Second edition 1999

British Library Cataloguing in Publication Data
A catalogue record for this book is available from the British Library

Library of Congress Cataloguing in Publication Data
A catalogue record for this book is available from the Library of Congress

ISBN 0 7506 1562 1

Typeset by Avocet Typeset, Brill, Aylesbury, Bucks
Printed and bound in Great Britain by Biddles Ltd,
Guildford and King's Lynn

Contents

Part 1   What advertising is about

Part 2   How the advertising business functions

Part 3   How advertising works in detail

Part 4   Advertising internationally

List of plates

The following can be found in the colour plate section located between pages 80 and 81:

Preface to second edition

When considering a second edition, an obvious question was, how much does the book need to be changed? The answer seemed to me to be a split one. Basic principles, not at all. My view on this was confirmed in an interview (*The Times*, 24 April 1998) with Chris Powell, 'who heads BMP–DDB, recently voted Britain's most successful agency by the industry ...' Asked whether advertising has changed much during his thirty years at the top, he replied, 'Actually, I don't think advertising has changed at all.' So there is much in this new edition that is the same – but a lot, too, that is different. Facts and figures have been updated wherever possible, but also massive changes in the way advertising is carried out, as distinct from how it is planned and created, are reflected. The chapters on the media now cover all the new developments, such as satellite television and the Internet. The chapter on printing methods has been totally rewritten in the light of the computer revolution which has come so far in such a short time. Also updated considerably are the international chapters, to acknowledge great developments in the worldwide promotion of global brands. Finally, new case histories and illustrations demonstrate contemporary ways of expression.

Acknowledgements are due to all the people who helped with the first edition, but in addition to Deborah Morrison of ISBA (the Incorporated Society of British Advertisers), under whose banner the book is now being published. Also to all the people and companies who helped with illustrations and case histories (listed on page xv).

Particular thanks are due to Mac Mackay, my business associate, friend and co-author of this edition.

Finally, to Tim Goodfellow of Butterworth-Heinemann, who 'stayed with it' patiently while the ISBA connection and all the other elements gradually came together.

John Wilmshurst

Acknowledgements

In preparing this book the following organizations have been very helpful; their courtesy is greatly appreciated:

The Advertising Association
The Advertising Standards Authority (especially for the abridged version of the Code in Chapter 9)
The Incorporated Society of British Advertisers
The Independent Television Companies Association
For permission to reprint the extracts on pages listed below, the author would like to thank the following publishers:

p 106 Associated Business Press, Ludgate House, Fleet Street, London EC4, from *The Business of Advertising* by David Farbey, copyright © 1979. p 374 George Allen & Unwin, from *International Marketing* by S. Majaro, copyright © 1977. pp 59, 60, 191, 198 from *Advertising* by Kenneth A. Longman, copyright © 1971 by Harcourt Brace Jovanovich, Inc., reprinted by permission of the publisher. p 69 NTC Publications, from *Accountable Advertising* by S. Broadbent, copyright © 1997. pp 71 reprinted by permission of Macmillan Publishing Company, from *Offensive Marketing* by J. H. Davidson, originally published by Cassel and Co. Ltd., copyright © J. H. Davidson, 1972. pp 86, 94, 95, 103, 195 McGraw-Hill, from *Advertising: What it is and how to do it* by R. White, copyright © 1980. p 78 McGraw-Hill Fogakasha Ltd, USA, from *The Marketing Communications Process* by Wayne M. Delozier, copyright © 1976. p 188 The Creative Business Ltd, from *Creative Advertising* by D. Bernstein, copyright © 1974.

The authors would in addition like to thank Vance Packard for permission to reprint the extracts on pages 15 and 24 from his book *The Hidden Persuaders*, copyright © 1957 by Vance Packard.

Thanks are due to the advertising agencies and their clients who kindly supplied material for the colour plate section.

Part 1

What advertising is about

Chapter 1

This advertising business

'. . . advertising grew naturally out of the social, economic and commercial developments which took place at an earlier stage in our history.'
T. R. Nevett, *Advertising in Britain – A history,* Heinemann, 1982

By the end of this chapter you will:

- Appreciate the long history of advertising and how it became the force it is today;
- Have an overview of how the business is made up;
- Understand its size and importance in modern life;
- Have a grasp of how it fits into the economic and social scene.

1.1 The space age business from the mists of time

As this book first took shape in the 1985 first edition, the 'information technology' revolution was already under way. Cable television was widespread in the USA and about to start trials in the UK. Satellite television was waiting in the wings. Direct response TV advertising through computer links was being developed. A mere ten years later, all these things had become commonplace. Now we have a new set of possible ways of advertising available, from fax to the Internet, and who knows what else.

Advertising is an inescapable part of our lives and very much involved in the rapidly changing technology of the world we live in.

But advertising in one form or another has been with mankind ever since trading began. Certainly it was well established in ancient Greece and some actual examples were recovered from under the volcanic ash that preserved the ruins of Pompeii.

1.1.1 The origins of modern advertising

Advertising as we know it however stems from that earlier time of rapid change, the Industrial Revolution. Historians argue about the dates when this began and ended but for our purposes it can be said to have happened in the UK during the second half of the eighteenth century and the first half of the nineteenth.

During that period a number of things produced the climate in which advertising could develop:

1   Population expanded rapidly from 6 million in 1740 to 12 million by 1821. Improvements in agricultural methods meant fewer workers were required in the countryside at the same time as industrial development provided more jobs at better wages in the towns.
2   This growth and concentration of population was accompanied by improved transport systems. Better roads, then canals and railways, made the movement of goods more efficient. This in turn meant that the processes of distribution and selling became much cheaper.
3   Thus the ingredients for mass production and eventually mass marketing were coming into being.
4   Printing had existed since the fifteenth century (the earliest surviving British advertisement was produced by Caxton about 1477). But during the eighteenth century, newspapers had developed strongly from 25 titles with combined circulations of 1,500,000 in 1700 to 258 titles with combined circulations of 16,085,000 in 1800.[1]

In the early days particularly, the number of readers was probably much larger than the circulations would suggest. Some copies were available in coffee houses and reading rooms, where each would have been read by very many people.

At the beginning of this period, advertising in newspapers was one insignificant method amongst many more important ones – including posters, broadsheets and tradesmen's 'cards' (sheets containing not merely their name and address, but listing their wares). There were even 'advertising engines' – horse-drawn wooden towers covered with posters – as well as 'sandwich-men' who carried boards in front and behind them on which advertisements could be placed. The latter were a regular feature of city life well into the twentieth century and occasionally reappear even today. However, during the first half of the nineteenth century, advertising in newspapers developed very rapidly indeed. Dr Nevett[1] has been able to chart this growth from the House of Commons Accounts and Papers, since advertising during this period was subject to a tax.

In 1800 the revenue collected was £76,668 14s 0d representing 511,258 advertisements. By 1848 there was £142,674 2s 0d collected representing 1,902,322 advertisements (the rate of tax changed over the period).

Advertising in the press – newspapers and an ever-growing number and variety of magazines – assumed the major role among all the other media. In terms of share of total expenditure it still retains prominence as we enter the second millennium (*see* Section 1.3.2) in spite of the growth of first the cinema, then radio and television. (Radio was the last of these three to carry advertising in the UK although in many other countries it was an important advertising medium before television came into being.)

1.2 The development of advertising as a business

The commercial potential of advertising in a growing number of newspapers and periodicals was quickly grasped by many of the prospering businesses that developed to serve the expanding populations of the fast-growing industrial towns. These many *advertisers* placing the advertising in a wide range of advertising *media* waited only for the third partner to come into being – the *advertising agencies*. These three groups constitute the main sections of 'the advertising business' – the advertisers spending money to communicate with their markets, and finding it useful, then as now, to use advertising agents to place their advertisements in the wide range of media.

1.2.1 The early advertising agencies

It has usually been considered that the original role of advertising agencies was not their present one of serving the advertisers' interests (*see* Chapter 6).

However, Dr Nevett[1] makes a strong case that their role has in general never been greatly different from what it is today, although there may have been some aberrations along the way.

> What the advertiser needed, therefore, was someone who could keep track of the rapid changes taking place in the newspaper world, advise on the suitability of a particular journal, write the copy if required, simplify accounting procedures and ease cash flow problems by granting credit. These were the services offered by the early agents; and as newspapers began granting them commission, advertisers were able to benefit in effect 'free of charge'.

According to Nevett, the 'space farmers' – agents selling space for a single publication, or a small number of publications – only came into being much later (around the end of the nineteenth century). Even then this was regarded by many as undesirable and the already established alternative system of the agent acting on behalf of the advertisers much to be preferred. Even so Nevett quotes Paul Derricks, head of a well-known advertising agency, stating in 1907 that of the 336 firms calling themselves advertising agents: 'A close scrutiny of the list would prove that according to the modern accepted definition of the term, fully 300 of 336 are not to be considered as advertising agents'. This was because all kinds of people sold space on behalf of the media without in any way offering the service we would now expect of an advertising agency. So that although Mather and Crowther (later Ogilvy Mather) had a staff of 100 in 1894 and were already offering an in-depth service, many 'agencies' were little more than space brokers.

It was well into the twentieth century before fully-developed advertising agencies were operating on any significant scale. The 'full service agency' (*see* Sections 1.3.1 and 6.2.6) did not really emerge until the middle of the twentieth century. By the 1980s it was already no longer regarded as the indisputable norm. A wide variety of types of agency now exists, to suit the differing needs of advertisers (*see* Chapter 6).

Advertising agents first appear in the records during the late eighteenth century, the earliest known being William Tayler (from an advertisement he himself took in the *Maidstone Journal* in 1786). James White, friend of Charles Lamb founded an agency in 1800. In 1812 the partnership of Lawson & Barker started, soon to be known as Charles Barker and continuing under the same name to this day. (In 1981 the Charles Barker group was the tenth largest agency in Europe in terms of gross income, but later lost that status – the agency business is a very volatile one.)

1.2.2 Some early advertisers

Newspapers could and did sometimes survive without advertising revenue but increasingly became dependent on it. Advertising agents certainly cannot exist on their own. But the real basis of the rapidly growing advertising business was the advertisers who financed it all.

Some of today's big spenders on advertising are companies who were already using advertising early in the nineteenth century – Crosse & Blackwell, Schweppes and Hedges and Butler among them. At that time, according to Nevett, the most important category of advertising was auctioneers' notices with 16 per cent of the total, followed by retailers with 13 per cent. Medical products advertising represented only 6.5 per cent although then and since they attracted a disproportionate amount of attention because of their outrageously extravagant claims such as that for Dr Roberts' 'Poor Man's Friend' ointment in 1855, offering … a certain cure for ulcerated sore legs, if of 20 years standing, cuts, burns, scalds, bruises, chilblains, scorbutil eruptions, and pimples on the face, sore and inflamed eyes, and cancerous tumours …'

Dr Nevett notes, 'By mid-century there were some obvious changes in the advertisement columns, reflecting the growing division between manufacturing and retailing. More retailers seem to have been using the newspapers …' This division grew of course and as mass manufacture developed, the 'typical' advertiser became the manufacturer using advertising both to create demand amongst his consumers but also to exert pressure on retailers to stock his products.

Only in the mid-twentieth century have we seen a substantial check in this development. The growing size and power of large retail chains has switched the emphasis back to retailers' advertising expenditure. This point is discussed in Section 2.3.5.

However, this brief look at history shows that there is nothing new about retailers investing in advertising expenditure on a large scale. Thus Heals spent £6,000 in 1855 and by the early years of the twentieth century Gordon Selfridge was spending £36,000 on promoting his new shop even before it opened.

Nor is the 1980s' emphasis on 'below-the-line' promotion (*see* Chapter 8) anything new. As Nevett says, 'When Jesse Boot opened a new shop, he hired a brass band, sandwich-men to parade the street, a Salvation Army man (normally employed by the company as a packer) to walk around with a bell proclaiming the merits of Boots' products and sometimes a coach-and-four carrying advertising placards, quite apart from using the more normal methods of bill distributing and festooning the upper storeys of his shops with signs.' David Lewis in Liverpool in 1886 chartered the *Great Eastern* as a floating exhibition to promote his stores (it attracted some half million visitors).

1.3 The current advertising scene

These developments taking place over many centuries but with increasing pace in the past 150 years, have produced a complex and highly sophisticated business. Basically the pattern established during the nineteenth century is unchanged. Advertisers, both manufacturers and retailers, continue to spend increasing sums of money on promoting their products. A strong development in recent years, however, has been the increasing expenditure on 'cause' advertising (*see* Section 2.3.12) and advertising by the government (*see* Section 2.3.9). Many companies too spend massive sums of money not simply on product promotion but also on 'corporate' advertising, to communicate with a wide range of audiences in order to improve and maintain good relationships with them – advertising being used as part of the company's public relations activity (*see* Section 8.7).

The top UK advertisers in 1996 (according to Register–MEAL, listed in the Advertising Association's *Marketing Yearbook* for 1996) are shown in Table 1.1.

Table 1.1 *Top twenty advertisers 1996*
TV expenditure reflects an average discount of 3.5%. Comparisons with previous years should be made with caution

| Rank | Advertiser | Total £'000s | Advertising Expenditure | | | |
			TV %	Radio %	Press %	Other %
1	British Telecommunications plc	123,030	75.6	2.2	18.8	3.4
2	Dixons Stores Group Ltd	98,476	6.8	6.2	87.0	–
3	Procter & Gamble Ltd	75,783	95.4	0.6	2.9	1.1
4	Vauxhall Motors Ltd	73,263	37.5	5.4	49.1	7.9
5	Kellogg Co of GB Ltd	68,502	93.8	0.7	3.5	2.0
6	Ford Motor Co Ltd	68,177	53.1	4.1	38.9	3.9
7	Unilever Lever Brothers Ltd	62,653	82.4	–	16.9	0.7
8	Procter & Gamble Health & Beauty	50,913	84.6	2.0	12.9	0.5
9	Renault UK Ltd	50,328	52.8	5.5	26.6	15.2
10	Peugeot Talbot Motor Co plc	49,459	48.8	1.3	43.0	7.0
11	Rover Group Ltd	42,622	44.9	2.1	43.2	9.8
12	Citroën UK Ltd	41,763	50.3	0.1	48.0	1.6
13	Unilever Birds Eye Wall's Ltd	41,695	87.2	–	8.8	4.0
14	Nissan GB Ltd	41,366	55.3	3.0	30.6	11.1
15	Unilever Elida Faberge Ltd	39,995	89.8	0.2	4.9	5.1
16	Boots The Chemists Ltd	37,671	47.8	0.4	48.2	3.6
17	Pedigree Petfoods	37,334	91.2	–	1.7	7.1
18	Mars Confectionery	37,100	83.5	2.8	8.2	5.5
19	McDonald's Restaurants Ltd	35,281	80.9	10.7	2.5	5.9
20	Coca Cola GB & Ireland	35,138	73.6	11.0	3.2	12.2

Source: AC Nielsen–Meal

In 1981 Britain had the biggest advertising expenditure in Europe, according to a *Financial Times* article of 19 October 1982. Current expenditures of European countries are shown in Table 1.2.

1.3.1 Advertising agencies in the 1990s

During the middle of the twentieth century, advertising agencies really came of age with the development of the 'full service agency' (*see* Section 6.2.6). The bigger agencies were able to provide their clients not only with advisory, selection and buying services in connection with the media plus a full range of design and writing support (the 'creative' aspect), but also many other services. They were able to arrange or even carry out market research, offer advice on all aspects of marketing (*see* Chapter 6) and help on a wide range of other promotional activities such as public relations and sales promotion. This increasing sophistication was coupled with an increasingly international bias. As more and more large companies became 'multinational' – operating in many different countries – their agencies found themselves following suit. This in turn led to many joint ventures and ultimately mergers and thus larger and larger advertising agencies with huge 'billings' (the term used for the total amount of advertising placed by an agency on behalf of its clients).

In 1996, Europe's top twenty agency networks were as shown in Table 1.3.

A few years earlier the number of American agencies in the list would probably have been larger. The USA, with its enormous markets and highly developed manufacturing and retailing operations had the most sophisticated advertising agencies which tended to follow their clients round the world, opening up local offices to serve them. However, more recently there has been a reaction to this, with local agencies tending to start up and grow very rapidly.

A phenomenon of the 1980s and 1990s in fact has been the frequent formation of new agencies, often by 'breakaway' groups of senior executives leaving an established agency to form their own company and probably taking some of the original agency's business with them. Whilst this has always happened from time to time over the years, it has been particularly marked recently.

Another strong recent development – in reaction perhaps to the concentration of agencies into bigger and bigger multinational groupings offering a full range of services – is a measure of fragmentation. Clients can now – in the UK at least – readily buy their media through one company, creative help from another, sales promotion from a third and so on. This so-called 'à la carte' approach is discussed further in Section 6.1.

A major, fairly recent change has been loss of control of media buying by the agencies. According to Sean Brierley[2] in *The Advertising Handbook* (Routledge, 1995) '… around 60% of all media expenditure was handled by a separate agency …'. The growth of the 'media houses' or 'media independents' has been very great. On the client side, more and more large companies are bulk buying their time and space to achieve better cost effectiveness – and, incidentally, putting increasing pressure on agency margins.

1.3.2 Advertising media in the 1980s

As hinted at the beginning of this book, rapid developments are taking place in advertising media. In particular the predominant position that the press has held since the Industrial Revolution is being eroded by the newer 'electronic' media.

Table 1.2 *Advertising expenditure in Western European countries*[1]

	Austria	Belgium	Finland	France	Germany
Advertising expenditure 1995					
Per capita US$	183.8	170.3	211.9	175.2	261.5
Total US$ (million)	1,665	1,703	1,087	10,188	21,410
Per capita ECU	144.9	134.1	167.0	138.0	206.0
Total ECU (million)	1,313	1,342	857	8,026	16,868
Per capita local currency	1,946	5,272	973	896	394
Total local currency (million)	17,630	52,743	4,993	52,115	32,218
Distributors of total advertising expenditure in local currency (million)					
Newspapers	8,033	13,910	2,925	12,725	15,513
Magazines	3,078	12,308	733	11,901	6,237
TV	3,678	16,985	1,016	17,455	7,663
Radio	1,709	4,261	163	3,635	1,318
Cinema	-	711	6	332	333
Outdoor	1,132	4,569	150	6,067	1,154
Distribution of total advertising expenditure as a percentage of total					
Newspapers	45.6	26.4	58.6	24.4	48.2
Magazines	17.5	23.3	14.7	22.8	19.4
TV	20.9	32.2	20.3	33.5	23.8
Radio	9.7	8.1	3.3	7.0	4.1
Cinema	–	1.3	0.1	0.6	1.0
Outdoor	6.4	8.7	3.0	11.6	3.6

Notes: 1 These data have been derived from national sources to produce a comparable series. They are net of
              discounts, include agency commission and press classified advertising but exclude production costs.
          2 Except per capita data, Italian local currency data are in billion units.
          3 1995 figures.
          4 USA is shown for purposes of comparison.

Source: The European Advertising & Media Forecast

Percentage of households with:		*Household equipment*			
Compact disc	32	20	35	64	21
Freezer	66	57	83	81	48
Dishwasher	36	22	42	44	44
Telephone	88	81	90	95	98
Microwave	34	10	71	56	55
Washing machine	83	85	82	90	94
		Western European television data			
Homes with TV sets (%)	99	98	96	98	99
As a percentage of TV homes:					
Homes with VCR	68	54	69	68	62
Homes with full cable service	37	90	30	9	81
Homes with teletext	58	24	44	_	63
Daily reach, all TV (%)	67	85	85	83	87
Average daily viewing (mins)	143	159	148	193	195

Notes: 1 Data refer to German language television only.

Table 1.4 compiled by the Advertising Association shows expenditure
in the UK by media from 1991 to 1996.

By 1996, press advertising had dropped in five years to just over 60% of

Ireland	Italy	Netherlands	Porlugal	Spain	Sweden	Switzerland	UK	USA
167.6	104.9	231.4	123.6	122.3	220.8	415.3	234.2	377.3
602	5,996	3,575	1,221	4,799	1,958	2,923	13,614	97,876
132.0	82.6	177.0	97.4	96.4	173.9	318.9	184.2	297.1
474	4,723	2,735	962	3,782	1,542	2,245	10,706	77,068
105	161,800	372	19,061	15,492	1,481	491	150	377
376	9,252	5,740	188,320	607,894	13,133	3,457	8,713	97,876
220	1,939	2,730	26,350	191,486	8,109	1,962	3,571	36,479
15	1,520	1,402	32,286	94,661	1,626	607	1,601	12,200
92	5,250	1,131	100,104	229,204	2,415	318	2,827	36,961
28	306	264	13,130	59,832	310	90	313	11,165
3	–	25	400	5,015	96	34	60	–
19	237	188	16,050	27,696	577	446	341	1,071
58.5	21.0	47.6	14.0	31.5	61.7	56.8	41.0	37.3
4.0	16.4	24.4	17.1	15.6	12.4	17.6	18.4	12.5
24.5	56.7	19.7	53.2	37.7	18.4	9.2	32.4	37.8
74	3.3	4.6	7.0	9.8	2.4	2.6	3.6	11.4
0.8	–	0.4	0.2	0.8	0.7	1.0	0.7	–
51	2.6	3.3	8.5	4.6	4.4	12.9	3.9	1.1
45	8	66	2	29	66	45	20	–
97	63	60	52	24	78	69	39	–
23	32	16	27	14	50	46	19	–
83	90	98	79	86	96	98	92	99
63	22	43	24	35	68	27	66	–
90	89	93	91	95	74	96	91	–
99	99	98	99	99	98	94	98	98
68	67	68	54	60	70	62	87	75
37	–	96	–	3	39	79	9	61
39	60	75	–	32	73	56	56	–
87	80	69	83	91	72	71[1]	76	–
200	80	157	159	214	139	129[1]	194	242

the total, with TV remaining fairly constant at 31.5%. Commercial radio stations have grown in number in recent years and are therefore taking slightly more advertising revenue. With the arrival of digital television and the pro-

Table 1.3 *Top twenty European agency networks ranked by European billings in 1996*

Rank 96	Rank 95	Agency	Billings ($m) 1966	Billings ($m) 1955	Change (%)	Income ($m) 1966	Income ($m) 1955	Change (%)
1	–	Publicis Communication	4,616	4,270	7.4	676	624	7.6
2	4	Young & Rubicam Europe	4,497	4,004	10.9	512	489	4.5
3	3	Ogilvy & Mather Europe	4,163	3,939	5.3	462	438	5.1
4	1	Euro RSCG	4,128	4,010	2.8	620	602	3
5	5	BBDO Europe	3,700	3,500	5.4	n/s	n/s	–
6	7	McCann-Erickson	3,680	3,137	14.7	517	470	9
7	8	Grey Europe	3,056	2,872	6	n/s	n/s	–
8	12	DMB&B Europe	2,763	2,300	16.7	n/s	n/s	–
9	9	Bates Europe	2,728	2,653	2.7	n/s	n/s	–
10	10	Saatchi & Saatchi Advertising Worldwide	2,616	2,599	0.6	327	325	0.6
11	13	Ammirati Puris Lintas	2,400	2,200	8.3	241	n/a	–
12	14	Lowe and Partners Europe	1,732	1,560	9.9	233	223	4.2
13	15	Lee Burnett Europe/Middle East/Africa	1,450	1,300	10.3	210	183	12.8
14	6	BDDP Paris	1,202	1,258	–4.6	190	188	1
15	17	TBWA	1,071	935	8.1	141	132	6.2
16	–	FCB Europe	1,051	n/a	n/a	131	n/a	n/a
17	19	Testa International	745	693	7	93	87	6.4
18	18	The GGT Group	n/a*	732	n/a*	n/a*	93	n/a
19	20	Bozell Worldwide	586.5	431	36.1	95	70	35.7
20	–	FCA!BMZ	530	510	3.7	82	66	19.5

*The 1996 figures for the GGT Group are not supplied because of the acquisition of the BDDP network.

fusion of new channels, TV is likely to take an increasing share of advertising. This is the pattern in the UK and it will vary in other territories (*see* Chapters 18 and 19). Government attitudes have a strong influence – some do not allow TV advertising, for example, and many restrict what may be advertised and to whom. Cigarette products have a total ban in the UK and there are still limits on what may be advertised to children. Generally, however, the UK experience suggests a probable neutral environment.

1.3.3 The growth of 'below-the-line' promotion

One further change to be noted is the shift in emphasis to 'below-the-line'. The latter term owes its origin to the fact that it was customary for advertising agencies to invoice their clients by first listing all advertising booked

Table 1.4 Total advertising expenditure by medium and by type

	£ million						Percentage of total					
	1991	1992	1993	1994	1995	1996	1991	1992	1993	1994	1995	1996
By medium												
National newspapers, incl. col. suppl.	1,121	1,155	1,220	1,336	1,433	1,510	14.7	14.6	14.8	14.7	14.6	14.3
Regional newspapers, incl. free sheets	1,628	1,640	1,715	1,871	1,963	2,061	21.3	20.7	20.8	20.6	19.9	19.5
Consumer magazines	506	466	448	499	533	583	6.6	5.9	5.4	5.5	5.4	5.5
Business & professional magazines	708	746	714	785	897	1,018	9.3	9.4	8.7	8.6	9.1	9.6
Directories	504	523	551	589	639	692	6.6	6.6	6.7	6.5	6.5	6.5
Press production costs	417	427	438	472	514	550	5.5	5.4	5.3	5.2	5.2	5.2
Total press	**4,884**	**4,957**	**5,085**	**5,552**	**5,979**	**6,413**	**64.0**	**62.6**	**61.8**	**61.1**	**60.7**	**60.6**
Television, incl. prod. costs	2,295	2,472	2,604	2,888	3,125	3,333	30.1	31.2	31.6	31.8	31.7	31.5
Outdoor & transport, incl. prod. costs	267	284	300	350	378	426	3.5	3.6	3.6	3.9	3.8	4.0
Cinema, incl. prod. costs	42	45	49	53	69	73	0.5	0.6	0.6	0.6	0.7	0.7
Radio, incl. prod. costs	149	157	194	243	296	344	2.0	2.0	2.4	2.7	3.0	3.2
Total	**7,637**	**7,915**	**8,232**	**9,086**	**9,847**	**10,590**	**100.0**	**100.0**	**100.0**	**100.0**	**100.0**	**100.0**
By Type												
Display advertising												
Press[1]	2,875	2,951	3,008	3,241	3,463	3,645	37.6	37.3	36.5	35.7	35.2	34.4
Television	2,295	2,472	2,604	2,888	3,125	3,333	30.1	31.2	31.6	31.8	31.7	31.5
Other media[2]	458	486	543	646	743	843	6.0	6.2	6.6	7.2	7.5	7.9
Total display	5,628	5,908	6,154	6,775	7,331	7,822	73.7	74.7	74.8	74.6	74.5	73.9
Classified advertising[3]	2,009	2,006	2,078	2,311	2,515	2,768	26.3	25.3	25.2	25.4	25.5	26.1
Total	7,637	7,915	8,232	9,086	9,846	10,590	100.0	100.0	100.0	100.0	100.0	100.0

Notes: 1 Including financial notices and display advertising in business and professional journals, but not advertising in directories.
2 Outdoor and transport, cinema and radio.
3 Including all directory advertising.
For expenditure on Direct Mail (£1,404m in 1996) see page 124.

Source: The Advertising Association's _Advertising Statistics Yearbook 1997_, tables, 3.1.1, 3.1.3, 4.1.1 and 4.1.2. Please see this source for definitions.

on their behalf in the main media (press, cinema, posters, radio and TV). On these activities the agency drew a commission which paid for its services (*see* Section 6.7).

At this point a line was drawn so that commission could be recorded. Then the other expenditure 'below-the-line' followed – point of sale material, sales literature and so on. On these the agency did not draw commission from suppliers and so usually charged a service fee for this part of their work. From this purely administrative convenience have derived the terms:

>   Above-the-line – all main commissionable media
>   Below-the-line – other, non-commissionable activities

An increasingly important ingredient of 'below-the-line' has been sales promotion – the use of special price offers and other kinds of incentives (gifts, competitions, trading stamps, etc.) to stimulate sales (*see* Section 8.4). It is this particular aspect of below-the-line expenditure that has been developing enormously.

Thus as early as 1978, Chris Petersen was pointing out the enormously more rapid growth of below-the-line promotion compared with that of above-the-line advertising.[3] Petersen quotes a Harris International Marketing Survey showing sales promotion expenditure growing from £545 million in 1974 to £1,853 million in 1977. Advertising Association figures showed a growth of advertising expenditure through agencics of £1,000 million in 1974 to only £1,630 million in 1977, a growth of 63 per cent only against the 240 per cent increase in sales promotion over the same period. The precise figures are suspect as comparisons are difficult and accurate expenditures on sales promotion difficult to compile.

Indeed, in 1988 the Advertising Association and the Institute of Sales Promotion jointly conducted a survey 'aimed at developing a useful set of definitions and techniques for measuring this difficult area'. A statement in the 1996 *Marketing Pocket Book* published by the AA went on to say that using a restricted definition (i.e. rather than a very loose one) suggested that expenditure on sales promotion in 1987 was of the order of £1,500 million, of which some £1,000 million was non-price-related promotion. This casts some doubt on the heady optimism of the early leaders of the sales promotion boom in the 1970s and 1980s.

1.4 Attitudes to advertising

As the preceding sections indicate, advertising has been a growing feature of the commercial scene (and hence inevitably of the social scene also) over the past two centuries. The development of television has meant that most people regularly encounter advertising in one of its most dramatic forms right in their own home. Inevitably this has produced a few raised eyebrows and some vociferous protests from people who worry about its impact on individual lives and on the social fabric.

These fears were highlighted for many in the popular book by Vance Packard.[4] In a typical passage, Packard says:

> This book is an attempt to explore a strange and rather exotic new area of modern life. It is about the way many of us are being influenced and manipulated – far more than we realise – in the patterns of our everyday lives. Large scale efforts are being made, often with impressive success, to channel our unthinking habits, our purchasing decisions, and our thought processes by the use of insights gleaned from psychiatry and the social sciences. Typically these efforts take place beneath our level of awareness, so that the appeals which move us are often, in a sense, 'hidden'.

What Packard was really highlighting was the growing reliance, as he saw it when the book was first published in the 1950s, on the findings of the then popular motivational research, now largely absorbed into qualitative research (*see* Section 17.2.1). Many people have taken it however as an indictment of advertising in general, even though Packard himself says later in the book:

> ... a great many advertising men, publicists, fund raisers, personnel experts, and political leaders, in fact numerically a majority, still do a straightforward job and accept us as rational citizens (whether we are or not). They fill an important and constructive role in our society. Advertising for example not only plays a vital role in promoting our economic growth but is a colourful, diverting aspect of American life ...

He also qualifies the possible effect of advertising on people's behaviour thus: . . . it is false to assume that there is any single or major reason why people buy – or don't buy – a product. A host of factors enter in, such as quality of the product, shelf position and sheer volume of advertising ...'

A less emotive view of the way most people, at least in the UK, view the role of advertising in their lives, is provided by research regularly carried out on behalf of the Advertising Association.[5] The report on the 1981 survey includes the following 'Summary and Conclusions':

> Advertising remains extremely low on people's list of concerns. Few people talk about it, fewer still hold strong opinions on the subject, and a tiny minority (2 per cent) feels that a major change is needed in this area. This contrasts with 34 per cent demanding change in the Government, 23 per cent change in education, 30 per cent in trade unions and 11 per cent in politicians.
>
> Seventy-seven per cent of the sample approve of advertising and 16 per cent disapprove (7 per cent have no opinion). This follows the trend shown by attitude surveys since 1972, of a continuing increase in the proportion of the sample approving of advertising and a decline in the proportion disapproving. In 1972, of the sample 67 per cent approved and 24 per cent disapproved. It is also clear that young people are more

Table 1.5 *Approve/disapprove of advertising*
Base: All adults 15+

| | Total | Sex | | Age | | | | | |
		Men	Women	15–24	25–34	35–44	45–54	55–64	65
Approve a lot (4)	298	170	128	78	83	51	33	26	2?
	29%	34%	24%	46%	41%	30%	21%	20%	13
Approve a little (3)	507	233	275	77	90	87	84	68	10
	49%	47%	52%	45%	44%	51%	53%	53%	51
Disapprove a little (2)	98	42	56	6	9	12	25	13	. 3:
	10%	8%	11%	4%	5%	7%	16%	10%	16
Disapprove a lot (1)	60	23	38	2	6	10	8	12	2
	6%	5%	7%	1%	3%	6%	5%	9%	12
Don't know	68	33	35	7	16	10	9	9	1
	7%	7%	7%	4%	8%	6%	6%	7%	8%

Source: The Advertising Association's *Advertising Statistics Yearbook*, 1997.

> strongly in favour of advertising than older ones; 89 per cent of the 15–24 age group
> approved, as against 6 per cent disapproving.
>   Only 10 per cent of the sample disliked advertisements in newspapers and maga-
> zines, and only 15 per cent disliked TV commercials. These figures again form part of a
> trend which has continued for many years. In 1972, of the sample 12 per cent disliked
> press and magazine advertisements, and 24 per cent disliked TV commercials.
>   A very small proportion of the sample expressed consistent attitudes of disapproval or
> dislike towards advertising. Second interviews with all identified 'strong disapprovers' who
> would consent to a further interview (two-thirds of those who qualified) found that the
> main reasons for disapproval of advertising were centred around a dislike of the stereo-
> typed life-styles shown in advertisements, a fear that other people might be misled by
> advertisements, a dislike of the quantity of advertising, or disapproval of some specific type
> or technique of advertising. Very few of the sample disapproved wholeheartedly of advertis-
> ing, very few were in favour of further restrictions on advertising, and none at all were in
> favour of the total prohibition of any kind of advertising.

Later surveys (see Tables 1.5 and 1.6) show continuing consumer
acceptance of advertising as a useful part of everyday life. It has its critics
but they are a small, though sometimes noisy, minority.

	Social grade				Work status		
AB	C1	C2	D	E	Unemployed	Not unemployed	Retired
64	84	77	48	26	89	181	28
31%	30%	31%	28%	20%	28%	33%	16%
82	142	126	91	66	155	265	86
39%	51%	51%	54%	51%	49%	49%	49%
26	25	14	15	18	30	39	29
13%	9%	6%	9%	14%	10%	7%	17%
17	12	13	6	13	20	23	17
8%	4%	5%	3%	10%	6%	4%	10%
20	14	18	9	7	21	33	14
9%	5%	7%	5%	5%	7%	6%	8%

1.5 The economic and social role of advertising

In spite of overwhelming approval by most people (*see* Section 1.4), advertising is sometimes criticized along the following lines:

1 It is a waste of money that would be better spent on price reductions or product improvements.
2 It encourages people to spend money they can ill afford on things they would be better off without.
3 It frequently appeals to the less attractive emotions, such as envy, snobbishness, etc.
4 The sheer weight of advertising 'forces' people to buy things they would not otherwise buy.

Criticism of the sort listed above led to the production of a British Labour Party Green Paper, which proposed in particular a tax on advertising and the setting up of a 'National Consumers' Authority' financed from the proceeds of the tax. The advertising industry in the UK has for long believed in voluntary controls by the industry itself (*see* Chapter 9), and produced a spirited reply to the Green Paper.

This document, 'A Commentary on the Labour Party Green Paper on

Table 1.6 Trends in public opinion of advertising 1966–1996
Base: All adults 15+

	1966	1969	1972	1976	1980	1984	1988	1992	1996
Approve a lot	22	35	25	26	30	35	30	28	29
Approve a little	46	44	42	47	47	42	51	48	49
Disapprove a little	14	10	14	11	10	8	10	9	10
Disapprove a lot	11	6	10	8	6	7	3	5	6
Don't know	7	4	9	8	7	8	6	10	7
	100	100	100	100	100	100	100	100	100
Approve	68	79	67	73	77	77	81	76	78
Disapprove	25	16	24	19	16	15	13	14	16
Don't know	7	4	9	8	7	8	6	10	7
	100	100	100	100	100	100	100	100	100

Source: The Advertising Association's Advertising Statistics Yearbook, 1997.

Advertising of March 1972' was published by the Advertising Association in October 1972, and contains the case in favour of advertising in reply to criticisms of the kind referred to above. Some of the points made are the following:

1   The consumer not only has the power to choose but exercises it ruthlessly.
2   The consumer has spending power nowadays for many goods and services over and above the necessities of life. Industry responds by offering a wide variety of such products to suit as many tastes as possible. No one would want, or can afford, them all. People have to choose.
3   The consumer can pick and choose what advertisement he wants to consider. It is well known that his mind and eye shrug off instantly those of no interest to him.
4   The process of advertising … achieves no more than an interest to try the product and, if that product does not live up to expectations, it is not bought a second time.
5   In general economics, the contribution of an efficient low-cost communication system lies in the fast pay-off of investment cost, the avoidance of wasteful production hanging about in the warehouses, the maintenance of steady production and therefore of employment.
6   The special value of advertising is its cheapness and rapid spread of product information.
7   Consumer attitudes may not be as the writers of the paper would like them to be. They are, however, the product of the material betterment of the mass of the population over the last century. They are the consumers' own choice, and industry and advertising have merely responded to their needs and wishes with products, services and communications. The communications have not created the attitudes and to restrict the communications will not change the attitudes.

More recently, the argument was discussed in a paper by S. C. Littlechild of the University of Birmingham.[6] He suggested that the various arguments by different schools of economists, in turn depend on varying psychological theories as to what determines people's purchasing behaviour. In particular:

> *Galbraith's view, that advertising creates or changes tastes, reflects the psychological theory of behaviourism. Kirzner's view, that advertising reveals opportunities for satisfying tastes, is consistent with Gestalt psychology. Shackle's emphasis on imagination is closer to the psychoanalytic view, and suggests a role for advertising in stimulating the creation of opportunities for satisfying tastes. For both Shackle and Kirzner, but in contrast to Galbraith, advertising certainly affects behaviour, but it does not determine it. It is an aid to choice rather than a substitute for it. The consumer is an active rather than passive*

participant. As Foxall (1980) puts it: 'Anyone who has tried to persuade others knows that consumers' attention is not simply there for the asking; and attention is only the beginning of a perceptual process which is fully capable of screening out unwanted messages at any stage'. It would therefore be incorrect to see the consumer's pre-advertising preferences as the 'real' ones: they might rather be seen as 'immature' and in course of development to their full potential.

Thus it seems likely that whether advertising is seen to be beneficial or harmful, socially or economically, depends very much on one's view of how people behave. The research quoted in Section 1.4 suggests that the average consumer – in the UK at least – is not much bothered either way and is quite prepared to accept advertising as a normal part of the environment in which he or she lives.

There is in fact a strong case for arguing that advertising is an essential facility if there is to be freedom of choice for consumers. Such freedom implies the necessity for businesses to have efficient means of placing their products and services before the public so that the choice can be made based on knowledge of what is available. A further point frequently made is that advertising makes it easier for a wide range of media to exist without government support (and hence control), since many existing media would not be viable if the readers or viewers had to carry the full cost.

These arguments, which raged very powerfully in the 1970s and 1980s, towards the end of the millennium seem extraordinarily dated and academic. Advertising in all its forms has become an accepted part of the scene and plays an ever more prominent role. The 'market economy' way of running things has virtually no rival with the collapse of the old 'command economies', notably the Soviet bloc. Even the communist-run People's Republic of China has encouraged the growth of a capitalist-type market economy, albeit within a much more rigid political system than elsewhere. Advertising is here to stay, virtually unquestioned, for the foreseeable future.

1.6 Summary

1 Advertising in one form or another has been around since the beginning of recorded civilization.
2 However, advertising as we now know it started to develop as the Industrial Revolution took place.
3 During this period the three main types of participant in the advertising business – advertisers, media and agencies – emerged and by the end of the nineteenth century were clearly recognisable in something near their present form.
4 The advertising scene gets increasingly more complex, e.g. as 'elec-

tronic media' (radio and TV) develop and as advertising becomes used for an increasingly wide range of purposes.

5 Whilst there are always those who argue that advertising is economically wasteful and socially undesirable, this is not the majority view and the arguments used depend ultimately on (partly subjective) judgements on either side about the nature of the way people make purchasing decisions.

1.7 References

1 Most of the figures quoted in the early sections of the chapter are from *Advertising in Britain: A History* by Dr T. R. Nevett (Heinemann, 1982).
2 Brierley, Sean, *The Advertising Handbook*, Routledge, 1995.
3 Petersen, Chris, 'Promotions Boom in Confusion', *Marketing*, September 1978.
4 Packard, Vance, *The Hidden Persuaders*, new edition, Penguin, 1981.
5 *Public Attitudes to Advertising 1980–81*, Advertising Association, 1982.
6 Littlechild, S. C., 'Controls on Advertising: an Examination of some Economic Arguments', *Journal of Advertising*, Vol. 1, No. 1, January–March 1982.

1.8 Further reading

More detailed and factual arguments are available (and frequently updated) in the various studies and guidance notes published by the Advertising Association. In particular the Advertising Association's Handbook contains a wide range of figures and reviews many aspects of the whole UK advertising business.

The Brierley book – reference 2 above – gives an excellent journalist's eye view of the business. Full of examples and anecdotes which help to bring it to life for those with no direct experience.

Dr Nevett's book is a must for an understanding of how the advertising business developed in the UK (and elsewhere the development must have been largely parallel) and is really the only authoritative source.

The Shocking History of Advertising by E. S. Turner (Michael Joseph, 1982) is an amusing mainly anecdotal account of some aspects.

1.9 Questions for discussion

1   'Advertising preserves freedom – for the consumer, for the media and for the marketplace'. This is the title of a talk you are going to give to a group of local businessmen. Write notes for your address.
2   What do you consider to be the two most vital stages in the development of the advertising business as it now operates?
3   Why did advertising agencies emerge and what is their essential role?
4   How do you account for the growing emphasis on below-the-line expenditure in the UK in the 1980s?
5   What do you see as the most significant development in advertising during the 1990s?

Chapter 2

What advertising does

'Advertising . . . attempts to inform and persuade a large number of people with a single communication.'

Kenneth A. Longman, *Advertising*, Harcourt Brace Jovanovich Inc., 1971

By the end of this chapter you will:

- Be aware of advertising's strengths and limitations;
- Recognize the different categories of advertising;
- Appreciate the many different tasks that advertising performs;
- Understand the relationship between advertising and marketing.

2.1 What advertising is

Advertising comes in so many forms and carries out so many different tasks that the common factors may not be obvious. They are however very simple. What distinguishes advertising from other forms of promotional activity *(see* Chapter 8) is:

1   *Advertising presents a totally controllable message.* Since the advertiser pays for the space (in newspapers, magazines, posters, etc.) or the time (radio and television) in which his advertisement appears, he has the right to insist on his message appearing exactly as he chooses, when he chooses and how he chooses, subject to the law and voluntary codes of good taste *(see* Chapter 9).

This is quite different from the situation which obtains if we use, for example, radio or television to transmit a message which we do not pay for. An interesting new product may well be featured in the news on television but it will be the producer not the advertiser who decides *if* it will appear, *when* it will appear and *how* it will appear. Having once appeared, it will no longer be news and will then no longer be featured. An advertisement however can be transmitted for as many times as the advertiser is prepared to pay.

2   *Advertising delivers messages to large numbers of people at low cost per 'contact'.* Sending someone to seek out a prospective customer in order

to talk to them personally is very expensive. We may not even know who to talk to because we do not know precisely who will be interested in our message.

3 *Advertising is a fast method of communicating with many people at the same time.* Using a sales team to call personally or by telephone on large numbers of people will take a long time. Even with such methods as letters posted or delivered directly to households, it is not easy to achieve a simultaneous delivery. Advertising can achieve this, often at short notice, through, for example, radio.

To summarize *Advertising delivers controlled messages to many people simultaneously and at low cost per message.* (NB Whilst the above is generally true, many publications have a wide 'pass-on' readership and so it may be many months before *all* the readers have seen the advertisement.)

2.2 The limitations of advertising

Advertising is often spoken of, especially by its critics, as being of almost magical potency. Vance Packard[1] for example says: 'Large scale efforts are being made, often with impressive success, to channel our unthinking habits, our purchasing decisions, and our thought processes ...'

Packard and the many quotations and similar writings which have followed from his book have given a very strong impression of the 'power of advertising'. Yet there are many examples of quite massive advertising expenditures which have failed to achieve their objective. Advertising's power lies in its ability to transmit messages – it is the nature of the message that determines whether advertising can succeed or not. Even more important is how people respond. Consumers are increasingly sophisticated and sceptical. They cannot easily be manipulated and will generally only respond to advertising that offers them some tangible or emotional benefit. In addition to this fundamental limitation advertising, *because* it addresses many people at once, cannot adjust to suit individual taste and interests in the way that a salesman can for instance. So an advertisement that charms and enthuses some of its audience may bore or annoy others. In winning over some customers we may lose others. It seems likely in any case that the way in which advertising works may be quite complex and as yet not clearly understood (*see* Chapter 16).

Similarly anyone who fails to understand an advertisement cannot ask questions as they would of a salesperson. Some people (e.g. regular television viewers) may have seen a particular advertisement so many times that they become irritated by it. Yet other people may have seen it only once or twice and are still trying to grasp its implications. Existing users, potential buyers and people who will *never* buy, all see the same advertisements. We cannot easily beam advertisements at some but not all, nor can we change the content of advertisements to suit individual requirements or viewpoints.

2.3 The many categories of advertising

Because of its ability to deliver messages cheaply and effectively, advertising is very widely used in many different ways. Here are some of them. Where possible figures are given to indicate the share of total advertising expenditure each represents in the UK (the breakdown will vary from country to country). (*See* Table 2.1.)

2.3.1 Personal

Individuals and families buy space in their local newspaper to sell their car or the furniture they no longer need, to find owners for their puppies or kittens, to announce the birth of their baby or their daughter's engagement.

We are *all* advertisers some time in our lives.

2.3.2 'Classified' advertising

A high proportion of advertising space, in regional and local newspapers especially, is concerned with jobs, cars and houses. Advertising is the standard method by which companies find staff, car dealers sell cars and estate agents find buyers for their clients' houses.

The term 'classified advertising' (or sometimes 'small ads') is used to distinguish this type of advertising – usually classified under headings such as Jobs Vacant, Cars, etc. – from the bigger 'display' advertisements usually standing on their own.

2.3.3 Manufacturers' consumer advertising

This is what most lay people mainly associate with the term 'advertising'. It accounts for much of the glossy, high-spending repetitive advertising on television and so is the most obvious form of advertising. It is the way in which large manufacturers communicate directly with their 'end user' customers (as distinct from the wholesalers, retailers, etc. to whom they sell directly and from whom the 'end user' ultimately buys). This is the advertising of food, drink, tobacco, clothing, cars, household goods, toiletries and leisure goods. Into this category it is also convenient to put – although not strictly manufacturers – books, magazines, etc. along with tourism and entertainment.

Out of a total media advertising expenditure in 1980 of £2,562 million this accounted for £1,077 million – only 42 per cent. Of that, over half – £544 million – was spent on television advertising however; hence the strong impact and apparent dominance of this type of advertising.

Table 2.1 *Annual adjusted Register-MEAL advertising expenditure by product category (press and TV – £m at current prices)*

Product category	1988	1989	1990	1991	1992	1993	1994
Agricultural & horticultural	17.6	24.0	22.2	20.0	22.0	22.4	23.2
Charity & educational	15.4	19.5	23.7	25.5	28.6	30.6	31.7
Drink	198.0	218.7	223.3	199.7	202.3	180.0	176.8
Entertainment	53.3	88.5	108.4	100.0	104.1	79.8	101.6
Financial	367.5	379.8	367.7	312.0	284.7	329.6	430.7
Food	494.3	503.6	526.7	524.1	561.2	559.4	538.5
Government	86.0	93.8	90.0	84.7	75.6	60.8	61.5
Holidays, travel & transport	131.0	138.4	138.6	159.5	172.7	198.7	193.5
Household appliances	107.0	99.7	85.5	81.8	77.3	76.2	68.7
Household equipment	81.5	84.1	77.0	63.8	58.7	68.9	81.5
Household stores	178.8	179.3	197.5	211.4	241.8	230.2	241.4
Institutional & industrial	133.5	177.4	140.7	123.5	85.3	88.6	77.8
Leisure equipment	141.5	159.8	164.0	163.4	156.5	149.3	184.3
Motors	283.0	322.4	323.7	322.9	364.9	405.2	440.8
Office equipment	96.5	100.1	95.9	78.1	135.1	162.6	228.0
Pharmaceutical	78.9	90.4	97.3	99.2	106.2	149.5	162.2
Publishing	121.3	123.3	133.4	121.9	134.0	150.6	145.7
Retail & mail order	369.4	394.2	405.8	434.2	515.7	643.8	694.7
Tobacco	47.1	44.0	50.0	42.9	30.9	24.1	29.1
Toiletries & cosmetics	148.2	168.9	173.6	182.9	207.7	230.9	265.9
Wearing apparel	36.9	39.2	38.8	38.1	45.0	37.9	43.9
Other	37.2	35.2	30.1	24.6	17.5	–	–
Total	**3,224.0**	**3,484.3**	**3,513.7**	**3,414.3**	**3,627.8**	**3,878.9**	**4,221.4**

Source: The Advertising Association's *Advertising Statistics Yearbook* 1995, table 19.2, quoting *The Advertising Forecast*

2.3.4 Services advertising

Over the past decade or so there has been a huge increase in expenditure on the advertising of 'services' or 'intangibles'. In particular, financial organizations such as banks and building societies have joined insurance companies in a much more proactive approach to the marketplace. Educational establishments, charities and travel also spend significant sums (see Table 2.1).

2.3.5 Retailer advertising

For many decades – since the turn of the century and into the sixties – it was leading manufacturers who dominated the marketing scene with their branded and heavily advertised products. Retailers were glad to stock them. With the disappearance of resale price maintenance and the growth of large retail chains however, this situation has altered. More and more retailers are developing their 'own label' brands and are themselves advertising heavily. Customer loyalty is increasingly to retailers rather than manufacturers.

Total media advertising expenditure by retailers in 1970 was £56 million by comparison with manufacturers £250 million out of a total of £554 million. Manufacturers were spending 45 per cent of the total and retailers only 10 per cent. In 1980 the total expenditure was £2,562 million, of which manufacturers spent £1,077 million or 42 per cent whilst the retailers' share, at £436 million, had climbed to 17 per cent.

In 1994 retailer advertising remained at 16.5 per cent of the total.

2.3.6 Trade advertising

As well as communicating with their 'end user'/consumer customers, manufacturers (including suppliers of services, e.g. holiday tour operators) also use advertising to communicate with the wholesalers, retailers, etc. who are their immediate customers. Much of this advertising will be in the 'trade press' specialist publications addressed to groups such as grocers, chemists and druggists, travel agents. These people need to be informed of new products, price changes, etc. and to be persuaded to deal with one supplier rather than another. Because the publications are low-circulation this does not represent a high volume of expenditure.

2.3.7 Industrial (business-to-business) advertising

The advertising most of us see (because it is intended that we should and aimed accordingly) is concerned with consumer products and services and appears in newspapers and widely-read magazines, on radio and TV, in the cinema and on posters. However, there is a very important category of advertising that is seen only by much smaller groups of people and appears mainly in much more specialized media.

This is industrial advertising (sometimes more accurately referred to as 'business-to-business' advertising). It includes the advertising of goods and services for commerce, industry, government and other institutions (e.g. hospitals, schools, hotel and catering chains). The customers are not individuals buying for themselves or their families, but executives or officials taking (probably collective rather than individual) decisions to purchase such items as factory machines, office equipment and vehicles or bulk supplies of stationery, raw materials and components. Accountancy and other professional services, including training and staff recruitment; software design; advertising; and market research, are examples of intangibles that fall into the same category.

Because the audiences are smaller and more specialized such advertising tends to appear in specialist publications like *Professional Engineering, Business Equipment Digest, Farmers Weekly* rather than in national newspapers or on television (although *some* industrial advertising does use the latter).

In 1980 industrial advertising accounted for £289 million, or nearly 20 per cent of the total. Remember also however that industrial marketing normally uses salesmen (and highly specialized and well-paid salesmen at that) much more extensively. The *total promotional cost* will therefore be much more closely in line with the relative importance of industrial markets.

2.3.8 Corporate advertising

A substantial proportion of the advertising carried out by companies is not designed directly to promote products. Rather it aims at encouraging people to have a clear understanding of what the company stands for – its 'corporate image' as it is often called. Alan Wolfe[2] has described corporate advertising thus: 'The purpose of this communication has less to do with pushing a company's goods or its shares, than to establish or preserve an environment in which the company can go about its lawful business'.

Therefore British Petroleum have spent large sums of money to tell the British public that the company is investing millions of pounds on their behalf on exploration and other developments that will benefit us all in years to come: their advertising also tells us that BP is not only an oil company but is effectively in many other types of business.

Many major companies, including Sony and ICI, promote the company name in such a way that all of their products benefit from the values attached to their 'corporate identity'. 'Intel inside' is an example of how a company can use advertising to encourage sales of its customers' products by attaching to them the values of its own.

Philips' 'Simply Years Ahead' campaign promoted the idea that anyone buying *any* Philips product gains access to all the technological know-how and productive excellence that Philips stands for.

Such advertising can have a number of objectives; in particular:

1   To give 'added value' to the products of the company.
2   To encourage people to trust and enjoy dealing with the company.
3   To encourage shareholders, 'the City' etc. to think well of the company.

It can be seen that advertising of this type may well be fulfilling a public relations objective (*see* Section 8.7).

2.3.9 Government advertising

The government used to be the biggest single advertiser in the UK if all direct advertising by the government (£53 million in 1980) and that of the nationalized industries (£52 million in 1980) was added together. However, many of the nationalized industries have since been privatized and this dominance has declined somewhat. (See the government expenditure figures in Table 2.1.)

2.3.10 Financial and savings advertising

Banks, building societies, insurance companies advertise their services. Companies publish their annual reports. All of this added up to £289 million in 1980, or 19.5 per cent of the total. By 1994 the figure of £430.7 million was down to 10.2 per cent of the total.

2.3.11 Charity and educational advertising

Charities advertise to gather in funds (Oxfam, The Salvation Army and Mencap are well-known examples), inform supporters and educate the public. Educational establishments are listed in the same category to give the relatively small total of £7 million in 1980. However, this is misleading as much charity advertising uses newspaper space or poster sites donated free. The 'Charity and Education' category was at £31.7 million by 1994.

2.3.12 Cause advertising

An increasing feature of the present day is the use of advertising to promote *causes* (sometimes referred to as advocacy advertising). Advertising is used to seek support for preventing the destruction of wildlife (e.g. Save the Whales), for helping political prisoners (Amnesty International) and for many other campaigns to marshal public support for a particular cause. Political parties similarly use advertising to win support for their policies and gain votes in the next election.

2.3.13 Recruitment advertising

The figures in Table 2.2 indicate the importance of advertising to recruit staff. These figures only cover classified advertising, but many companies also use display advertising to recruit and this would make the total figure even more impressive.

2.4 Advertising and marketing

We mainly associate advertising with encouraging people to buy products or services. Yet, as the previous Section indicates, much advertising is not at all of this character. Recruitment advertising, cause advertising, much government advertising, even corporate advertising to some extent is not part of a marketing process leading to profitable sales.

Having registered the point however, it remains true that most advertising *is* part of a marketing process. It is therefore with this context in mind that the rest of this book is written since in any event the principles of effective advertising do not change as we move from a situation where profitable transactions are the aim to one where they are not. So where does advertising fit into this process? The question is dealt with more fully in Chapter 5, but here is a brief indication.

The whole marketing process can best be defined as the profitable application of a company's resources to satisfying the needs of its customers. To satisfy the needs of its customers, a company must not only supply good products but also ensure that they are suitably priced, readily available and well presented. All of these aspects have to be acceptable to customers but also in some way perceived by customers as being 'better' than anything offered by competitors. There has to be a *competitive differential advantage*.

This approach is often referred to as the marketing concept and the whole process can be briefly expressed as in Figure 2.1.

The concept of advertising operating as part of the marketing mix is explored in more depth in Section 5.2.

Advertising is then one way of carrying out *the promotion* part of the marketing mix. Alternative ways include personal selling, sales promotion and public relations. These are dealt with in detail in Section 5.2.2 and in various later chapters.

2.5 The varied tasks of advertising

In its marketing context, advertising may have a wide variety of specific tasks assigned to it and a valuable discipline when considering expenditure on advertising is to ask 'What is it intended to achieve?'

2.5.1 A checklist for advertising objectives

This question can be pursued in detail by applying the following checklist:

Table 2.2 *Newspaper classified advertising by type*

	£m 1989	1990	1991	1992	1993	1994	% of total 1994
Recruitment	592	522	335	320	357	463	33.5
Property	248	260	276	255	236	246	17.8
Automotive	209	223	226	233	253	278	20.1
Other	309	342	366	388	388	396	28.6
Total	**1,357**	**1,347**	**1,204**	**1,196**	**1,234**	**1,383**	**100.0**

Source: The Advertising Association's *Advertising Statistics Yearbook* 1995, tables 5.7.1, 5.7.2

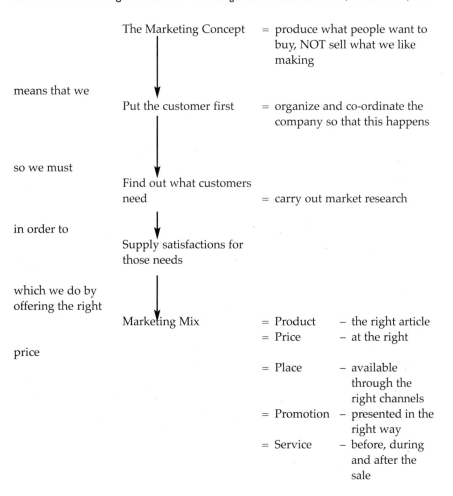

Figure 2.1 *The Marketing Concept*

1   To what extent does the advertising: aim at the target of *immediate sales*?
    – Perform the complete selling function (take the product through all the necessary steps towards a sale)?
    – Announce a special reason for 'buying now' (price, credit terms, etc.)?
    – *Remind* people to buy?
    – Tie in with some special buying event?
    – Stimulate impulse sales?
2   Is the advertising intended to: produce *short term* sales by moving the prospect, step-by-step, closer to a sale (so that when confronted with a buying situation the customer will ask for, reach for, or accept the advertised brand)?
    – Create awareness of a product or service?
    – Create a 'brand image' or favourable emotional disposition toward the product?
    – Implant information or attitude regarding benefits and superior features of the product?
    – Combat or offset competitive claims?
    – Correct false impressions, misinformation and other obstacles to sales?
    – Build familiarity and easy recognition of products?
3   Is the advertising intended to:
    – Build '*long term* customer loyalty'?
    – Build confidence in the company and its products which is expected to pay off in years to come?
    – Build customer demand which places the company in a stronger position in relation to its distribution?
    – Ensure universal distribution?
    – Establish a new product range nationally?
    – Open up new markets?
4   To what extent does (or should) the advertising aim to:
    – Hold present customers against the inroads of competition?
    – Convert competitive users to the advertiser's product?
    – Cause people to specify the advertiser's brand instead of asking for the product by a generic name?
    – Convert non-users of the product type to users of the advertised product?
    – Make steady customers out of occasional or sporadic customers?
    – Increase consumption among present users by (a) Advertising new uses of the product? (b) Encouraging greater frequency or quantity of use?
5   Does the advertising aim at some specific step which leads to a sale?
    – Persuade prospective buyers to write for literature, return a coupon?
    – Persuade prospective buyers to visit a showroom or exhibition, ask for a demonstration?
6   How important are the 'supplementary benefits' of advertising?
    – In aiding salesmen in opening new accounts?

- In aiding salesmen in getting larger orders?
- In giving salesmen an entrée?
- In building morale of company sales force?
7   Is it a task of advertising to impart information needed to consummate sales and build customer satisfaction?
- 'Where to buy it' advertising.
- 'How to use it' advertising.
- Special announcements (a) new models and features, (b) new prices, (c) special terms, quick delivery, etc. (d) new policies (guarantees etc.).
8   To what extent does the advertising aim at building confidence and goodwill for the company among:
- Customers and potential customers?
- The trade (distributors, dealers, stockists)?
- Employees and potential employees?
- The financial community?
- The public at large?
9   Specifically what kind of image does the company wish to build?
- Product quality, dependability
- Service
- Family resemblance of diversified products
- Growth, progressiveness, technical leadership.

When the advertising is part of a properly conceived marketing plan (*see* Section 5.5) the answers to these questions will of course arise naturally from that plan. However, in some situations, e.g. recruitment or cause advertising, the checklist may need modifying to suit the particular situation.

2.5.2 Checklist for non-commercial advertising

Many of the above questions will still apply even when the advertising is not part of a strictly commercial activity, although some modification may be necessary. Items 8 and 9, for example, may need a change of emphasis. A charity may need to appeal to its volunteers and its subscribers, a political party to its staunch supporters, as well as to the 'public at large'. All kinds of organizations will want to build an image. Increasingly, in fact, all kinds of organizations who are non-commercial in the sense that they do not make a profit now use similar language and procedures. The National Health Service has customers, state-funded schools have marketing plans, charities use direct marketing techniques.

Still, some of the questions in their checklist might be different, e.g.:

To what extent does the advertising foster and encourage support from:
- contributors
- voluntary workers

- beneficiaries
- employees
- official fund-holders?

Advertising to discourage drug abuse, smoking or drinking and driving might ask:
　　To what extent is the advertisement aimed at:
- raising awareness of the problem
- suggesting ways of dealing with it
- changing the attitudes of users (drinkers, smokers, etc.)
- giving support to the 'advisers' (parents, doctors, teachers, etc.)

2.6 Summary

1 Advertising differs from other forms of promotion in that:
　(a) Since it is paid for, it is totally controllable.
　(b) It delivers messages to large numbers of people at low cost per 'contact'.
　(c) It is a fast method of communication with many people at the same time.
2 Advertising is a powerful method of communication but not all-powerful.
3 The many categories of advertising include:
　(a) Personal.
　(b) Local 'classified' advertising.
　(c) Manufacturer's consumer advertising.
　(d) Retailer advertising.
　(e) Trade advertising.
　(f) Industrial advertising.
　(g) Corporate advertising.
　(h) Government advertising.
　(i) Financial and savings advertising.
　(j) Charity and educational advertising.
　(k) Cause advertising.
　(l) Recruitment advertising.
4 Whilst advertising is used in a variety of situations most of it is concerned with some form of marketing and has to be considered as an element in the marketing mix.
5 Advertising within a marketing context can carry out a variety of tasks, from generating immediate sales, to creating a favourable attitude towards a company or a product.

2.7 References

1 Packard, Vance, *The Hidden Persuaders*, new edition, Penguin, 1981.
2 Wolfe, Alan, *Corporate Advertising*, edited by Janet Mayhew, IPA, 1983.

2.8 Further reading

The Advertising Association publishes each year a detailed breakdown of advertising expenditure. On a more regular basis, expenditure figures derived from monitoring of advertising in the main press media and on television in the UK are published by MEAL and by British Rate and Data. Some other countries have their own equivalent of these publications. NTC publish an excellent annual *Marketing Pocket Book* full of useful statistics.

Examples of the many different kinds of advertising may be gleaned from the magazines *Marketing, Marketing Week* and *Campaign,* as well as from daily newspapers such as *The Times* and *The Financial Times* and TV programmes like 'The Money Programme' (BBC 2).

Advertising Made Simple by Frank Jefkins gives a good basic but comprehensive view of the whole advertising business.

2.9 Questions for discussion

1 Suggest examples of advertising campaigns that fit the various categories listed in Section 2.3.
2 Advertising is used as a means of solving a wide range of business problems. List the kinds of tasks which you believe advertising is well suited to perform and describe a situation in which you feel it is unlikely to be effective.
3 Describe briefly what you regard as the distinctive features of advertising as compared with other forms of communication.
4 How strong is 'the power of advertising' and does it increase or inhibit consumers' choice?
5 Take a recent newspaper or magazine and analyse the advertising to see how it fits into the categories described in this chapter.
6 Describe how the government uses advertising for the benefit of society.

Chapter 3

How advertising happens

'The development of an appropriate advertising strategy is essential to good advertising.'
Edmund W. J. Faison, *Advertising: A Behavioural Approach for Managers*

By the end of this chapter you will:

- Realize why advertising has to be a carefully planned activity;
- Understand the need for clear advertising objectives that can be measured;
- Be aware of the meaning and importance of positioning;
- Know how the advertising process works;
- Be able to approach planning advertising and setting budgets with confidence.

3.1 Determining the role of advertising

Chapter 2 examined the various roles which advertising can fulfil. The question now to be considered is how we go about selecting the appropriate role in a particular situation.

Basically, we do it by asking questions, such as:

1 Whom do we need to communicate with?
2 What do we need to tell them?
3 Why do we need to tell them (what effect are we trying to produce)?
4 Where is the best medium to deliver the message?
5 When is the best time to deliver the message?
6 How can we best get our message to them? (i.e. through which advertising media?)

When we are dealing with a product or service, then usually the answers will develop naturally out of the marketing plan (*see* Chapter 5 for the relationship between advertising and marketing). Sometimes however advertising will be used for other purposes, e.g.

1   As part of a public relations campaign, designed to develop improved knowledge and appreciation of an organization and its activities (*see* Section 8.7).
2   As a straight piece of information, as when new legislation is introduced and the government has to inform people of its implications.
3   For recruiting staff.

But whatever the purpose of the advertising we still have to answer the *who? what? why? where? when?* and *how?* questions in order to be able to develop effective advertising.

3.2 The need for planning

Advertising must be a planned activity, never a haphazard one. The 'asking questions' approach outlined in Section 3.1 is a beginning. We continue by developing such questions in greater depth, along the following lines:

1   What is the objective of advertising in this particular situation? There may be more than one task (e.g. to make customers more aware of the product *and* to secure wider retail distribution).
2   What is the audience we are communicating with? We must be very clear what our 'target audience' is. There may be more than one, in which case can we communicate with them all at once; or do we have a number of quite separate communication tasks to do?
3   What is the message we have to convey? It may well be different for each audience; consumers may need to be told of the product's performance, whereas dealers will be more interested in the profit they can make; in an industrial context the factory manager will want to know that a machine will give him fewer breakdowns and higher output, and the financial director that it will reduce capital outlay and hence reduce overdraft charges. It is usually essential to establish what is the *benefit* readers/viewers/listeners will receive if they respond to the message.
4   What is the best medium? Is this a job for television, the press, posters (*see* Chapters 11–14) or some kind of 'below-the-line' activity? (*see* Chapter 8).
5   What is the best timing and frequency? Do we need to advertise now, in 3 months time, in 6 months time, over what period? Is it better to have a short sharp burst or would a larger campaign 'spread thin' be better (sometimes called the 'drip' approach)?

6   How much should we be spending?
7   How can our message be expressed most effectively?
8   Is it a job best done by advertising or should some other method of
     communication be used? (*see* Section 5.2.2).

3.2.1 Quantified objectives for measurable results

One of the problems often associated with advertising is that the costs are
all too obvious but the gains not very clear. This difficulty can be minimized if the objectives are spelled out very clearly in terms to which
numbers (quantities) can be attached.
    Examples of quantified objectives are:

1   To produce direct sales of £100,000, i.e. orders are to be received from
     people replying directly to the advertisement totalling this amount or
     more.
2   To increase the number of people who have knowledge of specific fea-
     tures of our product or information about our company from 15 per
     cent of the population to 25 per cent.
3   To produce enquiries from genuinely interested potential customers at
     a cost of not more than £9.50 per enquiry.
4   To achieve a situation where at least 60 per cent of our target audience
     can 'recall' (remember to at least a limited extent) our advertisement
     up to 2 weeks after it has appeared.

    If we advertise in order to 'increase sales' or to 'keep our name before
the public' or similar vague intentions then it will not be possible to determine whether we did or did not achieve our objective and therefore
whether the money was or was not well spent. Also it will be much more
difficult to produce advertising specifically designed and well suited to
carrying out the appropriate task. It should be noted that increased sales
are not necessarily an indication of successful advertising except in the case
of 'direct response' advertising where purchase is made direct from the
company solely as a result of the customer seeing the advertisement. In
most cases there are many other factors involved which also influence sales
e.g. the amount of shelf space in retail outlets compared with that given to
competitive brands, the number and value of retail outlets, the amount of
competitive activity taking place (including price changes, new products,
etc.).
    As we shall see later (Section 16.2), advertising is one of many factors
which influence people in taking steps towards a sale. The final steps may
be taken after a considerable time lag, which can make it extremely difficult to relate sales to the advertising that helped to bring them about (but
was not solely responsible).

Similarly in business to business marketing, the personal contact of the salesperson may be by far the most potent force. Yet advertising has a value in making the customer more receptive and the salesperson's task easier. It is this change in receptiveness we must try to measure if we want to know what contribution advertising has made to the end result.

One way in which we can measure the effect of advertising on sales is, of course, to use advertising in one area and not in the other (control) areas; assessing the difference made by advertising (*see* Chapter 17).

Alternatively in certain cases it may be possible to disentangle the effect on sales of one influence (e.g. advertising) from all the other influences by using complex mathematical models and computer programs. This technique is known as *econometrics*. It demands a very large 'data base' and tends to be *very* costly, although costs can be expected to decrease as suitable software and data banks become more readily available (*see* Chapter 17).

3.2.2 The importance of integrated campaigns

It may sometimes be appropriate for a single advertisement to be produced for a specific limited objective. Obvious examples are the private sale of a car or the recruitment of a person to fill a particular job vacancy. Usually when we are dealing with product advertising and almost certainly when advertising has a public relations content then this 'one-off' approach is inappropriate. The advertising will continue over a period of time, its effect will be cumulative. In this – the most frequent – situation we need, not just an advertisement or a series of advertisements, but a *campaign*.

This term is used to describe a carefully planned series of advertisements expressing a consistent theme and each building on the other.

A further dimension is added by the fact that it is rare for advertising to be the sole method of promoting the product or service. Typically there are leaflets and brochures, often below-the-line material, sometimes exhibition stands. Frequently the advertising itself will appear in a number of different media – a campaign running on TV *and* on posters *and* in the press is not at all uncommon. Imagine each of these different forms being designed by a different designer each with his own theme, colour scheme and central creative idea. The result would be chaos and confusion. Clearly the opposite must apply, each part of the campaign must be consistent with the others and all must reinforce each other. We must have an *integrated* campaign.

3.3 Advertising strategy

Often it has to be decided what emphasis shall be given in the way a product is advertised. A good example from the fairly recent past was the introduction of 'mobile telephones'. Initially, it was the *idea* of mobile telephones that was promoted. A famous Vodaphone campaign had the theme 'How to be in when you're out'. Later the various companies were competing on the basis of low-cost equipment or the attractions of their particular tariff structure to specific groups of people, the market for mobile phones and acceptance of their benefits now being well-established. The early promotion of the general concept of a whole new type of product is often referred to as 'generic' promotion, whereas the later competing for share of an established market is 'differentiation'.

An important factor here is that in the early stages of growth of a new kind of product, sales can only be developed by encouraging the innovators amongst the population to adopt it. Once it becomes generally acceptable (as the camcorder was rapidly doing in the UK in the 1990s) then the various manufacturers each want to capture the maximum share of the subsequent rapidly growing market.

Other advertising strategy considerations include the various ways in which a market can be expanded by:

1   Increasing the amount used at one time (BT encouraging customers to chat on the phone and thus make longer calls – see the Case History provided in the colour plate section for further information).
2   Increasing the frequency of use (turkeys at other seasons not just the traditional Christmas roast).
3   Increasing the number of uses (e.g. use yoghurt in preparing food as well as by itself).
4   Increasing the number of users (Johnson & Johnson encouraging grown-ups to use their baby talcum powder).
5   Increasing product choice (e.g. confectionery manufacturers such as Mars introducing ice-creams based on their original brands.

3.3.1 Positioning

It is often valuable to consider how a product is to be 'positioned' relative to alternative products. As the 'low budget' one or the 'exclusive' (expensive) one. As advanced or conservative, e.g. Volvo cars tend to emphasize the safety and long-life characteristics which will appeal strongly to some car purchasers. Other makes will stress economy, ease of parking or performance. For many years during the 1970s and into the 1980s the Tesco supermarket chain in the UK presented itself as the low-price store, whereas Sainsbury's (with a similar range of merchandise and largely comparable prices) stressed quality and value for money. By the early 1990s, both were claiming high quality but Tesco then changed tack completely (and with considerable initial success) by instituting a 'loyalty' scheme which enabled regular customers to build entitlement to discounts – rather like the well-established frequent flyer programmes used by many airlines. Most other major supermarket chains, including Sainsbury's, felt obliged to follow suit. Chapter 4 contains examples of how detailed understanding of customers' needs enables products to be presented to them in the most appealing way – this is another aspect of positioning.

3.4 Implementing the strategy

Advertising strategy is the core of the planning process. It determines what the essential purpose of the advertising and associated activities is to be. However, the strategy has eventually to be converted into tactics – how is the strategy to be implemented, by whom, by what means, when and at what cost? At this stage the process splits into two streams – the creative aspect (what is the message to be and how is it to be expressed) and the media aspect (through what channels, using what size, length, frequency, etc. is the message to be transmitted).

The procedures and people involved are considered in more detail in Chapter 6. The detailed aspects that have to be dealt with are reviewed at length in subsequent chapters. Here we give merely a brief outline of what happens next.

Having arrived at a set of advertising objectives and established a budget, we are faced with decisions on how to implement them. (It works the other way round too, of course, for if the budget is set by the 'task' method (*see* Section 3.5), we must have some idea early on of how the objectives will be reached in order to work out the approximate cost.)

3.4.1 The creative task

Section 2.2 listed the key questions that determine the outcome of the advertising planning process. The creative stage of producing advertising campaigns is concerned with two of them:

1   What is the message we have to convey?
2   How can our message be conveyed most effectively?

Advertising a new burst-proof tyre will call for different treatment from reminding customers of the existence of a brand of baked beans or canned soup. But, of course, these questions must be answered in the light of the answers to some of the other questions, in particular:

1   What is the objective of advertising in this particular situation?
2   What is the audience we are communicating with?

Telling doctors about a new drug is clearly a different proposition from announcing a new pop CD or persuading companies to consider leasing vehicles rather than buying them. The advertising budget and the choice of media will also have a bearing. Above all the creative teams will be guided by the advertising strategy that has been developed. They will develop their ideas, not in a vacuum but knowing what the objectives are; whether the advertising is to be generic (mobile telephones are very useful devices) or brand-differentiating (Travelphone gives you better coverage of the UK). They will know that depending on whether the product is to be positioned as 'up-market' (expensive, exclusive) or 'down-market' (cheap, moderate quality, for everyday use by everybody) so it will need to be presented appropriately.

In addition, the advertising that finally emerges must of course have the following attributes:

1   Be able to command attention against all competing influences. People do not generally watch television and read newspapers primarily to see the advertisements (although they may well buy certain specialist magazines at least partly for that purpose).
2   Be able to sustain interest. Boring or dull advertising is unlikely to exert much influence.
3   Be memorable.

How this process actually happens is dealt with in Chapters 5 and 6.

3.4.2 How media decisions are made

Nowhere is the choice of methods more varied than in the media aspect of the job. A wide variety of kinds of media are available, including the following:

Broadcasting (TV and radio) – *see* Chapter 12
The Press (newspapers and magazines, both consumer and trade) – *see* Chapter 11
Outdoor (posters – on buses, trains, etc.) – *see* Chapter 13
Direct Mail (sending out letters through the post) – *see* Chapter 8
Exhibitions – *see* Chapter 8

If we want to reach financial directors of large companies, for example, we may choose between newspapers (such as *The Times* and *The Financial Times*), magazines (the accountancy journals, *The Economist* and so on), or direct mail. Usually the selection must be made in four stages, as follows:

1 What kind of media (from a list including the above)?
2 Which particular medium (which newspaper, which radio stations, etc.)?
3 What size/type of space, how much time, how many posters of what size, what frequency of appearance over what length of time?
4 How much will our budget permit us to buy?

Later these areas are investigated in more depth (*see* Chapter 7) but here, as an example of the kind of approach, a short look can be taken at the way in which one newspaper or magazine might be selected rather than another. This is done by progressively narrowing down the list of possible publications to find the one that will reach the maximum number of the target audience (though sometimes it may be better to concentrate on only a small section of the target audience, to gain maximum impact). Sometimes, of course, 'maximum number' will conflict with 'lowest cost' and a compromise may have to be decided upon. This is normally a progressive process going through a number of stages as follows:

1 Select those publications that are likely to reach as many of the target audience as possible.
2 Establish the cost of reaching those readers (often on a 'cost per thousand readers' basis).
3 Arrive at the best publication in terms of maximum number of readers within the target audience at lowest cost per thousand.
4 Consider whether any supporting publications are needed (for example, the 'best buy' publication may reach only 65 per cent of the target audience; to use a second would reach a further 25 per cent).

Sometimes other criteria have to be taken into account, e.g. a particular product may need illustrating in colour (fabrics, paint), whereas the 'best buy' may only carry black and white advertisements.

3.4.3 The importance of concentration

It has just been suggested that it is important to select the 'best buy' rather than to advertise in all publications that reach the target audience. This is one example of an important general principle in advertising – that of concentration. (Part of the folklore of advertising is that successful advertising is a matter of concentration, domination and repetition. We inevitably discover in practice that these admirable objectives often need to be tempered by considerations of what is possible within a restricted budget if profit is to be achieved.) It may be very tempting to try to cover all the options but this is never the most effective use of money. In general it is better to: (a) use the one best publication rather than many, (b) publish a small number of large advertisements rather than many small ones, and (c) reach a small part of the total potential market strongly rather than all of it with a feeble message. The aim should always be dominance, if need be in a carefully chosen sector, rather than to be just 'one of the crowd' of advertisers.

3.5 Deciding on advertising budgets

One of the questions posed in Section 3.2 was 'How much should we be spending?' This is absolutely crucial, for how much we have to spend will have a big influence on what kind of advertising we can do. It is not much use thinking of national television if the budget comes out at £5,000. Unfortunately it is a particularly difficult question to answer.

Up to a point we can arrive at it by way of the break-even approach. Since our promotional costs are probably an important element in our variable costs, we can plot them against anticipated sales and try to assess at what point further promotional expenditure would show diminishing returns. But, in the first place, there is likely to be a fair amount of guesswork in it (how else can we arrive at the level of 'anticipated sales'?). More important however, is that we are still dealing in total promotional costs. These may well include the expense of a sales force, sales literature (sometimes very costly indeed in the case of high-technology industrial products) and other forms of sales promotion. In a sense adding, say £30,000 to the advertising budget means operating with one less salesperson. What is the correct approach to this difficult question?

Some well tried approaches exist, the main ones traditionally being the following:

1   *Arbitrary Methods.* While, clearly, they cannot be recommended, many
    companies simply pick a figure 'off the ceiling' or on the basis of
    'that's what we can afford'. Sometimes 'inertia', as Simon Broadbent
    describes it, becomes an important element. What we are spending
    seems to work, so why change it (if it ain't broke, don't fix it)?
        Often this approach is extended by using a modifier to adjust for
    increases in media cost due to inflation.
2   *Percentage of Sales.* An 'easy' and superficially attractive method is to
    allocate a proportion of sales revenue to advertising. But which sales
    revenue? Last year's, this year's, what we anticipate next year? All are
    used by various companies in various ways. The method has the advant-
    age of making calculations easy – if anticipated turnover is £X,000, then the
    advertising budget is Y per cent of £X,000. But the underlying assumption
    is either that the level of sales is directly determined by the level of adver-

tising expenditure or that advertising is a luxury you buy according to how much profit you are making. A variant of this approach, often used in a fairly predictable market, is to allocate an amount for advertising on a per unit basis, e.g. 5 pence per case or per dozen of anticipated sales. There is an obvious danger that declining sales can lead to declining expenditure and so on in a vicious spiral. Conversely in a booming market rapidly increasing sales can lead to far higher expenditures than are necessary. All such approaches also need an answer to the question 'What should the percentage be?'

3   *What Competitors are Spending.* Clearly competitive expenditure cannot be ignored, since it may provide, especially for a company entering a new field, a good general guide to the kind of expenditure that may be necessary. But it can be very misleading:

(a) Because it assumes that competitors know what they are doing when, in fact, their level of expenditure may be hopelessly uneconomic and based on sheer guesswork.

(b) Because companies in the same field have a quite different promotional mix, e.g. in the cosmetics field Avon concentrate on direct selling, Boots rely largely on 'captive' customers in their own retail outlets, and many others spend heavily on advertising because it is the only way they can communicate directly with 'end users' and also because they can only obtain retail distribution by convincing retailers that demand will be generated by the advertising

4   *On a ' Task' Basis.* If it can be decided what task(s) advertising needs to perform in the particular circumstances, a suitable advertising programme can be worked out and costed to give the budget necessary to achieve the task(s). In principle this must be the correct approach, but unfortunately there are always many ways of achieving the desired result, often with wildly different costs. It is not easy to decide what concentration of advertising is necessary to achieve a particular effect.

To establish an advertising budget Dr Simon Broadbent[1] suggests asking the following four questions (which are, in fact, a combination of most of the above approaches):

1   What can the product afford?
2   What is the advertising task?
3   What are competitors spending?
4   What have we learned from previous years?

In an example he suggests that the approach might give answers such as the following:

1   £175,000 is all that is allocated in the preliminary budget.

2   £230,000 would achieve the advertising exposures regarded as desirable.

3   £200,000 will buy a share of advertising equal to the product's share of the market.

4   £200,000 was spent last year, but there are indications that brand share is responsive to the amount of advertising support.

Dr Broadbent goes on to say, 'You can imagine the discussions which take place around the range of £150,000 to £230,000. Ultimately, the decision will lie in the character of the firm. The conservative firm will settle at a low figure, the thrusting, expansionist firm will invest in its future.' In his later book *The Advertising Budget*[3], Dr Broadbent stresses that advertising budgets are evolved as part of the total marketing planning process and budgets are normally arrived at by a long process of discussion and argument. This means that personalities and relative power ('clout') within the organization may also play a part in what is finally agreed.

3.5.1 Other budgeting methods

The total number of methods available is endless and they are explored at length in an IPA publication.[2] Some of the more important, in addition to the 'traditional' methods already listed, are:

1   *The Marginal Return Approach.* This is only really practical in simple advertising situations such as direct response where the cost of additional advertising can easily be compared with the additional revenue it generates. It then makes sense to increase expenditure all the time sufficient additional profit results from it.

2   A somewhat similar approach is the *Cost per Capita* method where – as is sometimes the case in industrial or consumer durable markets – the advertising cost of gaining an additional customer can be calculated (e.g. by analysing coupon returns and the resulting volume of business).

3   *Matching Brand Share to Advertising Share.* Here advertising expenditures are adjusted to relate to the 'share of voice', i.e. the particular advertiser's share of total expenditure in that market to his projected brand share. This assumes a direct relationship between such expenditure and the market shares achieved. (Section 3.5.2 quotes figures from the IPA study[2] indicating how advertising expenditures tend to reflect the competitiveness of markets.)

4   *Marketing Model.* If a mathematical relationship can be developed (*see* Section 17.4.1 on econometrics) between the various elements in the marketing mix, it can be used to predict the optimum levels of advertising expenditure. It is, however, extremely difficult to achieve this

because of the vast number of variables involved. Such relationships have to be worked out for each different market situation – there seem to be no 'universal' models.

5   *The 'Total' Approach.* This is akin to Broadbent's approach in Section 3.5 but takes account of a larger number of factors. As the IPA study puts it: '... an attempt is made to take into account and blend all the influences on the advertising appropriation, namely:

(a) past sales
(b) forecast sales and profit requirements
(c) production capacities
(d) market environment – competitors, economy, political trends
(e) product performance – adequacy, perception of quality, etc.
(f) sales force strength
(g) distribution strength and problems
(h) seasonal factors
(i) regional factors
(j) availability and cost effectiveness of media
(k) trends in the market as revealed by research

In a practical sense, this method is one of the more realistic in that a careful review of all eleven factors will inevitably lead to a comprehensive understanding of every element in advertising/marketing. Decisions on advertising expenditure levels will stem from a review of those elements germane to brand performance in the period under review.'

3.5.2 Advertising to sales ratios (the AS ratio)

It should be apparent from the above that advertising expenditures as a proportion of the marketing mix and of sales revenue will vary enormously from one market to another.

The IPA study[2] expresses it as follows:

> The AS ratio is of course a percentage expression of advertising expenditure to sterling sales turnover. It can either be expressed in terms of sales value at retail selling prices (RSP), or at manufacturers' prices (MSP).
>
> In itself, the AS ratio should not be used as a method for setting an advertising appropriation. The AS ratio for a market category is an average, and for competitive brands it will vary according to product and company circumstances.
>
> It is of use as an order-of-magnitude guide in the sense that if an advertising appropriation is developed for a product which is substantially different from its market or competitors, then the basis of the appropriation working can be checked.

Alan Wolfe of Ogilvy Mather has prepared a useful guide to AS ratios for different market categories and comments:

As a generalization, it can be suggested that a brand in a static market in a relatively comfortable position compared with competition will be spending at or slightly below its market average, while brand leaders in a competitive battle will be spending at or slightly above its market average. A new product has been known to invest as much as 100 per cent of sales in its launch period.

On this basis, a brand leader in a moderately competitive situation is likely to be spending 5 per cent–10 per cent of sales, while investment in a highly competitive market could cost as much as 15 per cent–25 per cent. This compares with a generic market expansion campaign by a monopolist which often needs less than 1 per cent.

An analysis of AS ratios across 85 consumer goods and service markets in 1973 (see Table 3.1) revealed the direct relationship between intensity of competition and size of AS ratio. Threequarters of the markets had ratios lower than 8 per cent, although of course for individual advertisers the AS ratio will be higher.

3.6 The advertising process

The matters discussed in this chapter are not a series of separate aspects,

Table 3. 1   *Approximate advertising to sales ratios by market (85 Consumer goods and services 1973)*

Classification	AS Ratio	Markets	
	%	No.	%
Non-competitive	0.0–0.9	20	24
Light competition	1.0–1.9	15	27
	2.0–2.9	8	
Medium competition	3.0–3.9	4	23
	4.0–4.9	7	
	5.0–5.9	3	
	6.0–6.9	4	
	7.0–7.9	2	
Heavy competition	8.0–8.9	4	26
	9.0–9.9	3	
	10.0–10.9	4	
	11.0–11.9	2	
	12.0–12.9	4	
	13.0–13.9	3	
	14.0 and over	2	
Total		85	100

Source: IPC Marketing Manual MEAL

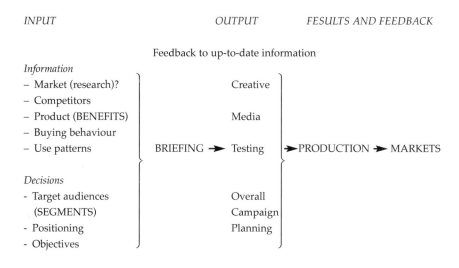

INPUT   OUTPUT   FESULTS AND FEEDBACK

Feedback to up-to-date information

Information
– Market (research)?   Creative
– Competitors
– Product (BENEFITS)   Media
– Buying behaviour
– Use patterns   BRIEFING ➤ Testing   ➤PRODUCTION ➤ MARKETS

Decisions
- Target audiences   Overall
   (SEGMENTS)   Campaign
- Positioning   Planning
- Objectives

Figure 3.1 *The Advertising Process*

but part of a total coherent process, with each part of it affecting all the other parts.

Figure 3.1 shows one 'model' of how the process works. We start by gathering a great deal of information – about markets, about competitors, about our own product (and indeed all aspects of our marketing activity). (*See* Chapter 4.) Using this information we must make decisions about positioning, decide on our target audiences (which will involve considera-tion of market segments) and decide on clear-cut objectives. These should be quantified so that results can be measured (*See* Chapter 5). From all this we can develop a clear briefing to the advertising planners, so that creative and media aspects can be developed as part of an overall campaign plan (*see* Chapter 6). Their ideas must be turned into appropriate material (artwork, tapes, films, etc.) – the production stage (*see* Chapter 15). Finally, the impact of all this must be observed and fed back into the system, so that we can know whether objectives have been achieved and also whether the information needs to be modified before briefing the subsequent stages of the campaign (*see* Chapter 17).

3.7 Summary

1   To be effective, advertising must be carefully planned and many ques-tions must be asked in order to establish:
     who do we need to communicate with?

what do we need to tell them?

how can we best get our message to them?

2   Advertising must be aimed at achieving specific objectives.

3   These objectives must be quantified so that the advertising may be clearly directed and its effectiveness measured.

4   The advertising plan must be based on decisions regarding strategy and positioning.

5   From these decisions the creative and media aspects of the advertising campaign may be logically developed.

6   A further aspect of planning is to decide on the appropriate budget – this may well involve using a number of different methods of calculation to arrive at the optimum result.

7   Advertising can best be viewed as a process in which information and decisions (on strategy etc.) lead to a briefing which forms the basis of creative, media and overall campaign planning. From this the advertising is produced and finally its effectiveness must be measured and fed back.

3.8 References

1 Broadbent, Dr Simon, *Spending Advertising Money*, Business Books 1975, second edition, 1981.

2 *Setting Advertising Appropriations*, IPA, 1978.

3 Broadbent, Dr Simon, *The Advertising Budget*, NTC Publications Ltd and IPA, 1989. A very comprehensive review of all aspects, including modelling.

3.9 Further reading

Dr Broadbent's book is exceptionally good, especially on the media aspects, but also on the whole concept of planned advertising. His later book, *Accountable Advertising* (Admap Publications, 1997), is also invaluable as a professional's guide to effective advertising.

Offensive Marketing by J. H. Davidson (Pelican, 1987) gives a good review of the whole marketing process, but with heavy emphasis on promotion and contains good case histories on how strategies are developed. Davidson's later book *Even More Offensive Marketing* (Pelican, 1997) is also excellent.

Advertising by Winston Fletcher (Teach Yourself Books) and *Advertising: what it is and how to do it* by Roderick White (McGraw-Hill, 1980, third edition, 1993) both have good readable chapters on the planning process.

3.10 Questions for discussion

1 You are preparing a memo to your managing director on advertising for your company. Outline the many ways of calculating the budget and recommend the method you prefer.
2 Select three current advertising campaigns with which you are familiar and discuss what objectives you think they might be trying to achieve.
3 As agency account executive you are called to a meeting to discuss a new perfume which your client, a leading manufacturer, plans to launch. List the information you will expect to take away and describe which details will be particularly useful in preparing a brief to (a) the creative department and (b) the media buying department.
4 Outline briefly some of the factors that go to producing an effective advertising campaign.

Chapter 4

Picturing the market

'Identify your customers, find out everything you can about them and then a lot more.'
Winston Fletcher, *A Glittering Haze*, NTC Publications, 1992

By the end of this chapter you will:

- Appreciate that successful advertising is based on information about the market;
- Understand the meaning and importance of benefits;
- Realize that we must study how our customers buy and what our competitors are offering them.

4.1 The need to know

All readers of spy thrillers will be familiar with the 'need to know' principle. To preserve security each member of the team is told only what he or she needs to know to carry out their part of the task. That way the danger of secrets being leaked or squeezed out under pressure is minimized.

In advertising, the situation is almost the opposite. To quite a large extent, the more people know, the better they can carry out their task of producing good advertising. At the end of the day we have to achieve good communication and that depends on a clear understanding of the people we are communicating with. It is a well-established (and obvious) principle of teaching or public speaking that the material, method of delivery and choice of words must be carefully selected to match the needs, expectations and ability of the audience. Teaching 5-year-olds is quite different from lecturing to post-graduates; an after-dinner audience of bankers is quite a different proposition from a talk at the young mothers coffee morning.

Exactly the same applies with advertising only more so because there is an essential difference. If we 'get it wrong' with a face-to-face audience, their reactions tell us so. They look bored, shuffle or cough; they may ask questions or in other ways indicate that they are not clearly understanding what we say or that the information we are delivering is not what they want. We can then change or add to what we are saying.

People receiving advertising messages cannot do this, so we may be unaware that our message has gone wrong. This means we have to be totally certain in advance:

1 Who are the people we need to address? What is their present level of knowledge or understanding? What kind of language and concepts do they normally use? How do they like to be addressed?
2 How will our product help them and how (from their point of view) does it compare with other products?
3 How do they go about buying our kind of product and how are the decisions taken? We also need to be clear about whether it *is worth* spending money on advertising, so we shall also need to know such things as:
   (a) How big is the market for this kind of product?
   (b) Is it growing, declining or static?
   (c) Is there a market for our particular type of product?
   (d) What competitors are there and how do their products compare with ours?

4.2 Is there a market?

The success of any commercial venture is primarily dependent on whether the product or service being offered has a market. What is meant by saying 'is there a market?' Some examples may help. As this section was being written in 1983, the butter industry in the UK was in considerable difficulty because less butter was being consumed as more and more people switched to margarine. The reasons included:

1 Butter had become much more expensive than margarine.
2 Margarines containing 'polyunsaturated fats' were believed by many medical researchers to be less liable to contribute to heart disease than butter and this had received considerable publicity.
3 Some newer margarines, such as Flora and Krona, had been developed which were more acceptable to consumers for use instead of butter than were the 'traditional' margarines.

   Interestingly, the promotion of Flora had been largely based on the health aspect (it is made from polyunsaturated fats such as sunflower oil) whereas Krona was advertised in such a way as to draw attention to its 'butteriness' (although direct comparison with butter was not allowed).

Thus the market for margarine – provided it met certain requirements was very buoyant, whereas the market for butter was in decline.

In 1996 the picture has changed somewhat. Butter is no longer perceived as quite so harmful; indeed, some experts have suggested that certain non-dairy fats can be *more* harmful than butter. This may change the market for fats quite considerably and offers a good example of how necessary it is to monitor markets continuously.

Similarly bread consumption has declined steadily since World War II and the high demand for the 'standard white, sliced, wrapped loaf' has been replaced by a much lower demand for a wider range of more specialized types of bread.

In 1983 video-tape recorders were in a boom situation but in 1996 this has peaked and been followed by a similar boom in camcorders and, more outstandingly, in mobile telephones.

Clearly it is going to be easier to get a response from advertising a product in a market which is growing than in one which is static or in decline. So we need to establish, probably through market research, what is happening in our particular market.

4.3 Who is buying?

If mobile telephones are being sold in large numbers, what kind of people are buying them? Old or young, male or female, wealthy or not so wealthy?And what are they using them for? Business (predominantly the case originally) or personal (increasingly so)? Are they used on a regular basis or only for emergencies? The answers to such questions will help in making many decisions, including prices for selling the instruments, for the standing charge and for the charge for time used.

By asking these questions and many more we can establish as precisely as possible what kind of people we are dealing with and what we need to offer them. The more we know about them, the more effectively our advertising can communicate with them.

4.3.1 Some customer profiles

Every two years the Institute of Practitioners in Advertising runs an Advertising Effectiveness awards scheme. The winning campaigns are featured in a series of publications titled *Advertising Works*[1]. This series of case histories provides many illustrations of customer profiles'. The 1980 volume, for example, enabled comparisons to be made of the target for a number of drinks.

Lucozade, the glucose carbonated drink marketed by Beecham had been 'positioned' (*see* Section 3.3.1) mainly as a drink for those, especially children, recovering from illness. However, the incidence of child illness had been declining steadily over 10 years. The drink was often used – as a 'pick-me-up', mainly by women – in health as well as after illness. It was therefore decided to seek to widen the market by repositioning the product and the new target audience was defined as: 'Active women between the ages of 18 and 35 who care about the health and well-being of themselves and their children.'

Schloer apple juice, another Beecham product, saw its target audience as: 'Housewives, primarily those with a growing family, 25–45 years old, with middle-class values or aspirations.'

Campari, imported by Findlater Matta, had in the past, set out deliberately to attract adventurous and discriminating drinkers. They were a minority of discoverers who enjoyed flaunting their sophistication and took pride in the knowledge that Campari did not appeal to all tastes. The brand's user profile was upmarket and slightly older. Unfortunately, an ageing, middle-class market did not provide sufficient scope for Campari's ambition for volume. Campari needed a more stable and democratic base. This *meant recruiting new, younger, mass-market trialists from among the socially mobile, high-spending, heavier drinkers with the discretionary income to spend drinking in pubs in the evenings.* (Present author's emphasis.)

These examples illustrate the importance which successful advertisers attach to a clearly-defined (and often quite subtle) appreciation of who their advertising is to be aimed at. The definitions of target audience are of course not simply dreamed up or arrived at by discussion – although much discussion is involved – but based on known facts about who the consumers are (or could be) and what are their habits, spending patterns, attitudes, aspirations, etc. These facts must be sought out normally through market research (*see* Chapters 16 and 17).

For example, a survey[2] carried out in 1978 by IPC Women's Magazines Ltd entitled *Alcoholic Drinks for the Home – Who Buys What?* included the breakdown shown in Table 4.1.

In the 1995 *Advertising Works 8* we read that the typical malt whisky drinker only buys three bottles a year, is middle-aged, rather conservative and not easily influenced. By contrast, the introduction of lemonade laced with alcohol in 1995, such as the 'Hooch' brand, caught on so rapidly with teenagers as to cause public concern and calls for controls.

A different but equally useful way of viewing the market is illustrated by the Cadbury's Roses story in *Advertising Works 8* 1995. Their main competitor, Quality Street, had achieved a dominant position in the market as the assortment for sharing with the family. Cadbury's counter-attacked by positioning Roses as the ideal 'informal gift' ('say thank you with Roses'). Between 1979 and 1990 Roses moved from a poor second to Quality Street to leader in its sector.

Table 4. I   *Buying alcoholic drinks for home consumption or to give as a present*

	total	age of housewife					social class			
		15–24	25–34	35–44	45–54	55–64	AB	CI	C2	DE
sample:										
unweighted	1464	201	331	291	315	326	176	376	500	412
weighted	2047	199	488	440	470	450	269	536	679	563
ever buying (%)										
anyone in household	77	81	81	80	74	70	85	81	76	70
housewives	68	72	74	72	64	60	76	72	67	61
men	60	62	69	67	59	42	70	65	62	47

Source: IPC survey, 1978.

4.4 Our product and its benefits

We have to have a clear understanding of our product. This may sound silly – of course we understand our product, we may think. After all, we designed it, made it and have been selling it for years. First though, we must understand what a product really is – and in talking of product we include what are sometimes called services. The intangibles like haircuts, air travel, insurance, need to be viewed as products just as do tangible items such as drinks, cars and machine tools. To understand what the product is we must recognize the difference between what we produce and what our customers buy. A drill manufacturer may sell ¼ inch steel drill bits. What his customers are paying money for is the ability to produce ¼ inch holes. (Which means incidentally that in the not far-distant future a laser device or something of the kind may enable us to make holes much more simply in which case the market for metal drills will disappear.)

When we buy steak at the butcher's we pay money, not for a rather sickening lump of bleeding raw flesh, but for the knowledge of the succulent meal it will become and the satisfied looks on the family's faces when they have eaten this. An ancient adage in the advertising business recognizes this – 'sell 'em the sizzle, not the steak'.

In *Marketing Management,* Professor Philip Kotler[3] defines a product as, 'A bundle of physical service and symbolic particulars expected to yield satisfactions or benefits to the buyer'.

4.4.1 The importance of benefits

What we design into a product is *features* – such as a more powerful drill motor, or a tenderized steak. What our customers buy are the *benefits* of faster, easier drilling or of steak which is easier to prepare and pleasanter to eat.

A key aspect of understanding our market in order to communicate effectively with it is defining what are the most important benefits which our customers can obtain from the products we offer them. This can be a complex matter because the same product may deliver a number of different benefits to different people. What we see as the main benefits may not be those that appeal to our customers. It is the *perceived benefits,* the ones that our customers feel to be important that are the benefits we must identify and concentrate on in our advertising.

To appeal to a wider group of customers the benefit offered by Lucozade became the fact that it 'helps the body to regain its normal energy level' rather than simply being 'easier to take in sickness'[1] (*see* Section 4.3.1). From the 'regain normal energy rate' idea (when we are active this rate oscillates vigorously; when we are tired it is flat and depressed) this developed into the creative theme of the advertising which strongly presented the benefits of Lucozade.

The benefit of Krona margarine was presented as the fact that it is 'the first margarine with a taste and texture indistinguishable from butter'. (*See* Fig. 4.1.) The advertising makes no mention of the highly sophisticated technology and carefully selected ingredients that went into its manufacture. Those features are not what the customers buy.

Campari was advertised as being 'enjoyable whatever you choose to drink it with, but especially with soda or lemonade'.

Similarly, Roses is an easy and inexpensive way to say 'Thank you very much' and the early Vodaphone advertising offered trades and professional people a way to be 'In when you're out'.

4.4.2 Knowing our competitors

In understanding how our products and their benefits appeal to our customers we must of course also take account of our competitors. For example, the two margarines (Flora and Krona) and the three drinks (Lucozade, Schloer and Campari) (referred to in Section 4.3.1) each have many competitors. That is to say someone who buys and uses these products has many alternatives from which to choose. It is therefore important to have a clear and detailed understanding of what are the benefits of each of the competitive products, as well as our own. Sometimes differences are very slight and very subtle. There may even be no measurable difference at all in physical attributes or measurable performance.

Yet the customers will want to choose a product which best suits their needs – psychological and emotional as well as physical – and which they can be comfortable with as an expression of their particular personality and individuality. So products need to be *differentiated* from each other

The margarine that raised questions in an Australian parliament.

In Sydney Australia, several years ago, an extraordinary rumour started amongst housewives.

It grew to such proportions that the New South Wales Government became involved. And it all began over something as simple as a margarine.

So successful did this margarine become, that housewives were even buying it by the caseful. People were taking it off lorries when it was delivered at supermarkets, to be certain of buying some.

All this activity led to the Minister of Agriculture being asked questions about the product in parliament.

For the rumour was that it wasn't margarine at all. Its taste was that good.

The counterpart of this Australian Margarine is on sale in Britain.

It's called Krona.

Figure 4.1   *A press advertisement for Krona margarine. The television campaign used the same theme (see Section 3.2.2 on integrated campaigns). Source: Broadbent, S., Advertising Works, Holt, Rinehart and Winston, 1981*

(Section 2.4 referred briefly to the need to establish a *competitive differential advantage*.) Sometimes it is the promotion element in the marketing mix – and advertising in particular – that carries the main burden of establishing the difference.

The task of advertising is then to establish *added value* by highlighting those perceived benefits which make the product more desirable to its chosen target audience than the competitive products are. Krona is not just 'any old margarine', Campari not 'any old drink', British Airways not 'any old airline', Esso not 'any old oil company'. Each has a clearly distinguishable personality and set of attributes. Each is expected by its customers to deliver certain benefits which it clearly offers. All of this is often summed up by saying that a product or a company has a clear 'image'. People will find it more difficult to know what to expect from a company which they see and understand only 'through a glass darkly'. Good advertising polishes up the mirror and focuses the lens through which the customers view the products being offered to them.

Once more of course, the knowledge of what competitive products are being offered must come from a detailed study of the market-place – market research again! We have to know in particular what customers see as the alternatives. If they do not buy from us, who will they buy from? Which products do they prefer – and why? Which do they like least – and why?

Having gained this clear understanding of what is on offer and what is preferred by each group of customers (and there will often be many groups with different preferences) we have to decide which group to aim at with which benefits highlighted. This involves consideration of positioning (*see* Sections 3.3.1 and 4.3.1) and of market segmentation – the differing requirements of different groups (segments) within the total market.

4.5 How do people buy our product?

In order to select and transmit appropriate information in the most suitable manner to our target audience we must have some knowledge of what is involved for them in the buying process. What information do they work with in making their decisions? Is it an instant 'impulse' decision or carefully considered over a long period? Do they buy frequently and in doing so develop a habit of buying particular products and 'favourite' brands or do they reconsider which one to buy 'this time'? Do they actively seek out our product or service (as for example when they need a plumber because the tank is leaking) or must we first stimulate the interest of an initially passive audience?

Longman[4] suggests three different models of the marketing and advertising situation, the one we use being determined by the following factors:

1   The purchase cycle – its length, regularity, and its responsiveness to advertising.
2   The brand decision – whether it reflects conscious commitment, automatic choice, or something in between.
3   The purchase decision – how much deliberation and 'shopping around' it involves.
4   The relationship between time of purchase and time of use – on-premise consumption as compared with home inventory and regular or sporadic use at home.
5   The brand's competitive market position.
6   The functions assigned to other marketing activities for the brand.

Clearly answers to these questions can only come from a detailed study of the market-place and how customers purchase and use the product. Longman's suggested three models are:

1   *Brand Switching Model.* Where the purpose of advertising it to encourage purchasers of a type of product used regularly (margarine or coffee for example) to 'switch' from one brand to another or alternatively to encourage continued purchase of their existing brand.
2   *Purchase Cycle Model.* Here the purpose of advertising is to induce people who do not normally or regularly use the product to change their behaviour by using it. The irregularly used type of food product (e.g. some types of meat or dessert) are examples where advertising of the reminder type ('Why not give them . . . for a change') could be appropriate. It could be said that the brand switching model applies where there is a fixed purchase cycle, whereas here we are trying to influence the purchase cycle by encouraging more frequent or more regular usage.
3   *The Attitude Model.* Here, there may be no purchase at all unless we can encourage people to change their attitudes. New products in particular may involve the need to encourage people to accept change (video recorders, word processors). Existing attitudes may cause resistance to purchase (e.g. of exotic or unfamiliar foods). The attitude model will of course also apply to much of the public relations or 'corporate image' type of advertising.

Several of the current theories on how consumer choices are made and the part advertising is thought to play in the process are examined in some depth in Chapter 10.

4.6 Advertising and 'the trade'

Section 2.3.6 referred to trade advertising – directed at 'the trade' to influence them to stock and sell our products. Section 5.4.1 considers the influ-ence of distribution patterns – making it easy for our customers to obtain our product from a local shop (e.g. groceries), a distributor (e.g. farm machinery), in some cases direct from the manufacturer (e.g. Land's End clothing) or on their own doorstep (Betterware household goods). These choices can be summed up in a chart (*see* Figure 4.2).

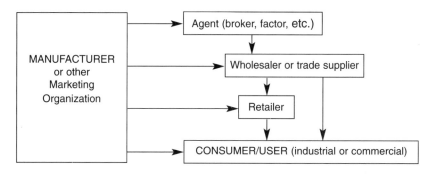

Figure 4.2   *Some alternative routes to the customer*

Which type of distributor, retailer, etc. (often collectively called 'middlemen' or, increasingly, 'resellers') is used is a decision based on a number of factors:

1   *Cost.* Selling direct saves money which would have to be paid as dis-counts to resellers (or lower prices enabling them to add their own 'mark-up'). However, selling direct carries its own costs – for a sales force or advertising, delivery costs, etc.
2   *Control.* Using resellers may be attractive from other points of view but means that the manufacturer loses direct contact with his ultimate cus-tomers. The large supermarket chains for example are increasingly building their own 'customer franchise' – groups of customers who always shop with them and buy what products they offer rather than choosing to buy particular manufacturers' products and then finding a stockist who has them on his shelves.
3   *Special Facilities.* Where, for example, after-sales service is important (cars, domestic appliances, office equipment) or where customers need to see products on display (kitchens and bathroom fittings) the manufacturer may need to use resellers to provide these facilities for him.
4   *Access to Markets.* In some cases the reseller has access to a market that the manufacturer would find it very difficult and expensive to estab-lish for himself (e.g. a manufacturer of building products who devel-

ops some of them for do-it-yourself use). So a manufacturer may need to use advertising:

(a) To reach to market directly without using resellers
(b) To encourage resellers to stock his products:
   i)   by letting them know through trade advertising about, for example, the profits he could bring them
   ii) by ensuring through consumer advertising that the products will sell: the promise of this will often help to persuade a reseller to stock
(c) To support resellers already stocking his product, either by advertising from manufacturer to consumer (see (b) above) or by providing promotional material – ranging from advertising artwork or blocks to point of sale material – or by contributing financially to the reseller's own promotional activity.

Often a manufacturer wanting to sell his products through a reseller will need to do all of these things. For example, a food manufacturer selling his products through supermarket chains may well need to:

1   Advertise his products to the consumer, e.g. on television (knowing incidentally that resellers will also see and be influenced by such advertising).
2   Provide point-of-sale leaflets, stickers, etc. to the supermarkets.
3   Arrange periodic sales promotional activity (*see* Chapter 8) – often worked out individually with each store group in turn ('tailor-made promotions').
4   Make an allowance within the total financial deal for a contribution through local and/or national advertising by the supermarket chain.

How much of the total promotional budget to allocate to each of these activities is an important consideration (*see* Section 5.4.1).

Although the above is most obviously necessary where the reseller is a retailer, it may be no less important where the reseller is a distributor of industrial equipment such as machine tools or an agent (e.g. in computer software).

4.7 Case study

The Roses story

One of the award-winning campaigns recorded in *Advertising Works 8* (1995) concerns the progress of Cadbury's Roses chocolates from its repositioning in 1979 to market dominance at the end of 1993.

Background

Prior to 1979 the chocolate assortments market in the UK had developed into three sectors: the premium sector (hand-made chocolates and the more expensive Continental assortments); mainstream (the traditional boxed chocolates such as Black Magic) and economy, dominated by the 'twist wraps' (Quality Street and Roses).

The two brands differ slightly in that Quality Street includes more toffees, some of them unwrapped, and is marginally less expensive. In 1969 Quality Street had repositioned itself as the ideal brand for 'sharing with all the family'. This left Roses in an awkward situation as 'more special (and expensive) than Quality Street but not as special as the mainstream assortments'.

Consumer research reactions included;

> 'Roses are more of a luxury'
> 'They are too expensive for everyday'
> 'Roses would make me feel guilty'

With a brand share a poor second to Quality Street, Roses needed a new and clearly defined position. The one adopted was the 'informal gift', lying between Quality Street's 'sharing with the family' and the more 'romantic' boxed chocolates.

The theme was developed into the 'Thank you very much' campaign – catchy music by The Scaffold – from 1970 onwards. It moved Roses into first place in terms of advertising recognition and sales.

As early as 1979 research was recording consumer statements like:

> 'It's a way of showing gratitude for what they've done for each other, isn't it?'
> 'Small gift, an ideal way of saying thank you.'

Advertising Works continues: 'From being clearly behind in the 1970s, Roses became the "most preferred" brand and the one bought "most often".'

4.8 Summary

1   Successful advertising campaigns are based on clear information about the market.
2   There must be a recognition of where the product fits into the market – how it needs to be 'positioned' – who will buy it and what benefits it delivers.
3   It is also necessary to be clear what competitive products are available and how ours can be differentiated from them.
4   We need to understand how people buy our product in order to determine which of the various models of advertising is most likely to be applicable.
5   In addition to communicating benefits to the end users we may often also have to use advertising to ensure the support of 'the trade'.

4.9 References

1 Broadbent, Dr Simon [Ed], *Advertising Works*, Holt, Rinehart and Winston, 1981.
2 *Alcoholic Drinks for the Home – Who Buys What?* IPC Women's Magazines, 1978.
3 Kotler, Philip, *Marketing Management – Analysis Planning and Control*, third edition, Prentice-Hall, 1976.
4 Longman, Kenneth A., *Advertising*, Harcourt Brace Jovanovich, Inc., 1971.

4.10 Further reading

Advertising Works provides many most valuable case histories that demonstrate how successful campaigns are grounded on detailed understanding of the market. A new edition is published every two years, the most recent (No. 9) in 1997.

IPC publish a number of reports that throw light on how a particular market works, as do other publishers, TV contractors, etc.

The Economist Intelligence Unit's Retail Business and the Mintel reports, both issued monthly, contain regular reports on a wide range of markets in the UK and EIU also publishes an EEC-wide equivalent.

There are a number of very useful 'sources of sources' designed to help in finding suitable sources of information about markets. One is the *UK Marketing Source Book*, published by NTC.

4.11 Questions for discussion

1 Explain the benefits, and who benefits, when the government runs a successful fire prevention campaign.

2 Identify two products whose sales are developing rapidly in your country and discuss:
  (a) why this seems to be taking place
  (b) what part advertising appears to be playing in the development

3 What advertising campaign are you personally most conscious of at the present time? What benefits does it appear to be offering and to whom?

4 During the past decade there have been a number of changes in the pattern of distribution of goods and services to the consumer. Identify two major changes that have taken place and state what you consider to have been the main causes.

5 Which of the advertising models listed in this chapter seem to you to be the most applicable to the purchase of:
  (a) breakfast foods
  (b) family cars
  (c) home computers
  (d) banking services
  (e) word processors

6 What sources would you use to gather market facts and information on the market for:
  (a) a chocolate bar
  (b) lap-top computers

7 Charles Revson is quoted as saying, 'In the factory we make cosmetics, in the Drug Store we sell hope.' Explain what is meant by this statement.

Part 2

How the advertising business functions

Chapter 5

Planning advertising campaigns

'Advertising can actually do a great many different things. The range of situations in which it may be used is very wide, and for each situation there is a variety of different strategies and different media.'
Simon Broadbent, *Accountable Advertising*, NTC Publications, 1997[1]

By the end of this chapter you will:

- Understand when advertising is the best promotional tool and when something else would be more effective;
- Be able to set about planning advertising with confidence;
- Appreciate the different ways in which advertising is managed in large organizations.

5.1 The importance of objectives

In Section 3.2 the point was made that advertising must be a *planned* activity. Simply spending money on advertising will achieve little or nothing unless:

1 We are very clear why we are spending it – we must know what our objectives are.
2 It is spent in such a way as to make it likely that the advertising will help carry us towards those objectives.

These two requirements in turn lead to a third:

3 We must measure whether the desired objectives are or are not achieved (*see* Chapter 17 for ways of carrying out the measurement).

A much-quoted aphorism – alleged to have been uttered by Lord Lever, one of the first advertising 'big spenders' – is, 'I know that half the money I spend on advertising is wasted. The trouble is, I don't know which half.' This counsel of despair is unacceptable in today's climate and most committed users of advertising on any scale put considerable effort and expenditure into measuring results.

Although things have moved on since Lord Lever's day, many people still find it difficult to evaluate the returns in sales and profit from advertising expenditures. This is because it *is* difficult. That should not, however, mean that we do not do it. Broadbent[1] suggests that:

> Advertising is still run differently (that is, from other corporate expenditures). It is hardly understood by many who pay for it; its objectives are set in communication terms; its budget is subject to whims; no one is too sure about the real returns – and so advertising budget recommendations are not much trusted.

There are two necessary steps to overcoming this problem:

1   Set objectives which are realistic, achievable and measurable.
2   Put the appropriate (and often complex and difficult – there's the problem) measurement mechanisms in place.

Measurement techniques are examined in Chapters 16 and 17, so here we look at the kinds of objectives that advertising may be expected to meet and how we go about planning campaigns that can be measured. Note that we will almost always be thinking in terms of advertising *campaigns* rather than individual advertisements. (Recruitment advertising and some kinds of direct response advertising may be among the exceptions to this rule.)

In Section 2.5 we gave an extensive list of all the tasks advertising can perform but in a campaign planning context we normally need to look at it somewhat differently, Sev D'Souza[2] suggests:

> In most advertising strategies there will be a section on campaign objectives. Invariably it will include some of these tasks:
> – Make an impact
> – create awareness
> – communicate messages
> – evoke an immediate response (sell off the page or get more information)
> – create favourable impressions
> – remind consumers
> – fulfil needs
> – change perceptions (mental repositioning or overcome prejudice)
> – reinforce attitudes
> – consolidate a position

- *enthuse the staff and the trade*
- *encourage trial.*

The problem we then have is turnng these tasks into targets that can be measured. For example, what is meant by 'awareness'; how much 'awareness' should a given expenditure generate in order for it to be justified (in the case of an existing product we may be wanting to increase or sustain awareness rather than create it). In order to measure things such as this we typically must do research before and after to establish, for example, how many of our target audience were aware of the product before and how many after the campaign (*see* Chapter 17). There is a further problem, however. When we have measured this kind of advertising effect, how can we be sure of its effect on sales? – an increase in awareness of a product people hate might not do much for sales and profits, and all kinds of other factors, from the weather to competitive activity, may have an influence on the result. For this kind of reason, Broadbent stresses the importance of using 'modelling' (mathematical analysis of sales trends, etc.) as the ultimate measure.

Advertising Works 6 (1991) contains a case history showing how Knorr set out to increase sales of their stock cubes in Scotland. Fairly complex research and analysis was able to demonstrate that advertising did between 1982 and 1990 increase sales volume sufficiently to pay for itself 1.8 times over. So in this case, whilst increasing awareness was an important function of the advertising, the real measure was the increase in sales. But measuring sales alone could have ignored the influence of many other factors. The model used took account of pricing and distribution of Knorr and competitors' products, new varieties, seasonality and competitive advertising.

So, as well as setting objectives in terms that can be measured, we need in the end to be able to make judgements on whether the advertising expenditure was justified.

There are situations even now where absolutely precise measurement of results may be difficult to achieve. As Hugh Davidson[3] points out, 'The trouble is that advertising is only one of the many variables which also affect sales. Indeed, an advertising campaign is itself influenced by four sub-variables – the content of the message, the amount of money placed behind it, the choice of media and the amount of competitive activity.' Davidson concludes that, 'The evaluation of advertising still relies heavily on the personal judgement of experienced executives.' Whilst many advertising executives would go some way with Davidson on this, most would want as much quantitative measurement as possible on which at least partly to base their 'personal judgement' since otherwise such judgements can become disastrously subjective (*see* Chapter 17).

We should also consider whether, even if advertising does achieve the desired result, some other method might achieve it better or at lower cost (for example recruitment of staff can be carried out through Job Centres, by using recruitment agencies or even 'on the grapevine').

5.2 Advertising in a marketing context

Not all advertising is directly concerned with marketing (*see* Section 5.1). However, a very high proportion of it is and we therefore need to consider the planning of advertising within a marketing context. Public relations is considered in Section 8.7 and brief reference is made there to the use of advertising in that context.

Marketing managers tend to approach decisions about advertising and other forms of promotion in three stages:

1   What is the right marketing mix?
2   What is the right promotional mix?
3   How can we most effectively carry out the promotional programme we have decided on?

5.2.1 What is the right marketing mix?

The concept of the marketing mix is dealt with at length in the author's *The Fundamentals and Practice of Marketing.* Here is a brief summary of its main implications.

Whilst there are many ways of expressing the marketing mix concept, an easily-understood and memorable one is 'The 4 Ps and the S'. The 4 Ps first:

> Product – making the right product (or service) available
> Price – at the right price
> Place – through distribution channels convenient to our customers
> Promotion – and presented in the way that appeals to them best

The marketing mix theory says that all four of these elements are important and that each must be right – and in the correct balance with each other – if customers are to be fully satisfied. And winning satisfied customers is what marketing is all about! The most effective way to win customers is to offer them an advantage – in any or all of these areas – over what competitors are offering (*see* Section 2.4). The fifth ingredient – the S – is for *service* which is very important in many situations; whether pre-sales service (providing information, costings, specifications, etc.) or post-sales service (such as repair and maintenance, training of operators, advice on operation). Sometimes service of some kind is supplied right through every stage of the buyer/seller relationship.

The relative importance of these ingredients varies enormously from one situation to another. Sometimes – with sophisticated technical equipment for example – it is all-important that the performance of the product is exactly right for the job. Price is a secondary consideration and place and promotion relatively unimportant. Pre- and post-sales service may be vital. With many consumer products on the other hand – soft drinks for example – the products are rather similar anyway and what counts most is how they are promoted and how widely they are distributed. The service element hardly enters the picture. Philip Kotler[4] suggests the following as markets where promotion will be especially important:

1 Products are alike, thus leading manufacturers to try to differentiate them psychologically.
2 Products are in the introductory stage of the life cycle, where awareness and interest must be built, or in the mature stage, where defensive expenditures are required to maintain market shares. (See the author's *The Fundamentals and Practice of Marketing* for an outline of the Product Life Cycle Theory.)
3 Products are sold on a mail-order basis
4 Products are sold on a self-service basis.

5.2.2 What is the right promotional mix?

Within each of the '4 Ps and the S' further decisions have to be made. Here we are specially concerned with the promotion aspect – how products or services are presented to customers. Under this heading are sometimes included matters like visual design and packaging. But primarily we are concerned here with methods of *communicating* with customers. Methods used are:

Personal selling
Advertising
Sales Promotion
Public Relations

Each of these has its advantages and disadvantages and their relative importance varies with the particular case. We have to choose the appropriate promotion techniques and build the best 'promotional mix'.

Personal selling enables a *dialogue* to take place and it is known that two-way communication (where the customer can ask questions and the salesman can react to the particular situation) is more effective than one-way communication such as advertising. On the other hand a salesman can deal with only a small number of people and each 'contact' costs a lot of money. Also it takes a long time for the sales force to get round and talk to everybody we need to communicate with.

Advertising delivers a message cheaply to a great many people very quickly but presents problems if we need discussion or if the message needs to be changed to suit each customer. And of course advertising cannot negotiate a contract, carry out a survey of the customer's needs or arrange a trade-in. Generally speaking it cannot take an order – although some advertising (like the bargain pages in some newspapers or direct response advertising in a wide range of media) does complete the whole selling job. People read the advertisement, are convinced and send off an order with a cheque or their credit card number. But this is the exception rather than the rule.

Sales promotion (*see* Section 8.4) is a term covering a whole variety of things including cut price offers; premium offers (gifts given with the product or in exchange for tokens included in the packaging) 'loyalty points such as Air Miles or other entitlement to discounts, cash or other rewards accumulated through purchases; competitions ('win a holiday in the Bahamas'); as well as more complex affairs like the highly successful Tesco 'computers for schools', whereby shoppers collected vouchers with purchases and gave them to schools attended by their children or grand-children; the schools assembled sufficient points to exchange them for a computer for the classroom. Sales promotion techniques are good at pro-ducing activity and interest at the point of sale. Cut price offers for example induce people to take one product off the shelf rather than another and to go to one petrol station rather than another. The other strength of sales pro-motion is that it tends to get dealers and stockists involved in a rather less passive role than the one they normally adopt. Indeed, many sales promo-tion campaigns are deliberately designed to stimulate 'the trade' into greater activity in support of a particular product or range of products. Sales promotion schemes can indeed be aimed solely at people in the trade or at members of the sales force.

Public relations (*see* Section 8.7) is also a very broad term but one of its main facets is press relations which is concerned with disseminating (mainly favourable!) information about a company and its products through 'the media' (radio, TV and the press especially) not by paying for space as with advertising, but by providing news items or stories that the media will feel are of interest to their readers, listeners or viewers. An advertisement says precisely what we want it to say and we know that it *will* be published and *when* it will be published. Sending a press release to a newspaper on the other hand is no guarantee that our story will be pub-lished nor that if published it will be used in the way we would wish. An advantage is that favourable comment in the editorial columns has the weight of authority of the publication behind it and so is more believable than an advertisement where people know that it is *us* saying how won-derful our product is.

5.2.3 Carrying out the programme

The final stage is how will the selling, advertising, sales promotion or public relations work? If we are to use salesmen, how will they operate; how will they be equipped (with literature, visual aids, information); what advantage can they offer to customers over their competitors? If we decide that advertising is necessary, what media shall we use; what message will it carry; how can the message be most effectively stated – words, pictures, cartoons, case-histories of satisfied customers, or what?

In all these decisions we must bear in mind that cost is involved and every time we add to the cost, then extra sales must be generated that more than recover the cost.

For example, if we were selling cars we could put a simple black and white message in the motoring magazines stating the fuel consumption. The cost of setting up the advertisement would be small. But if we felt that the styling, colour, etc. of the car was all-important, then we would have to pay for expensive photography (perhaps with model fees and travel to some exotic location) and the printing of the advertisement itself would cost considerably more. These are just a few of the considerations and some of the limitations that have to be worked with.

5.3 The particular strength of advertising

Advertising therefore has to justify its place in the promotional mix, and in turn in the marketing mix, in preference to or alongside the other possible methods of promotion. Section 5.2.2 indicated some of the bases of comparison.

Kotler[4] suggests that advertising has the following particular distinctive qualities, 'especially when it comes to brand and institutional advertising'.

1   '*Public presentation.* Advertising, unlike personal selling, is a highly public mode of communication. Its public nature confers a kind of legitimacy to the product and also suggests a standardized offering. Because many persons receive the same message, buyers know that their motives for purchasing the product will be publicly understood.

2   *Pervasiveness.* Advertising is a pervasive medium that permits the seller to repeat his messages many times. It also allows the buyer to receive and compare the messages of various competitors. Large-scale advertising by a seller says something positive about the seller's size, popularity and success.

3   *Amplified expressiveness.* Advertising provides opportunities for dramatizing the company and its products through the artful use of print,

sound, and colour. Sometimes the tool's very success at expressiveness may, however, dilute or distract from the message.

4   *Impersonality.* Advertising, in spite of being public, pervasive, and expressive, cannot be as compelling as a personal salesman. The audience does not feel obligated to pay attention or respond. Advertising is only able to carry on a monologue, not a dialogue, with the audience.'

5.4 Promotional strategy

Marketing management making decisions about the place of promotion, and advertising in particular, have to make strategic judgements as well as taking into account cost-effectiveness and the kind of considerations indicated in Sections 5.2 and 5.3.

5.4.1 The influence of distribution patterns

In many marketing situations contact between the manufacturer of a product or the supplier of a service and the people who use it is indirect (*see* Section 4.6). A typical pattern is shown in Figure 5.1.

Figure 5.1

In this situation, decisions have to be made about the kind of promotional activity which is necessary and the weight of promotion to be applied at each stage. Promotional techniques can be used to persuade wholesalers, retailers, distributors, etc. to put the product into stock (*selling in* or push strategy). They can also be applied at the user end of the chain to persuade or encourage the users to demand the product (*selling out* or pull strategy). What happens at the point of purchase can also be vitally important and is described by the term merchandising.

Merchandising involves paying close attention to all the activities that take place in-store; designed actively to sell goods at maximum profitability. It includes:

Selection of products to be stocked
Stock control

Store layout, lighting and decor
Space allocation and merchandise location
Traffic flow (the way customers are encouraged to move around the store)
Display
Promotional activity
Pricing policy

Whilst merchandising is obviously vital to retailers and other resellers it is also a vital link in the chain for manufacturers and other marketing organizations. To some extent their interests are the same – how can we sell maximum volume at maximum profit? But there is also conflict. The manufacturer is concerned to move his products rather than those of his competitors. The retailer is interested only in achieving maximum turnover and/or profit and is not too concerned about whose products he uses to achieve it.

Thus the *manufacturer's viewpoint* is likely to be that merchandising is vital because: (a) his whole marketing activity only begins to take effect when customers actually purchase the product; and (b) he can achieve a higher sell in rate if he helps the retailer to sell out. The *retailer's approach* will concentrate on identifying his most profitable lines and giving them appropriate emphasis and identifying less profitable lines so as to eliminate them from his stocking list or to take steps to improve their profitability.

Because of this difference in emphasis, the manufacturer's view of merchandising is likely to be a narrower one, concentrating on ensuring that his products are in stock, well displayed and (when appropriate) priced and promoted as planned. However, manufacturers need to be aware of the much wider spectrum within which these activities must take their place.

5.4.2 The factors influencing promotional strategy

There are four main factors to be taken into account when deciding on promotional strategy:
1 *The nature of the product and its market(s).* For example, the kind of packaging, advertising and in-store activity suitable for pop records would clearly not be appropriate for expensive authentic jewellery. Promotion of pharmaceuticals to doctors, weapons to the military or security services to banks each have their own peculiar requirements.
2 *The stage in the product life cycle.* Marketing theory postulates that virtually all products have a life cycle, passing through a series of stages and following an S-curve pattern (see *The Fundamentals and Practice of Marketing*, Chapter 4 for more details[5]).

It is generally acknowledged that advertising is likely to be at its most cost effective when used in the growth stage to capture a maximum share of an already rapidly growing market. Large advertising expenditures used to slow up the decline will usually be unprofitable (but may sometimes be necessary to protect turnover). Similarly using advertising to generate the market for a hitherto unknown product tends to be very costly (but may be worth it to a company which has the capital to invest). Many large marketing organizations habitually do spend money 'up front' in this way and the readiness of Japanese companies to invest in promotion to generate markets and wait years for the 'pay-off' is often put forward as a key element in their success.

3 *Nature of the buying process.*
   (a) the relative importance of resellers and the way in which users make purchases will determine, for example, whether a 'push' or 'pull' emphasis is desirable
   (b) where and what kind of promotion is likely to be most effective depends on consideration of a purchasing decision model, such as:

| **Felt Need** | $\rightarrow$ | **Search Process** | $\rightarrow$ | **Evaluation** | $\rightarrow$ | **Purchase Decision(s)** | $\rightarrow$ | **Post-purchase Feelings** |

   (see Chapter 16 for a review of some theories on how advertising works.)
4 *Competitors promotional activity.* Whilst we must never simply follow a competitor's lead or 'outspend' for the sake of it, competitive activity must be monitored, evaluated and reacted to.

5.5 Advertising campaign planning

It should be very clear by now that successful advertising is not a hit and miss affair, but an activity which demands careful analysis, decision-making and planning. At the broad 'global' level we may talk about 'marketing communications strategy'. Thus M. Wayne Delozier[6] uses this term when he says, 'The five basic steps in the formulation of marketing communications strategy are the following:

1 Assess marketing communications opportunities.
2 Analyse marketing communications resources.
3 Set marketing communications objectives.
4 Develop and evaluate alternative marketing communications strategies.
5 Assign specific marketing communications tasks.'

Delozier's points 1–4 correspond approximately to what is described in this book as:

1 Picturing the marketing (*see* Sections 4.1 and 4.2).
2 Comparing the merits and appropriateness of the various promotional methods (*see* Sections 5.3 and 5.4).
3 Setting promotional objectives (*see* Section 5.1).
4 Evaluating results (*see* Section 5.1 and Chapter 17).

Arriving at what actually has to be done and ensuring that it gets done (sometimes referred to as the tactics) will now be dealt with. How is advertising planned in practice?

The word *campaign* is used to indicate that well-conducted advertising is a continuing planned set of activities with a definite purpose not a series of disjointed happenings. A good advertising campaign plan must:

1 Clearly state the objective of the campaign.
2 Define precisely how much it is necessary or appropriate to spend (*see* Section 3.5).
3 Establish what messages have to be communicated to which target audiences and for what purpose (*see* Chapter 3).
4 See that advertising and all other promotional activities (personal selling, sales promotion, point of sale and merchandising, public relations, etc.) are all properly co-ordinated in an integrated campaign (*see* Section 3.2.2).
5 Evaluate performance against targets at all stages (*see* Chapter 17).

5.5.1 Advertising campaigns and marketing strategy

The total process may then be pictured along the following lines:

Marketing Strategy
↓
Promotional Strategy
↓
Advertising Strategy
↓
Advertising Tactics
↓
Testing Proposals
↓
Execution/implementation
↓
Evaluation and feedback

5.6 The management of advertising

The whole of this chapter is concerned with the need for advertising to be a planned activity. This means that it must be managed, not left to chance. Then the question arises – who manages it and how do they go about it?

5.6.1 The organization of advertising

Where the responsibility for advertising management rests within an organization depends on a number of factors, in particular:

1   The size and complexity of the organization.
2   The importance of advertising within the marketing mix and the volume of activity it involves.

Thus a small organization where advertising is relatively unimportant may not have any specialist people or departments. Advertising may be just a small part of the many responsibilities carried by the owner/proprietor (e.g. a small garage or restaurant) or of the sales director (e.g. of a medium-sized capital equipment manufacturer).

On the other hand in a large company marketing fast-moving consumer goods there is likely to be a very large and complex organization. Where there is a wide range of products responsibility for co-ordinating all the promotional activities connected with each product – or small group of products – usually rests with the *brand manager* (product manager is an alternative term). Thus the organization might be something along the lines shown in Figure 5.2.

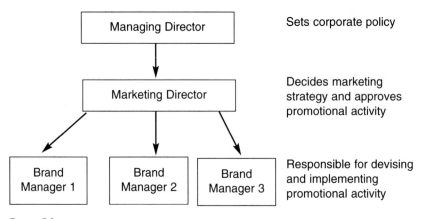

Figure 5.2
Source: Farbey *The Business of Advertising*

In between these extremes comes the type of organization shown in Figure 5.3 (found for example in consumer durables companies and in some industrial marketing companies).

Farbey[7] in Chapter 7 of *The Business of Advertising* lists eleven types of organization.

Case History: BT Advertising Campaign – It's Good to Talk

Because of pressure from its regulatory body OFTEL, together with increasing competition, BT prices have had to reduce dramatically. So to keep revenues growing, increased telephone usage is the obvious strategy. Since over 90 per cent of UK households are BT customers, this means growing the whole market.

Two previous campaigns had had some success in this, but in 1993/94 it was recognized that there was a need to tackle underlying barriers to calling if a real step-change in phone usage was to occur.

It's good to talk

24 hr Freefone 0800 800 020

1 BT

Famous and much-loved actor Bob Hoskins shows how 'It's good to talk' in the BT advertising campaign that transformed telephone habits and gave BT over £200 million of extra profit.

Agency: *Abbott Mead Vickers*

There are two main barriers to a better appreciation of phone communication:

1 Men tend to use the phone in a very functional way, whereas women tend to be more 'chatty'. Because many men cannot understand women's usage, they try to restrict it and act as 'gatekeepers' to the phone.
2 High price perceptions inhibit usage. Although BT *call* charges have fallen, perceptions remain high because *total* phone bills keep rising (because of extra use).

The 'It's good to talk' campaign aimed to use Bob Hoskins – a familiar actor to whom most people could easily relate – to put over the benefits of developing good relationships through talking on the phone. It also related call charges to everyday low-cost items.

Evaluation of the campaign showed that every 100 TVRs in any given month produced an eventual return of 1.75 per cent of monthly sales. The campaign generated a substantial increase in calls per line and prolonged rise in call durations.

Overall, the campaign produced an advertising-generated income of £297 million. With hardly any variable costs, this is pure profit and represents a return on investment of 6 to 1.

Post-campaign research indicated that there was a substantial increase in the degree of relaxed attitudes towards using the phone – particularly among men – and women feel correspondingly less guilty about using the phone.

BT price perceptions fell steeply, and people claimed to use the phone more and for longer as a result of seeing the advertising.

As the magazine *Marketing* said of the campaign, 'Perhaps the word "campaign" does it an injustice ... it is actually a piece of social engineering.'

Case History: The Andrex Puppies

Launched in 1972, the 'Puppies' advertising campaign for Andrex toilet tissue is the longest-running UK campaign apart from the PG Chimps. Using a 'constant drip' media strategy of 100 GPPs per week, 52 weeks in the year, it has – over more than 25 years – become Britain's favourite advertising.

People say of the advertising things like, 'You see the puppy pulling it all about to show how strong it is, and yet at the same time it is soft and gentle'; 'If someone says toilet paper, then Andrex is the first name that comes to mind. It's got the best adverts and it's been around the longest.'

Devised by JWT, the campaign is based on strongly focusing the *rational* attributes of the product – softness, strength and length – through the puppies' expression of the strongly linked *emotional* qualities – warmth, trust, charm, maternal, safe – so that these qualities become the embodiment of the brand. Thus the puppies sustain continued interest whilst still conveying very strongly the product's essential physical qualities.

The advertising strategy

The *advertising strategy* is described as follows:

- *Long-term:* To make consumers believe that Andrex offers the best in softness, strength and length, which when combined with the emotional appeal of the puppy, make Andrex unbeatable.
- *Short-term:* To pick up and emphasize individual attributes or the emotional appeal to build on the long-term proposition.

Results

Not only is Andrex very widely recognised and loved, it has been extremely successful in supporting a dominant share of the hotly contested toilet tissue market. In spite of the entry of Kleenex Velvet in 1982 (Andrex until then was unchallenged in product quality) and the growth of 'premium private label' tissues (largely at the expense of 'standard private label'), Andrex sustained a 32 per cent volume market share. Thereafter it also went into decline, partly because of the increasing quality of premium private label, but also because the advertising message was diluted and spread across a number of products (kitchen towels, etc.) with varying themes. Market share dropped to just over 21 per cent.

With the re-emphasis on the puppies in the 'Puppy Patrol' series, the trend has been reversed, and by 1997 market share was over 22 per cent and rising. Customer recognition of and loyalty to the advertising remains extremely strong.

2 Andrex

Stills from the famous and highly successful 'Andrex Puppies' TV campaign – the longest-running UK advertising ever apart from the PG Chimps.

Audi quattro. However slippery.

No car grips wet tarmac like an Audi quattro. Permanent four wheel drive means a tight hold on even the ugliest of roads.

Audi

3 Audi
Advertisement featuring the Quattro to further Audi's position as technologically innovative ('Vorsprung durch Technik'). Tracking studies show increasing association with 'technologically advanced', etc. and sales in 1997 were 17 per cent up in a market growing only 7.3 per cent overall.
Agency: Bartle Bogle Hegarty. *Audi 'Eel'*, Photographer: Kevin Griffin.

4 Boddingtons
Turned by Whitbread, who purchased it in 1989, into a national brand after 200 years in the north-west. The campaign generated high spontaneous awareness of the brand in an increasingly competitive market.
Agency: Bartle Bogle Hegarty.
Boddington's 'Flake', Photographer: David Gill, Model Maker: Gavin Lindsey.

5 Levi's Saw Tooth Western Shirt

One of a series of award-winning advertisements to reinforce Levi's in style and women's magazines throughout Europe as a highly desirable heritage item. Designed by Bartle Bogle Hegarty using creative photography of specially commissioned sculptures.
Levi's Wood, Photographer: Kevin Summers.

6 Olivio

Olivio (Van den Bergh Foods) was struggling, five years after launch, to justify a premium price in a market dominated by own label copies. In 1996 the brand was relaunched with advertising highlighting the longer life potential of Mediterranean-style diets. Market share doubled within six weeks and Olivio has subsequently reversed a 60:40 own label:branded sales ratio.
Agency: Bartle Bogle Hegarty. *Olivio 'Chianti'*, Photographer: Max Forsythe.

french

connection me

fcuk fashion

7 French Connection
Designed by GGT in 1997 to build a strong brand for French Connection by breaking the conventional mould of merchandise/model-focused advertising. The heavy poster campaign in and around London resulted in greatly increased brand awareness, an almost immediate increase of 12 per cent and enough sales of T-shirts carrying the slogans to almost in itself pay for the campaign.

8 Waterstone's
Aimed at Waterstone's existing users and other 'inner-directed' potential heavy book buyers. Immediate, but so far anecdotal, response has been very positive from customers and Waterstone's own staff.
Agency: GGT.

9 Cadbury's Creme Egg

Launched in the 1920s, the product really took off in the 1970s. The 1997 campaign was designed to reinforce previous success and to reinvigorate, refresh and re-engage the consumer (mainly 16–24-year-olds). In 1997 the product achieved 97 per cent distribution with sales growth of 9 per cent in 1997 and 10 per cent in 1998. *Agency:* GGT.

10 Renault Clio

'Papa' and 'Nicole' from the famous TV campaign for the Renault Clio car which, as well as doing a great deal for Renault's sales and image in the UK, became part of the national folklore. *Agency:* Publicis.

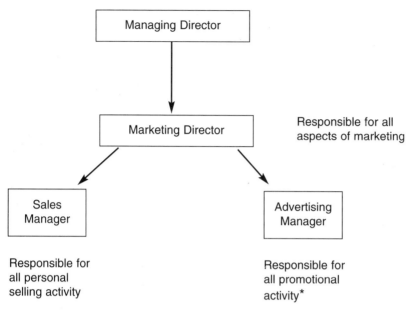

Figure 5.3
Source: Farbey *The Business of Advertising*

5.7 The role of the advertiser and the importance of briefing

It should be noted that the whole of this decision-making and planning is clearly and totally the responsibility of the advertiser, although he may seek information and other help from his agency.

The advertiser's main role (and hence that of the advertising manager, brand manager or whoever is responsible) is to ensure that the agency is provided with a clear-cut briefing (*see* Section 3.6 and Figure 3.1). It also involves selecting an appropriate agency (*see* Section 6.5) and monitoring and supervising the agency's work (*see* Section 6.8) to ensure that its response to the briefing is appropriate and that the creative and media proposals it produces are likely to bring about the desired results. It will also be necessary to monitor the production of these proposals to ensure that their implementation is (a) as envisaged in the proposals and (b) carried out at reasonable cost.

The other half of the partnership – the role of the agency – is examined in the next chapter.

5.8 Case study

Advertising is only part of the answer

Around 1993 Safeway, the UK supermarket group, decided that young parents were their unexploited market and forecast that they have enough spending power to guarantee Safeway's growth until the new millennium. Over £20 million a year was spent on an advertising campaign featuring toddlers Harry and Molly, who spoke to each other in adult 'voice-overs'. The couple became very popular and the advertising achieved an exceptionally high 60 per cent recall rate.

However, Safeway failed to hold its market share in the face of aggressive growth by rivals Tesco and Sainsbury. *The Times* refers to serious underinvestment and comments, 'To make life easier for the mothers of young families, the company has gone to astonishing lengths. But none of this counts for anything if customers come to the stores and find empty shelves, fresh food with short sell-by dates and an erratic mix of prices.'

An outstanding example of how advertising can support and enhance the rest of the marketing mix but cannot succeed on its own.

Source: *The Times*, 'Corporate Profile: Safeway', 9 March 1998.
Note: By early 1998 Harry and Molly had outgrown their roles and new models had to be found – another hazard of successful advertising?

5.9 Summary

1   Advertising must be a planned activity directed at clear objectives.
2   Advertising may take place within a marketing or within a public relations context.
3   In a marketing context we have to decide the appropriate role for advertising within the promotional mix which in turn is an aspect of the marketing mix.
4   The role of promotion (and of advertising in particular) is determined by:
   (a)   the nature of the product and its market(s)
   (b)   the stage in the product life cycle
   (c)   the nature of the buying process
   (d)   competitors promotional activity
5   Advertising campaigns must be properly planned and this is typically

the role of the advertising manager or the brand manager depending on the company and its type of market.

6 The planning activity leads to a briefing which must be clearly communicated to the advertising agency, whose response must be carefully monitored.

5.10 References

1 Broadbent, S. *Accountable Advertising*, NTC Publications, 1997.
2 D'Souza, S. Chapter 2 'The roles of advertising', in *How to Plan Advertising* (ed. D. Cowley), The Account Planning Group, Cassell, 1989.
3 Davidson, J. H., *Offensive Marketing*, Pelican, 1972, Chapter 13.
4 Kotler, Philip, *Marketing Management*, third edition, Prentice-Hall, 1976, Chapter 15.
5 Wilmshurst, John, *The Fundamentals and Practice of Marketing*, 3rd edn, William Heinemann, 1995.
6 Delozier, Wayne M., *The Marketing Communications Process*, McGraw-Hill Fogakasha Ltd, 1976.
7 Farbey, David, *The Business of Advertising*, Associated Business Press, 1979. (Chapter 1 deals with the roles of advertising and Chapter 7 with management approaches.)

5.11 Further reading

The Fundamentals and Practice of Marketing[5] discusses clearly and simply the marketing mix and the role of promotion and advertising within it and is a good basic text for those wishing to get a clear grasp of the wider aspects of marketing.

Offensive Marketing[3] gives some excellent examples of a variety of promotional approaches – though primarily in a fast-moving consumer goods context.

Davidson's later book, *Even More Offensive Marketing*, (Penguin Books, 1997) is also excellent.

The weekly journals *Marketing*, *Marketing Week* and *Campaign* provide a flow of up-to-date examples of advertising campaigns.

The Incorporated Society of British Advertisers (ISBA) publishes a booklet 'Advertising Briefing Procedure' which is a useful practical guide.

How to Plan Advertising (Cassell, 1989–95) is an excellent book on this aspect.

Philip Kotler's European edition of *Principles of Marketing* was published in 1996.

5.12 Questions for discussion

1   As the brand or product manager of one of your own company's product groups you have to propose the advertising appropriation and programme for the forthcoming year. Which factors will you take into account in formulating your recommendations?

2   'Good advertising starts with a good brief.' Discuss this statement describing the constituent parts of an advertising brief and defining who provides them.

3   Identify and discuss an advertising campaign that appears to be part of a purely marketing exercise and one that appears to have broader public relations objectives.

4   How important a place would you expect promotion to occupy in the marketing mix for:
    (a)   electric shavers for women
    (b)   a new form of electric light bulb that is much more expensive but uses less electricity and lasts longer
    (c)   satellite telephones for use in cars
    (d)   compact disc players

5   For each of the products in Question 4, what forms of promotion would you expect to be most important?

6   Using an actual example of an advertising campaign (e.g. from *Advertising Works – see* Section 4.9) write brief notes of what the campaign plan would be likely to contain, using points 1–5 listed at the end of Section 5.5.

Chapter 6

How advertising comes into being – the role of advertising agencies

'… the problem is altogether less how to find an agency than finding the right one.'

Jim Ring, *Advertising on Trial*, Pitman, 1993

By the end of this chapter you will:

- Understand why and when advertising agencies have an important role;
- Appreciate what an advertising agency is and how it operates;
- Have an awareness of the different departments that make up an agency and what they each do;
- Be able to set about choosing an agency with confidence;
- Understand the basis on which agencies are paid and how to negotiate an appropriate method of remuneration.

6.1 Who needs an advertising agency?

Once the advertising objectives have been set and a briefing prepared, *someone* has to act on the brief, interpret it and convert it into actual media bookings, artwork, films, etc. so that things happen and messages get communicated to the correct target audiences in the market-place. Perhaps it is because a high proportion of the writing is done by advertising agency people that books on advertising tend to *assume* that an advertising agency will be involved. Also of course it is true that the majority of advertising *is* produced by advertising agencies on behalf of their clients.

It is worth remembering, however, that it is perfectly possible for an advertiser to produce and place its advertising without using an agency. Many newspaper and magazine publishers do everything 'in house', as do some large retail chains, for example. Many smaller advertisers work directly with the media without using an agency. Local car dealers, house selling agents, etc. will supply 'copy' direct to their local newspaper who will design an advertisement, prepare any illustrations that are required, do the typesetting and produce the artwork ready for printing, all as part of the service the advertiser gets when he buys the advertising space.

There is also an intermediate solution where instead of delegating the job to an advertising agency, the advertiser uses a variety of suppliers. In some countries, especially the USA and the UK there is a superabundance of such suppliers. An advertiser can use a 'creative consultant' (also described as 'creative boutiques', 'creative hot-shops', etc.) to write and design the advertisement; a media buying organization (a 'media shop') may recommend a media schedule and buy the media; photography, artwork, etc. may be purchased directly from the appropriate specialists. Thus instead of buying what a particular agency has to offer (the table d'hôte approach) the advertiser can select what he wants from the 'menus' offered by the various suppliers (the à la carte approach as it is sometimes called).

In the UK it is indeed now quite common for an advertiser to use only part of the service offered by its advertising agency and to buy the rest elsewhere (e.g. agency creates the campaign, media house places it).

There is no one of these approaches which is definitely and invariably better than another. Each has its advantages and disadvantages, listed by Roderick White[1] in Table 6.1.

Jim Ring takes a slightly different look at the same choice. See Figure 6.1.

One other advantage which traditionally came when big-spending advertisers used an agency was a financial one. Agencies could obtain a commission from the media which the advertiser could not and this commission, partly or totally, financed its work on the advertiser's behalf. Thus the advertiser could be said to be getting the work cheaper from an agency than by using one of the other methods. The 'commission system' is discussed more fully in Section 6.7 but at least in the UK and the USA the pressures of the 'fair trading lobby' have partially outlawed the commission system and made it possible for the commission paid by the media to be passed on to advertisers. Thus this financial consideration is no longer a major one.

Whilst it is a useful 'quick-reference' source, White's table does of

Table 6.1

	Agency	Specialist services	Do it yourself
Advantages	All-round skills. All-round experience. Objective outsider's point of view of your business. You can learn from others' mistakes. They do the whole job for you. Continuity of work contact.	You can pick the real experts for each part of the job. You can fill the gaps in your capabilities, without having to buy the complete service of the agency. May be cheaper. May be faster.	Everything in your control. Full understanding of your problems. Learn as you go along (no embarrassment at lack of knowledge). May be faster. Probably cheaper.
Disadvantages	Lack of specific knowledge of your business (usually). Cannot devote all their time to you. May do a poor job for a small client. Probably expensive to use.	Need careful control and co-ordination: this needs experience. Require extra careful briefing – every time. Difficult to get extra services in a hurry.	Easy to make mistakes – no one available to cross check. Lack of required skills. Lack of specialized know-how. Limited view – no outside knowledge to provide a different viewpoint or stimulus.

course over-simplify and a senior advertising agency executive has commented as follows:

> ... there are points which are obviously not correct, e.g. stating that agencies are 'probably more expensive to use' makes too many unsupportable assumptions. Saying that agencies 'usually lack specific knowledge of your business' is nonsense. Because they employ planners, account executives, etc. and a generally larger number of creative people the chances are that there is far more specific knowledge available. Many people move around the agency world specialising in cars, finance, retail, tobacco, drink, fashion, food, etc.
>
> Commenting that they 'cannot devote all of their time to you' also seems questionable, since the erroneous impression is given that, therefore, specialist services do give all their time, which is untrue. In both cases, if this is listed as a disadvantage, then it also deserves to be listed as an advantage on the grounds of cross-fertilisation of ideas, which most other authors mention.
>
> Under advantages of a specialist service, he omits to mention that one is normally guaranteed the attention of very senior people or the principals in many cases.
>
> Under the disadvantages side he omits to mention the very real danger of either creative or media requirements being given unfair dominance in planning by specialists.

	Creativity	Cost	Speed	Size of job	Client expertise
Full-service agency	✓✓✓	✗✗✗	✓	Large only	Valuable
Specialist Service	✓	✗	✓✓✓	Small only	Crucial

Figure 6.1 *Agencies versus the rest*
Source: Ring (1993) *Advertising on Trial.*

See also the points listed in Section 6.4.

So whether to use an agency or not is a matter for individual companies to decide for themselves. As a broad indication, a company with a wide range of highly technical products calling for special writing skills, by technically informed people, but where clear presentation is more important than exciting creative approaches may often opt for a 'do-it-yourself' approach. A company dependent on developing a high level of awareness of its products through an exciting 'brand image' is more likely to buy in specialized talent. When this need is allied to a requirement for media buying skills, then an agency rather than creative specialists (whether individuals or companies) is likely to be the answer. It would still be possible to buy in creative help from one source and media help from another. The advertiser then has to exercise overall control, as Roderick White[1] points out. This in itself calls for considerable skill and experience and in addition may 'lock up' a great deal of senior executive time.

White gives a useful guide (*see* Table 6.2) to decision-making on how to tackle the advertising task.

In the end one of the key advantages of using an advertising agency may be what has been described as 'one-stop shopping'. Instead of having to deal with a whole range of different suppliers, a close relationship with an agency makes it possible for a single briefing to be given to one person (or at least a small group) who then assumes responsibility for seeing that all the different aspects of the job are set in motion and the desired end result achieved in a planned and coordinated manner. Thus a high degree of delegation is achieved, enabling the advertiser's staff to concentrate on those tasks that only they can do. This is especially true when there is a close working relationship built on mutual understanding and trust – the reason why 'client/agency relationships' are so important (*see* Section 6.8).

Table 6.2

Factors to consider	Questions to ask	Decision directions
1 Experience	Do I know about advertising?	If yes, do-it-yourself is a possibility.
2 The task	Is it simple or complicated?	If simple, do-it-yourself is a possibility.
	Am I sure *what* it is?	If 'no', you probably need an agency.
3 Money	Would my account interest an agency?	Probably!
4 Confidence	Do I need a second opinion?	If 'yes', try an agency.
5 Workload	Is there likely to be a mass of detail involved?	If 'yes', try an agency.
6 People	Do I have people who can do it for me?	If 'no' try an agency or specialist

6.2 What is an advertising agency?

In the light of the diversity of sources of help now available to advertisers, it is perhaps necessary to state what it is that distinguishes an advertising agency from any of these other organizations.

An advertising agency may consist of one or two individuals or it may be a large multinational corporation employing thousands of people. Turnover, or 'billing' as the agency world calls it, may range from tens of thousands of pounds sterling to many millions (*see* Section 1.3). Billing incidentally, although it is the traditional way of assessing an agency's turnover, can be misleading. In essence it is simply the amount of money spent by the agency with the media on behalf of its clients. When agency remuneration was almost entirely by commission (*see* Section 6.7) this gave a reasonable indication of its 'real' turnover – in other words, how much money it received for performing services on its clients' behalf or putting it another way, how much of the money passing through its books actually 'stuck' as opposed to being passed straight on to the media. With fee income becoming more and more important as a source of agency income and with agencies no longer forbidden (*see* Section 6.7) to split or pass on commission, billings may give an increasingly false picture.

As soon as it gets beyond being more than one or two people working on their own and becomes a company of some size, an agency has to carry out many of the same functions as any other business – it will have accountants, secretaries, receptionists, personnel people; it will have a board of directors and a company secretary.

What really makes it an advertising agency as distinct from any other kind of business is that it has four groups of people exercising four distinct specialisms (although in the very smallest agencies, some of the specialisms may reside in a single person, who will have a dual or treble role). These specialisms are:

1   Account management
2   Creative
3   Media
4   Traffic and production
5   Account planning

If one or other of these specialisms is missing, the company is not strictly speaking an advertising agency in the full sense of the term (although by 'buying in' e.g. creative help or media expertise it could still exercise all the functions of a fully-fledged agency). So let us briefly look at each of these in turn.

6.2.1 Account management

Advertising agencies have 'clients' rather than 'customers' but an alternative description used in describing which clients an agency works for is the term 'account'. Agency people refer to 'working on the Guinness account', 'winning the Fiat account', and so on. Each client or account has one or more people responsible for overseeing the agency's work on its behalf.

Typically there is an account director (who may or may not be a 'real' director of the agency within the meaning of the *Companies Act* – it may be a courtesy title) with ultimate responsibility for several accounts. Heading up to him or her will be a number of 'account executives' (called account managers in some agencies) each of which has a much smaller number of accounts to look after. An account executive may indeed have only one big account and the business of a very big advertiser may even be split into sections (e.g. on a product by product basis) with an account executive for each. A very busy account executive may be supported by one or more assistant account executives (traditionally a training ground for people on this side of the agency business).

The account management role consists of:

1   Acting as the liaison between client and agency – this aspect being essentially a sales function.
2   Establishing in conjunction with the client an appropriate brief and then ensuring that that brief is correctly passed on to all necessary people and departments within the agency (often via regular 'contact reports' which record meetings, telephone calls, etc.)
3   Being the focus of all the agency's work on the client's behalf, ensur-

ing that it is properly co-ordinated, produced on time, etc. In some cases the account management team are responsible for planning the advertising campaigns for their clients; in other cases there may be a special group who carry out this task for all clients.

It is often said that the account executive represents the agency to the client and the client to the agency – a difficult, demanding but exciting and rewarding role. As Winston Fletcher[2] puts it: 'Client service executives are the agency's representatives at most meetings with clients. They therefore need to be clear thinking, articulate, confident, likeable, hard-working and above all capable of listening to and understanding a client's problems, and convincing the client that the agency's solution to those problems, when it has been produced, is the right one.

6.2.2 The creative department

The agency's brief (*see* Section 5.7), emanating from the client, is discussed with the account management's staff and probably refined in the process. It then gets fed to the various other departments of the agency for them each to make their special contribution. One of the first to be involved (usually in parallel with the media department) is the creative team.

The brief will indicate that a particular message – the proposition – has to be communicated to a particular audience (there may be multiple propositions for a series of audiences). The task of the creative department is to turn a proposition, which may be banal or at least not very dramatically expressed, into a compelling, exciting message that will not merely inform but also persuade, stimulate and motivate the people that receive it.

There are typically three aspects to this:

1   What is the central idea or form of expression round which the message will be built (the 'creative concept')?
2   What words will be used to express it (the 'copy')?
3   How will the message *look*; what pictures or diagrams will be used, how will they be arranged on the page (the 'design' or 'layout'); what action will take place on the screen?

Thus the creative teams consist broadly of two sets of people, copywriters and designers. Once the broad 'creative treatment' is agreed – both copy and design – then other specialists come into their own such as *typographers* who are skilled in the selection of style of lettering (typefaces) and the appropriate sizes and arrangements of the actual words to convey the message as clearly as possible. There are people who specialize in writing scripts for television commercials, designers who specialize in packaging and point of sale material, and so on.

6.2.3 The media department

This also has two sides to it. There are media specialists in the *planning* of 'media schedules' i.e. selecting the best advertising media to reach the desired target audience(s). Recommendations also have to be made about size or length of press advertisement or broadcast commercial, whether to buy maximum size or maximum frequency, etc. (*see* Chapter 14).

The other aspect is that once the client has accepted, probably after discussion and minor modifications, the media department's proposals, someone has to negotiate with the media and buy the space and/or time at the most advantageous rates. They may also have to negotiate for favourable timing or positions, the most favourable spread over the period concerned, etc.

Thus media departments often consist of media *planners* and media *buyers*. In smaller agencies these two functions may be carried out by the same individuals (who may then be called planner/buyers) but it is well to recognize that they are separate specialized functions.

Increasingly media selection is based on a vast mass of data about audience figures, readerships, buyers characteristics, and so on. So media departments will often include specialists in the processing of this mass of data (which is now very largely available in electronic/digital form).

6.2.4 Traffic and production

So far the departments looked at have been mainly preoccupied with ideas – on what advertising should say, how it should look, where it should appear. But at some point these ideas have to be turned into actual material – usually artwork or film-scripts – something from which the media can work in order to reproduce the ideas the creative people have generated. In addition, newspapers and magazines appear on particular dates and radio and TV transmit at particular times. So there is a logistics problem which is twofold:

1   All the various activities of the agency eventually have to be carried out to a set timetable with an ultimate deadline of the day the advertisement appears. Someone has to keep track of each job – from briefing through creative media and production departments – to ensure that the final deadline is met. Built into the time-scale must be a number of days to allow for the client to see and approve material at each stage, for any necessary modifications to be carried out, etc. The term used in the agency world for this control and time-keeping aspect is *traffic*.

Traffic staff work in close liaison with the account executives but are normally responsible for keeping meticulous records and time-tables so that they can signal any dangerous delays or hold-ups to enable appropriate action to be decided on. Much of their time will be spent 'chasing' material through the various agency departments and outside suppliers.

2   The material actually has to be *produced,* i.e. turned from a set of ideas ('copy and layout') into something tangible – a metal printing block, 'finished artwork' from which a printer can work, or a film which can be screened (*see* Section 15.2). So there has to be a group of people – the production staff – who ensure that all this happens. Their expertise lies in their knowledge of how printers and other suppliers operate, in what form material needs to be supplied to them, and so on.

In many agencies the traffic and production functions are combined. In small ones either or both may be exercised by the account management staff. But somewhere, somehow these vital contributions have to be made, because otherwise all the brilliant creative ideas can come to nothing, either because vital dates are missed or because the execution is botched (by poor printing, ill-prepared artwork or similar horrors). The creative spark of the business is where the glamour resides, but it is the unsung heroes in traffic and production departments that make it all happen.

6.2.5 The planning department

Sometimes called the Account Planning Department, this takes on a very specific and important part of what had traditionally belonged to the account management team. It developed from the availabilty and increasing use of market research techniques to 'flesh out' and interpret for the creative people the all-important customer's point of view. In *How to Plan Advertising* (Cassell, 1995) the role is described as follows:

> Within an advertising agency – and on a smaller scale within an account group – it is the responsibility of the planner to keep in touch with the real world. In many cases, other members of the team have a good understanding of the context in which advertising is received, but the planner's access to social and demographic trend data, and direct access to consumers through quantitative and qualitative research, enables them to provide the agency and account team with a (hopefully) objective view of the world outside. This essential background knowledge can be considered at two quite distinct levels, as follows:
>
> 1   What is life like out there and how is it changing?
> 2   How do people (in particular the target audience) feel about their lives?

6.2.6 Other departments

Most agencies of any size will have other specialist departments, depending on the kind of clients they have and any specialism they offer.

Fletcher[2] lists the following which 'larger agencies will often include within their organization':

> Television production
> Merchandising and promotion
> Marketing
> Market research
> International
> Public relations
> Conferences and exhibitions

White[1] also lists:

> Contracts (with TV and radio actors, personalities, etc.)
> Home economics
> Direct mail
> Audio visual

It must be stressed that these are not essential to all agencies but are as it were the 'optional extras' which enable them to offer a more specific service to their clients without having either to have these services performed by non-specialists or to buy them in from outside. The latter course is, however, perfectly possible and many agencies do it for at least some of their clients' requirements.

There was in the 50s and 60s a vogue for the 'full service agency' (*see* Section 1.3.1). This was when agencies competed for clients on the basis of offering the broadest possible range of services. Since then a number of things have developed:

1   Many specialist companies have grown up who can provide a much higher level of expertise than is achieved by most agencies trying to do everything.
2   More advertisers now have their own specialists in, for example, the analysis of market research information and the development of strategies.
3   The economics of the business have become much tougher and agencies now have to ensure that each department makes a profit in its own right. This has resulted in many former agency departments being either closed down or 'hived off' as separate units or even separate companies. J. Walter Thompson in London, for example, owns

Lexington Public Relations Ltd and the British Market Research Bureau Ltd. An advantage of having a separate company is that it can more easily take work from people who are not clients of the parent agency, thus making it easier to achieve a profitable turnover.

6.3 How advertising agencies operate

There are two basic approaches to achieving a viable working arrangement between an agency and its clients. In the first virtually all contact is between the account management staff and their opposite numbers in the client's advertising or marketing department. They then brief their colleagues, vet the results, if necessary modify them to ensure that they meet the client's brief, then present them to the client. There is very little contact between other agency staff and members of the client's staff. The system has the advantage of clear-cut lines of communication and of well-defined responsibility. Disadvantages are its rigidity and the possibility that as things pass backwards and forwards along a perhaps lengthy chain of communications:

(a)   messages may be misunderstood and important nuances lost
(b)   agency staff such as creative people can become rather unenthusiastic because they are so 'remote from the action'. If their ideas get turned down there can be resentment at the account management staff who may be perceived as not selling the ideas strongly enough.

To overcome these hazards an increasingly popular alternative approach is to have what White[1] describes as a nuclear account group *(see* Figure 6.2). Each member of the team, which may number between say five and ten people is free to discuss any aspect of the account with the others (and may frequently talk direct to the client).

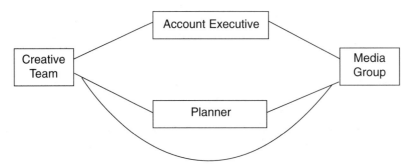

Figure 6.2
Note: *this function may be carried out by the account executive

6.4 What kind of an agency for which client?

If it is assumed that it has been decided that an agency *is* necessary, the question immediately arises – which agency? Once again the answer depends entirely on the needs of the advertiser concerned. The decision will probably turn mainly on the following factors (the order of importance will vary from one situation to another):

1 *Level of expenditure.* It is desirable for an advertiser to be spending enough money to carry some degree of relative importance compared with the agency's other clients. A company spending £10,000 is in the nature of things unlikely to get the best level of service from an agency most of whose clients are in the £1 million and upwards class.

2 *Location/accessibility.* If there needs to be frequent consultation and regular contact it may be felt necessary for the agency to be located where such contact is easy. This may not necessarily be in the same town, but at least will be at the end of a good rail or air route or linked by a motorway.

   In addition, some advertisers, especially those operating on a local or regional basis, may feel that an agency from the same area will have a better understanding of local conditions. In the UK London was for many years seen as the centre of the universe as far as advertising agencies were concerned and those in other areas had difficulty in proving themselves (although there have always been some strong agencies in other main cities). In recent years there has been something of a swing which has meant much new business going to regional agencies rather than to London-based ones. (Consequently a number of London-based agencies have acquired bases in other big cities by taking over existing agencies already well-established there or by starting up subsidiaries from scratch.) The increasing power of electronic communications, from e-mail to video-conferencing, means that the problems of distance are diminishing all the time.

3 *Specialism.* There are advertising agencies that specialize, e.g. in 'financial advertising' (for banks, insurance, etc.) and the placing of statutory advertising of company reports, share issue prospectuses, etc.: advertising for staff recruitment; direct response advertising. Some agencies specialize in 'industrial' or 'business to business' advertising. There are even those who concentrate on particular areas of products such as medical or agricultural. Some advertisers will see this kind of specialism as important, although others may want the benefit of a broader perspective and a wider range of experience.

4 *Type of help needed.* An advertiser seeking help from an advertising agency needs to be very clear what kind of help is required. It can fall

into various categories:

(a) *Creative* – the ability to produce brilliant creative ideas that will transform an undifferentiated product into a highly distinctive one, very largely through the way it is advertised (Equitable Life insurance, Orange telecommunications, Mr Kipling cakes for example). Not all advertising needs this 'creative spark'; in many instances – with technical products for example – clear straightforward communication of benefits is much more important (e.g. Psion palm top computers, most capital goods advertising).

(b) *Media* – the main service an advertiser may seek from the agency is skill in selecting and buying time and space. Very considerable sums of money may be saved – or extra value obtained – in this way and some agencies are very much stronger in this area than others.

(c) *Administrative* – one of the frustrations often expressed by advertisers is that their agency is not very businesslike over the precise accuracy of copy, delivering material (e.g. sales literature) on time, invoicing accurately, etc. When there is a large volume of multiple activities (advertising in many media, catalogues and leaflets, direct mail, exhibitions, etc.) firm grasp of logistics can be vital.

(d) *Marketing* – whilst most large advertisers these days have their own staff skilled in market research, market analysis, targeting audiences, defining market segments, etc., many do not. With smaller advertisers the number needing help in this way can be quite high. In this situation the agency can offer access to a pool of valuable expertise and information that the advertiser does not have.

Few agencies operate at the highest level of skill and efficiency in *all* of these areas (though most of them would claim to). Thus the advertiser has to be very clear what his priorities are (e.g. is sheer logistical efficiency more important than the ability to produce earth-shattering creative ideas, or is one good idea worth suffering a few irritating administrative lapses for?).

The Incorporated Society of British Advertisers (ISBA) has a publication *Managing the Advertiser/Agency Business Relationship*[3] in its 'Best Practice' series. It recommends that companies seeking a new agency should 'write down the precise objectives they wish to achieve from the relationship.' It also quotes the … 'old agency saying that *accounts are won by creativity but lost by administration.*'

The ISBA, jointly with the IPA and the DMA, publish a 'pitch guide' for best practices on cases where agencies are judged on the basis of a competitive pitch.

6.5 Choosing an agency

If the choice of an agency is so important how can advertisers approach the task of getting it right?

The ISBA publication (*see* Section 6.4) suggests an approach setting the following questions:

1   Define the objectives, as above.
2   Draw up a shortlist of agencies using sources such as ISBA and IPA, the quarterly Advertiser and Agency List published by British Rate and Data (BRAD), the Advertising Agencies Register or similar advisory companies.
3   Reduce to an even shorter list – ISBA suggests four at most (many people would say two or three).
4   Set these few agencies a project which ... 'should relate to your longer-term requirements but should be limited in scope and presented to all the agencies in the form of a tightly written brief.
5   Treat all the contenders in the same way and score them against a checklist. Mark their method of dealing with you, the way in which the presentation was carried out, the way they responded to the brief and the quality of their strategic argument. Assess their media thinking and creative ideas, their administrative system and above all, the way they propose to charge for their services ... Finally, judge them as colleagues. Make sure that you have met the full team who will be working with you and that you are clear on their individual responsibilities.'

The ISBA's view on how to conduct the last two stages is:

This information will probably enable the client to whittle down the list to around half a dozen agencies, who should be contacted and asked for a full agency presentation. At this stage the question of speculative campaign pitches arises. A number of agencies refuse to do these as they represent a considerable drain on an agency's resources in time and money which can only be indirectly financed by existing clients. If the client wishes to see creative ideas and campaign concepts (and this is by no means always the case), he would normally do so only with agencies which have survived through to his final shortlist. Ethically he should at this stage also undertake to pay an agreed fee for such presentations.

The client should by now be left with a final choice of about three contenders, and should go back to each agency for more detailed discussions, bearing in mind the points initially raised in the definition of the most suitable agency for his business. The agency should be asked to field the account team it would propose to handle the business, and detailed talks should be held with each to determine background, experience, skills and character. Another useful check is (with the agency's knowledge) to speak to one of their existing clients to get a working view of the agency's strengths and weaknesses. Equally illuminating is to speak to a client who has recently left the agency to discover his reasons for doing so.

6.6 Appointing an agency

Once the appropriate agency has been chosen great care has to be paid to setting up the relationship in the right way. Not only is it important to settle on the appropriate method of payment (*see* Section 6.7) but there are two other key aspects which are best made clear at this point:

1   What is actually expected of each party in terms of services to be provided, information to be made available, etc.
2   The technical and legal 'nitty-gritty' of matters such as ownership of copyright, termination of contract, etc.

Both the ISBA and the IPA (representing the advertisers and the agencies respectively) favour an actual written contract to cover these aspects which really do need to be made absolutely clear at the outset if misunderstandings are not to develop and give rise ultimately to an unnecessary and expensive breach in the relationship (*see* Section 6.8).

The IPA booklet (1) suggests:

> The client should by now be able to make his final choice but this does not constitute an appointment, which only follows after detailed discussion and the drawing up of a formal contract. Most agencies are reasonably flexible in their approach to handling their client's business, as these businesses by definition will vary considerably. It is, however, imperative that a legal document exists, detailing the framework of the agreement which the client and agency have negotiated. It is particularly important that the client selects the method of remuneration best suited to his needs (e.g. commission or fee, or combination of both).
>
> The contract should typically cover the period of appointment, the services the agency agrees to provide, approvals and authority, scale and method of charges, terms of payment, copyright, legal liability and agreed arbitration procedures in case of dispute. The IPA publish a useful booklet on the technicalities of agency/client agreements, which should be read by the prospective client.
>
> Of all the headings covered in a contract (which should be reviewed by competent legal advisers) the complex subject of copyright deserves special mention and careful attention. As a general rule copyright rests with the individual artist, designer or photographer unless otherwise assigned and the client in commissioning work is granted reproduction rights for a specific job. Further use of the same material in a different task could, unless otherwise agreed, be subject to further copyright charges.
>
> Normally an agency employed artist will assign ownership and copyright to his employer but this should be checked and included in the contract. The matter becomes further complicated if the agency buys in creative work from third party sources and the question of ownership and copyright in such instances should also be included in the agency/client agreement. The whole subject becomes of particular significance if at some stage the client and agency decide to go their separate ways. It is then in the client's central interest that he have a binding agreement on ownership and copyright to cover termination of an account. To neglect this facet is to court disaster, expense and acrimony.

6.7 How advertising agencies get paid

It is important to understand that what advertising agencies have to sell is time. Their main cost is for the salaries and office accommodation of their staff (together with telephone, travel expenses and all the other things those people use). Most other outgoings – media costs, artwork, films, etc. are charged out to clients anyway. So it is primarily people who have to be paid for and whose costs the agency has to recover (with something over and above to provide profits of course). Experienced, gifted and therefore well-paid people it is true, but fundamentally no different in principle from plumbers, garage mechanics, accountants and solicitors. If the agency's staff spend time on a client's work, the cost of that time has to be recovered in just the same way as if a garage repairs a customer's car or an accountant does an audit.

The problem is, how best to do it? As we have seen (*see* Sections 1.3.3 and 6.1) agencies were traditionally paid by commission. The agency booked space with the media on the advertisers' behalf. The media paid a commission to the agency, in return for which the agency 'sorted out' the client, helped him to determine what kind of advertising was necessary, designed and wrote it for him, did whatever production work was necessary, etc.

Always, however, there was a problem. The commission system worked very well for advertisers spending reasonable sums of money 'above-the-line' (*see* Section 8.1) and needing reasonable amounts of help. Some, however, needed a great deal of help and for excellent reasons (e.g. an industrial advertiser using specialized media to reach markets with very small numbers and hence inexpensive media rates) did not spend much on media. Or their requirement was such that most of their expenditure was 'below-the-line'.

Two approaches developed over the years to cope with this problem:

1   The agency would ask the advertiser to pay an *additional* commission to that paid by the media (e.g. 20 per cent rather than the standard 15 per cent).
2   The agency would cost the time spent and charge the advertiser a fee (from which any commissions received from the media were deducted).

Thus, the 'commission system' and the 'fee system' developed side by side. Some people have always argued that the fee system was the most rational and fair (each client paying for the time spent on his behalf) but the commission system had many advantages, including:

1   Traditional and well understood.

2   Simple and easy to operate.
3   In spite of its conceptual imperfections it worked well in most cases.

More recently the matter has been complicated by pressures from the Fair Trading lobbies in many countries which have led in some of them to the commission system being declared an unfair commercial practice and one that may not be enforced.

Thus in the UK for example it used not to be possible for an advertiser to deal direct with the media and obtain the commission that might have been paid to the agency. (Commissions were payable only to 'recognized' agencies – those who fulfilled certain conditions laid down by the media owners.) Advertisers may still choose to operate the commission system of course but they must now decide in discussion with their agency which is the best approach.

6.7.1 Commission or fee – which works best?

In 1973 a working party was set up by ISBA (the Incorporated Society of British Advertisers) to examine and report on these alternatives. The working party report summarized the history of the commission system as follows:

> Initially, the evolution of the Advertising Agency was from their very first work as space brokers, when they received commissions from media of as little as 2½–5 per cent. However, in the 1930s and 1940s these figures had risen to a general 10 per cent level.
>
> As advertising became more sophisticated, agencies offered to advertisers a free layout and copy service within their commission terms, but they also received some commission from their blockmakers for the illustrations they put into advertisements.
>
> In the late 50s and early 60s, mainly influenced by American practice, most of the UK national newspapers increased commission to agencies to 15 per cent. Most popular weekly and monthly magazines have subsequently come into line at the 15 per cent level but some industrial, trade and technical weeklies and monthlies still keep their commission at the 10 per cent level. The traditionally 'free' services, offered by the Agencies, of providing copy and layouts, still purport to be covered by the commissions received from the media, but other services carried out by Agencies, such as artwork, typesetting, blocks and other services bought in from outside suppliers are charged to clients at net cost plus 17.65 per cent a percentage which usually gives the Agency 15 per cent on the gross. Publications which offer only 10 per cent commission to Agencies are dealt with in a similar manner to bring the Agencies' commission up to 15 per cent equivalent.

The report went on to consider the advantages and disadvantages of the two systems. The commission system was thought to have the following disadvantages:

1 The effort required by the Agency may bear no relationship to the 15 per cent commission.
2 Big accounts subsidise smaller accounts.
3 Profitable accounts subsidise less profitable accounts.
4 The need to operate within 15 per cent commission may result in work being carried out by employees who are of too low a calibre.
5 Agencies are encouraged to pad the work load in order to appear to be earning their keep.
6 There is a temptation for an Agency to recommend an increase in advertising budget in order to boost Agency income.
7 The commission system leads to a lack of objectivity in Agency media recommendations and to discrimination against recommending below the-line activity.
8 Agencies on the 15 per cent commission system tend to expand their services as their revenue increases whether or not their clients want the extra services, the final result being that many clients are paying for services they do not want.
9 In times of inflation and rising media costs, Agency revenue is provided with an automatic hedge against inflation at the expense of the advertiser.
10 Advertisers are forced to use a recognized Agency and are precluded from performing work 'in house' or using 'freelance' services.

(*Author's note*: this was when the commission system was still enforceable.)

The arguments against the fee system were listed as:

1 The fee system is basically a cost-plus system which breeds inefficiencies; the commission system is a discipline on the Agency to keep down costs.
2 The fee system could lead to a price war between Agencies and thus of a skimping of service to clients; it could also lead to a deterioration in the standards of advertising.
3 The fee system is complicated to administer and needs to be constantly reviewed.
4 The settling of fees can lead to friction between Agencies and their clients.
5 With a fee system media cutbacks are no longer all savings – the Agency fee still has to be paid.
6 With a fee system the client can be tempted into undue haste in Agency dealings because actual time spent becomes more directly built into the fee.
7 The commission system is an incentive to the Agency to increase the client's business and thereby to increase billings.
8 With the commission system Agencies are obliged to compete for

business on the basis of quality rather than price.

Client and agency together, taking these points into account and taking note of the requirements of each client's particular situation must arrive at the best system for each advertiser.

Since that study was carried out there has been significant movement in the direction of:

1   Greater reliance on fees rather than commission.
2   Where commissions are still the basis, then a level significantly lower than the traditional 15 per cent is common. Jim Ring suggests that 5–6 per cent is often the sort of level arrived at by negotiation, although the book was written when the pressures of recession were bearing very heavily on agencies. Ring also suggests that increasingly advertisers are looking to pay their agencies at least partly on the basis of results:

'... the media buying activities of agencies are increasingly assessed in such a way, and there is a growing inclination on the part of advertisers to put other aspects of the account on that basis. In practice this usually means providing the agency with a basic income and adding a performance-related bonus.' He goes on to discuss the problems involved, but concludes: 'As it becomes gradually more possible to evaluate advertising activity ... the impact of the advertising should be the criterion on which agency fees are based, in short, payment by results.'

6.8 Working effectively with an agency

Having selected the correct agency, agreed terms and conditions (including an appropriate method of payment) and made the appointment, what then?

Roderick White[1] suggests:

Running a client-agency relationship is, like a marriage, a matter of give and take. The best clients do their best to provide the agency with all the information they can, and to share their thinking with them. Their objective is to work with the agency. For this to happen, of course, the agency has to earn, and keep, the client's respect. Less satisfactory clients treat the agency as just another supplier, employed to produce a product to a specification, to be kept firmly in its place and to be screwed down financially if possible. The idea of a constructive partnership, in which the agency can contribute something that the client lacks, is barely considered.

If you consider the amount of sheer hard work – on both sides – that goes into the business of finding and appointing an agency, it seems to me that it is very firmly in the interest of both parties to build a relationship that works. The investment in management time required to select an agency, and the length of time likely to be involved in the *learning process before the agency both fully understands the client's market and knows how to work with the client's organization, dictate that agency changes are best made infrequently. Like marriage, agency relationships should not be entered into with divorce in mind, even though their expected life span may be rather shorter than even the average American marriage. It is, after all, quite possible for a client to be with an agency for 50 years or more, though this is pretty rare.*

The ideal basis for a client–agency relationship is one of mutual respect. If this can be backed by the expectation of high standards of performance, and a cooperative effort to attain these high standards, the result should be good advertising. If it is not, it is important to have a system for reviewing the relationship to see what is going wrong. That is why an increasing number of clients and agencies have a system of regular reviews, not just of advertising plans and campaigns, but of the relationship and how it works: to assess gaps in performance (on both sides), and the strengths and weaknesses of the relationship. By doing this, it is possible to eliminate most of the small problems that can eventually lead to the breakdown of confidence and cooperation, and to ensure that both sides are contributing fully and effectively to the task of producing the best possible work on the account. Advertising is, above all, a cooperative effort.

Similarly an IPA booklet[4] 'Getting the most out of the client-agency partnership' suggests: 'It takes two to make a successful partnership but only one to louse it up.' The best practice seems to be to try to build a joint team of people drawn partly from client, partly from agency – who work closely together as one team.

The IPA booklet supports the idea of regular meetings (some agencies and clients call them 'harmony meetings') purely for the purpose of reviewing how the partnership is working. The IPA booklet suggests the following checklist:

1   Are the client's corporate objectives and the marketing objectives that derive from them, entirely clear to both parties? Have the marketing and communications tasks been quantified, together with their financial and profit implications?
2   Are the marketing and communications planners fully informed about relevant factors in the commercial environment, particularly:
         actual and potential customers
         product advantages and limitations
         competitors
         current or predictable marketing problems
         product and marketing development plans?
3   Has sufficient lead-time been allowed for planning purposes?
4   Has the agency's creative policy been fully thought through and discussed in relation to the defined communications tasks?
5   Do the various creative manifestations (whether advertisements in paid media, explanatory literature, direct mail shots, audio-visual and other sales aids, exhibition stands or press publicity) express the policy effectively?

6 Have the media plan and budget been fully thought through and discussed? Are both agency and client convinced that they are as cost-effective as available information will permit?

7 If results in one area or another have not come up to expectations, has there been a serious effort to find out *why*, instead of shrugging it off or explaining it away?

8 Is there sufficient readiness not just to change for change's sake, but progressively to improve performance within an agreed long term policy?

9 Is the level of financial and administrative control satisfactory on both sides?

10 Is the level of client–agency communications – in both directions – as good as it should be?

11 Is there mutual understanding and respect between the individuals working on the account, on the client and on the agency side?

'A 'hair-letting-down' summit meeting between client and agency to discuss these points, say once a year, can help to dispel the kind of misunderstandings that culminate in the laborious and time-consuming search for, and indoctrination of, a new agency that have already been described.'[4]

The last point is a good one. Some clients take the view that the best approach is to change agencies frequently to 'get a fresh approach'. The amount of time and effort involved in seeking, appointing and briefing a new agency as compared with working to get the best from the one you have seems to make occasional 'harmony meetings' much the better approach.

6.9 How agencies get business

Since an advertising agency is basically a profit-making commercial operation like any other, growth is likely to be one of its objectives. This means that a lively, vigorous agency will be seeking new business. Fundamentally, this situation is no different from any other similar kind of company trying to get new business. There have to be new business targets, marketing plans for achieving them and executives charged with the task of implementing them.

On the other hand, members of the professional body – the Institute of Practitioners in Advertising (the IPA) – agree to act in many respects like other professions such as solicitors, accountants, architects. For example, they undertake not to deliberately approach clients of other members to attract their business: a rather strange attitude for people devoted to highly competitive activity on behalf of their clients!

Fortunately, reasonable compromise is possible. There are always clients around who are seeking a new agency and there are many ways of making one's own agency highly visible to them – especially through promotional techniques such as advertising and PR. The activity of agencies by its nature is newsworthy – getting a new client, launching a new campaign, etc. usually gets good news coverage.

Farbey[5] has a useful chapter 'Business Development for Agencies' which explores this topic in depth. He suggests that agencies need to produce a new business plan with targets of new business sought or expected from:

1   Existing clients, now using other agencies for other products.
2   Other existing clients with possible extra assignments.
3   Close contacts of the agency.
4   Companies with which the agency does not have contact.

Farbey then continues:

> A programme can be drawn-up for each group, and a very wide and varied range of activities mounted, though it should be emphasised that new business is an opportunistic matter, which consists of creating or finding opportunities. Some of these may happen by design, and many will not, which is not to argue against a methodical approach, but rather to say that method will need to combine with fortune.
>
> It is necessary perhaps to define what new business activity substantially is. In essence, it is a contact-making function, aiming at decision-makers among prospective clients, and seeking to convert those contacts into a formal new business solicitation. As such, it follows four main stages: identifying contacts, making contact, presenting the agency and presenting for business. The plan will begin by establishing which sort of potential clients the agency like to handle. These might be industries allied to the existing expertise of the agency, or new categories which the agency feels would extend its capability.
>
> When analysing target prospects, a vital consideration for the agency is to identify not just likely companies, but also the key individuals within those companies. In this, advertising is no different to other types of industrial selling. In essence, who are the decision-makers? For normal product-based advertising, there may be three tiers of decision-maker.
>
> 1   The advertising management, or advertising manager.
> 2   The marketing management, or marketing director.
> 3   The company top management, perhaps the chairman or managing director.
>
> There may often be more individuals involved than that. Agency policy within an advertiser is a complex matter, and no two advertisers approach the question of how to select an agency in exactly the same way. The main question is that of the ultimate decision-maker. Who has the real power to select or reject an agency, in the last count?

The all-important stage which this systematic activity normally leads to is the presentation where the agency tries to project to its prospective client how its services would benefit the client. This is the other side of the picture from the one outlined in Section 6.5, 'Choosing an agency'.

6.10 Summary

1 Advertisers have to decide whether the programme of promotional activity they need to carry out can best be accomplished:
   (a) in-house
   (b) using an advertising agency
   (c) using other specialist services
   or of course a combination of two or three of these approaches.
2 A fully-fledged advertising agency has departments concerned with:
   (a) Account management
   (b) Creative
   (c) Media
   (d) Traffic and production
   but a 'full service agency' may have many other specialist departments.
3 Each client has to decide which agency is most appropriate by deciding what kind of help it needs, as well as considering size, location, etc.
4 Choosing an agency should be a logical step-by-step process exercised with great care and the appointment made in such a way that each party knows exactly what to expect from the other.
5 Because of the time and upheaval involved in changing agencies it is important for both parties to devote much attention to ensuring that the partnership continues to work successfully over many years.
6 Agencies, like any business, need their own programme of business development.

6.11 References

1 White, Roderick, *Advertising: what it is and how to do it*, McGraw-Hill, 1980 (third edition, 1993).
2 Fletcher, Winston, *Advertising*, Teach Yourself Books, 1978.
3 *Managing the Advertiser/Agency Business Relationship*, Incorporated Society of British Advertisers.
4 'Getting the most out of the client-agency partnership', Institute of Practitioners in Advertising.
5 Farbey, A. D., *The Business of Advertising*, Associated Business Press, 1979.

6.12 Further reading

Both the White and the Farbey books mentioned above give much further detail on this whole topic.

The Practice of Advertising, edited by N. A. Hart and James O'Connor, (William Heinemann, 1978) has chapters on 'The Advertiser' and 'The Advertising Agency'.

The ISBA has a very useful 'Best Practice' guide to managing the advertiser/agency business relationship.

6.13 Questions for discussion

1   Put the case for and against using an advertising agency for any commercial or non-commercial organization with which you are familiar.

2   Show how an advertising agency and its client should work together so as to produce an effective advertising campaign. Illustrate your answer with examples from *either* a consumer product *or* an industrial product *or* a service.

3   Write a brief outline of what you consider to be the main role and functions of an advertising agency.

4   Discuss to what extent advertising agency staff can legitimately be regarded as 'professionals' like accountants, lawyers and architects.

5   As the Advertising Manager of a major toy manufacturer, you and your management have become unhappy with your advertising agency and have decided to consider moving the account. Write a memorandum to your Managing Director stating how you propose to go about the selection and detailing your selection criteria.

6   You have just applied to an advertising agency for a job as an account executive. Describe the way in which an advertising agency is usually organized and how the account executive fits into the organization.

Chapter 7

Where advertising appears

By the end of this chapter you will:

- Appreciate that the advertising medium affects the advertising message;
- Recognize the complexity over the variety of which medium to choose;
- Be able to judge the pros and cons of the main media;
- Appreciate the rapid expansion of media choice facing today's advertiser;
- Understand the changing face of the management of the main media;
- Have had an introduction to how advertising is bought and sold.

7.1 The importance of the medium

Earlier chapters have focused on the need to be clear about what audiences we want to aim our messages at (*see* Chapter 4), what we expect to happen as a result of those messages (*see* Chapter 5), what the messages should contain and how we might go about getting them expressed in the most cost-effective way (*see* Chapter 6). However, no message can be of any value if it is not transmitted and received effectively. The channels of communication have to be correctly selected so that they deliver the appropriate messages to the right people as effectively as possible. That effectiveness has two key aspects:

(a) *The clarity of the message*: the communication channel must be such as to give the message the best chance of being expressed clearly.
(b) *The breadth of coverage*: the channel must communicate with as many of the target audience as possible at the lowest cost.

This becomes a very complex decision for two main reasons:

(a) *Channel clarity is largely judgemental*: decisions about which channel communicates most clearly are largely judgemental, and it is sometimes not easy to determine precisely which is the most cost-effective.
(b) *Channel proliferation continues*: there is an ever-increasing number of channels to choose from.

The importance of this selection process gave *media* a place in the Output column of the model of the advertising process in Section 3.6.

That views of advertising effectiveness are both mixed and complex is illustrated by the on-going debate about the effect of advertising on the consumption of cigarettes. A working paper by Martyn Duffey, *Advertising and Cigarette Demand in the UK* (UMIST 94 08, 1994), concluded that advertising effects were always estimated to be negative: '… no evidence has been found in this research to back up the view that aggregate cigarette advertising serves to expand total demand for cigarettes. On the contrary, the results presented here suggest that the general effect, if one exists, of brand advertisements … may have been to restrain aggregate demand for cigarettes.' One may be slightly perplexed as to why this might be the case, until one realises that cigarette advertising in the UK must carry prominent health warnings. The working paper went on to state that 'cigarette advertisements may paradoxically reinforce and disseminate the health education message through their warnings content'. It must be said that this view conflicts with the Health Committee statement that advertising undermines the health education message.

This chapter examines some of the factors involved in selecting and buying space or time in the media most appropriate to a particular communications task.

7.2 Selecting media

Section 1.3.2 gave an indication of the relative importance of the main advertising media in the UK and the way in which this emphasis is changing. The relative importance varies from country to country. The figures in the table in Section 1.3.1 indicate in a crude way *which* media advertisers regard as most important but do not tell us why *they* make this choice. That will be a reflection of the clarity of the message and the breadth of coverage.

The breadth of coverage is the more obvious, although sometimes difficult to evaluate as precisely as we would like. For example, using TV

Note: *Advertising medium* is a term usually used to describe each channel of communication; *advertising media* describes them all collectively. (While media is the plural of medium, many advertising people do not distinguish clearly between them and may be heard to talk about an 'advertising media'.)

advertising was once considered as ideal for many consumer advertising campaigns but sadly it can be very wasteful as markets fragment. If one looks at the TV landscape in many markets, one sees that there are very few, if any, channels that directly target a given audience. Even targeting children is not as easy as one might imagine. Children do watch TV – that is, of course, until they reach the age of 11, after which their viewing lessens as they are distracted by other interests. But fragmentation is at its most rife: The Disney Channel, although not taking advertising, is one of the more recent channels to target children and their families – particularly mums. The Children's Channel and Nickelodeon are considered correct for any four- to nine-year-olds but this is not necessarily the case, as both appeal to different ages between the BARB reported four- to nine-year-old age group. Sky One and The Cartoon Channel might not both be correct if your target is both boys *and* girls. If only children could be relied upon to stick to the same channel for long periods; unfortunately they are notorious channel-hoppers. What is known is that they are programme watchers. The children's market has fragmented to the stage where new methods need to be found to reach the specific target and gain distinctiveness from competing advertising messages. Sponsorship, co-production and advertiser-supplied programming are already appearing as alternatives to traditional advertising.

The problem of market fragmentation and targeting is being addressed by the launch of what has been called the 'fourth wave of electronic media'. The first was licence fee television, the second commercial terrestrial television, then came broadly based subscription channels either from satellite or through cable, and now the fourth, being the TV equivalent of the glossy magazine – 'the single-interest channel for everything from healthcare to cars. While having potential for precisely focused advertising, they are also a splendid opportunity for sponsorship – although this is only an emerging field.

Clearly, when deciding how to spend money on advertising, the advertiser (advised by their advertising agency) will seek to 'maximize' that expenditure. In other words, the advertiser will want to ensure that for every pound spent, they are getting the maximum impact on the maximum number of the target audience.

This latter point, in theory, is fairly easy to arrive at. One simply counts the number of readers or viewers and divides by the cost. Thus one of the most common rule of thumb measures of advertising value for money is 'cost per thousand', i.e. how much money does it cost to reach each 1,000 readers or viewers or listeners with our message, using that particular medium?

In practice it is more difficult. This is because normally quite expensive research techniques are needed to determine the size of the readership or audience. In addition, the 'audience' for a TV station may not be quite what it seems at first sight.

Thus those listed as readers of a particular magazine are those who claim that they saw that particular magazine during a particular period of time. That does not mean that they read the whole of that magazine and certainly does not necessarily mean that they saw any given advertisement. Similarly, someone listed in the figures as watching a particular television programme does not necessarily watch with great attention the advertisements that interspersed it.

So we find the term 'opportunities to see' (OTS) being used; for this is what we really get for our money. Not X thousand readers but Y thousand people who have an opportunity to see our advertising. For example, if one were to consider a TV listings magazine carrying next week's TV programmes, while one person might purchase the magazine, it is likely to be read by the whole family, putting the OTS perhaps three or more times higher than the circulation figure.

How many of them *do* see and the interest that they pay to any advertisement will depend on the nature of the medium and their relationship with it. For example, an enthusiastic hobbyist may buy a magazine about cameras or computing in order to read the advertisements. They may be of as much interest as the editorial. On the other hand one can assume that people buy their daily newspaper or watch TV primarily for the sake of the editorial content or the programmes. In this case the advertisements will very much take second place and may even be seen as an intrusion.

Other factors, such as how well the medium lends itself to the clear and forceful expression of the message, will also have a bearing on the value of that medium to the advertisers.

7.3 Advertising media compared

Table 7.1

	Advantages	Disadvantages
Television	Reaches a very wide audience ...	... but unselectively (although an increasing number of channels, including cable etc. modifies this slightly)
	Sight, sound and colour gives dramatic possibilities	Expensive both for time and film production
	Can be used regionally (14 different stations/areas in UK)	(30 second peak spot across the network costs over £20,000; a film will probably cost over £50,000)
		Transient message
National Press	Message received at home in a relaxed atmosphere	
	High national coverage ...	... but needs more than one paper to achieve it

	Advantages	Disadvantages
	Authoritative editorial atmosphere	Mainly black and white only, little drama
	Can cope well with detailed information	Demonstration of product very difficult
	Audience profile can be varied (by contrast with TV)	
	Messages carry urgency …	… but are read in a hurry (not quite so true of the Sundays)
Local/Regional Newspapers	Strong reader loyalty	Over 1,000 titles in the UK so complex/expensive to use on a wide scale
	High coverage within specific areas	Generally poor readership data
	Regional flexibility	High production costs
Magazines	Selective readerships	Reading may be spread over weeks/months
	Reader involvement (especially in 'enthusiast' publications)	Long copy and cancellation dates
Outdoor (Posters and Transport)	Low cost per 1,000	High printing costs (but acceptable if used on a big scale)
	High coverage and OTS Big posters give high impact	Long booking and cancellation lead times
	Sites can be booked very flexibly	Poor audience research
	Colour and size = drama	
Radio	Local area coverage with high OTS among listeners	Expensive as a national medium in the UK
	Impact and immediacy	Relatively small audiences (as percentage of population) in the UK (but in some countries is the best way of reaching most of the population)
	Speed of appearance (short lead times)	Audiences may not listen intently but use as 'audio wallpaper'
Cinema	Selective local coverage	High production costs (many copies of films have to be made as well as original)
	Excellent coverage of 15–24 year-olds	Limited value otherwise in UK
	Impact of big screen with sound, movement and colour	Slow build-up of audience because attendance is low and infrequent

	Advantages	*Disadvantages*
Electronic media/Internet	Principally sight, but with sound and some colour movement dramatic possibilities are developing	Generally poor viewership data
	Interactive medium permits direct response	Consumer confidence in security low but improving
	Able to track audience movements through the media	While possible to direct Internet audience to information, can be difficult to gain large OTS without support from other media
	Message permanent and can be down-loaded by audience (i.e. screen-savers, text, etc.)	Not a mainstream media with broad customer appeal: but developing
		Speed of movement through the media depends on sophistication of technological link
		No universal computing language yet agreed – material written in *Java Script* may not be read by systems written in the more universal *html*

7.3.1 The growth in media choice

The vast increase in the portfolio of media over the past 20 years means that there is now something for everybody. There are television channels dedicated to sport and music, radio stations playing diverse musical styles, and magazines for every interest. Alongside this has been an explosion in the number of advertisements shown on TV. In 1985, if an individual watched television for an entire day, he or she would be exposed to 200 different advertisements; with the growth in cable and satellite by 1995, this figure had risen to a potential 4,500 – a 3,000 per cent increase.

If one looks at the growth in other forms of media, one can see the breadth of choice, particularly when you think that digital cable and satellite will be offering up to 200 channels by the end of the millennium. (*See* Section 12.2.)

7.3.2 The increasing cost of TV advertising[1]

Taking a 25-year perspective, the cost of TV advertising has been rising to such an extent that there is now tremendous pressure on both advertiser and agency alike. The gap between the amount of advertising a brand

Table 7.2

Media	1975	1995
Press		
National dailies	9	11
National Sundays	8	10
Regionals	1,450	1,829
Consumer magazines	1,079	2,457
Business publications	2,126	5,378
Radio		
BBC	1–4	1–5
BBC local	✓	✓
Independent local radio	Capital & LBC	150
Independent national radio	✗	4
Pirate	✓	✓
Community	✗	✓
TV		
BBC1	✓	✓
BBC2	✓	✓
ITV	✓	✓
Channel 4	✗	✓
Night-time	✗	✓
GMTV	✗	✓
Satellite	✗	✓
Cable	✗	✓

needed and the amount of advertising a brand *could afford to buy* has been growing. In the US in 1965, three-quarters of all commercials were 60 seconds long; by the mid-1990s, nearly half of all US commercials were 15 seconds long.

There has been a similar trend in the UK. By the mid-1990s, 43 per cent of all commercials were under 30 seconds long. But shortening the advertising is only one way to pad out an advertising budget shrunk by media inflation. Another is to cut the Television Ratings (TVRs), and here we can see the most dramatic impact on major brands. (*See* Section 12.3.3 for more information about Television Ratings.)

While there are fewer advertising messages broadcast, the other problem recognized is that these messages are not hitting their targets like they used to.

Take the market for cars. Be it in Australia, Britain, the US or Germany, we find a startling fact. Even allowing for inflation, it took twice as many dollars to sell a car in Australia in the late 1980s as it did in the late 1970s. The same is true in the US. In Britain, it took three times as much.

Across the world at the end of the 1990s, it is taking two or three times as much advertising to sell each barrel of beer as a decade earlier. This

Table 7.3

Brand	TVR (1965)	TVR (1990s)	Change (%)
Persil	9,000	2,273	395
Kellogg's	7,125	2,691	265
Cadbury's Dairy Milk Chocolate	4,111	627	655
Quality Street	2,466	1,073	230
Guinness	4,716	1,415	333

points to a reduced productivity for advertisements. In part, this comes from the reduced weight of advertising that has forced brands to operate on inadequate advertising expenditure. The big brands listed in the Table above averaged about 5,000 TVRs a year in the mid-1960s. That produced about 28 minutes of television advertising a year per consumer for those brands against each of their target consumers. By the mid-1990s, a typical brand was closer to 600 TVRs a year, generating just 3.5 minutes of advertising. While some might suggest that 28 minutes was a needless extravagance, 3.5 minutes is certainly too little.

New competitors have added to the problem. In the UK lager market between 1988 and 1994, the number of brands increased by 67 per cent. Each of those new brands is bidding up the price of existing brands' television airtime, and so reducing the amount of expenditure per brand. The net result is a fragmentation of the total advertising market for lager in the consumer's mind.

In this confused and fragmented situation, the existing brands have an enormous advantage because, as the battle rages, consumers have tended to stay loyal. In established markets from lagers to baked beans to soup, we see that leading brands in the 1940s are still brand leaders in the late 1990s. This is due to the fact that brands established when quality differences were more easily perceived are harder to subsequently displace with basically similar products.

The annals of marketing are littered with new product failures. Only 15 per cent of grocery products sold in the US come from brands introduced since 1970 – the rest are over 25 years old. We have moved into the era of the giant super-brands, the new 'haves' of the marketing world. The 'have-nots' are the new, minor, or declining brands with 3.5 minutes of television every 365 days struggling to keep on the supermarket shelves.

With the relative failure of above-the-line advertising to help them, it is not surprising that more of them are switching their marketing funds into below-the-line activities. This was something that was reported particularly in the recession of 1992, mirroring what happened in the early 1980s. However, studies show that most below-the-line campaigns at best bring forward sales among existing users. They nearly always fail to build brand values that provide the long-term basis for a premium position in the market.

The challenge, therefore, for advertising in the new millennium is to create new strategies to help brands in very different circumstances than before. We are moving from an age of advertising *creativity* to the era of advertising *productivity*.

7.4 The ownership and management of the media

Attention was drawn in Chapter 1 to the fact that the advertising business consists of three main groups – the advertisers, their agents and the media. Thus the media operate as separate businesses in their own right. Unlike most businesses they have two distinct and separate groups of customers, their readers, listeners or viewers and their advertisers. These two groups are interdependent since advertisers buy space or time in order to reach the readers/audiences. So the amount of advertising media owners can sell and the price they can command is very dependent on the size and nature of their readership or audience.

7.4.1 The management of newspapers

Although they are interdependent, these two aspects of the business are normally managed quite independently. Thus a newspaper will have an editor who is responsible for deciding the content of the newspaper, in particular what goes into the editorial columns. However, they will normally have a large degree of control also over the volume and in particular the positioning of the advertising. That is to say they will decide which pages should carry advertising and which not, how much on each page and where in the paper the 'advertising pages' shall fall. Their main responsibility is to the readers, but in putting their interests first they are also serving the newspaper's best interests. By giving their readers what they want they ensure

1 A high readership.
2 That they will be ready to pay a good price for the paper.
3 That they will purchase regularly.

From the newspaper's point of view, the former is often the most important point because high readership – especially of the right quality – means that advertisers will want to place their advertising in the newspaper. This means a high advertising revenue and this in many cases represents a higher proportion of the newspaper's total income than does the 'cover price' (what the readers pay).

It is the advertising manager's responsibility to seek income for the newspaper – largely from advertising revenue. However, and particularly in local newspapers, there is an increasing trend to carry loose inserts in addition to advertising. At the *Eastern Daily Press* in Norwich, for example, they have a whole department dedicated to the management of their loose inserts on behalf of clients. With increasing sophistication of print production and of distribution management, they can target inserts to particular socio-demographic groups or districts.

The advertisers are the advertising managers' customers, and to them the paper's readers are primarily a 'benefit' that can be sold to those advertisers. Whereas the editor is responsible for a team of newsgatherers, journalists and feature writers, advertising managers have teams of sales staff. Typically they will have a group of salespeople (advertisement representatives) who visit large advertisers and agencies to discuss their marketing plans and recommend where their paper might be able to 'deliver' their desired target audiences at an acceptable price. They may well also have a team of 'telesales' staff who operate banks of telephones and take down the verbal requests for classified advertisements that flood in to most newspapers every day. A high proportion of advertising revenue, especially for local newspapers is for jobs, cars, houses, as well as the 'personal' advertisements for people who have a litter of cats or a used washing machine to dispose of or are seeking to earn extra cash by tutoring children or carrying out repairs. Increasingly in recent years this telesales activity has changed from the passive acceptance of requests from advertisers to a very active, even aggressive, selling of additional space.

Many newspapers have a third management function, that of circulation. The circulation manager has responsibility simply for selling more copies of the newspaper. This is most frequently achieved through a wide variety of promotional techniques ranging from advertising – often on television – to price-cutting cover price (as *The Times* did in the late 1990s to 25 per cent of the usual cover price), introductory cut-price subscription offers, money-off promotions ('go to France for a £1 with Stena-Sealink') and competitions ranging from bingo to lottery-related scratch cards to more sophisticated fantasy league football.

Obviously a key factor in determining how many copies are sold is the paper's contents (the product). This is the editor's responsibility and can lead to problems in determining a clear marketing policy through a split between 'production' (editor) and sales (circulation manager).

7.4.2 The impact of freesheets

A somewhat different emphasis arises in the case of the rapidly growing 'freesheets'. These are mainly local newspapers with a high proportion of advertising and relatively little editorial matter. They are delivered free to people's houses and *all* their income comes from advertising. They have the advantage to advertisers that their circulation (though not necessarily their readership) can be known very accurately since they can be delivered to selected neighbourhoods. However, the quality of their editorial and the level of readership may be suspect (although the quality of many of them is improving all the time as they take a higher proportion of local press advertising revenue).

Many freesheets are published by companies who already publish a 'traditional' newspaper and the effect of this is to increase the dependence on advertising revenue. Often over 90 per cent of the revenue will come from advertisements, the rest from copy sales.

The schemes used by some to gain new advertising customers can be less than scrupulous. One business freesheet telephoned companies saying that they had been offered a new business award and were entitled to free editorial and advertising at a 'significantly discounted rate'. (In effect, this amounted to advertising editorial or 'advertorial', the basis of much editorial in some freesheets.) A journalist undertook to complete a telephone interview and the design department would produce an advertisement and artwork at 'no extra cost'. While the offer seemed too good to miss, the practice did not meet expectations.

One advertiser reported, 'Although the journalist made the interview and our advertising copy was sent to the design department, the article and advertisement returned for approval carried many inaccuracies, both factual and typographical. When the final advertorial and advertisement appeared, some of the errors had been corrected but some new ones had been inserted. Not a happy experience.'

Fortunately, although this event is a cautionary tale for the unwary, it was a rarity and the majority of freesheets are much better managed.

7.4.3 The management of radio and television

Most newpapers in the UK are owned and run on an entirely commercial basis by independent companies (many of them part of large multinational groups). Their activities are only circumscribed by company law and other laws of the land (advertising is also subject to the voluntary code system – *see* Chapter 9).

Since 1 January 1991, the Independent Television Commission (ITC) has been responsible for controlling all aspects of independent commercial TV in the UK, taking over the previous responsibilities of the Independent Broadcasting Authority (IBA) and the Cable Authority. The BBC operates as a complete separate network and does not accept advertising, being entirely financed by an annual licence fee (£91.50 in 1998) being paid by every household with a colour TV set. There is a reduced fee for a black and white set. The BBC does produce advertisements for its own programmes of course!

Each of the sixteen UK contractors holds their licence for about ten years. The last re-allocation was in 1991, when licences were awarded on a tender basis to the highest bidder, subject to a quality threshold. Twelve licences remained with their existing contractors, four changed hands – those for the south-east (from TVS to Meridian), the south-west (from TSW to Westcountry TV), the London weekday service (from Thames to Carlton), and the national breakfast service (from TV-am to GMTV).

During the last few years there has been a considerable consolidation of advertising sales within ITV, mainly as a result of changes of ownership of the ITV franchises. Carlton, Laser and TSMS have been responsible for selling the various regions.

Commercial radio is under the control of the IBA, which is a quasi-independent body appointed by government to supervise the proper implementation of the laws under which the 204 independent radio stations that are Radio Authority licensees operate.

There have been some notable changes of late, with the activities of some radio stations to mirror the activities of newspapers' circulation management function. Given that in 1995 more people listened to the commercial Pepsi Network Chart Show than to the once-dominant Sunday evening BBC chart show is evidence of the changes in radio listening. For the first time, commercial radio was marketed on a national level by a £2.8 million campaign. Radio 1 FM (BBC) fought back with a £2 million advertising campaign of their own.

7.4.4 The management of other media

It would be impossible and unnecessary to describe in detail how all the many other media operate, but they all to varying degrees incorporate one or both of the two functions – editorial and advertising indicated in the previous two sections.

Magazines function similarly to the newspapers. Most have twin sources of revenue but the freesheets (*see* Section 7.4.2) have only advertising income as do controlled circulation magazines. These, although they were established earlier, are in effect a kind of freesheet. The term normally refers to specialist, usually industrial magazines, which are mailed direct to a carefully selected readership who pay no subscription. Because the readership *is* carefully selected, with the needs of certain advertisers in mind, they are prepared to pay such a good price for advertising that it can meet the whole of the magazine's necessary income.

Some other media obviously only have advertising revenue and the editorial function is totally absent, as with posters and transport advertising. In the cinema, whilst the two functions are there, they are even more widely separated. Indeed cinema advertising is sold by separate companies who have no direct connection at all with the producers of films, or the cinemas that show them (most cinemas in the UK are owned by the distributors). Similarly poster contractors (the people that own or rent the sites and are responsible for sticking up the posters as appropriate) sometimes sub-contract the sales functions to other companies acting on their behalf.

Media owners have a great understanding of what their readers/ viewers want, because they have to cater for them every day; therefore, that knowledge and understanding can be harnessed for advertisers' benefit. For example, Simple Soap used advertorials and infomercials, put together exclusively by the media owners. While they are involved in promotional activity, like ferry tickets for a £1, they can add value at the more sophisticated end with, for example, the development of a TV sponsorship property – as Lego Duplo (children's building bricks) did for *TotsTV* with a scheme developed by the programme producers which now forms an integral part of the opening credits. While all the creative work on a campaign should not be produced solely by media owners, creative ideas that are campaignable can be supplemented with media owner developed solutions.

7.5 How advertising is sold

In Sections 7.4.1 and 7.4.3 reference has been made to the fact that advertising has to be sold like any other commodity and that newspapers, TV contractors, etc. recognize this and invest in the appropriate staff and organization.

Selling space or time effectively depends on a number of things, in particular:

1   Having a medium with a good, well-defined audience which represents a potential market to some advertisers.
2   Identifying clearly who these advertisers are and how to influence them. On the latter point the media have to decide for example whether to concentrate their sales effort on potential advertisers or their advertising agencies (most often they will have some contact with both). In each case who must be contacted? In the advertiser's company it is the advertising manager, brand manager or sales director; in the agency the media staff or the account planning staff. Often again it will be a multiple set of contacts.
3   Making available appropriate information on readership or audience (*see* Section 7.2).
4   Presenting this information – in the form of clear benefits to advertisers through reports, sales literature, etc.

5   Having a clear, appropriate and well-presented pricing structure. A key
     feature of media selling has traditionally been the *rate card*. This gives
     both 'mechanical' information (details of the form in which advertise-
     ments are to be supplied – blocks, artwork, etc. together with sizes
     where appropriate) and also details of costs – traditionally the 'page
     rate' (the cost for a whole page of advertising, followed by half page,
     quarter page, etc. costs) and the 'column rate' (the cost per centimetre
     depth across a single column of type). In addition the rate card will
     give details of the costs of colours in addition to black, copy dates i.e.
     when 'copy' is required to allow printing in time for the publication
     date; and perhaps some information on circulation, readership, etc.
        In the case of broadcasting, rate cards give details of how costs
     vary according to 'length of spot' (15 seconds, 30 seconds, etc.) and
     according to 'time segment' (afternoon, early evening, late evening).
     The latter is important because both the size and quality of the audi-
     ence varies – and charges vary accordingly.

In order to encourage advertisers to use their medium, media owners
may offer a range of additional services, including:

> media research
> assistance with evaluating results
> 'merchandising' support such as providing low-cost point-of-sale
> material, extra copies of multi-page advertisements at low 'run-
> on' rates.

For a large part of the twentieth century, 'card rates' were firm and
there was little room for negotiation. Increasingly, however, competition
between media has increased and social attitudes have changed so as to
make rates enforced by the seller unacceptable. So that the rates indicated
on the media's promotional material and what is actually paid will be a
function of:

1   Demand for that type of advertising (e.g. there is high demand for TV
     advertising in the pre-Christmas period).
2   The volume of alternatives, especially when new advertising media
     first become available.
3   The Advertiser's (or his agency's on his behalf) skill in negotiating –
     see Section 7.6.3.

7.6 How advertising is bought

The purchase of advertising time or space may be – and frequently is –
carried out directly by the advertiser. The advertiser may be an individual

wanting to dispose of a used car or let a room. It may be a local retailer, estate agent or firm seeking employees. A high proportion of total purchases of advertising will be of this character. Typically the volume of advertising and sums of money involved may be small (although cars, jobs and houses advertised in local media, mainly by local firms and individuals, represent a high proportion of total advertising expenditure). In these cases the requirement is usually fairly clear-cut, the choices not too wide and the advertiser will feel quite confident in dealing direct with the media.

In other cases, very large sums of money are involved, the choices very complex and the decisions difficult to arrive at. It is in these situations that advertisers are likely to seek help and advice from their agencies or, more recently, from media buying specialists.

Whichever way it comes about, the media purchasing process in these cases tends to be a complex one, consisting of three main stages (assuming that a clear advertising strategy and budget have already been arrived at).

7.6.1 The inter-media decision

The inter-media decision is the choice of which of the various *types* of media is best for the task in hand. This decision is based on a series of factors clearly established in a checklist issued by the Media Circle. In brief they are:

1   *Reach.* The extent to which the various media are capable of reaching the target market. All things being equal, one with high reach will be preferred to one with low reach.
2   *Creative Scope.* The extent to which the medium offers the capability of achieving e.g.
      colour
      movement
      sound
      detailed description
      the appropriate social situation
3   *Sales history.* Taking account of any past experience which indicates a correlation between advertising in particular media and sales success.
4   *Marketing flexibilily.* In terms of
      regionality
      timing
      couponing/sampling
5   *Trade Reaction.* The extent to which advertising in a particular medium will encourage dealers to carry stock (to some extent in recent times dealers have been more impressed by their suppliers' commitment to TV advertising than to say magazines).

6   *Competitors Use of Media.* If most competitors use a particular medium heavily, it may be decided either to be 'in the swim' following suit or to be different in the hope of being more conspicuous by doing so.

7   *Size of Budget* (*see* Section 3.5). This may determine what is possible even if the use of some other medium is desirable (e.g. TV advertising – in 1984 – is hardly feasible on a national scale for a budget of less than £400,000).

8   *Cost-Effectiveness.* The ultimate criterion is to reach the maximum number of the target audience at lowest cost and maximum impact. However, as the Media Circle checklist points out, this can be a complex comparison to make effectively and convincingly.

7.6.2 The intra-media decision

Having decided which *type* of media to use (the inter-media decision), it will often then be necessary to decide which of the alternatives within this type to use, e.g. if magazines, which magazines to use (the intra-media decision). This becomes largely a matter of comparing costs and readerships. One must be aware of not giving too much attention to the intra-media decision just because the numbers are so often available to make that judgement manageable and reassuring when the inter-media decision may seem nebulous and therefore worrying. Clearly, the inter-media decision is the more important.

7.6.3 Negotiating

Once it has been decided which media to use it becomes a matter of shrewd dealing, negotiating and hard bargaining to achieve the best buy for money. This is quite different skill from the earlier two stages and for this reason agencies often split their media specialists into media planners and media buyers. It was the comparative weakness of many agencies in the buying area that was partly responsible for the rapid growth of specialist media houses whose main expertise lies in their ability to achieve good value for money from media expenditure.

It will be apparent that there is a great deal more to be said about the whole business of selecting suitable media to carry advertising messages to the selected target audiences. Chapter 14 looks in more detail at media selection and buying. Chapters 11–13 study in more depth the way the main media operate in the UK (including how the vital readership and audience figures are provided). In some countries the whole media scene will be completely different from what obtains in the UK and a brief review of some of those differences is made in Chapters 18 and 19.

7.7 Summary

1   Media selection is based on both breadth of coverage and on whether or not the message that one wants to convey is communicated clearly by that media. It is recognized that fragmentation of audiences and the growth of media choice within any given channel makes media selection more difficult.
2   The main media are recognized as having a variety of positive and negative characteristics that must be taken into account when making media choices, particularly as the cost of TV advertising continues to escalate.
3   Newspaper management has changed of late, making the way that this medium is used change – for example, loose inserts are becoming more popular in some areas.
4   The changing role of the Independent Television Commission has had an impact on independent commercial television in the UK, with the changing ownership of ITV franchises leading to a consolidation of advertising sales.

7.8 References

1   Extracted from *Forensic Marketing*, edited by Gavin Barrett, published by McGraw-Hill in association with the Marketing Society.

7.9 Further reading

Broadbent, Dr Simon, *Spending Advertising Money*, Business Books, 1975. Broadbent's book is exceptionally good on the whole aspect of media choice.

Media Planning by J. R. Adams (Business Books Ltd, 1971) is equally good but concentrates more on the mechanics of media scheduling.

Martin Davies' *The Effective Use of Advertising Media*, (Business Books, 1981) is not so valuable as its title would suggest on the topic of media selection – the other two books are very much better in this respect. It does, however, contain much valuable information on sources of data, the way media are organized, etc. Insights into the relationships between agencies, advertisers and the media are provided by quotations from a postal survey that Davies carried out.

Aaker, David A. and Myers, John G. *Advertising Management*, Englewood Cliffs, NJ: Prentice Hall, 1982.

7.10 Questions for discussion

1 Imagine you were deciding to advertise a new mobile phone. What
   media would you choose. Explain your choice and indicate why you
   would exclude other media from your campaign.
2 Given the recent changes to the management of independent television in the UK what are the implications for advertisers?
3 While the cost of advertising on television has increased, it does offer
   better value for money. Discuss.
4 What do you consider to be the main qualities of a good TV time
   buyer. (Compare your answers with Section 14.5.)

Chapter 8

Advertising and its stablemates – below-the-line promotion

By the end of this chapter you will:

- Have reviewed some cases illustrating the importance of below-the-line promotions;
- Recognize the breadth of direct marketing;
- Have reviewed the recent advances in direct mail;
- Have gained an insight into how to make exhibitions more successful, especially overseas;
- Recognize the impact of price promotions on consumer sensitivity to such promotions;
- Understand how merchandising and point of sale have a crucial role in the marketing of many products;
- Have a broad understanding of the impact of PR and realize how public opinion can often be manipulated;
- Appreciate that while sponsorship is growing in popularity – especially TV sponsorship – it does need careful evaluation.

8.1 Above- and below-the-line

It was once customary for advertising agencies to invoice their clients by first listing all advertising booked on their behalf in the main media (press, cinema, posters, radio and TV). The agency drew a commission on these activities from the media owners, who paid for its services. (Increasingly these days, agencies are paid by an agreed fee, rather than by commission.)

At this point a line was drawn on the invoice so that commission could be recorded. Then the other expenditure 'below-the-line' followed – point of sale material, sales literature and so on. The agency did not draw a commission on these from suppliers and so usually charged a service fee for this part of the work. From this purely administrative convenience have derived the two terms:

- *Above-the-line*: all main (commissionable) advertising media.
- *Below-the-line*: other (non-commissionable) publicity activities.

Who first used the terms is uncertain – Procter & Gamble is one company to which the honour is sometimes given.

Above- and below-the-line are convenient terms because they have been widely used and understood over many years in the advertising business. They provide a useful shorthand that often overcomes the necessity to reel off a long list of media and methods.

To limit any possible confusion it is probably safer to refer to above-the-line *advertising* and below-the-line *promotion*. That still leaves us with the potential problem that one of the most important sets of below-the-line techniques is called *sales promotion* (*see* Section 8.4).

To help explore the distinction further, let us consider the manufacturers (or suppliers – especially if the 'product' is an intangible service) and their relationship with the consumers or users. On the left is the manufacturer, on the right the consumer:

Manufacturer (—————————————————) Consumer

The line between them is a continuum or line of communication; and, like all lines of communication, the shortest, most direct route with the clearest and most relevant message will be the most effective. If the manufacturer produces an advertisement of some kind, that advertisement is in fact a communication between the manufacturer and one single consumer. Even though advertising generally communicates with a 'mass audience', it does so one at a time. (If you view your audience as a grey mass, your advertising is likely to be viewed in the same way.)

So along this line from left to right the manufacturer speaks to the consumer; and this can be achieved by advertising. But this is not, by any means, the only method of communication available. For example, the package says something about the product. So does the price. So does the type of store that stocks it. So does the type of person whom your customer sees consuming it. So may the behaviour of the manufacturing company – how its other products perform, how it treats its workers, how it treats its immediate environment. Public relations, the transmission of the company's non-advertising communication to its publics (*see* Section 8.7), is clearly important in this respect. Finally, and probably most importantly, the loudest message of all is that delivered by the product itself – performance.

Along the line from right to left, in the opposite direction, the consumer speaks to the manufacturer – often through research. Market research is the message from the consumer telling the manufacturer if a product is bought, how often, where, in what quantities and when. Attitude research delivers a somewhat less direct message, telling the manufacturer what the consumer thinks and feels about the product, why it is not bought, and, with luck, why it is.

There are many aspects to communications and all are parts of the marketing mix – the *product,* its *price,* where it is sold – (*place*) and the means by which customers find out about the product and are persuaded to use it (*promotion*). One ingredient in the mix – promotion – no matter how 'right', how well planned and executed cannot make up serious shortfalls in the rest of the mix.

If we return to the communication line between a manufacturer and its customer, we can regard 'advertising' as messages close to the manufacturer but distant from the consumer at the point of purchase, while sales 'promotion' (an important aspect of below-the-line promotion) comprises messages closer to the consumer when the decision to buy is being made.

This is summarized neatly by Hugh Davidson in *Offensive Marketing* (1987), referring to one specific aspect of below-the-line publicity:

> The role of [sales] promotion is to encourage purchase by temporarily improving the value of a brand. It is part of the overall marketing mix, and ties in with advertising, product performance, and pricing. In general, the purpose of advertising is to improve attitudes towards a brand, while the objective of promotions is to translate favourable attitudes into actual purchase. Advertising cannot close a sale because its impact is too far from the point of purchase, but [sales] promotion can and does.

Remember, the foregoing is only a generality. There are many instances where advertising can close a sale, e.g. 'direct response' advertising, where a telephone number is given for placing orders or an order form is clipped from the magazine carrying the advertisement.

'Promotion' unfortunately has a range of meanings. It can be used to describe the marketing communications aspect of the marketing mix (*see* above) or more narrowly, as in sales promotion. In its very broad sense it includes the personal methods of communications, such as face-to-face or telephone selling, as well as the impersonal ones, such as advertising. When we use a range of different types of promotion – direct mail, exhibitions and personal selling – we describe it as the *promotional mix.*

8.2 Direct marketing

Under this heading are a number of marketing activities that can occasionally cause some confusion. Direct mail and mail order are the two most often confused (the terms tend to be used indiscriminately in place of each other). Yet direct marketing is an all-embracing term that includes telephone marketing (telemarketing) and door-to-door distribution.

Mail order is simply what it says it is – the process of ordering goods by mail and often, though not necessarily, having them delivered through the mail as well. Typically the ordering is done from a catalogue produced by a 'mail order house' and for many people it is a convenient method of shopping, encompassing the ease and comfort of choosing at home without having to go to the shop and often doing so on attractive credit terms.

More recently a variant has developed known as 'direct response marketing' or 'selling off the page'. Instead of ordering from a catalogue people do so from an advertisement in a newspaper or magazine which, like the catalogues, give details and attractive illustrations of the products. The media has expanded to include independent radio, where there are so many more local stations developing (Section 12.6), and which is particularly suited for selling music; television, where the medium has coined the term *Direct Response Television* or DRTV (Section 12.8), and the newer electronic media on the Internet (Section 12.2.2). The future lies in the possibility of being able to sit at home yet wander through a virtual shopping mall with credit card on the PC keyboard. Whatever the system for viewing the products, the mechanism for ordering and delivery is very similar.

Direct mail on the other hand is simply using the postal service to deliver messages to a selected target audience. What then *maybe* happens is that the recipient can order goods directly (a combination of direct mail and mail order). More frequently the 'mailing shot' – the letter and its enclosures – will be the first in a sequence of events. The recipient will be invited to send for further information and/or invite some kind of personal call, e.g. to provide a demonstration or to give further details of the product being offered.

Direct mail, indeed, does not necessarily call for any immediate response at all. Some organizations, e.g. hotel chains and airlines, use it as a means of keeping in communication with their regular customers (in which case it can be regarded as part of their public relations activity – *see* Section 8.7).

8.2.1 The growth of direct marketing

Expenditure on direct marketing has grown considerably recently, as figures taken from the 1998 *Marketing Pocket Book* illustrate (Table 8.1).

According to the Direct Marketing Association's Census, in 1996 £6.6 billion was invested by clients in all forms of direct marketing. This was an increase on £5.5 billion the previous year. While some of that rise may be accounted for by better research, other indicators support the view that

Table 8.1   *Constant 1990 prices (£m)*

	1991	1992	1993	1994	1995	1996
Direct mail (at current prices)	895	945	904	1,050	1,135	1,404
Door-to-door distribution	265	300	310	317	327	–
Telemarketing	55	62	75	90	108	–
Total	1,215	1,307	1,289	1,457	1,570	–

Source: Direct Mail Information Service (DMIS)

below-the-line is an upward curve. According to research by BT/Channel 4, 19 per cent of television commercials carried a response phone number in 1995, rising to 23 per cent in 1996 and 25 per cent in 1997. More DRTV means more phone calls, more people involved in call handling, and ultimately more database activity.

In the USA, the communications revolution has enabled larger volumes of information to move around the country at ever lower costs. Activities that rely on information flows are springing up thousands of miles from the big city centres where they were once based. There has been a surge in the range of marketing and sales activities as an increasingly competitive economy forces companies to devote more effort to customer relations. These forces have fuelled relocation of telephone calling centres across the country; North and South Dakota have been among the states to benefit.

8.2.2 The limitations of direct marketing

Any limitations of direct mail spring almost entirely from the sheer difficulty of carrying it out correctly. In particular:

List-building
A direct mail campaign is only as effective as the list of names and addresses to which the material is posted. Building a good list usually entails a great deal of research and keeping it up-to-date calls for more effort and dogged determination than most people are prepared to give it. Any list rapidly becomes of limited value unless it is regularly and rigorously 'cleaned' to remove people who have died, moved house, changed jobs, been promoted and so on. The wide availability and cheapness of computerized record systems makes the mechanics of keeping and updating lists much less of a chore than it once was, but does little to ease the *management* of the list.

Until recently, direct mail was especially valuable for 'specialized markets' where a relatively small number of buyers for particular products could be identified. It was less useful for products with a widespread consumer market, because of the difficulty of selecting potential customers out of the population as a whole and establishing relevant names and addresses to eliminate the otherwise high wastage. Although it was used (notably by Reader's Digest) it tended to be exceptional. This is being changed in the UK by the existence of the ACORN system (Area Classification of Residential Neighbourhoods) which enables mailings to be made to selected neighbourhood types (e.g. council flats or executive-type private housing estates). ACORN was developed by CACI Ltd and it is cross-referenced to the Target Group Index so as to offer selective mailings to people living in certain types of housing known to have a strong correlation with particular purchasing propensities. The key is the area post code system which enables quite small groups of houses to be pin-pointed.

Contents and presentation of material
The essence of effective direct mail is its personal touch. Yet there is always a temptation to cut costs by mass-producing stereotyped material. If this is done response rates drop dramatically and users then become disenchanted with the medium.

Ideally, whatever else is sent with it, there should normally be a letter addressed to the recipient by name, outlining benefits likely to be of interest specifically to that reader. There may thus have to be variants on the message. Again computers come to the rescue – it is very easy:

(a) to have a number of different messages which can be selected at will
(b) to insert individual names and addresses into a standard letter

The key is that the material should look and feel as though it is addressed specifically to the person receiving it. Clearly, as with list-building, this is an area where careful planning can pay off handsomely.

Critical factors in optimizing direct mail response
The role of the list as compared with the other factors involved in a mailing is well illustrated by the results of some tests carried out by Drayton Bird[1]. Mailings were sent out to twelve lists, all of which were thought likely to be successful. They also tested three prices, two ways to pay, different times for mailing, alternative ways of responding, and several creative approaches. The best combination of these factors produced a result 58 times as good as the worst combination. By far the most important factor in these tests was the choice of list. *See* Table 8.2.

8.2.3 Innovations in direct mail

Recognizing the fact that over 75 per cent of all mail handled by the Royal Mail is generated on a computer, Electronic Services is a positive response

Table 8.2

Factor	Difference between best and worst
List	× 6.0
Offer	× 3.0
Timing	× 2.0
Creative	× 1.35
Response	× 1.2

offering customers a new and relevant way to access the post. Sending mail via Electronic Services is quick, simple and easy.

All documents, along with the database of names and addresses of the people you want to send them to, can be transferred to the Royal Mail Electronic Mail Centre. You send the information for your mailing straight down from your internal computer systems. In fact, for maximum convenience, you even choose the method of transfer which is best for you: via a modem, direct line, a Value Added Network or even on disk.

Once Royal Mail receive your data the information is processed. The mailing is then printed, addressed, enclosed and put into the post for First Class delivery. Data sent by 6 p.m. will still be in the post that evening.

For the customer, Electronic Services means a big saving in time and effort as well as big money savings too because you are not relying on internal or external resources to move mail from A to B. It is a highly cost-effective way to get mail into the postal system.

8.2.4 Door to door distribution

Members of the Association of Household Distributors (AHD) are able to deliver unaddressed material to every home in the UK. Items include leaflets, brochures, coupons and samples, all of which can be targeted geographically and demographically. Households can be classified by town, region and TV area; by type of property or drive-time radius of retail outlets; by lifestyle or geodemographics such as MOSAIC or ACORN; and all are accessible by postcodes.

Methods of distribution:

- *The Free Newspaper* network offers delivery alongside the weekly free newspapers, and is estimated to cover 86 per cent of the UK. Some publishers offer mechanical insertion into the newspapers.
- *Royal Mail Door to Door* can reach every home in the country, including rural areas, delivered by postmen alongside the mail.

- *Solus distribution* means that a single item is delivered at one time – useful for unusual items or those with specific targeting requirements.
- *Shareplan* means that the item is delivered with up to four other non-competing items, and the cost is shared with other advertisers. These need longer lead times to co-ordinate targeting and timing.

8.3 Exhibitions

Under this heading we are lumping together what is in practice a very wide and very diverse series of events, ranging from major international trade fairs, to small local activities such as 'Ideal Home' exhibitions held in quite small communities. It covers agricultural shows as well as the many exhibitions – some very large, some very small – for specific sectors of industry or a particular profession (e.g. opticians who prescribe contact lenses).

Fundamentally, each of these is very analogous to a newspaper or magazine. Exhibitions have an organizer (the publisher), visitors (the readers) and exhibitors (the advertisers). Like newspaper or magazine publishers, an exhibition organizer has to be able to make available to his advertisers (exhibitors) a sufficient number of interesting contacts between himself and a suitable audience.

The main difficulties with exhibitions are to establish clearly:

(a)   how many people of the 'right' type visited the exhibition?
(b)   how many visited my stand and what was the effect of their visit?
(c)   was it worth the cost?

The last point is especially significant because exhibitions can be very expensive indeed and many of the costs may be hidden unless the exhibitor is very clear-sighted. An ISBA publication *Guide for Exhibitors*,[2] lists the following categories of cost likely to be incurred:

> Cost of space
> Stand design
> Stand construction
> Delivery and withdrawal of exhibits
> Entertainment (drinks, refreshments, etc. for visitors)
> Tickets and passes (for staff and also to customers if tickets are
>   provided free for them)
> Staff expenses

This may already add up to a somewhat frightening total and still ignores the 'cost' of lost business which sales staff might otherwise have won anyway had they not been tied up at the exhibition. In the light of these costs, a very clear set of benefits needs to be achieved *(see* Section 8.3.1).

The attendance at exhibitions should be logged by the organizer and is important information on which future planning may be based. But it is also essential for the exhibitors themselves to log the numbers and type of people who actually visited their stand.

8.3.1 The potential benefits of exhibitions

We have suggested that the cost of exhibiting may be very high. Fortunately the benefits may also be considerable. The ISBA *Guide for Exhibitors* booklet lists the following:

1 To publicize the Company image (long term benefit).
2 Meet existing customers and improve interest in products.
3 Meet potential customers, identify new sales areas/outlets.
4 Introduce new products/services.
5 Prepare the ground for future sales by inviting the appropriate author-ities, associations, ministries to the stand for talks.
6 Support local agent, evaluate his effectiveness, possibly appoint new agents.
7 Assess performance of competitors in terms of product, service and presentation.
8 Give lectures/meet top technicians.
9 Aid market research and long range planning (in former Iron Curtain countries almost the only way of reasonably assessing the possible state plans and meeting the end users and obtaining their reactions).
10 To take orders.

Of particular importance are perhaps the fact that products can actu-ally be seen and sometimes even demonstrated in a relaxed atmosphere and that many of the prospective customers (a) are in a 'buying mood' and (b) may often be people the exhibitor's sales force might not normally meet.

8.3.2 The popularity of exhibitions

The expenditure on UK exhibitions has grown some 33.5 per cent since 1990 to a £1.016 billion business by 1995, one-quarter of which were private events organized by a single company, whereas all others were open to any company wishing to participate. Around two-fifths of all 1995 UK exhibitions were held at the National Exhibition Centre (NEC) in

Birmingham and a third in London (Earls Court or Olympia).

In 1990, a quarter of all overseas exhibitions were UK company/DTI joint ventures. While this proportion had declined to approximately 20 per cent by 1995, expenditure had grown to £347 million. (*Source*: The Incorporated Society of British Advertisers, Exhibition Expenditure Survey, 1995.)

In the US, most convention centres are run by contractors who organize everything to do with the show – from providing workers to rebuild stands to hiring out of equipment. A few tips for anyone organizing an exhibition in the US include:

- Many cities in the US are firmly in the hands of the unions, so it is well worth finding out the 'rules' before hand.
- Always get the US-based freight forwarder's contacts and phone numbers.
- Arrange to get your consignment at the destination a day before you need to start setting up – even if it costs a little more.
- Make contact with the organizers' office as soon as possible – it is first come, first served with the workmen, so if you should be last, quality may suffer.
- Be prepared with 'beer tokens' (cash) to give to the correct people.
- If TVs, videos and fridges are needed, buy them, don't hire them. It may be cheaper.
- Don't accept the bill handed to you by the organizers at the end of the show unquestioningly. If you are concerned, say so. They do try it on.
- Keep the workmen's stomachs full – this way you might avoid the standard four tea breaks in addition to the lunch hour.

8.4 Sales promotion

8.4.1 Clarification of terms[3]

Let us consider Michael. Twenty years ago Michael had the opportunity to work on a product that was quite important to him at the time, and in fact still is. The product needed to be packaged and presented properly in order to find its right place in the market. To promote and market it successfully, its plus points had to be stressed and its many weaknesses minimized. Furthermore, the product had to be communicated in the right way to a very specific and well-defined target audience, brought to their attention in an innovative way, then married to an incentive of some kind to make the audience really want it.

Sounds like a familiar brief for a product launch, requiring the skills of a sales promotion or direct marketing agency? In fact, you'd be wrong. The product that was quite important to Michael was Michael, and the results of Michael's endeavours would quite obviously make a big difference to his career prospects and his future.

Without really appreciating it, Michael was using the techniques to find his first job as a graduate in a then emerging discipline, which was a blend of sales promotion and direct marketing. Obviously the letters of introduction he wrote were direct mail. The special offer was the opportunity to meet a potential new recruit to the world of communications. This marriage of sales promotion and direct marketing resulted in a six out of twenty uptake. If we all achieved a 30 per cent 'Yes, I would like to try' strike rate from our sales-promotion/direct-marketing approaches, we would all be rich. This example, for which we have Michael Ingrams of the Ingram Company to thank, serves to illustrate several points.

The blurred line between sales promotion and direct marketing probably does not exist. The experienced practitioner trying to use all methods at his disposal will easily move from one methodology to another. Twenty years ago, though, the terminology did not really exist, and neither did the technology. Twenty years ago 'below-the-line' as a whole was only just emerging. Within this ill-defined categorization direct-marketing techniques were being used, though they were not called by that name. Everything that *was not* advertising was just called 'below-the-line'.

The second point to come from this example relates to that blurred line. If there was a blurred line over those two decades, then it was between above- and below-the-line rather than between sales promotion and direct marketing. A generation of excellent practitioners has since grown up bridging the two areas.

As the classic debate has always found, above-the-line and below-the-line have many similar objectives, and may therefore overlap. Indeed, as we have already seen, the two disciplines are interdependent. By the same token, sales promotion and direct marketing often intrude into each other's territories. If, as a broad generalization, one can say that the objective of sales promotion is to increase take-off of a product or service through the addition of added value, while direct marketing seeks the same result by addressing its target audience personally either at home or in the office, it becomes apparent that the two disciplines can borrow quite heavily from each other.

There is actually nothing frightening or terribly complex about either discipline. The best professional exponents in any field 'know their stuff' and can advise on the best course of action. Some activities start life as a sales-promotion exercise and then are carefully planned to develop into a potent database marketing opportunity.

For example, consider Sealink Auto Club. The brief was to develop a promotional technique that would generate loyalty among motorists. By joining the club, consumers could take advantage of a 20 per cent rebate on the cost of their car-ferry travel, as well as being offered various other promotional benefits. However, once Sealink had enrolled members and put their details on computer, it had an invaluable database for direct marketing purposes.

That there are areas of overlap between sales promotion and direct marketing is clear. Sales promotion, by and large, would regard direct marketing as a specialized and potent part of its armoury, while direct marketers would acknowledge promotional techniques as a critical adjunct to their skills. Both can theoretically operate without the other, as roast beef can exist independently of horseradish sauce, but the magic is missing.

However, for our purposes, we can regard sales promotion as consisting of an offer that has tangible advantages not inherent in the usual product or service in order to achieve marketing objectives. So sales promotion is a stimulus or motivating influence to *buy* and is treated separately from direct marketing.

8.4.2 Price promotions and advertising

Economists have developed two conflicting theories about the effects of advertising on consumers' price sensitivity. One suggests that advertising leads to product differentiation, thereby reducing price sensitivity, whereas the other states that advertising increases competition by providing information to consumers, in turn increasing price sensitivity. One might reconcile these opposing views by suggesting that advertising affects consumers' price sensitivity through its influence on two moderating effects: (a) advertising can increase price sensitivity by expanding the number of brands considered; and (b) it can also reduce price sensitivity by increasing the relative strength of brand preference. It does seem to be that a price-oriented advertising message increases consumers' price sensitivity, while a non-price-oriented message decreases price sensitivity.

Several theories suggest that price promotions may have a negative long-term effect on consumers' behaviour. Consumers who buy on promotions are likely to attribute their behaviour to the presence of promotions and not to personal preference for the brand. Increased promotion in a category is likely to lead to a perception that the key differentiating feature of brands is price. This can lead to an increased reliance on sales promotion for choosing brands. Furthermore, frequent dealing in a category may condition consumers to look for promotions in the future, thereby making them more promotion-prone.

In considering the long-term impact of promotions and advertising on consumer brand choice behaviour, Mela and others[4] ran a study to develop and empirically test a model. More specifically, they set out to find if consumers responsiveness to marketing mix variables changes over time, and if so, why. To address these issues, they used a unique data set that included store environment and purchase history of more than 1,500 households for just over eight years for one frequently purchased consumer packaged product in one market.

They noticed that, at least in their data set, consumers had become more price- and promotion-sensitive over time. They found two segments of consumers: loyal (relatively less price-sensitive) and non-loyal (price-sensitive), and that the size of the non-loyal segment had grown over time. They concluded that this suggests that a larger number of consumers had become more price- and promotion-sensitive over time.

Quarterly advertising and promotion policies of brands were used to help explain these changes in consumer behaviour. The results confirm the conventional wisdom that, in the long run, advertising reduces consumers' price sensitivity while promotions increase consumers price and promotion sensitivity. These effects are significantly larger for non-loyal consumers than for loyal consumers. In general, compared to the 'good' effects of advertising, promotions have significantly larger 'bad' effects on consumers' price and promotion sensitivities. They suggested that although increased promotional spending may make consumers more price-sensitive over time, competitive reactions limit any shifts in market shares.

8.4.3 Sampling

Sampling, for so long the Cinderella of the marketing world, has found some success in recent years. High-profile exercises, like Pepsi offering a million samples as part of a mid-1990s challenge, caught the headlines. However, research towards the end of the 1990s at the fundamental end of the £300 million a year medium – through the letterbox – is more significant. Research carried out through the Research Society of Great Britain's (RSGB) Omnibus Survey concludes that the doorstep delivery is the best advertising medium for launching new products, and the third most effective medium overall, behind TV and magazines.

Within the panoply of through-the-door advertising (direct mail, door-dropped leaflets, samples and coupons) samples emerge as the favourites for product trial and launches. Of the housewives sampled, 94 per cent thought sampling gave a better idea of the product and 43 per cent drew a distinction from advertising, which they claimed did not influence them. Sampling was considered the most useful medium by 44 per cent when manufacturers launch new products, compared to 16 per cent in favour of TV. When housewives were asked to recall advertising from the previous two months, 81 per cent nominated TV ads, 59 per cent magazine ads and 55 per cent leaflets through the door. Advertising leaflets through the post scored 40 per cent and cinema ads came bottom with a 12 per cent recall.

Samples score well because consumers like something for nothing. It takes the risk out of trying something new. Uniquely among marketing methods, sampling breaks down the adversarial psychological barrier between buyer and seller.

However, direct mail has inherent advantages over sampling in terms of hitting scattered groups of consumers who fit a target market profile. While mass markets are more cost-effective for sampling, with niche products one has a high wastage. It will be important to balance cost per item with cost per response.

Ever more sophisticated lifestyle databases, which can carry up to 300 items of profiling information on each household, are a double-edged sword for sampling. On the one hand, they allow clients to make more precise judgements about which addresses to target, right down to their postcodes. On the other, they strengthen the argument for direct mail in terms of pulling out named individuals with similar profiles at individual addresses nation-wide.

Moreover, sampling suffers from two other key drawbacks. First, it is unsuitable for a number of product categories, such as financial services, drink and tobacco. Second, clients have long memories of the bad old days when verifying whether or not samples had actually arrived was a constant problem.

8.5 Sales literature

It is rare that a product does not need some kind of printed material to support the advertising with further informative and/or persuasive material. Leaflets or brochures giving detailed information about the product and its benefits may be necessary in helping the customer to decide on purchase. If there is a range of products then catalogues or 'range leaflets' may be called for to help customers to decide which is the best product in the range for his or her purposes.

Once the sale is complete, the customer may need further material giving information on how to use, how to maintain or obtain service, etc. and often we shall want at that stage to give information on further products which the customer might be interested in.

The relative importance of such material will vary enormously from one situation to another and the emphasis given to it in promotional mix and budget allocation terms will vary accordingly. Defence equipment, capital goods generally and innovatory consumer durables all need large amounts of support literature. On the other hand candy bars and canned soups need little or none. Like so many other aspects of the promotional task, it is a matter of considering what is necessary or desirable in the light of the nature of the product and the way in which customers purchase and use it.

With the development of the Internet and the growing number of people who can access the network, many companies are putting their sales literature on the Internet. Many advertisements today carry the company's webpage address so that sales messages can be accessed from the company's point of view cheaply and from the customers' point of view quickly. With developing systems, such sales collateral can be made attractive through sound and movement as well as providing direct response mechanisms. The person accessing the information can make their own hard copy off their own printer if they wish.

8.5.1 Letterbox marketing

Letterbox marketing has always seemed to be the poor relation of marketing. While marketing directors happily expound the merits of their latest TV, radio or press campaign, a new leaflet door-drop campaign doesn't seem to have the same allure. However, while the medium is never realistically likely to be as sexy as TV, new research claims that targeting consumer doorsteps could be more effective at attracting attention than mass-media marketing.

Research by the British Market Research Bureau (BMRB) for trade body the Association of Household Distributors (AHD) published in January 1996 reveals that consumers read, often keep and act upon promotional material that arrives through the letterbox. The findings revealed that 85 per cent of people glanced at leaflets and 65 per cent were actually moved to act, either buying a product or visiting a store, in response to a door-drop. This compared favourably with the attention given to TV and press advertising; 64 per cent of respondents agreed that they didn't take much notice of TV adverts and 80 per cent that they flick over adverts in magazines or newspapers.

The rationale behind these findings is that letterbox leaflets cannot fail to get noticed. Press advertising may be passed over as consumers search for news and entertainment. TV advertising builds brand personality but suffers when entertainment takes the focus off the brand. BMRB reports that consumers in the survey claimed to like TV advertising without necessarily paying attention to the advertiser's message.

8.6 Merchandising and point-of-sale material

8.6.1 An overview

In many marketing situations the contact between the manufacturer of a product or supplier of a service and the people who use it is indirect.

A typical pattern is:

Marketing → Reseller or → User
organization   intermediary

In this situation decisions have to be made about the kind of promotional activity that is necessary and the weight of promotion to be applied at each stage. Different promotional techniques can be used to persuade wholesalers, retailers, distributors, etc. to take the product into stock (a *selling-in* or *push* strategy). Similarly, they can also be applied to the user end of the chain to persuade or encourage the users to demand the product (a *selling-out* or *pull* strategy). What happens at the point of purchase (or point of sale, POS) can also be vitally important, and is described by the term 'merchandising' which demands close attention to all activities that take place in-store designed to actively sell goods at maximum profitability. It includes:

- the selection of products to be stocked
- stock control, i.e. making sure there are the right quantities of each item
- store layout, lighting and decor
- space allocation and merchandise location
- traffic flow
- display
- promotional activity
- pricing policy

While merchandising is obviously vital to retailers and other resellers it is also an important link in the chain for manufacturers and other marketing organizations. To some extent their interests are the same – how can we sell maximum volume at maximum profit? But there is also a conflict. Manufacturers are concerned to move their products rather than those of their competitors. Retailers are interested only in achieving maximum turnover and/or profit and are not too concerned about whose products they use to achieve it.

Thus the *manufacturer's viewpoint* is likely to be that merchandising is vital because:

(a) their whole marketing activity only begins to take effect when customers actually buy the product
(b) they can achieve a higher sell-in rate if they help the retailer to sell out.

The *retailer's approach* will concentrate on identifying their most profitable lines and giving them appropriate emphasis, and identifying less profitable lines so as to eliminate them from the stocking list or to take steps to improve their profitability.

Because of this difference in emphasis, the manufacturer's view of merchandising is likely to be a narrower one, concentrating on ensuring that their products are in stock, well displayed and (when appropriate) priced and promoted as planned. However, manufacturers need to be aware of the much wider spectrum within which these activities must take their place.

An important part of the manufacturer's end of this merchandising aspect is to ensure that they provide what is necessary to make their products stand out at point of sale. This will not only include designing packaging so that products will be dramatic and easily recognizable but include also the provision of *point-of-sale material* such as:

1 Racks or bins for the display of material (where necessary, designed to assist in self-selection).
2 Stickers, posters, labels and 'shelf-talkers' – which carry a message on a mobile – to act as reminders and tie in with above-the-line advertising (although in many modern self-service stores the scope for this may be very limited). However, modern technology is altering the picture somewhat.
3 Identification, on the pack and/or elsewhere, of current sales promotional activity.
4 Provision of any necessary leaflets, catalogues, etc. to assist customers' decisions to buy.

However, dealers often find themselves in the situation of being overwhelmed with the amount of display material offered by suppliers. The more sophisticated they are, the more conscious they are that they need to get maximum turnover from each square metre of shelf space, the more selective they will be. Concerned more with profits than with which brand actually sells best, manufacturers need to convince retailers that their display will increase profits. Using POS material to feature a national promotion (especially if it is to be heavily advertised) is one way of doing this, but its apt design is crucial if it is to be used and not discarded.

In some cases POS promotion is used to persuade people to shop at one particular point of sale rather than another. The petrol promotions are intended to encourage people to buy their petrol or oil from one company's site (or sites) rather than another. Trading stamps are another way of building such brand or company loyalty. So are the so-called 'loss leaders' that many retail outlets feature, when one or more items are heavily marked down in price and featured in advertising, or put on posters in the window, etc. to tempt people into that outlet in preference to a competitor's. Naturally the hope is that, once in, they will buy other items besides the featured 'loss leader'.

8.7 Public relations

Public relations is both a whole professional activity in its own right and also a series of specific techniques. In an advertising context the use of some of those techniques as alternatives to or supplements to advertising will often be considered, e.g. new cars are promoted through appraisals by newspaper motoring correspondents as well as by advertising. On the other hand much advertising is used as part of a 'corporate public relations' activity.

Here a brief introduction to both aspects is given. But first another definition.

8.7.1 What public relations is

For many years the Institute of Public Relations defined public relations as 'the deliberate planned and sustained effort to institute and maintain good relations between a company and its public'. Public relations is not a haphazard business, it is not merely the use of gimmicks or the razzmatazz of a launching party, but it is conscious decisions, plans for the future accurately charted, a constant monitoring of a sustained programme of communications that gives a company or a product a good feeling in the minds and hearts of its customers. This good feeling must be constantly reinforced to ensure that a company will have a score of bonus points for the occasion when a problem arises.

Richard Branson and his 'Virgin' brand name can seem to do no wrong and the brand has been able to span music recordings, international passenger and freight airlines, soft drinks, personal finance, and UK railways. Even when their railways are singled out as being poor performers the Virgin brand endures in part through the charismatic Mr Branson and in part through well-organized press and public relations. When the big, bad British Airways has a go at undermining their transatlantic passenger business, the press sides with Branson and he invariably comes up on top in the public eye.

However, much PR activity (including 'corporate advertising') is aimed at the many other groups, apart from customers, who can have an influence on a company's successful operation.

Ideally PR should always be two-way. As well as talking to our public we should listen to what they think of our product and how they see our company.

8.7.2 The seven stages of public relations

To achieve these desirable ends public relations must always be a carefully planned activity. A fully efficient PR campaign consists of the following stages:

1   State the problem or the aim.
2   Do the research.
3   Identify the public.
4   Select the media.
5   Monitor the effects.
6   Look to the future.
7   Maintain financial checks at all stages.

1 *State the problem or aim*

This first stage sounds self-evident, but it is a sad fact that managements may be coerced into sponsoring a gymkhana or supporting a Christmas bazaar with no planned idea of what PR they should be aiming for. Management should at all times be listening to how their products or services are viewed by the customer and how their company is seen by society. This latter question of corporate image is a big one including within it a company's livery and stationery, logo, printed material, etc. A company must be sensitive to how they are viewed and PR should always endeavour to be two-way – speaking to its public and listening to what its public has to say. This brings us on to the second stage of PR – research.

2 *Research*

The methods of doing research will be found in Chapter 16 but as well as these accepted channels of research there is much to commend informal research. A sales director can learn how his customers and potential customers are dealt with when he rings the phone in his general office; a word with the police will often illuminate a transport manager on how his drivers are regarded on the road. Listening and reading are important sources of information in the PR universe.

3 *Identifying the Publics*

When a company has established its PR aim and done the research, then it will need to identify the people to whom it wishes to speak. The launching of a low calorie vegetable-based margarine could be aimed at slimmers, or health enthusiasts, mothers of families or any number of groups of people. In the PR world each of these groups of people is called one of the publics. Figure 8.1 is a diagram of the PR universe. Note that the arrows of communication are two-way. Opinion formers are an important part of PR. They are the out-front people in a community, the chairman of the parent teacher association, the mayor, the vicar, the leader of the Women's Institute, local councillors and dignitaries. It is necessary for a company to have good relationships in the City, so that the funding of a new venture, or assistance in difficult trading conditions may be more easily achieved. The 'don't tell 'em nuffin' approach to competitors will rebound on a company, whereas a friendly and communicative approach to competitors will facilitate understanding within an industry and the mutual tackling of

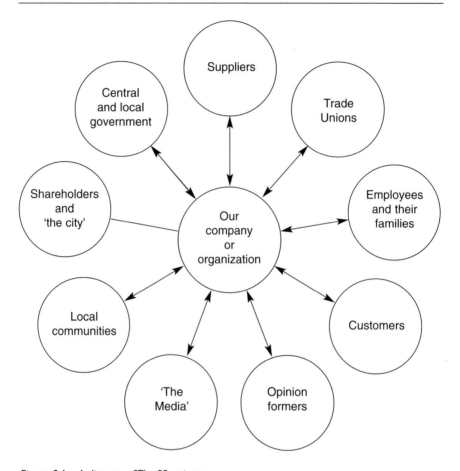

Figure 8.1   *A diagram of The PR universe*

problems within that industry. Good communications with Government officials are very important and can often be crucial in overseas situations.

4 *Select the media*
Types of media that can be used include the following:

PR Media
Direct Contact   Briefings
                                  Education
Briefings   Professional recommendation
                                  Research Papers
'The Media'   Social responsibility programmes
– Press   'Badging' (T-shirts, car stickers, etc.)
– Broadcasting

Advertising	Print (brochures, annual reports)
Lobbying	
Audio-visual and Films	Events (conferences, seminars, visits, open days)
Sponsorship	Competitions
Newsletters	Databanks (Teletext etc.)

There is a constant change of emphasis in the different media used and the new tools coming to hand now include cable and satellite television, audio-visual films, increasing numbers of radio stations and data banks.

5 *Monitoring*
Public relations is never cheap. It is highly labour intensive, and very skilled labour at that, and constant monitoring must be maintained to ensure that the declared aim is being achieved at an acceptable cost.

6 *The Future*
We have just said that vigilance must be maintained to ensure that our declared aim is being achieved. But our aim may well change. The product image that Singer sewing machines worked at a hundred years ago was of a model that would not wear out but now the image of a sophisticated multi-use machine is more appropriate. At the time of going to press the banks are presenting themselves as caring and listening, but with interest rates falling and the value of money rising they may well change their image to safety, security and extensive service departments.

7 *Maintaining financial checks at all stages*
It is difficult to quantify the effects of PR but unless this is undertaken seriously much money can be wasted. For example, on a stand at an inappropriate exhibition or trade fair, on a misguided sponsorship scheme or a costly seminar. The watchword is constant vigilance.

8.7.3 The use of PR techniques to promote products

Much of what has been said about PR so far has been talking largely of using certain techniques to project a favourable impression of the company. This in itself will contribute an important dimension to the successful promotion of products. Sony or Philips can sell their products more readily because their companies and names are highly regarded.

However, PR techniques can also be used very effectively to achieve much more specific promotion of products. For example, new products, especially if they involve new technologies (such as the microchip) or achieve things which could not be done before (such as a new drug), are often newsworthy and hence may be featured in the editorial columns of the press or in radio and TV programmes or news broadcasts.

As well as making products widely known (at no direct cost, by contrast with advertising which would often cost a great deal to achieve the same coverage) products featured in this way carry the authority and independent endorsement of the publication or feature writer, the broadcast channel or presenter. It is of course possible for this to backfire. The newspaper or TV programme may not like the product or may highlight its less desirable features. But good products offering genuine benefits are more likely to gain than to suffer.

Products which are no longer new may, of course, find it more difficult to be featured in this way. Then we have to look for such things as:

1   *Application stories.* New ways in which the product is being used, new problems it is solving ('XYZ adhesive overcomes space shuttle ceramic tiles' problem').
2   *Orders and expansions.* Large overseas contracts, new factories providing employment.
3   *Visits.* Royalty or other visiting dignitaries seen using the products ('President tries his hand with ABC Bulldozer').
4   *Sponsorship.* (*See* Section 8.8.)

8.7.4 Advertising with a social dimension

Whatever the motivation, companies are increasingly affiliating with causes such as AIDS awareness, breast cancer research and prevention, domestic violence and rape awareness and prevention, drug abuse prevention, gay rights, literacy, sensitivity to mental and physical disabilities, racial harmony, and wildlife conservation. Such advertisements – variously referred to as 'cause-related marketing', 'cause marketing', 'mission marketing', 'passion branding', 'social issues marketing' or 'corporate social marketing' – appear to be growing in popularity among consumers. In a recent survey,[5] 64 per cent of American adults surveyed said they believe that cause marketing should be a standard part of a company's activities; 78 per cent said that they would be more likely to buy a product associated with a cause that they care about; and 84 per cent said that cause marketing creates a positive company image.

8.7.5 How the media influence the audience[6]

The media have a crucial role to play in forming, and then reinforcing, crowd behaviour and this is probably even more true of TV than the press. Many people have long since ceased to believe everything they read in the papers, which they rightly suspect as partial. But so often with TV, for the majority of people, 'seeing is believing'.

This is particularly dangerous when, as now, too many news and documentary producers appear to have lost any sense of obligation to present an objective picture. Instead, they frequently use the tricks of their trade to push a subjective and often prejudiced line. This tendency to dress up opinion with all the trappings of objectivity is highly dangerous.

By rights, all journalists ought to be trying to do two things: to report the facts, so far as these are obtainable; and to explain the workings of the world in terms that the layman can understand. Many journalists do still try to do this as best they can but media ethics, never pure as the driven snow, are thought to be slipping – and too many journalists these days seem to have other agendas. Some writers suggest that the tabloids have degenerated into adult comics. However, even in the quality press and the broadcast media, objective reporting and commentary is on the wane. Instead, much reporting is motivated by the following.

Political propaganda
In any democratic society, a vital function of the media is to provide an outlet for different political viewpoints. It seems foolish, therefore, to complain – as some do – that almost all newspapers take a strong political line. So long as this is clearly apparent to readers and is confined to comment, it is entirely healthy. However, it becomes thoroughly unhealthy when the barriers between reporting and commentary break down. Through selective reporting and the manipulation (even invention) of quotes, it is relatively easy for propaganda to masquerade as news. Taken off guard, the public can be fed a line without realizing it. The most disgraceful example this century was provided by *The Times* in the late 1930s. Deeply committed to appeasement, the paper resorted to suppressing hostile reports on Nazi Germany, even when these emanated from its own correspondents in the field.

Another dramatic example of media manipulation of the facts was provided by the American media giant NBC, when it tried to provide visual evidence of how dangerous the 'side saddle' petrol tanks on General Motors lorries could be. On the news, viewers saw the lorry crash and the petrol tank explode. What they didn't see were the news-hungry journalists putting dynamite in the tank to get the effect they were after.

The most notorious case in recent years was the BBC's initial TV news report on the bombing of Libya. That piece was reported as: 'Britain is braced tonight for a wave of terrorism after British bases were used by American bombers …' That may have been the universal opinion in the BBC canteen, yet it was politically coloured speculation, not news. As events turned out, it was completely wrong. For many, it was a sorry performance.

Admittedly, the furore over that particular report has since led to the

BBC tightening up its act – at least in its main news bulletins. Sadly, it is clear that the manipulation of news elsewhere continues unabated. Documentaries and investigative reports usually claim to be objective. In fact, they are almost always 'scripted' in advance, and therefore reflect the prejudices of the programme makers. To viewers subjected to half an hour of planted quotes and heavily edited interviews, it may be far from obvious that they are being force-fed propaganda.

Sensationalism

Everyone knows that the tabloids are sensationalist – and by those standards the quality press and broadcast media may seem models of decorum. In fact, they are far from immune to the same pressures. The days when the public was starved of news – when scarce bulletins from London were read to tatters in village pubs – are long gone. Nowadays, all the media are competing ferociously in conditions of over-supply. With the best will in the world, they have to dress up reports and tickle popular prejudices to attract attention.

A casual glance at any quality paper will show this to be so. Sex sells. Royalty sells. 'Human interest' sells. At one stage, even the BBC routinely ended its main news bulletins with a sick child and a talking duck. All of which might seem quite harmless, and often is.

The problem is that serious newspapers feel the need to present this sort of nonsense in a serious way. The tabloids will happily feed for weeks off the seamier elements of a political sex scandal. The broadsheets, covering the same story, will feel the need to invest it with false importance. The fairly trivial affair of an unknown junior minister and his secretary will quickly blow up into a moral crisis, a political crisis for the government, and a personal crisis for the Prime Minister.

The same tendency to sensationalism is evident in many other fields. Global warming, the oil glut, BSE – all are areas where very inconclusive scientific 'evidence' has been manipulated to build up a major story. Read the newspapers' letters column and you will occasionally find an eminent scientist complaining that contradictory evidence has been suppressed. It seems that it has. Meat is dangerous, we hear, but Russian nuclear waste is not! The media know that their customers enjoy believing that the world is coming to an end, or at the very least that they are being poisoned. Stories pandering to such desires are gold dust – and mere facts or academic rebuttal appear not to be allowed to interfere. The medium is indeed the message.

Public concerns are so often manufactured by the media – with more than a little help from those with a vested financial or political interest. Those endless 'reports out today' are not ferreted out by investigative journalists. Many are deliberately planted in the media to sway public opinion, and often have as much objectivity as a PR company's press releases. If they are repeated in the media unchallenged, it is out of cynicism as much as out of laziness. On dull news days, they are far too useful to be thrown away. Nor can journalists afford to lose important sources of information by rubbishing what they have to say.

Pack-hunting
Journalists, too, like to go with the crowd. They hunt in packs. This is most obvious in the tabloids. But again, the quality press and the broadcast media are moving in the same direction. The media campaigns that sink ministers (or even army generals) on 'moral' grounds would have far less impact if the quality media did not feel obliged to muscle in on the action. When they do so, they reveal more interest in the exercise of power than in any sense of news values.

The periodic lynching of public figures is the most blatant example of media pack-hunting. However, the fact that journalists tend to allow their colleagues to dictate the news reaches much further afield. An admired report or broadcast will inevitably attract copy-catting, followed by a series of spin-offs developing the story from a variety of different angles. In no time at all, a gigantic construction is created which bears almost no relation to events in the real world. It's news simply because it's news.

There are several recent examples, hung on the flimsiest of pegs. At the end of the 1980s, the media decided collectively that a major watershed had been reached. The 1980s, we were told, represented individualism, money, power and ambition in their most virulent forms. In stark contrast, the 1990s were to be 'caring-sharing' years characterized by community values, selflessness and compassion. If nothing else, all this guff filled up a great deal of airtime and column inches whenever the real world was quiet.

When part of Windsor Castle burned down in 1993, the media decided to make it into a symbol for the House of Windsor. In no time, a huge fuss was manufactured on 'the decline and fall' of the monarchy. Conferences were organized, books and special supplements churned out, special reports filled the TV screens. The public, however, wasn't buying, so this story had to be abruptly retired – just like herpes, when AIDS took over as the perennial sex disease, or nuclear winter, when global warming took over as the apocalypse story. The end of the world has its fashions too.

But even apocalypse is not without its financial opportunities. Remember the oil story of the mid-1970s? Everyone was convinced that the world was running out of oil. Politicians and media alike combined to contrive an 'oil shortage' and 'energy crisis'. Both of these were a complete myth. The media blew up the story to such extremes that financial experts were soon predicting that the price of oil would hit £70 a barrel within a couple of years. Oil companies soared in price. Banks lent billions to Third World nations with oil potential. Billions more were invested in oil substitutes. And still more billions were invested in drilling new wells and developing new ways of pumping oil from marginal sources. This was the time that Japanese manufacturers of small cars got their first toehold in the big-car American market.

This pattern was to reverse itself. Soon, all the frantic investment in new oil production would mean a glut of surplus oil on the world market. The price of oil would fall, not rise as predicted.

Now the situation is reversed. The media have a new story – this time it's global warming. And the idea that the world is awash with oil, that there's so much of it, no one wants it or cares about it. There is a feeling that it's not good to own it or invest in it. After all, oil is bad for the world environment. It produces greenhouse gases that trap heat and endanger the world's eco-system. And so the story goes on. After all, it makes a decent news story for a slow day and it gives a lot of people something to do!

8.8 Sponsorship

Increasing sums of money are being invested by organizations of all types and sizes in sponsoring sporting and cultural activities. Thus something that could once have been regarded perhaps as a minor PR medium is rapidly becoming a distinct and important form of promotion in its own right. The reasons for this include perhaps a desire to contribute to the good of society (and to be recognized as doing so).

Usually, however, there are more specific objectives involved. For example in the UK, advertising of cigarettes on television is forbidden. By sponsoring sporting activities such as cricket (e.g. 'the Benson & Hedges cup') the manufacturers were able to retain their presence on TV, together with many mentions of their names in a wide range of other media. At the same time they stand to gain from the association of the brand name with an activity which has healthy connotations and their contribution to its success is seen by many as a laudable activity. Others of course may take the view that such contributions amount to a somewhat cynical flaunting of the spirit of the law. The total effect, however, is likely to be overwhelmingly good rather than bad for the companies concerned and for their products.

Often the link between sponsors and the activity concerned is much more direct such as oil companies and motor racing, sportswear manufacturers and tennis and the potential benefits of such an association are obvious. The issues involved are summed up neatly in the following extracts from another ISBA booklet *Guide to Sponsorship*[7]:

> ... sponsorship is the provision of financial or material support by a company for some independent activity (usually related to sport or the arts) not directly linked to the company's normal business; but support from which the sponsoring company would hope to benefit.

Sponsorship is usually undertaken to develop a more favourable attitude towards the sponsoring company or its products within a relevant target audience such as consumers, trade customers, employees, or the community in which it operates.

Advertising's main function is the direct promotion of a company or its products in space or air time bought for that specific purpose. But in sponsorship, the company's name could be incidental to the main activity, playing a supportive role to the event or individual being sponsored. Sponsorship works largely through indirect communications. While on the other hand, this means that it can appear as less overtly commercial, on the other, it means that impact and memorability are likely to be considerably less in the short term; something to be borne in mind when setting objectives.

The booklet goes on to stress that:

Careful and accurate identification of objectives is essential to a successful sponsorship operation. The aim should be to establish realistic, common-sense goals which are based on the fundamentals of marketing communication, and which will be capable of some form of evaluation.

It also suggests that:

Typical objects might be expressed as:
To increase brand awareness among consumers.
To improve consumer image of company in terms of modernity, warmth, concern, etc.
To increase goodwill and understanding among trade customers.
To enhance company's image in local community.
To raise employees' morale and company loyalty.
To create favourable awareness of the company among young potential future consumers.

As with all forms of promotion, having established the objectives, it is necessary:

(a) to make as accurate and detailed an assessment of the cost as possible.
(b) compare it with the cost of alternative methods of achieving the same results.
(c) monitoring and assessing results and again comparing with costs.

The latter may be especially difficult with sponsorship, because of the essentially low-key and indirect nature of some of the results looked for. For this reason alone considerable caution is necessary before investing heavily in this type of promotion. However, many organizations clearly believe that the investment in sponsorship can be a very good one. On Thursday 23 August 1995, *The Times* was given away free for one day only with more than double its print run to 1.5 million thanks to Microsoft, which underwrote the estimated £300,000-plus cost.

As an illustration of the size of the market, Table 8.3 summarizes the UK expenditure on sponsorship.[8]

Table 8.3

	1990	1991	1992	1993	1994	1995	1996
Market size (£m)	230	238	239	250	265	285	302
No. of sponsorships	–	759	659	745	818	946	987

A view on the changing fortunes of the corporate sponsorship can be seen in Table 8.4, which reviews the number of involvements in sponsorship by various sectors.[9]

Table 8.4

Sector	1995	1996
Sports goods/clothing	76	125
Alcoholic drinks	124	106
Automotive trade	81	87
Banks/finance	61	65
Insurance	67	58
Grocery	44	43
Communications	36	42
Soft drinks/water	30	40
Tobacco	26	34
Media	32	27

8.8.1 Sponsorship, advertising and word-of-mouth

In a world in which star endorsements can cost many millions of pounds, one can begin to question the validity of risking so much of the marketing budget when one false move on the part of that star can not only wipe out the monetary investment but actually rebound directly on the brand's proclaimed values. Even if potential sponsors manage to allay their fears about existing skeletons in the star's cupboard, how do they legislate for that moment of madness in front of the world's press which characterised Cantona's actions when he leaped on someone in the crowd?

It is likely that, to an increasing extent, marketers and brand-builders of the future won't have to worry about this question. Paradoxically, future success will depend not upon persuading stars to put their name to your brand but rather upon persuading real people to tell their friends, family and work colleagues about it. There has been a rapid decline across society in levels of trust in the institutions which govern British lives. Now, we are seeing this growing distrust extend to almost every organization, institution and public body. In an increasingly complex and commercially-oriented world, consumers are becoming more and more cynical and distrusting of every corporate body and communication with which they come into contact. Instead, they are turning increasingly to the one source of advice and counsel which they feel to be above commercial activity – their friends and family. Of course, word-of-mouth endorsement has always been a powerful marketing channel. Perhaps in the future it will not simply become a necessary and consciously managed one within the marketing armoury, but the key channel for brand-building. Its deployment will require new skills and techniques compared with those with which many are currently familiar.

8.8.2 TV sponsorship

There seems little doubt that the TV sponsorship market will continue to grow in both volume and value. The number of deals done will continue to increase but the business will spread across more channels. Satellite and cable stations will compete even more fiercely for their share of business; already programme sponsorship is far more important as a portion of revenue to non-terrestrial channels than it is to either ITV or Channel 4. The spectrum of sponsors will also widen. Already there are many more companies that have used programme sponsorship to access TV for the first time. With entry-level costs falling, this trend is likely to continue. Also, the range of programmes sponsored will broaden, as fears of supporting contentious shows diminish.

On the ITV network in 1995, game shows and factual/information programmes contributed much in terms of the number of programmes being supported (44 per cent), but others were spread across all genres. Regionally, the ITV picture is very different, however, with deals heavily concentrated on sports programmes, information services and other factual shows.

The balance on the other channels naturally reflects their programming bias. For example, on Sky in 1998, most programme sponsors were connected with sport. But even on heavily thematic channels (MTV, NBC Superchannel, etc.), the range of programmes attracted much wider sponsors. And the range of sponsors supporting those programmes also got wider.

In 1995, ITV was still responsible for the bulk of UK television sponsorship in value terms. According to Carlton Television Sales, ITV annual sponsorship revenue reached £29 million (nearly 60 per cent of total UK TV sponsorship).

Programme sponsorship sales expanded, but not in the exciting way forecast by ITV a few years previously. Satellite and cable have been more involved in sponsorship, with NBC and Superchannel doing well, and with UK Living/UK Gold new entrants in this area. MTV found it relatively straightforward to attract sponsors, with around 10 per cent of its total ad revenue coming from programme sponsors. At United Artists Programming, which sells Discovery and Bravo channels, there has been some activity, where important deals were done with IBM, Foster's and Simpatex in the last quarter of 1995.

European Business News picked up four sponsors: Volvo, ABB, Chase Manhattan, and the State of Georgia (promoting venues for the Olympic Games). With new channel launches coming fast and furious, it is probable that satellite sponsorship business will increase. Despite tiny audiences, cable-only channels, too, are beginning to attract mass-market national sponsors.

Associated Newspapers' Channel One has arrangements with HSA (healthcare), Vauxhall Masterfit, Debenhams, Amarula, MGM and SmithKline Beecham supporting lead series. SelecTV meanwhile has sponsorship for reruns of *Birds Of A Feather* (from Surf). Even Live TV – despite its disastrous launch – attracted big-name sponsors. BP sponsored its Rugby League World Cup coverage while Nescafé supported the British Ice Skating Championships.

The position of agencies still concerns some. In the US, ad agencies and PR companies control television sponsorship. But in the UK, many programme sponsorship deals are still done directly between broadcasters and advertisers.

Most deals eventually involve a range of intermediaries, including advertising agencies, PR companies, media independents or sponsorship specialists – but often only when the pieces need to be put in place. Agencies are slowly recognizing the advantage in actively seeking sponsorship opportunities.

8.8.3 Sponsorship needs better research

Sponsorship is still a business with as much room for error as success, according to new research commissioned by *Marketing* and published in November 1995.

A set of 1,000 telephone interviews were conducted by Audience Selection asking respondents two simple, unprompted questions: first, if they knew who was responsible for sponsoring a certain event, programme or venue (for example, the London Marathon) – and second, if they were aware of what a particular sponsor or brand name stood for (for instance, Carling as a beer or Frosties as a breakfast cereal). The sample was representative of the UK.

There were two clear winners. The first, PowerGen's sponsorship of the ITV Weather, was correctly identified by 51 per cent of interviewees. There was good knowledge across both the age range (62 per cent of 15- to

24- year-olds and 56 per cent of 45- to 54-year-olds) and the class range (60 per cent of ABs, 43 per cent of DEs). As PowerGen was the first and most publicized sponsor of a TV programme, this is not surprising. Not far behind them were the 43 per cent who named Diet Coke as the sponsor of the ITV Movie. And Diet Coke can take heart from the fact that 79 per cent of the sought-after 15- to 24-year-old age group got it right.

At the other end of the recognition scale comes insurance company Direct Line, whose sponsorship of the Eastbourne Ladies Tennis Championship in 1995 failed to register even a blip – thus posing the question, why tennis for an insurance company?

Table 8.5

		Sponsorship awareness	Male (%)	Female (%)	Brand awareness %
PowerGen	ITV National Weather	51	57	45	86
Diet Coke	ITV Movie	43	49	38	95
Carling Black Label	English Premier League	32	48	17	99
Sharp	Manchester United FC	26	42	12	68
Coca-Cola	League Cup	22	32	12	98
Commercial Union	London's Burning	16	16	16	84
Frosties	Gladiators	15	16	13	93
Budweiser	World League, American football	12	19	5	92
Pepsi	The Network Chart Show	9	13	5	97
Heineken	The Rugby World Cup	6	9	3	99
Fosters	Oval Cricket Ground	6	13	0	90
Green Flag	England Football Team	6	12	0	13
Nutrasweet	The London Marathon	4	6	2	80
Labbatts	Apollo Theatres	3	4	2	70
Lloyds Bank	Young Musician of the Year	2	3	1	91
Lilt	Notting Hill Carnival	2	2	2	89
Wella	Baywatch	2	2	2	71
Guinness	The Royal Ballet	1	1	0	97
Direct Line	Ladies Tennis, Eastbourne	0	0	0	75

Source: Audience Selection

'Tennis is a family game which appeals to both men and women,' said a spokeswoman for Direct Line. Despite the lack of awareness in the *Marketing* research, the spokeswoman insists the sponsorship was a success. Direct Line repeated the exercise again the following year.

However, if you want more than to simply feel good, then a careful match is vital. A popular brand with a popular event works almost before it has begun, as Diet Coke shows. The ITV film season began in 1993 and was the first sponsorship of a strand that included a creative bumper. With ratings like 14.8 million for the film *Pretty Woman*, both sides of the deal got what they wanted.

A spokeswoman for Diet Coke says 'Sponsorship offers something a little bit different from traditional advertising; event sponsorship is taking advantage of a unique opportunity. It has worked hard and has continued to increase awareness'.

Even if you don't have the purchasing power and visibility of Coca-Cola, a marginal brand matched with a popular event can hope, eventually, to achieve higher brand awareness through the deal. It is important to get good matchmaking: the fit is between understanding what motivates your target audience and looking at areas where you can become commercially involved. It is also important to understand the imagery or associations that can be reflected from the sport or event.

Where there is no obvious connection between the event and the product or its audience, the benefits are hard to quantify. For instance, Wella's sponsorship of *Baywatch* receives only a 2 per cent recognition rate, perhaps because a brand associated with women is sponsoring a programme that has great attraction for men and children. Sports sponsorship by brewers makes sense – men like sport and beer – but do *Baywatch* fans spend a lot on their hair?

8.9 Back to the promotional mix

To make effective use of any of these techniques, they must be considered

Table 8.6 *Percentage of annual marketing budget allocated to specific activities*

	1994 (%)	1995 (%)	Change (%)
Press advertising	17.70	16.00	−10
Television	18.40	14.80	−20
Radio	2.30	2.40	4
Outdoor media	2.50	3.10	24
Exhibitions	4.70	5.80	23
Direct marketing	13.40	15.60	16
Telemarketing	n/a	2.70	
Sales promotion	14.60	12.20	−16
Loyalty schemes	3.80	2.40	−37
Sponsorship/hospitality	7.70	4.50	−42
PR	5.40	10.20	89
Market research	5.40	5.40	0
IT	1.40	2.00	43
Other	2.70	2.90	7
	100.00	100.00	

Source: Marketing Forum, reported in *Marketing*, 11 January 1996

– along with above-the-line media – as part of a total promotional mix, itself part of a marketing mix, aimed at achieving specific marketing objectives (*see* Chapter 5).

The aim is to select that series of methods (or just occasionally one only) that will enable us most effectively to communicate the necessary messages to the necessary people in order to bring about the objectives.

8.10 Case studies

8.10.1 Whatever happened to Barum?

The Barum name was supposed to revolutionize pharmaceutical sales, offering up to 40 per cent less than the market leaders; all that without consumer advertising.

Barum, from Wrafton Laboratories, an ambitious attempt to create a new market between the massive over-the-counter brands and the cheaper, but lower quality, private label offering was launched in mid-1994. It tried to take a single brand name across eighteen different product categories, from analgesics and antacids to depilatories.

Sadly, it failed twelve months later.

As an incentive to stock Barum, one that undercut the brand leaders by between 20 per cent and 40 per cent, retailers were offered very high margins of up to 60 per cent. This strategy failed to pay off. While the company was able to achieve reasonable distribution shortly after launch, Barum failed to win repeat orders. While it persuaded Sainsbury's and Safeway to accept one of the analgesic lines, the multiples remained unconvinced.

The company had a marketing budget of just £50,000, which was too small to stretch to consumer ads. The company accepts that national distribution through the multiples would have created more cash to invest in marketing communications. A company spokesman said, 'It is likely that we tried to launch too many products too quickly and the brand was probably stretched across too many different categories. We may have got our pricing wrong too.'

While they may have been able to have reduced their price differential between Barum and the other brands and still retain their USP (Unique Selling Proposition) they appeared still to be seriously underfunded to attempt realistic consumer advertising. While it is possible to launch a new brand without such support (Patak's and Müller are two examples), as the then senior vice-chairman of the Chartered Institute of Marketing, Tom Brannan, commented, brands with a strong USP can survive with little consumer advertising, but the smaller the point of difference, the bigger the requirement for marketing support.

It seems that the company failed to communicate Barum's USP strongly enough. Better point of sale material and sampling programmes may have helped. The point of difference was not sufficiently powerful to encourage consumers to switch from the safety of established brands and they may have needed advertising to provide that reassurance to lure them.

8.10.2 Tesco switch to direct

In 1996, the food retailing giant, Tesco, decided to shift its £30 million advertising and marketing budget from above-the-line to direct marketing, increasing its activity below-the-line. The Tesco Clubcard, launched in February 1996, rapidly attracted over 6 million members in that year and remains at the forefront of the supermarket's marketing drive towards the millennium. Tesco was reported to be doing this to wrest the consumer's attention from rival Sainsbury's ABC card.

Tesco's spend on national TV and press advertising fell from £6.3 million in the third quarter of 1995 to £2.5 million in the same quarter the following year, according to Register-MEAL. As part of its more flexible approach to advertising brought about by the Clubcard initiative, it was able to spend more below-the-line. For example, in 1996 it was able to mail 3.5 million customer magazines to its top Clubcard members.

8.10.3 Political parties go for a direct approach

Pre-Christmas 1995, the Conservative Party sent out a direct mail appeal to 100,000 homes of Tory voters asking for donations to the Party. Although they had a low standing in the opinion polls and a number of internal troubles, they received more than £450,000 in donations, making this their most successful direct response campaign. Yet this was an appeal with a difference as it was themed around a lottery. Prizes included a £14,000 Rover 400 ('no prizes for guessing the colour', their mailing explained!) and a £4,000 Caribbean cruise. The more money supporters donated, the more chances they got to enter the draw.

For political parties, the attraction of direct marketing is that it allows them to make use of the rich data they already possess on their members and likely supporters and target them for specific messages. By targeting people who had bought shares in privatized services, the Tories were able to contact them to try to persuade them that they would lose out under Labour. The Liberal Democrats also launched a direct marketing campaign in key marginals they believed they could take from the Tories. Even before it took on the 'New' tag Labour was looking at ways to use direct marketing, offering members its own affinity card (in conjunction with the Co-operative Bank) as early as 1989 and making a habit of looking for new recruits among the ranks of trade unions.

All the parties are looking at more ambitious ways of using direct marketing, including campaigns aimed at specific social groups. These could include, for example, law and order literature aimed at homeowners who have been burgled and made insurance claims, campaigns on education for parents with children of school age, and literature on pensions targeted at OAPs. In this way they will be able to target directly, to support the broader mass-media messages of TV, press and posters.

8.10.4 Animated response link with Internet

Wallace and Gromit are successfully fulfilling their fans' desires for information and promotional items in a new link between Royal Mail and the Internet.

Taking time out from their busy schedule, Wallace and Gromit are featured in the 'Aardmarket', an exciting 24-hour Internet shopping facility, programmed and configured by The Mail Marketing Group, a UK-based direct marketing organization. The site was developed after Aardman Animations found that visitors to their existing website were frequently demanding access to Wallace and Gromit merchandise. Aardman Animations approached The Mail Marketing Group, who combined their experience with a team of Hewlett Packard experts and Aardman's creative talents to make the Aardmarket possible.

Unlike some on-line shopping facilities, Aardmarket shoppers can rely on a secure server to protect sensitive information such as address and credit card details. The mail marketing group processes the orders on a daily basis, with the help of Royal Mail, and Wallace and Gromit merchandise is despatched to a total of 236 countries. Orders can be tracked at every stage by the generation of a unique reference number for each order.

Visitors can call the site direct at http://aardmarket.aardman. com or link to it from Aardman's existing site, http://www. aardman.com.

8.11 Summary

1 'Above-the-line' referred to the main commissionable advertising media, while 'below-the-line' referred to other, non-commissionable publicity activities. While still used today, the line between the two areas is becoming much 'fuzzier, with some talking about 'through-the-line' activities to allude to the integration of activities – the cornerstone of successful campaigns.

2 Direct marketing has grown considerably of late to imply more than just mail order, and the term is used to include telemarketing and door-to-door distribution.

3 While the popularity of exhibitions is growing, there are many points of detail that have to be considered, particularly overseas.

4 The interaction of price promotions and advertising needs to be considered carefully if key brand values are not to be compromised.

5 Product sampling has grown away from being the Cinderella of the marketing world into becoming the favourite medium to launch products and for product trial and the third most effective medium overall.

6 Merchandising and point of sale is recognized as having a crucial role to play in the marketing of many products, but is of no value unless the retailer agrees to carry it!

7 Public and press relations is not the poor relation of the advertising world any more as we see how the media may influence the audience through propaganda and sensationalism, quite apart from the behaviour of a select few journalist rogues.

8 While sponsorship has grown in popularity of late, there is still much to be done in the evaluation of the effectiveness of sponsorship.

8.12 References

1 Bird, D., *Common Sense Direct Marketing*, second edition, Kogan Page, 1989.

2 *Guide for Exhibitors*, Incorporated Society of British Advertisers.

3 Taken from Wilmshurst, J., *Below-the-line Promotion*, Chapter 8, Butterworth-Heinemann, 1993.

4 Mela, C. *et al.*, *The Long Term Impact of Promotions and Advertising on Consumer Brand Choice*, Marketing Science Institute Working Paper 96–127, December 1996.

5 Reported in Drumwright, M. E., *Company Advertising with a Social Dimension*, Marketing Science Institute Working Paper 96–110, July 1996.

6 Adapted from Campbell, J. and Bonner, W., *Media, Mania and the Market*, Fleet Street Publications, 1994.

7 *Guide to Sponsorship*, Incorporated Society of British Advertisers.

8 RSL Sportscan, 1996.

9 RSL Sportscan, 1996.

8.13 Further reading

The sources quoted as references are each valuable on their own topics.

Further insight on direct mail is obtainable from *Direct Mail* by Robin Fairlie (of Reader's Digest) published by Kogan Page Ltd, 1979.

The best brief and very readable introduction to the whole field of public relations is *Teach Yourself PR* by Herbert Lloyd, (Hodder & Stoughton, 1980).

A Manual of Sales Promotion by J. Williams, (Innovation, 1983) is very comprehensive and practical.

Blattberg, Robert C. and Neslin, Scott A. *Sales Promotion: Concepts, Methods and Strategies*. Englewood Cliffs, NJ: Prentice Hall, 1990.

Kotler, Philip, *Marketing Management: Analysis, Planning, Implementation And Control* (7th Edition), Englewood Cliffs, NJ: Prentice Hall, 1991.

Smith, Ian, *Meeting Customer Needs* (2nd Edition), Oxford: Butterworth-Heinemann Ltd in association with the Institute of Management Foundation, 1994.

8.14 Questions for discussion

1 Review the four main methods of door-to-door distribution and list the advantages and disadvantages of each. If you were marketing carpet cleaning services, which would you choose and why?

2 List the criteria that you would look for in a company to handle your exhibition of lead crystal in Toronto, Canada.

3 John Smiths Bitter have run a 'no nonsense' advertising campaign for their beer promotions over recent years. This has manifest itself in a straight 13.5 per cent extra free on promotional cans. Discuss the long-term impact on brand values from such a strategy.

4 Outline why sampling has proved to be so popular as a marketing tool.

5 What arguments would you put forward to a retailer to convince them to carry your point-of-sale material ahead of the competition?

6   In a group, discuss examples of where you feel the media have influenced the audience.

7   How would you evaluate the effectiveness of sponsorship?

Chapter 9

How advertising is controlled

'Advertising, like any business, is governed by all general principles of law. In addition, it is regulated by various voluntary codes of standards and practice.'
Diana Woolley, *Advertising Law Handbook*, Business Books, 1976

By the end of this chapter you will:

- Appreciate why advertising needs to be controlled;
- Be aware how this is done in the UK and elsewhere through the law and, in particular, through the Codes of Practice;
- Appreciate the role of the Advertising Standards Authority and how it functions;
- Be familiar with the British Codes of Advertising and Sales Promotion.

9.1 Why control is necessary

Most people in the UK approve of advertising in general terms and it is control over the *truthfulness* of advertising that many see as necessary. Section 1.4 quoted a survey carried out in the UK in 1981 which included among its findings the fact that 24 per cent disapproved of advertising. The reasons for disapproval included the view that advertising portrayed too stereotyped an image of family life and that 'advertising makes people buy things they do not want'. (Perhaps significantly when the statement is expressed as 'advertising makes *me* buy things I do not want'. Only 15 per cent of the sample agreed with this statement!)

Thus there is a minority of people who disapprove of advertising *in principle*. Michael Barnes[1] in discussing a series of surveys carried out in the UK between 1961 and 1981 points out that: 'Common factors that appeared among the disapprovers who were contacted included: a high degree of family-centredness; low exposure to posters, cinema, commercial radio and magazines (other than Sunday colour supplements); political conservatism; and a tendency seriously to question the materialistic values of society.' (The point that it is possible to hold a view of economics that makes advertising non-beneficial was discussed in Section 1.5).

If some people do disapprove of advertising in principle there will naturally be some pressure to control, or even eliminate it, on these grounds alone.

Even if advertising is accepted in principle, however, there will be some types of advertising which are widely regarded as undesirable. In particular advertising which deliberately sets out to deceive by falsifying facts or claiming the impossible will stimulate urgent calls for some degree of control.

Finally, there are some members of society, notably children, who may be regarded as needing special protection from the highly persuasive claims made by advertising.

For all these reasons, in every developed society there has been a tendency right through the twentieth century for an increasing range of controls of one sort or another to be imposed. Eric Burleton[2] quotes *The Times* as suggesting in 1909: 'The best modern advertising has the publication of facts for its basis. The day of successful claptrap and vulgarity, still more the day of exaggerated and deceptive misrepresentation is quickly passing away. So far from these being fostered by advertising agents, the whole tendency of the best and most successful agents is to repress them.'

Section 1.2.2 refers to some of the outrageous claims made by advertisers in the previous century and changing customs and social attitudes make *us* no longer accept practices that were common in 1909.

9.2 How best to control advertising?

The question then is not whether advertising should be controlled but to what extent and by what method. Practice varies considerably on both aspects.

Eric Burleton[2] points out that in Europe for example countries fall into four broad categories from this point of view:

1   Countries with no self-regulation.
2   Countries with weak self-regulation.
3   Countries with strong legislation and some self-regulation.
4   Countries with strong legislation.

In 1998 the ASA sees the UK in an additional category.

Category 1. Includes most of the Eastern bloc (Bulgaria, Yugoslavia, Rumania, Czechoslovakia, East Germany*, Albania and Poland – Hungary has made a tentative start on a code of self-regulation).
Category 2. Applies to Greece and Portugal.

---

* East Germany and West Germany are now unified.

Category 3. Consists of Norway, Sweden and Finland. In Finland, for example, most TV and radio advertisements are pre-vetted by the TV and radio network. No children can appear in TV adverts. Tobacco and alcohol advertising is banned by law except in trade journals.

Category 4. Includes all the West European countries, although there are very considerable differences in the way the systems operate.

Most of these codes are based on the ICC Code of Practice, itself derived from the British Codes of Advertising and Sales Promotion.

The main arguments in favour of legal restraints are the obvious ones that unfair or unethical advertising affects the community at large and so the community as a whole, through the law, should exercise the necessary protection. It is also argued that to leave the industries concerned to operate their own regulatory system is unlikely to be tough enough to overcome the wide range of abuses.

The contrary argument runs that the law is cumbersome and expensive to operate and finds it very difficult to move quickly (because for example of the time it takes in most countries to get new regulations through the legislative procedures (the parliamentary systems or whatever)). Self-regulatory systems it is claimed have the advantages that:

1   The Committee of Advertising Practice, who write and enforce the Codes, are representatives of the advertising industry trade and professional bodies and are therefore able to judge what is reasonable and what is not. The ASA's Council, who judge whether or not an advertisement breaks the Codes, are, however, predominantly lay members and so have no axe to grind.

2   They are extremely flexible because necessary modifications of the system to meet changing circumstances can be quickly made once agreement is reached by all the parties involved.

3   Sanctions can be quickly and firmly applied (e.g. by the participating media owners refusing to accept advertisements which have been judged as unacceptable by the ASA Council) whereas legally applied sanctions can usually result only after lengthy legal proceedings.

In an increasing number of countries it seems that a balance between the two systems is evolving, with the main emphasis being on the self-regulatory approach. Whilst the systems vary somewhat from one country to another, the basic approach is normally fairly similar. By way of example, the British system is outlined in some detail in Section 9.6. Most other systems are in any case largely based on the British one.

9.3 The law and advertising

Advertising practices and the conduct of businesses related to advertising are affected by the law in a number of ways:

1   There are laws that affect any kind of trading activity, such as the law of contract and of copyright.
2   Some laws are specific to advertising such as those which regulate commercial broadcasting.
3   Laws relating to aspects of trading such as printing product details to be displayed on packaging, etc.
4   Laws which have a specific purpose (such as the control of gambling or of money-lending) which have detailed implications for any advertising which relates to the areas concerned.

What follows is a brief indication of some of the more widely significant aspects of the law as they affect advertising. A more detailed study should be pursued in the sources listed in Sections 9.8 and 9.9. In all cases British law is quoted and there will be significant differences in other countries in terms of what the law says and of how it is administered. British law can be derived from decisions in the courts over many years (sometimes centuries) in which case it is known as case law. Or it can be expressed in specific Acts of Parliament – statute law. Both are administered and interpreted by the courts.

Legal actions can be 'civil' where one citizen (or a company or other legal entity) takes another to law to obtain damages or other redress for a wrong they believe has been committed against them. A 'criminal' action is one where the police or some other representative of the state believes that a statutory law has been infringed (and a crime therefore committed). If a client does not pay an advertising agency's bills the agency can bring a civil action to recover the money. But if the agency's representative (unlikely event) were to physically attack the client in an attempt to make him pay, then a criminal law case might well be brought.

9.3.1 The law of contract

Central to any business activity is the notion that when someone has agreed to supply something or to carry out some task for an agreed 'consideration' (i.e. for a pre-determined payment or some other benefit) then they can be held to the agreement. The agreement may be in writing or purely verbal.

A quirk here is that the courts have decided that goods in a shop window at a marked price do not constitute a contract but merely an 'offer to treat' so that the shopkeeper can if he wishes refuse to sell at that price. A price in an advertisement is similarly regarded as an offer to treat. If the contract is broken then one of four types of legal redress may be obtainable:

1   The contract may be rescinded, removing all obligations from both parties.
2   The injured party may claim compensation for any work he has already done.
3   The injured party may be awarded an order by the court to enforce performance of the contract.
4   The injured party may claim damages to compensate him for the performance of any loss he has suffered through non-performance of the contract.

9.3.2 Advertising 'agents'

The important thing to recognize about advertising agencies is that as far as the law is concerned they are not 'agents' but 'principals'. That is to say that an advertising agency making a contract e.g. with a newspaper, is legally bound by the contract in *its own right* – it does not make the contract on behalf of its client. So that if for example the client went out of business after the advertising had appeared, the agency would be responsible for paying the newspaper for the advertising space.

9.3.3 Copyright

Since advertising is built around ideas, the ownership of those ideas is a crucial area. This is determined by the law of copyright. Usually the owner of any work is the writer or artist but when the work is produced in the course of his employment then the *employer* (e.g. the advertising agency for which he or she works) owns the 'copyright' i.e. the right to benefit from the work. Copyright exists in every literary, dramatic, musical or artistic work, every sound recording or film (cine or video), every radio or television broadcast. The existence of copyright means that the work is protected for a definite number of years (typically 50 years after the author's death) from being used or published or reproduced in any way without the owner's authority.

In the case of advertising material (copy, artwork, TV, films, etc.) produced by people not on the payroll of the agency, the copyright is normally transferred (assigned) to the agency through standard forms of agreement. Note, however, that copyright normally rests with the agency not the client – unless of course the client has insisted on a different arrangement.

Copyright in photographs rests with whoever commissioned them, but the photographer owns the negatives (unless his contract specifically says otherwise) and he may charge the copyright owner for use of the negative.

9.3.4 Trade marks and passing off

A trade mark is 'a device, brand, heading, label, ticket, name, signature, word, letter, numeral, or any combination thereof' (Trade Marks Act 1994). Once a trade mark is registered the owner is protected and no one else may use it. So most company and brand names are normally registered to obtain this protection. To be registered a trade mark must contain or consist of at least one of the following:

1 The name of a company, individual or firm represented in a special or particular manner.
2 The signature of the applicant for registration or some predecessor in his business.
3 An invented word or invented words.
4 A word or words having no direct reference to the character or quality of the goods, and not being according to its ordinary signification a geographical name or a surname.
5 Any other distinctive mark, but a name, signature, or word other than such as fall within 1–4 above is not registrable except upon evidence of its distinctiveness.

9.3.5 Trade descriptions

It is against the law in the UK and in many other countries to apply a false trade description to goods or to sell goods with a false trade description (so that, for example, retailers and importers are responsible for observing the law, not just manufacturers).

'A trade description is an indication, direct or indirect, and by whatever means given, of any of the following matters:

1 Quantity (which includes length, width, height, area, volume, capacity, weight and number), size or gauge.
2 Method of manufacture, production, processing or re-conditioning, e.g. home-made.
3 Composition, e.g. solid gold.
4 Fitness for purpose, strength, performance, behaviour or accuracy, e.g. waterproof.
5 Any physical characteristics not included in the preceding paragraphs, e.g. shape.

6 Testing by any person and results thereof, e.g. MOT tested.
7 Approval by any person or conformity with the type approved by any person, e.g. Design Centre award.
8 Place or date of manufacture, production, processing or reconditioning, e.g. Chateau Latour 1963.
9 Person by whom manufactured, produced, processed or re-conditioned.
10 Other history, including previous ownership or use, e.g. Government surplus.'[3]

More recent legislation in the UK applies these provisions to services as well as to goods.

9.3.6 Laws relating to advertising specific types of goods or services

There are many specific laws relating to certain types of business activity or certain kinds of products which directly or indirectly affect the advertising of them. They include:

> food products
> medical products
> cigarettes
> alcoholic drinks
> gambling
> consumer credit
> finance (e.g. insurance, unit trusts)

All of these are 'sensitive areas' e.g. for reasons of public health or because they are particularly open to deception or fraud. Similarly there are laws restricting the use of children in advertisements and specific restrictions on television advertising to children (*see* Section 9.4).

9.4 Legal control of radio and television advertising

Unlike other forms of advertising, the way in which advertising is used on radio and television in the UK is strictly regulated by the Independent Broadcasting Authority Acts.

Diana Woolley[3] summarizes the general restrictions on broadcast advertising as follows:

The Broadcasting Act controls advertisements quite strictly; it contains provisions which relate to the times when they may appear and on the frequency and duration of the time segments in which they appear, on the manner in which they are presented and on their content. The Act does not always specify the conditions but instead it empowers the Authority to impose restrictions.

The Authority has power to specify that advertisements must be excluded from certain broadcasts. At the time of writing, no advertisement might be included in:

1   *Religious services or programmes.*
2   *Formal Royal ceremonies or occasions and appearances of the Queen or Royal Family.*
3   *Programmes designed and broadcast for reception in schools.*
4   *Half-hour adult education programmes.*
5   *Certain current affairs and documentary programmes, including This Week and World in Action.*
6   *Such other programmes as the Authority may from time to time specify in particular or general terms. A recent example of this was the exclusion of advertising from radio broadcasts of debates in Parliament.*

The Act states that such advertisements as are permitted may be shown at the beginning or end of a programme or 'in natural breaks therein' but does not specify how frequently such breaks may occur nor how much advertising is to be allowed. But the IBA is empowered to issue directions as to the minimum interval which must elapse between any two periods of advertisements and the number of such periods to be allowed in any programme or item in a programme or in any hour or day. The IBA may also make rules on the amount of advertising to be permitted.

The Independent Television Commission and the Radio Authority also have their own Code of Advertising Standards and Practice and all radio and TV advertising is vetted before transmission. This is quite different from the situation with other forms of advertising (*see* Section 9.5) where there is no compulsory pre-vetting and the system of standards is a voluntary rather than a statutory one. The contents of premium rate telephone calls are the responsibility of the Independent Committee for the Supervision of Standards of Telephone Information Services.

All cigarette advertising, however, has to be cleared by the ASA before publication.

9.5 The British voluntary control system

In the UK advertising in all media (including sales promotion activity) other than radio and television is regulated by a voluntary control system. Twenty advertising trade associations join in a Committee of Advertising Practice (CAP) which is responsible for:

(a)   drawing up the Code
(b)   co-ordinating its implementation

(c) handling complaints from within the industry and from the public (competitive complainants are named, members of the public remain confidential).

(d) giving advice on the interpretation of the Code to those in advertising

Supervision of the CAP is by a body independent of advertising and charged with operating in the public interest. This is the Advertising Standards Authority (ASA) which is responsible for handling all complaints, for liaison with Government departments and outside organizations and for publicity, including advertising, of the self-regulation system. The ASA has an independent chairperson who is free to appoint a council of 12 people, at least half of whom (in practice two thirds) are independent of any advertising interest.

The British self-regulation system is financed by a 0.1 per cent surcharge on all display advertising. This resulted, from 1980 to 1981, in over £3 million being paid to the ASA from over 1,100 advertising agency and media collectors. In addition, media owners are generous in the donation of advertising space to publicize the ASA to the general public, as part of its regular and large scale advertising campaign in national and local print media.

The ASA carries out a regular research and monitoring programme across media sectors: direct marketing (list and database practice as well as advertising content), national and regional press and consumer magazines. It also keeps a special watch on specific product sectors such as slimming, health and beauty, alcoholic drinks, food and nutrition claims, car advertising, etc.

In 1997 the ASA checked a statistically based sample of over 6,000 advertisements in national and regional press and consumer magazines. It showed that compliance with the Codes was very high – 96 per cent. A similar sampling of posters showed 98 per cent compliance.

The system works quickly and effectively. The Secretariat evaluates every complaint, public or competitive and obtains comments and substantiation of claim if required from the advertiser involved. For public complaints a draft recommendation is put to the ASA Council. If the complaint is upheld, assurances are sought from the advertiser to modify the advertisement or withdraw it. If no such assurance is received media warnings are issued and publication of the offending advertisement is prevented. The ASA's monthly Case Reports are circulated widely to media, consumer organizations, government departments and the trade associations. Regular editorial comment on these reports appears in the public press.

In 1997 the ASA received 10,678 complaints, as a result of which they required 500 advertisements to be withdrawn after investigation. In recent years the total number of complaints has run at between 10,000 and 12,000, of which 10 per cent are from competitors and the remainder from the public.

The other self-regulation system in Britain is for television (including Teletext) and radio. Control of broadcast advertising has the power of the law behind it, but is closely integrated with a self-regulated system of pre-vetting. All television and radio advertisements must be pre-checked twice with the television or radio companies, first at script stage and second at the finished television or radio commercial stage.

Much more difficult to control is the rapidly developing use of the worldwide Internet for advertising across national boundaries. The ASA brought advertisements on computer and video games, CD-ROM and the Internet within its scope in 1995 and is part of an international network of self-regulatory bodies. The same sanctions, including adverse publicity and peer pressure, can be applied widely through these global links which are being constantly extended. (*See* the ASA publication *Interactive ASA* which is updated regularly.)

9.6 The British Codes of advertising and sales promotion

The following is an abridged version of the Codes, produced by the ASA for public information. It contains the essence of the thinking behind the Codes and many of its major rules.

THE BRITISH CODES OF ADVERTISING AND SALES PROMOTION
This summary of the Codes contains many of their major rules. Those involved in the preparation or publication of advertisements should refer to the Codes in full.

The Codes are published by the Committee of Advertising Practice (CAP) for the advertising industry and are supervised by the Advertising Standards Authority.

Introduction
The Codes contain all the rules by which the British advertising business has agreed that non-broadcast advertisements and sales promotions should be regulated.

They establish a standard against which any advertisement may be assessed, and are a guide to anyone who commissions, creates or publishes advertisements as well as to anyone who believes they may have reason to question what an advertisement says or depicts.

The first edition of the Codes was published in 1961. This booklet refers to the 9th edition published in February 1995.

Scope
The Codes' rules apply to:

- *advertisements in newspapers, magazines, brochures, leaflets, circulars, mailings, catalogues and other printed publications, facsimile transmissions, posters and aerial announcements*
- *cinema and video commercials*

- *advertisements in non-broadcast electronic media such as computer games*
- *viewdata services*
- *mailing lists except for business-to business*
- *sales promotions*
- *advertisement promotions*
- *advertisements and promotions covered by the Cigarette Code*

The Codes' rules do **not** apply to:

- *broadcast commercials, which are the responsibility of the Independent Television Commission or the Radio Authority*
- *the contents of premium rate telephone calls, which are the responsibility of the Independent Committee for the Supervision of Standards of Telephone Information Services*
- *advertisements in foreign media*
- *health-related claims in advertisements and promotions addressed only to the medical and allied professions*
- *classified private advertisements*
- *statutory, public, police and other official notices*
- *works of art exhibited in public or private*
- *private correspondence*
- *oral communications, including telephone calls*
- *press releases and other public relations material*
- *the content of books and editorial communications*
- *regular competitions such as crosswords*
- *flyposting*
- *packages, wrappers, labels and tickets unless they advertise a sales promotion or are visible in an advertisement*
- *point of sale displays except for those covered by the Sales Promotion Code – and the Cigarette Code*

Interpretation
The judgement of the ASA Council on interpretation of the Codes is final.

Conformity is assessed according to the advertisement's probable impact when taken as a whole and in context. This will depend on the audience, the medium, the nature of the product and any additional material distributed at the same time to consumers.

The Codes are primarily concerned with advertisements and promotions and not with terms of business, products themselves or other contractual matters.

The Advertising Code General Rules

- *all advertisements should be legal, decent, honest and truthful*
- *all advertisements should be prepared with a sense of responsibility to consumers and to society*
- *all advertisements should respect the principles of fair competition generally accepted in business*
- *no advertisement should bring advertising into disrepute*
- *advertisements must conform with the Codes. Primary responsibility for observing the Codes falls on advertisers. Others involved in preparing and publishing*

advertisements such as agencies, publishers and other service suppliers also accept
an obligation to abide by the Codes
• the Codes are applied in the spirit as well as in the letter.

Substantiation
Before submitting an advertisement for publication, advertisers must hold documentary
evidence to prove all claims, whether direct or implied, that are capable of objective
substantiation. Relevant evidence should be sent without delay if requested by the ASA. The
adequacy of evidence will be judged on whether it supports both the detailed claims and
the overall impression created by the advertisement.

If there is a significant division of informed opinion about any claims made in an
advertisement they should not be portrayed as universally agreed.

Obvious untruths or exaggerations that are unlikely to mislead and incidental minor
errors and unorthodox spellings are all allowed provided they do not affect the accuracy or
perception of the advertisement in any material way.

Legality
Advertisers have primary responsibility for ensuring that their advertisements are legal.
Advertisements should contain nothing that breaks the law or incites anyone to break it,
and should omit nothing that the law requires.

Decency
Advertisements should contain nothing that is likely to cause serious or widespread
offence. Particular care should be taken to avoid causing offence on the grounds of race,
religion, sex, sexual orientation or disability.

Advertisements may be distasteful without necessarily conflicting with the Codes.
Advertisers are urged to consider public sensitivities before using potentially offensive
material.

The fact that a particular product is offensive to some people is not sufficient
grounds for objecting to an advertisement for it.

Honesty
Advertisers should not exploit the credulity, lack of knowledge or inexperience of
consumers.

Truthfulness
No advertisement should mislead by inaccuracy, ambiguity, exaggeration, omission or
otherwise.

Matters of opinion
Advertisers may give a view about any matter, including the qualities or desirability of their
products, provided it is clear that they are expressing their own opinion rather than stating
a fact. Assertions or comparisons that go beyond subjective opinions are subject to the
rules on substantiation.

Fear and distress
No advertisement should cause fear or distress without good reason. Advertisers should not
use shocking claims or images merely to attract attention.

Advertisers may use an appeal to fear to encourage prudent behaviour or to discourage dangerous or ill-advised actions; the fear likely to be aroused should not be disproportionate to the risk.

Safety
Advertisements should not show or encourage unsafe practices except in the context of promoting safety. Particular care should be taken with advertisements addressed to or depicting children and young people.

Consumers should not be encouraged to drink and drive. Advertisements, including those for breath testing devices, should not suggest that the effects of drinking alcohol can be masked and should include a prominent warning on the dangers of drinking and driving.

Violence
Advertisements should contain nothing that condones or is likely to provoke violence or anti-social behaviour.

Political
Any advertisement whose principal function is to influence opinion in favour of or against any political party or electoral candidate contesting a UK, European parliamentary or local government election, or any matter before the electorate for a referendum, is exempt from the Codes' rules on substantiation, truthfulness, testimonials, comparisons and denigration. All other rules in the Codes apply. The identity and status of such advertisers should be clear. If their address or other contact details are not generally available they should be included in the advertisement.

There is a formal distinction between government policy and that of political parties. Advertisements by central or local government, or those concerning government policy as distinct from party policy, are subject to all the Codes' rules.

Privacy
Advertisers are urged to obtain written permission in advance if they portray or refer to individuals or their identifiable possessions in any advertisement. Exceptions include most crowd scenes, portraying anyone who is the subject of the book or film being advertised and depicting property in general outdoor locations.

Advertisers who have not obtained prior permission from entertainers, politicians, sportsmen and others whose work gives them a high public profile should ensure that they are not portrayed in an offensive or adverse way. Advertisements should not claim or imply an endorsement where none exists.

Prior permission may not be needed when the advertisement contains nothing that is inconsistent with the position or views of the person featured. Advertisers should be aware that individuals who do not wish to be associated with the advertised product may have a legal claim.

References to anyone who is deceased should be handled with particular care to avoid causing offence or distress.

References to members of the Royal Family and the use of the Royal Arms and Emblems are not normally permitted; advertisers should consult the Lord Chamberlain's Office. References to Royal Warrants should be checked with the Royal Warrant Holders' Association.

Price

Any stated price should be clear and should relate to the product advertised. Advertisers should ensure that prices match the products illustrated.

Unless addressed exclusively to the trade, prices quoted should include any VAT payable. It should be apparent immediately whether any prices quoted exclude other taxes, duties or compulsory charges and these should, wherever possible, be given in the advertisement.

If the price of one product is dependent on the purchase of another, the extent of any commitment by consumers should be made clear.

Free offers

There is no objection to making a free offer conditional on the purchase of other items. Consumers' liability for any costs should be made clear in all material featuring the offer. An offer should only be described as free if consumers pay no more than:

a)   the current public rates of postage
b)   the actual cost of freight or delivery
c)   the cost, including incidental expenses, of any travel involved if consumers collect the offer.

Advertisers should make no additional charges for packing and handling. Advertisers must not attempt to recover their costs by reducing the quality or composition or by inflating the price of any product that must be purchased as a pre-condition of obtaining another product free.

Availability of products

Advertisers must make it clear if stocks are limited. Products must not be advertised unless advertisers can demonstrate that they have reasonable grounds for believing that they can satisfy demand. If a product becomes unavailable, advertisers will be required to show evidence of stock monitoring, communications with outlets and the swift withdrawal of advertisements whenever possible. Products which cannot be supplied should not normally be advertised as a way of assessing potential demand.

Testimonials

Advertisers should hold signed and dated proof, including a contact address, for any testimonial they use. Testimonials should be used only with the written permission of those giving them.

Testimonials alone do not constitute substantiation and the opinions expressed in them must be supported, where necessary, with independent evidence of their accuracy. Any claims based on a testimonial must conform with the Codes.

References to tests, trials, professional endorsements, research facilities and professional journals should be used only with the permission of those concerned. They should originate from within the European Union unless otherwise stated in the advertisement. Any establishment referred to should be under the direct supervision of an appropriately qualified professional.

Guarantees

The full terms of any guarantee should be available for consumers to inspect before they are committed to purchase. Any substantial limitations should be spelled out in the advertisement.

Advertisers should inform consumers about the nature and extent of any additional rights provided by the guarantee, over and above those given to them by law, and should make clear how to obtain redress.

'Guarantee' when used simply as a figure of speech should not cause confusion about consumers' legal rights.

Comparisons

Comparisons can be explicit or implied and can relate to advertisers' own products or to those of their competitors; they are permitted in the interests of vigorous competition and public information.

Comparisons should be clear and fair. The elements of any comparison should not be selected in a way that gives the advertisers an artificial advantage.

Denigration

Advertisers should not unfairly attack or discredit other businesses or their products.

Exploitation of goodwill

Advertisers should not make unfair use of the goodwill attached to the trade mark, name, brand, or the advertising campaign of any other business.

Imitation

No advertisement should so closely resemble any other that it misleads or causes confusion.

Identifying advertisers

Advertisers, publishers and owners of other media should ensure that advertisements are designed and presented in such a way that they can be easily distinguished from editorial.

Features, announcements or promotions that are disseminated in exchange for a payment or other reciprocal arrangement should comply with the Codes if their content is controlled by the advertisers. They should also be clearly identified and distinguished from editorial.

Mail order and direct response advertisements and those for one day sales, home-work schemes, business opportunities and the like should contain the name and address of the advertisers. Advertisements with a political content should clearly identify their source. Unless required by law, other advertisers are not obliged to identify themselves.

The Sales Promotion Code

The Sales Promotion Code should be read, where appropriate, in conjunction with the rules in the Advertising and Cigarette Codes. The Specific Rules and the Introduction are common to both Codes.

The Sales Promotion Code is designed primarily to protect the public but it also applies to trade promotions and incentive schemes and to the promotional elements of sponsorships. It regulates the nature and administration of promotional marketing techniques. These techniques generally involve providing a range of direct or indirect additional benefits, usually on a temporary basis, designed to make goods or services more attractive to purchasers.

Protection

Promotions involving adventurous activities should be made as safe as possible by the pro-

moters. Every effort should be made to avoid harming consumers when distributing product samples. Special care should be taken when sales promotions are addressed to children or when products intended for adults may fall into the hands of children. Literature accompanying promotional items should give any necessary safety warnings.

Promotions should be designed and conducted in a way that respects the right of consumers to a reasonable degree of privacy and freedom from annoyance.

Consumers should be told before entry if participants may be required to become involved in any of the promoters' publicity or advertising, whether it is connected with the sales promotion or not. Prizewinners should not be compromised by the publication of excessively detailed information.

Suitability
Promoters should make every effort to ensure that unsuitable or inappropriate material does not reach consumers. Neither the sales promotions themselves nor the promotional items should cause offence. Promotions should not be socially undesirable to the audience addressed by encouraging either excessive consumption or inappropriate use.

Availability
Phrases such as 'subject to availability' do not relieve promoters of the obligation to take all reasonable steps to avoid disappointing participants.

If promoters are unable to supply demand for a promotional offer because of any unexpectedly high response or some other unanticipated factor outside their control, products of a similar or greater quality and value or a cash payment should normally be substituted.

Participation
Any factor likely to influence consumers' decisions or understanding about the promotion should be indicated. This includes a prominent closing date where applicable, limitations on availability of promotional packs, geographical and personal restrictions, and any proof of purchase requirements. Promoters must also include their full name and business address in a form which can be retained by consumers.

Administration
Sales promotions should be properly supervised, with adequate resources to avoid giving consumers any justifiable grounds for complaint. Ample time should be allowed for notifying the trade, distributing goods, collecting wrappers and the like, and for judging and announcing results.

Promoters should fulfil applications within 30 days unless participants have been told in advance that it is impractical to do so. Alternatively, they should be informed promptly of any unforeseen delays and offered another delivery date or the return of any money paid for the offer.

When damaged or faulty goods are received by consumers, promoters should either issue a replacement or offer a refund without delay. Goods not received should normally be replaced by promoters free of charge.

Promotions with prizes
Where prizes are involved in promotions, participants should be informed at the outset of any restrictions in the number of entries or prizes, whether there is a cash alternative, how and when winners will be notified and announced, how entries will be judged, who owns

their copyright, whether and how they will be returned, and any post-event publicity envisaged. Entry forms and goods required for proof of purchase should be widely available. Promoters should avoid exaggerating the likelihood of consumers winning a prize. A prize is won; a gift is given – promoters need to take care to avoid confusing the two.

Any rules should be clear, readily available and easily retained. The closing date should not be changed unless circumstances outside the reasonable control of the promoters make it unavoidable. The names, counties and entries of major prizewinners should be made available and, unless stated in advance, all prizewinners should receive their prize no later than six weeks after the promotion has ended. If the selection of a winning entry is open to subjective interpretation, a judge who is independent of the competition's promoters must be used. The identity of all judges must be made available on request.

Instant win promotion tokens or numbers should be randomly allocated to ensure participants have an equal chance of winning. Winners should get their winnings immediately or know immediately what they have won and how to claim.

Charity-linked promotions
Promotions claiming that participation will benefit registered charities or good causes should name the beneficiary and have their consent. The benefit should be accurately specified, and any limitations imposed on the promoters' own contributions should be stated. There should not be a limit to consumers' contributions, regardless of any target figure quoted, and any extra money collected should be given to the beneficiary on the same basis as contributions below that level. A current or final total of contributions made should be available to consumers on request. Particular care should be taken when appealing to children.

The above material, with additional detail, is contained in the ASA publication *Advertising under Control*, which is updated regularly, and copies are available on request.

9.7 Summary

1   Most people, in the UK at any rate, approve rather than disapprove of advertising.
2   Nonetheless there is considerable pressure from the disapprovers to exert some degree of control and even those who approve want control of excesses.
3   Control can be exercised through the law and/or through codes of practice. In most countries it is through a mixture of the two, with the balance varying from one country to another.
4   The advantages of voluntary control systems are held to be that they can be exercised more speedily and more flexibly whereas the law tends to be slow-moving and cumbersome.
5   In the UK there are some laws, in particular relating to broadcast advertising, but in the main a voluntary Code of Practice is operated, which has formed the model for similar Codes in many other countries.

6   The main provisions of the Code are listed (*see* Section 9.6).

9.8 References

1 Barnes, Michael, 'Public attitudes to advertising', *Journal of Advertising*, April–June, 1982.
2 Burleton, Eric, 'The Self-regulation of advertising in Europe', *Journal of Advertising*, October–December, 1952.
3 Woolley, Diana, *Advertising Law Handbook*, Business Books, 1976.

9.9 Further reading

Advertising Association Handbook, edited by Bullmore and Waterson, (Holt-Saunders, 1983) reviews many important aspects.

The Advertising Standards Authority issues a number of useful booklets, including the *British Codes of Advertising and Sales Promotion.*

Wilson, Richard M. S. and Gilligan, C. with Pearson, David J. *Strategic Marketing Management: Planning, Implementation And Control*, Oxford: Butterworth-Heinemann Ltd, 1992.

9.10 Questions for discussion

1   Explain, with reference to specific acts and codes, how legal and voluntary controls of advertising in UK complement each other to provide broad coverage of possible areas of abuse by advertisers.
2   Consider the arguments for and against the use of statutory rather than voluntary controls on advertising.
3   How does the control of advertising vary throughout Europe?
4   Discuss how the control of broadcast advertising differs from that of other forms of advertising in the UK.
5   Someone tells you that the British system of self-regulation is ineffective because the Advertising Standards Authority cannot fine or imprison anyone for malpractice. How would you answer him?

Part 3

How advertising works in detail

Chapter 10

How advertising is created

'The creative advertising man is controlled by a tight brief. It is determined by the nature of the marketing and advertising objective – the what, whens, whys and to-whoms. The brief states the proposition – itself a single entity – and requests its interpretation. This discipline is a creative necessity.'

David Bernstein, *Creative Advertising,* Longman, 1974

By the end of this chapter you will:

- Realize the importance of the creative ingredient in effective advertising;
- Be aware of what makes a good creative person and how to get the best from them;
- Be able to brief creative teams;
- Appreciate what makes a good advertisement;
- Understand the significance of the terms USP and brand image.

10.1 The nature of creativity in advertising

A picture may be painted, a poem written, a symphony composed for no reason apart from the desire or need of the artist to express himself. Success to the artist, writer, composer, may simply consist in getting somewhere near expressing the vision that impelled them to create something. Others may feel that success is only achieved when their audience, their 'public', responds to what they have created. But in any of these cases it is hard to be specific about what a picture, a poem or a symphony is *for*. It does not in the most literal sense have any specific purpose (although we could of course argue that life might often be rather pointless and certainly less rich if none of these things were created). To ask a creative artist what specific objectives his work was intended to achieve is usually irrelevant. If it is beautiful, moving, thought-provoking, exciting, stirring in its own right that is purpose enough.

An advertisement on the other hand can be very beautiful or exciting or amusing and yet fail utterly in its purpose. Conversely it may be banal or ugly and yet do what it set out to do. So 'creativity' must have a rather different meaning or at least a more limited one, in the advertising context than it has in the world of art. Advertising is created with very definite, quite specific aims in view.

10.2 The 'science' of advertising

One of the most famous and highly regarded books on the creation of advertising carries the title *Scientific Advertising*[1]. It was written in 1923 to promote an American advertising agency called Lord and Thomas, of which the author, Claude Hopkins, was a director.

The book opens with the statement 'The time has come when advertising has in some hands reached the status of a science.' Hopkins was a superb copywriter, much of whose experience was in mail order advertising. His claim to have established a scientific approach was based on such ideas, revolutionary no doubt in the 1920s, as:

> Do nothing to merely interest, amuse or attract. That is not your province. Do only that which wins the people you are after in the cheapest possible way.

> Treat (advertising) as a salesman. Force it to justify itself. Compare it to other salesmen. Figure its cost and result.

> Almost any question can be answered, cheaply, quickly and finally, by a test campaign. And that's the way to answer them – not by arguments round a table. Go to the court of the last resort – the buyers of your product.

> An ad-writer, to have a chance at success, must gain full information on his subject.

> Advertising without this preparation is like a waterfall going to waste. The power may be there, but it is not made effective. We must center the force and direct it in a practical direction.

It could now be strongly disputed just how 'scientific' advertising really is. For example, a fully scientific body of knowledge enables one to predict precisely what will result from a given set of actions. Advertising can rarely do that. Because at the end of the day the results of advertising depend on human reactions (emotional as well as rational) not on purely mechanistic responses. So prediction of results is often uncertain and developing advertising to achieve desired ends involves judgement as well as facts.

Nonetheless, in essence Hopkins was right. Advertising is not a matter of following the creative man's instinct or whim, not just a question of designing attractive pictures or coming up with bright ideas expressed in clever words. Rather it is a matter of expressing clearly defined ideas in a compelling way so as to attract and interest specified types of people in known situations and motivate them to react in a particular fashion. So the 'creative' writers and designers must operate within a framework of known facts, with set targets and subject to measurement of cost-effectiveness. As the above quotations illustrate, Hopkins caught the essential truth that the creation of effective advertising stems from hard logical thinking based on an assessment of the facts rather than ideas from the blue.

Nowadays there has been a great deal of research into the mechanisms of advertising (see Chapter 16) and most major advertising campaigns are based on highly detailed analyses of the facts of the situation. Still though there is the 'creative' ingredient. Still someone has to turn the bare facts and the bold proposition into a compelling message.

David Bernstein[2], a leading and highly regarded British 'creative man', sums up the paradox like this:

> The central core of our activities is creative. The basic decisions are judgemental. The results of our work depend on human behaviour. Thus advertising can never be a science. But if you are in advertising and accept our working definition, if you believe in advertising's role in the economy, if at the end of the day you want to feel that you have helped the man who pays your salary (i.e. the client) by at least pointing him in the right direction . . . then you'll have to try to make it a science.

10.3 What it takes to create effective advertising

Because the facts and the logic – the science – only take us so far; because there has to be the judgemental contribution and the turning of the dull proposition into the exciting message, 'creative' advertising people – the writers, designers and art directors – have a special contribution to make. What is the nature of that contribution and what are the peculiar characteristics of the people that make it?

10.3.1 The creative contribution – what is it?

Bernstein[2] offers a model of the creative process (see Figure 10.1) consisting of a double-ended funnel, with a wide entrance into which we pour all the facts and figures, eventually concentrating them into the proposition. (The 'offer' – expressed in basic terms – which the advertisement is making to the reader, listener or viewer.) This goes into the narrow central tube and emerges as the creative idea. The funnel opens up into a second 'mouth'

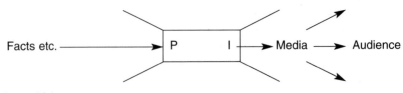

Figure 10.1

from which the advertising conveying the creative idea spreads out through the media to reach its audience.

The creative process consists of turning the proposition into an idea. So, says Bernstein: 'The proposition is arrived at through *reason* and P becomes I through *imagination*. The idea becomes an advertisement largely as a result of *craft'*. The creative department in an agency typically supplies both the imagination and the craft, although sometimes the functions are separated with a creative department supplying the imagination and an art department supplying the craft. At the latter stage the development of the form and shape of the advertisement consists of the hard graft of applying special skills to the mechanics of layout, detailed copywriting, typography, etc. But, says Bernstein, '... though the final execution is important and demands hard work, talent and imagination, it calls for none of that white hot intensity which brings into being something which wasn't there before.'

10.3.2 The creative contribution – who makes it?

The essential core of a good advertisement then is that it is an accurate but also an imaginative interpretation of the whole marketing strategy and in particular of the advertising proposition which has been developed from that strategy. At its height this imaginative leap can transform an ordinary product into an extraordinary one, or express a perfectly straightforward claim in a striking and dramatic way. For example, Oxo is a well-established brand of gravy flavouring, whose advertising claims it 'Gives a meal man appeal'. KitKat chocolate coated wafer is used by many people to accompany their morning coffee or afternoon tea so the advertising suggests, 'have a break, have a KitKat'. The ability to create dramatic and extraordinary expressions of ordinary statements is what makes a good creative person.

David Ogilvy, one of the 'father-figures' of modern advertising,[3] quotes research carried out at the Institute of California's Institute of Personality Assessment. They found creative individuals to have the following characteristics:

'Creative people are especially observant, and they value accurate observation (telling themselves the truth) more than other people do.

They often express part-truths, but this they do vividly; the part they express is the generally unrecognized; by displacement of accent and apparent disproportion in statement they seek to point to the usually unobserved.

They see things as others do, but also as others do not.

They are born with greater brain capacity; they have more ability to hold many ideas at once, and to compare more ideas with one another – hence to make a richer synthesis.

They are by constitution more vigorous, and have available to them an exceptional fund of psychic and physical energy.

Their universe is thus more complex, and in addition they usually lead more complex lives.

They have more contact than most people do with the life of the unconscious – with fantasy, reverie, the world of imagination.'

Ogilvy[3] describes his own experience of the creative process and creative people in the following terms:

The creative process requires more than reason. Most original thinking isn't even verbal. It requires 'a groping experimentation with ideas, governed by intuitive hunches and inspired by the unconscious.' The majority of business men are incapable of original thinking, because they are unable to escape from the tyranny of reason. Their imaginations are blocked.

I am almost incapable of logical thought, but I have developed techniques for keeping open the telephone line to my unconscious, in case that disorderly repository has anything to tell me. I hear a great deal of music. I am on friendly terms with John Barleycorn. I take long hot baths. I garden. I go into retreat among the Amish. I watch birds. I go for long walks in the country. And I take frequent vacations, so that my brain can lie fallow – no golf, no cocktail parties, no tennis, no bridge, no concentration; only a bicycle.

While thus employed in doing nothing, I receive a constant stream of telegrams from my unconscious, and these become the raw material for my advertisements. But more is required: hard work, an open mind, and ungovernable curiosity.

10.3.3 Can creativity be taught?

The creative input is the most vital ingredient in many advertising campaigns, if only because most of the other ingredients can be arrived at through careful analysis which is 90 per cent hard work (although even there the other 10 per cent of imaginative insight into the situation can make all the difference). With the creative aspect of things it is the other way round – imagination is the major part of it. We then have to ask where does it come from – do we have to look for people who 'just have it' or can it be taught? Referring back to Bernstein's analysis (*see* Section 10.3.1) it is probably true to say that the craft aspect of 'making a good ad' can be taught but the imagination aspect can only be encouraged. As is clear from the University of California studies quoted by Ogilvy (*see* Section 10.3.2) many of the ingredients of a good creative person are in-born characteristics.

Modern jargon would stress that they are predominantly 'right brain' people i.e. good at visualizing rather than verbalizing, strong on seeing patterns, remembering music, tending to the poetical as distinct from 'left brain' people who tend to be rational rather than intuitive, disciplined rather than individualistic. Since (*see* Section 16.6) 'right brain' activity is an important ingredient in how purchasing decisions are made, it is easy to see how vital this aspect may be. Of course all people have both left and right brain characteristics and differences between them are a matter of emphasis. So creativity is something that can certainly be encouraged (by producing the right working conditions and by removing some of the traditionally rigid attitudes toward properly 'disciplined' working). But it would be difficult to teach a predominantly 'left brain' person to become an outstanding creative person – in advertising or elsewhere. His destiny probably lies in some other direction.

When Ted Bell, Creative Director of the Leo Burnett agency in Chicago, started building his creative team he took on unseasoned schoolleavers. 'I was looking for punks', he said. 'I wanted kids who had no experience in the business, who didn't have a clue how to create ads. Kids who didn't know the rules and just wanted to do great ads. They had to have talent, excitement and raw energy about them. And a great love of great advertising.' (Quoted in *How to Succeed in Advertising, when all you have is Talent,* NTC Business Books, 1994.)

In *The Brothers – the Rise and Rise of Saatchi and Saatchi* by Ivan Fallon (Hutchinson, 1988), John Hegarty, one of the Saatchi creative team, says: 'Creativity is I believe an expression of insecurity, a desire to win approval. It is in a climate of self-doubt that the creative spark is forced and cajoled into fire.' (See the Bernstein reference in Section 10.6.)

Thus the creativity aspect is a wayward and difficult to define 'divine spark', perhaps not totally different from that which produces the visual arts or literature. The difference is that we always have to revert to the insistence on working within a clear brief, to achieve a clearly-defined objective. Creative people have to work in one way as free spirits but also within disciplines. As John McKeil puts it (*The Creative Mystique,* John Wiley and Sons, 1985), good creative people, as well as having great ideas, must '... have a few other things:

They can take criticism
They can take pressure
They can work wherever they have to
They can work on more than one thing at a time.

Not a very common combination, which is why really good creative people are so sought after and (if they are lucky) so well paid'.

So we come back, to the importance of the creative brief discussed in

Section 10.4. As Garry Duckworth says (*Excellence in Advertising – the IPA Guide to Best Practice*, Butterworth-Heinemann 1997):

> 'Creative briefing is pivotal because it represents the stage in the advertising development process where the strategic understanding developed by the account team reaches the people whose job it is to really crack the creative problem.'

10.3.4 Characteristics of creative people

Kenneth Longman[4] lists the following characteristics as being 'common to highly creative people':

> Perhaps the most important characteristic of creative people is an avid curiosity. There is very little in the world that does not interest them. They may be as interested in the ecology of the North Woods as in the behaviour of teenagers in a discotheque. They read books on a great variety of topics, they are always seeking to understand things in new ways, and they are not fussy about whether the data they receive are completely accurate.
>
> Along with this curiosity, creative people have vivid imaginations. They can generate a large number of ideas rapidly. They might, for instance, be able to think of seventeen words that rhyme with 'syntax' and do it in a minute or two. Of greater importance, their imagination enables them to see new relationships between the things their curiosity has led them to discover. They habitually come up with unusual answers to questions and original interpretations of events (a quality that has not always endeared them to their educators).
>
> This combination of curiosity and imagination leads highly creative people to make fewer black and white distinctions than other people. With more data on hand and more of an ability to conjecture, they can see almost any issue in shades of grey. Their particular talents also lead them to prefer complex situations to simple ones, things that are easily understood bore them.
>
> Creative people are also characterized by the ability to emphathize. They find it easy to 'feel the way it feels to feel that way', whether they are concerned with other people, animals, or inanimate objects. Their warmth shows up in their sense of humor, and they will often inject humor into situations where most people consider it inappropriate.
>
> Creative people are also enthusiastic. In fact, enthusiasm is the driving force behind their curiosity and imagination. It gives them a strong sense of mission and its frequent concomitant, a feeling of loneliness. It also leads them to trust in their own abilities. They generally feel less dependent on authority, less anxious about what they produce, and less concerned about salary and status than other people. Accordingly, they look for jobs that provide stimulation and challenge, a fact that probably has more to do with the high turnover of personnel in advertising agencies than anything else. When a very creative person changes jobs, it is less likely to be for the sake of money (though the change may be accompanied by a substantial raise) than for the sake of finding more interesting challenges and opportunities.
>
> Finally, creative people are flexible. They find it easy to shift gears and try a new approach to a problem. They delight in new challenges. They can relate isolated experiences to one another with facility. They are quick to separate the source of information and opinion from the content. They form their own judgements about any

information received and are much less influenced than others by attitudes toward the source of the information. In their flexibility, however, they are intellectually honest, and they are likely to stick to their guns when disagreement arises. Highly creative people are not prone to yield to group pressure except as a matter of expediency.

These qualities that creative people share are invaluable in designing both good and great advertisements. Without them, the odds are very much against success.

10.4 The importance of the creative brief

As well as highlighting the essential role of management on the advertising process (see Section 10.3.1) David Bernstein insists that 'discipline is a creative necessity' (*see* quote at head of chapter). Chapter 3 presented a model of the advertising process which indicated the importance of a brief based on a detailed analysis of a wide range of information, together with decisions on such things as segmentation and positioning. From this brief the creative people must draw both the information on which their imagination can work and the guidelines within which it must be disciplined to operate.

Maurice Drake, another leading British creative director, suggests[5] the following ingredients in what he refers to as the creative strategy:

> *Let one thing be clear. The discipline of a creative strategy is not a straitjacket to creative thinking. A good strategy – and there are many useless and unexecutable ones – allows the creative person to direct his thinking into the correct channels instead of just trying to pluck an idea out of the air.*
>
> *It is important that the strategy should be written by the creative people, naturally in consultation with the client contact and marketing departments. There is a good reason for this; the act of writing the strategy down means that the creative team fully understands the product, the marketing environment in which it must compete and the potential consumer. In addition, a strategy written in the creative department can be executed in an advertisement. That may seem a strange point, but many strategies written outside the creative departments are simply tidy documents that contain far too many elements and could never be executed within the confines of anything other than a documentary film or a leading article!*
>
> *So what should the strategy contain? In the main the contents fall under the following headings:*
>
> Why we are advertising
> *This sums up, as succinctly as possible, why the client is advertising at all. It may be to launch a new product. It could be to change the positioning of a well-established product, or to take advantage of a seasonal sales peak or extra use of the product in an area that varies from the national norm, or perhaps to achieve a fast rate of trial and sampling. In other words, that situation or circumstance upon which advertising can act and achieve results must be evident.*
>
> What the advertising must achieve
> *This is not a rephrased reiteration of the above, but a statement of what end result the*

advertising must have on the consumer. There lies the key difference between the general objective and the advertising objective. The latter is a means of achieving the former.

For instance, a general objective to raise brand share may be accomplished by an advertising objective to change a consumer attitude or misconception. The former is to sell more, and the latter is to convince consumers to desire more.

Prospect definition

This is the key to any good strategy. No product can be all things to all people. It is far more profitable to have a motivating effect on a specific group of consumers than to give a blunt-edged promise to an indifferent mass. This principle of consumer segmentation, which is so much part of modern advertising and marketing, throws great responsibility on the correctness and clearness of the prospect definition.

For that important reason it must be so much more than just a bald statement of the prospect's socio-economic grouping. This is part of it, but by no means all of it. Socio-economic grouping gives you some traditional guide to the prospect's habits, attitudes and disposable income. But imagine if you were asked to go out in the street and find a man in the C2–DE socio-economic group. You might find dozens with that description. But which one would you choose?

This is why the prospect definition must be so much more. It must be like a police identi-kit picture and description, so that the advertising can pin-point the most potential consumer.

Another factor is age, and in clearly defined limits – not something vague like '16–45', for the strata of appeal between those ages are infinite. Obviously the sex of the consumer is important, and whether married or single, and number in family. As far as possible the prospect definition should also cover consumers' aspirations, hates, loves, habits, anything that can help the creative people not only to identify them but to understand them.

Promise

This is the 'reason for being' of the product, which singles it out from competition in the teeming market place. This is 'why to buy'. Remember the famous Charles Atlas advertising: this did not just sell a body-building course on bigger muscles. All the others said that. It was the one that offered weak people the chance to be strong people, and in that promise reposed the seeds of its success.

Above all, the promise must be consumer-orientated not product-orientated. In one example an underarm spray that was a powder in an aerosol stated 'It's surprising what a little powder does for an underarm spray'. That was product-orientated. It was changed to 'Now you don't have to get wet to be dry'. See the difference – that's a consumer promise. And research proved it right to change it.

Reason Why

Obviously evidence as to why a promise is possible will strengthen the promise. It is not always possible to have an exclusive product difference, in formula, engineering, speed of experience. But one reason why, for instance, can be the number of people who have tried the product and found it to be all it promised.

In any case, the consumer must be given some firm basis for believing that the product will keep its promise. If the strategy is properly written and based on known facts, in whatever form a particular agency may choose, and if it contains this kind of information, it can only lead to better, more effective advertising.

Of the creative task Drake writes:

*So the creative task can be described as gift-packaging the truth. We have to make
the product news interesting enough to stand out and be seen among all its
competitors.*

*Working from the strategy, it is the creative person's aim to find new language, both
in words and visuals, to present the product and its benefits to the consumer. For it is
saying something that may not be unique, but in a unique manner, that marks the great
campaigns.*

*Let's take some examples. 'Palmolive makes skin look young again!' A good promise,
but hardly a new thought. But the creative man said 'Palmolive brings back that
schoolgirl complexion' – a visual imagination-provoking set of words, and a campaign
that made history. 'More people eat Heinz Beans than any other'. This could just have
sounded like a successful manufacturer patting his own back. But 'Beanz Meanz
Heinz' said exactly the same thing, but so memorably that it went into the language, and
the new spelling of 'Beanz' is now used more often than the standard dictionary
version.*

The task that faces every creative person says Drake is 'turning information into communication'. The creative 'inspiration' must be firmly
based on hard information and must have communication not 'artistic'
merit as its aim.

10.4.1 The influence of media choice

Advertising creativity is all about effective communication. But this has
another aspect – the media through which the communications will take
place. So although they each need to be considered in detail, they also have
to be thought of as part of a whole. Whilst the central creative idea (Beanz
Meanz Heinz or Palmolive's 'Schoolgirl complexion') does not change, the
way it is expressed may have to vary considerably depending on whether
the media schedule provides for a massive TV expenditure, posters, or
some small black and white spaces in newspapers. Some creative ideas
lend themselves to immediate impact whereas others (such as the classic
Benson & Hedges cigarettes campaign which featured the distinctive gold
pack in a wide range of increasingly surrealistic settings) achieve their full
impact by a gradual build-up over a long period of time.

It may of course work the other way round. If a creative treatment is
developed which is seen to have enormous potential but calls for specific
media treatment (e.g. large or unusual shaped spaces in newspapers for
example) then the media people may be required to plan accordingly.

Ideally the media and creative planning goes step-by-step and
hand-in-hand so that each can draw on and influence the other as necessary.

10.5 What makes a good advertisement?

The short but unhelpful answer is 'one that communicates the necessary message effectively.' It is unhelpful because there are often many different ways of achieving the end results. This means it is very difficult to produce good advertising ideas 'by the rule book'. Indeed Roderick White[6] quotes an American agency as claiming that it has the following rules for producing good advertising:

>rule 1 There are no rules.
>rule 2 There may be exceptions to rule 1.

White then goes on to suggest some rules of his own (a compendium in fact of guidelines put forward by various advertising pundits down the ages):

1   Every advert should embody a clear, straightforward proposition.
2   Say what you have to say in as few words as possible.
3   There is no place for humour in advertising.
4   Give the consumer credit for some intelligence.
5   Be original.

Some of these guidelines embody the thinking of David Ogilvy[3] who lists his own rules for 'How to Build Great Campaigns'. They run:

1   What you say is more important than how you say it.
2   Unless your campaign is built round a great idea it will flop.
3   Give the facts.
4   You cannot *bore* people into buying.
5   Be well-mannered but don't clown.
6   Make your advertising contemporary.
7   Committees can criticize advertisements, but they can't write them.
8   If you are lucky enough to write a good advertisement; run it until it stops pulling.
9   Never write an advertisement which you wouldn't want your own family to read.
10   The image and the brand – every advertisement should be thought of as a contribution to the complex symbol which is the *brand image*. If you take that long view, a great many day-to-day problems resolve themselves.
11   Don't be a copy-cat.

None of these 'rules' are universally agreed. For example, White points out that humour (his rule 3 and Ogilvy's rule 5) is often successfully used in advertising. He also comments on the fact that the strict application of his rule 1 – the so-called USP approach (*see* Section 10.5.1) – can be very limiting.

White's own first thought is probably correct, 'There are no rules'.

10.5.1 USP and brand image

The first of Roderick White's rules quoted in Section 10.5 refers to a 'clear, straightforward proposition'. The classic embodiment of this approach was propounded by one of the outstanding figures in advertising, Rosser Reeves. In his book *Reality in Advertising*[7] he discussed at length the idea of the Unique Selling Proposition or USP, developed at his New York agency Ted Bates & Company in the early 1940s.

The USP, says Reeves, is 'like Gaul, divided into three parts:

1   Each advertisement must make a proposition to the consumer. Not just words, not just product puffery, not just show-window advertising. Each advertisement must say to each reader: 'Buy *this* product, and you will get *this specific benefit*'.

This admonition, of course, has been on page one of almost every advertising textbook for the past 60 years; but as you will see, it is becoming almost a lost art, and more honoured in the breach than in the observance.

2   The proposition must be one that the competition either cannot, or does not, offer. It must be unique – either a uniqueness of the brand or a claim not otherwise made in that particular field of advertising.

One might assume that a unique proposition, in itself, would be a strong theoretical base for an advertisement. However, there are thousands of unique propositions that do not sell. Witness, a famous toothpaste once advertised: '*it comes out like a ribbon and lies flat on your brush*'. This was a proposition, and it was unique. However, it did not move the public, because it apparently was not of importance to them. So we come to the third part:

3   The proposition must be so strong that it can move the mass millions, i.e. pull over new customers to your product.

These three points are summed up in the phrase: *unique selling proposition*.

This is a USP.'

Ever since there has been endless discussion about whether all good advertising has to have a USP. David Ogilvy's 'brand image' approach is sometimes held up as an alternative – almost an opposite – theory. Says Ogilvy[3]: 'Build sharply defined personalities for their (your clients') brands and stick to those personalities, year after year. It is the total personality of a brand rather than any trivial product difference which decides its ultimate position in the market.'

In fact, 'brand image' and 'USP' advertising approaches are equally valid, depending on the situation. Nor are they mutually exclusive, a product may be advertised on the strength of a USP such as 'Persil washes whiter' and *also* have a strong brand image, which Persil for example undoubtedly has.

10.6 How creative departments work

David Bernstein[2] describes creative departments as 'disciplined anarchy'. On the one hand like any other business activity it needs some degree of structure and control to ensure that things get done and that deadlines are met. On the other hand the production of good advertising ideas comes from imaginations being given free rein (although within the discipline provided by the brief).

Says Bernstein, 'It is the creative director's job to maintain that state of disciplined anarchy. He has to institute controls and procedures while simultaneously encouraging the utmost flexibility'.

The argument has raged for years about the actual procedure by which advertising ideas develop. Do the words come first or the pictures – or the intrinsic idea or 'copy platform'. Do the writers lead the way and then ask the art directors to provide illustrations for their words? Or does design lead and copywriting as it were provide the captions? The answer is both and all possible combinations. Ideas can come from anywhere (even from outside the creative department). The normal practice now is for writers and designers to work as teams, often known as 'creative groups'. Jointly (if it is a two-person team) or collectively they absorb the brief, 'kick ideas around' until one or more useful ideas emerge, and then concentrate on one or more until they begin to take shape as viable creative ideas.

10.7 The craft of copywriting

Again, the records abound with 'rules' and probably few great copywriters consciously follow any or if so have their own set. Thus there are many examples of defective advertisements that break 'the rules'. Quoted here the ones listed by David Ogilvy, partly because he is in any case one of the great copywriters of all time, but also because his 'rules' (in a chapter[3] headed 'How to write potent copy') are redolent with important basic principles for successful advertising, quite apart from any immediate practical value.

Headlines

1   *The headline is the 'ticket on the meat'. Use it to flag down the readers who are prospects for the kind of product you are advertising.*
2   *Every headline should appeal to the readers' self-interest.*
3   *Always try to inject news into your headlines (free and new are the most powerful words you can use in a headline).*
4   *Use words such as how to, suddenly, now, announcing, introduce, it's here, just arrived, important development, improvement, amazing, sensational, remarkable, revolutionary, startling, miracle, magic, offer, quick, easy, wanted, challenge, advice to, the truth about, compare, bargain, hurry, last chance.*
5   *Always include the brand name in your headline.*
6   *Include your selling promise in your headline.*
7   *End your headline with a lure to read on.*
8   *Avoid tricky headlines (puns, literary allusions, etc.)*
9   *Avoid negative headlines.*
10 *Avoid blind headlines (the kind which mean nothing unless you read the body copy underneath them).*

These rules of Ogilvy's emphasize the important functions of headlines to:

(a)   *attract attention*
(b)   *win the reader's interest and involvement*
(c)   *make them want to read on* because they feel it will be worth their while to do so

Body Copy

1   *Don't beat about the bush – go straight to the point.*
2   *Avoid superlatives, generalisations and platitudes. Be specific and factual. Be enthusiastic, friendly and memorable. Don't be a bore. Tell the truth but make the truth fascinating.*
3   *Always include testimonials in your copy.*
4   *Give the reader helpful advice or service.*
5   *(Quoting Claude Hopkins) 'fine writing is a distinct disadvantage'. So is unique literary style. They take attention away from the subject.*
6   *Avoid bombast.*
7   *Write your copy in the colloquial language which your customers use in everyday conversation.*
8   *Resist the temptation to write the kind of copy which wins awards.*
9   *Resist the temptation to entertain.*

Most of this could be summed up by saying that good copy must be clear, simple, direct, appropriately expressed and relevant. Note that all these attributes can be learned and practised. That is why copywriting can be described as a craft whereas it may take near genius to produce an outstanding advertising idea.

10.8 The craft of advertising design

Wherever the basic idea comes from (*see* Section 10.6), sooner or later it will usually (unless it is for radio) have to take visual form. This frequently begins as a very rough pencil or felt pen scribble (known as a 'scamp') on a layout pad – or sometimes on whatever surface is at hand (blackboard, envelope, menu card . . .)

This will be developed, perhaps through various stages, to a 'finished visual' which will be detailed and accurate enough to convey a good impression of the end result. The finished visual accompanied by a type-script of the copy will normally be used for presentation, discussion and approval of the advertisement or campaign and will be used as a reference in preparing finished artwork.

10.8.1 The principles of good design

As with copywriting (*see* Section 10.7) the main rule is that there are no rules. A good designer may break all the rules and yet succeed, a bad one can follow the rules and produce something so mundane and uninspired as to be valueless.

Various attempts have been made, however, to express at least some of the elements commonly found in a good layout. Richard E. Stanley[8] for example suggests that it will include:

1   *Balance* 'gives stability to the ad so that it does not seem to "lean" one way or the other.'
2   *Contrast* 'makes the most important parts of the ad stand out'.
3   *Proportion* 'proper proportion avoids sameness and monotony.'
4   *Unity* 'makes the ad appear to be a unified whole rather than a series of disconnected parts.'
5   *Gaze Motion* '... positioning ad elements to suggest a certain viewing sequence. '

Kenneth A. Longman[4] states:

> Studies conducted during the 1930s by George Gallup and others conducted by Daniel Starch beginning in the 1920s, have demonstrated that one of the main requirements for an advertising layout is simplicity. The layout should have a minimum number of elements and should display symmetry and balance. Ads with many different elements, lengthy headlines, and a great deal of scattered copy tend to be poorly noted.
>
> More recently, studies of television commercials have produced analogous results. Here too, the basic principle is to keep the advertisement simple. The television commercial with a large number of changes of scene is not very successful.

Longman quotes Fairfax Cone (one of the founders of the Foote, Cone & Belding agency) as summarizing this principle with the words, 'It is the primary requirement of advertising to be clear, clear as to exactly what the proposition is. If it isn't clear, and clear at a glance or a whisper, very few people will take the time or effort to figure it out.'

It couldn't be better put.

10.8.2 Typography

An important aspect of the clarity referred to by Fairfax Cone is the ability to understand quickly the import of the headlines and body copy of an advertisement. The selection of the best size and style of lettering – the typography – can therefore be crucial. This may be decided by the designer or art director but frequently it will be the specialist task of the typographer – a designer who specializes in this highly important aspect of design.

10.9 Summary

1   Creativity in advertising is not concerned with producing a work of art, except by accident, but with very specific aims in view – to communicate a particular message to a particular audience as effectively as possible.
2   Although claims have been made that the creation of advertising is a science it is probably best regarded as a craft.
3   The function of 'the creative people' is to turn a possibly banal proposition, arrived at through reason, into a dramatic expression arrived at through the imagination.
4   Up to a point creativity can be taught or at any rate encouraged, but it does seem as though highly creative people tend to be strong in such personal characteristics as avid curiosity, vivid imagination, empathy and flexibility.
5   The useful exercise of the creative ability is very dependent on it being correctly channelled through a good creative brief.
6   Although guidelines can be offered as to what makes a good advertisement, a good layout or good copy, there are certainly no hard and fast rules.
7   The guidelines themselves can be summed up in the statement that advertising 'must be clear as to what the proposition is'.

10.10 References

1 Hopkins, Claude, *Scientific Advertising*, Crown Publishers, Inc., 1966.

2 Bernstein, David, *Creative Advertising*, Longman, 1974.
3 Ogilvy, David, *Confessions of an Advertising Man*, Atheneum, New York, 1963.
4 Longman, Kenneth A., *Advertising*, Harcourt, Brace, Jovanovich, Inc., 1971.
5 Hart, Norman A. and O'Connor, James [Ed], *The Practice of Advertising*, William Heinemann, 1978.
6 White, Roderick, *Advertising: What it is and how to do it*, McGraw-Hill, 1980 (third edition, 1993).
7 Reeves, Rosser, *Reality in Advertising*, MacGibbon and Kee, 1961.
8 Stanley, Richard E., *Promotion*, Prentice-Hall, 1977.

10.11 Further reading

Both Bernstein (British) and Ogilvy (USA-based) are worth reading for their clear insight into the underlying meaning and purpose of advertising. They see *patterns* where others merely tell how to do it. Ogilvy's book is in addition a fascinating glimpse of the personality of one of the world's leading admen. A more recently published work by Ogilvy is *Ogilvy on Advertising*, (Pan Books, 1983).

The Brothers, quoted above, gives insight into a more recent great creative man, Charles Saatchi.

Books of the 'how to do it' type abound. Among them are: *The Craft of Copywriting* by Alistair Compton (Business Books, 1979) which is clear, brief and to the point, not only about how copywriting is done but how a creative department functions and feels.

10.12 Questions for discussion

1　To what extent do you consider that talented creative people in advertising are 'born not made'.
2　Prepare your own list of guidelines for advertising copy-writers.
3　Select three current press advertisements and write a critique of each, saying what appears to be good and bad about each in terms of their creative content.
4　When an advertising campaign fails to work, the client usually blames the agency, but often this may be because the client has not adequately prepared his or her requirements for the campaign. What is the role of the client in creating an advertising campaign, and what should he or she do to ensure that the agency has the best possible chance of creating a successful campaign?

5   Draft a creative brief for the launch of a new brand of boiled sweets, indicating the key elements to be covered and describing the kind of detail the brief would contain.

6   How important do you consider 'creative ability' to be in the list of attributes to be considered in selecting a new advertising agency for a range of palm-top computers, and how would you assess it?

Chapter 11

The printed media

By the end of this chapter you will:

- Recognize the increasing variety of printed media;
- Understand how circulation and readership is evaluated;
- Understand the main geodemographic classification systems;
- Recognize the main characteristics of the press as an advertising medium.

11.1 A dazzling variety

The printed media, newspapers and magazines – usually referred to as 'the press' – offer a very wide range of publications of differing character aimed at different audiences. With the increase in titles and the further fragmentation of readership, the targeting has become an important issue for media planners. However, despite these changes, the printed media offer much better targeting than do the broadcast media (*see* Chapter 12), which tend to have much less variety and more homogeneous audiences.

The current situation regarding newspapers in the UK is summarized as follows:

- Nationally, there are six 'popular' daily newspapers, the *Today* newspaper having disappeared in 1994, and five 'quality' dailies.
- On Sunday there are six 'popular' newspapers and four 'quality' Sundays. There are six colour magazines circulated with the Sunday newspapers.
- Although listed as national newspapers, the *Daily Record*, *Sunday Post* and *Sunday Mail* are largely circulated in Scotland.
- In January 1997, there were 94 paid-for regional newspapers with a total circulation approaching 14 million.
- At that time there were over 1,000 free newspapers with a total circulation of over 26 million. Their revenue comes almost exclusively from paid-for advertising space or loose inserts. (*Note*: *Reaching the Regions*, first published by the Newspaper Society in 1995, listed a total of 1,439 titles!)

- The regional newspapers appear in broadsheet and tabloid formats, with publishing frequencies of mornings, evenings, Sundays, daily and weekly.

While the above summarizes the situation in the UK, it is unusual as the UK probably has the largest selection of press media, especially in relation to the population, in the world.

The complete list of all UK media that carry advertising is provided by BRAD (British Rate and Data).

The situation regarding magazines is still more complex. There are several thousand titles (5,352 alone are business titles) to be found in the UK, from the internationally renowned *Reader's Digest* to special interest titles like the British Sausage Appreciation Society magazine. The various types of periodicals are explained in more detail in Section 11.1.2.

11.1.1 The main categories of newspapers

'National' means a newspaper or magazine readily available throughout the country and aiming to satisfy the needs of readers in all areas. The number of national newspapers in the UK is very high compared with most other European countries and with the USA where each major city has its own (one or more) daily and Sunday newspapers, with very few of them having regular readers outside their own immediate areas.

'Regional' applies to publications with a much more local readership and with news coverage to match. Thus the *Yorkshire Post* is published in Leeds and has most of its readers in the Yorkshire area of the UK. It has a high quality of national and international news but also a considerable local news content. Its excellent business section concentrates on locally-based firms or those with strong local involvement. The *Guardian* on the other hand was originally the *Manchester Guardian* with similar local emphasis but a few years ago 'went national' and is now printed in London as well as Manchester and has an almost completely national and international emphasis. Some regional newspapers (the term 'local' is often used) have a very small area of circulation indeed. Because there are so many of them, for many years the Evening Newspaper Advertising Bureau (ENAB) and the Weekly Newspaper Advertising Bureau (WNAB) acted as centralized sales agencies. The two organizations have recently been merged into one.

The *Guardian* is a 'quality' newspaper like *The Times*, the *Daily Telegraph* and *The Observer* (a Sunday paper). They all have a highly literate approach with well-written items of news and comment. They deal with matters of moment in some depth and whilst some of the material is humorous and light-hearted, it is rarely flippant or superficial.

The 'popular' newspapers on the other hand deal in snappy headlines and very superficial coverage of news. Only the most immediately important national and international events will be dealt with and there is a much heavier emphasis on 'human interest' stories of crime, immorality, outstanding bravery, sporting or 'show-business' success or notoriety.

Obviously the readership of these newspapers varies accordingly. For example, the *Daily Telegraph*, with a circulation of some 1 million each weekday, has a readership of over 80 per cent ABC1 while the *Sun*, with a circulation of 3.8 million, has a 69 per cent C2DE readership profile[1].

11.1.2 Types of periodicals

There is an enormously variable spectrum of magazines – referred to as 'periodicals' because they tend to be published weekly or monthly rather than daily (somewhat confusing in the light of weekly newspapers). However, some clear-cut categories can be perceived.

General Interest Magazines
Reader's Digest, Weekend, Radio Times, are examples of publications which have a wide spread of readers, although of course the precise make-up of their readership will vary widely. Most of them have relatively high readership and are covered by the National Readership Survey (*see* Section 11.2.2). This means that they are easy to use on a selective 'fine tuning' basis as an alternative to newspapers in order to reach the right demographic balance of readers combined with other desirable characteristics. For example, *Reader's Digest* has a big 'pass-on' readership, is in circulation for a long time and has a particular editorial character. The latter is quite different from newspapers and different again from the 'TV listings magazines' . It used to be that there were only the *TV Times* (carrying independent TV programmes) and *Radio Times* (carrying BBC radio and TV programmes). With the advent of satellite and cable TV, the monopoly position of these two magazines has been eroded and many more listing magazines have appeared.

Household magazines
Publications such as *Ideal Home* and *Good Housekeeping* deal with a wide spread of topics to do with the home (cooking, gardening, decor, personal finance, etc.) Their readership, male and female, tends to be 'up market' and they carry a great deal of advertising for high quality durable and semi-durable products.

Closely related in their subject-matter, but more 'popular' in treatment and with a wider spread of readership are the 'shopping magazines' *Family Circle* and *Living* which are sold primarily through supermarkets – and incidentally can be used to advertise to shoppers of a particular chain of stores.

Women's magazines
While titles such as *Woman* and *Woman's Own* are aimed primarily at women they also have a significant male readership, as the pages carry articles of common interest. Although some magazines are of general interest, there are other titles with a different focus, giving advantages for advertisers.

Women spend over £350 million a year on their magazines, and for ten years their circulations have grown steadily while newspaper circulations and TV viewing have declined. While there have been new titles each year, some have been withdrawn. IPC decided to remove *Me* in mid-1994 just five years after its launch. It was pitched to challenge the leaders (*Woman* and *Woman's Own*) but it did not find its niche and keep pace with the more competitive environment of the 1900s. *Me's* demise in January 1995 was an indicator not just of its own weakness, but of the strength of the weekly women's magazine market. What sets it apart from other sectors is the cross-consumption of its readers. No other consumer magazine area has loyal readers who will purchase three or more rival magazines with similar themes, every week.

However, the growing differences between two particular titles have attracted much attention of late. *Marie Claire* and *Cosmopolitan* have dominated the women's monthly market for a number of years. Their 1996 circulation figures were 424,900 and 427,700 respectively. Tempting as it is to make straight comparisons between the titles, media buyers insist that to do so is to over-simplify how magazines work. Demographically, the audiences may be very similar but the readers will differ in their attitude to the world, to shopping, to how they dress. It has been suggested that *Marie Claire* provides a market that is more serious, one that is interested in clothes and world issues, while *Cosmopolitan's* readers are more glitzy and fun-loving. They therefore provide advertisers with different ways to sell products to different women.

Men's magazines
This description was once used narrowly to cover the 'girlie' magazines such as *Playboy* and *Penthouse*. However, in the late 1990s there was a surge in new general interest magazines for men. *FHM* (*For Him* Magazine), *GQ* and *Loaded* were among the leaders and the launch of *Men's Health* showed the growing interest in health issues.

Special interest consumer magazines
Almost any sport, hobby, leisure interest or specialized sphere of knowledge has a magazine for its devotees. They range from magazines for home computer or photography addicts, to anglers, model engineers and antique collectors. For firms marketing specialized products and services they represent an excellent way of directing their advertising very specifically, exclusively and therefore economically to those enthusiasts most likely to buy.

A feature of such media is that often readers will scan the advertising as avidly as the editorial. Camera enthusiasts for example are keen to know what lenses and other gadgetry are available. Magazines such as *What Car* and *What Camera* cater especially for those seeking comparative information to help them make purchasing decisions.

Contract magazines

Since May 1994, 80 new contract magazines had been launched by early 1995, according to the Association of Publishing Agencies. The most high-profile of these were retail titles. The boom began with the launch of Sainsbury's *The Magazine* in March 1993, since when it has been very successful. It emulates existing non-contract magazines in its quality and it is given a premium checkout position by Sainsbury's. In its first year it established sales of 325,000; it provided Audit Bureau of Circulation (ABC) figures to prove it and joined the National Readership Survey. The success of Sainsbury's title gave impetus to the retail contract magazine sector and magazines for Boots, Tesco, Safeway, Harvey Nichols and Iceland were quick to follow. And it is not just the retail stores that use contract magazines – Heinz has also used magazines as part of its mailing campaigns. Companies see them as fulfilling a principal means of communicating with their customers.

Trade magazines

Every kind of retail trade has its own specialist magazine (such as *The Grocer, Retail Jeweller, Chemist and Druggist*) which forms an excellent channel through which manufacturers and other suppliers can communicate with the distributors of their products. The advertising therefore tends to be mainly devoted to new products, the announcement of promotional campaigns, special incentive 'deals' for distributors and so on.

Technical and professional journals

Similarly most professions and fields of specialism have their own publication *The Engineer, Accountants Weekly, The Director* (monthly magazine of the Institute of Directors) for example. Not only do some of their readers buy special products and services connected with their profession but, more importantly, they are often key decision-makers on behalf of the organizations who employ them. For that reason, this category often tends to get merged with the next.

Industrial and business-to-business journals

Each area of industry and commerce also tends to have its own publications – such as *Farmers Weekly, Caterer and Hotelkeeper, British Printer, Brewing and Distilling International*. Advertisers wishing to communicate with industry often have a choice between the so-called 'horizontal magazines' – those reaching specialists in a wide range of industries (*Industrial Equipment News* for example) and 'vertical magazines' reaching many different types of executives in a particular industry.

The early 1990s saw hard times for business magazines; not only did the money put into advertising begin to fall but the business press's share of that budget began to decline from 10.7 per cent in 1989 to 7.7 per cent in 1993. As the UK came out of recession, advertising budgets began to grow once more but client companies were looking for value-added services. Advertisers began to look for sponsorship, inserts, advertorials and joint promotions as ways of extracting maximum value from their budgets – and publishers began to respond to that demand.

By the mid-1990s there was an increase in the editorial quality, circulation verification through ABC profiles, and the level of service given by advertising departments of business magazines. The Periodical Publishers Association introduced Business Magazine Week in February 1995. From there, the sector has gone from strength to strength.

Controlled Circulation

Because business to business advertisers are normally interested in communicating with people who have specific interests and who have powers of decision-making, many such magazines operate on a 'controlled circulation' basis. That is, no charge is made to the readers, but the entire revenue is derived from advertising. The publication is delivered free (normally by post) to all those who meet certain criteria such as level of seniority, professional qualification, job title or purchasing responsibilities.

An enormous advantage of such magazines is that their recipients are known very precisely, whereas the small circulation of many trade, technical and business journals means that they are not included in readership surveys. The only figure available, therefore, is the ABC certificated figure of circulation which is an inadequate source for choosing the best medium for a particular purpose.

11.2 Circulation and readership

The terms 'circulation' and 'readership' have been used and it is important to get quite clear the difference between them. Circulation means quite literally the number of copies of a particular publication that is circulated – that is how many are bought or given away free. Since each copy may be read by more than one person, the number of readers – people who see all or part of the publication – will be larger. It can be difficult to establish precisely what these figures are. In the worst case, the only figure available is what the publisher says his circulation is. But this figure may be misleading, perhaps because the publishers' records are not very accurate, possibly even because – since advertising rates depend on size of circulation and readership – the publisher may issue figures which are deliberately misleading. It is also sometimes important to know how many copies are bought as distinct from being given away as samples, for promotional purposes and so on.

11.2.1 Audit Bureau of Circulation (ABC)

The ABC, as it is known, is a non-profit-making company set up jointly in 1931, by advertisers, advertising agencies and publishers to overcome part of the problem. The great majority of publishers take part in the auditing system it carries out on the industry's behalf. The Bureau sends regularly to each publisher member forms for completion by independent auditors – usually the publisher's financial accountant. In addition, the Bureau's own auditors carry out random checks to ensure that forms are being correctly entered.

On the basis of this information, the ABC issues audited circulation figures. The figures for newspapers and general consumer magazines, audited yearly, show net sales at full cover price. Where any copies have been sold at less than normal price they are shown separately.

Specialized magazines may include certain free copies in the audited figures, but they are listed separately (the main ones being controlled circulation and free distribution to members of clubs and societies).

The ABC also issues Verified Freesheet Distribution (VFD) Certificates based on audits which check numbers of copies and the areas where they are delivered.

For business and professional magazines and specialist consumer ones, the ABC may issue further information based on the Media Data Form. This is completed voluntarily by publishers and is not audited. It provides a breakdown of circulation, geographically and by type of subscriber. Thus it would give valuable information to advertisers in an industrial magazine as to whether it would be likely to reach people able to influence a particular type of purchase.

The ABC also administers the Exhibition Data Form which audits attendances at exhibitions in terms of numbers and type of visitors.

11.2.2 National Readership Surveys Ltd (NRS)

In the UK, a number of joint bodies supported by the advertising industry are responsible for basic readership/audience research for the main media. For newspapers and magazines, readership research is commissioned by National Readership Surveys Ltd (NRS Ltd). Its Board of Directors consists of four directors each representing the Newspaper Publishers Association (NPA) and Periodical Publishers Association (PPA), three directors representing the Institute of Practitioners in Advertising (IPA) and one director representing the Association of Media Independents (AMI), plus a non-voting director representing the Incorporated Society of British Advertisers (ISBA).

The survey uses a sample of 37,500 from all adults of 15 or over living in England, Scotland and Wales, and 280 titles are measured. Readership can be related to a whole range of factors, such as TV viewing habits and ownership of consumer durables.

People interviewed are shown the 'mastheads' – the titles as they normally appear on the publication – of a series of newspapers or magazines and are asked by the interviewer: 'I want you to go through this booklet with me and tell me for each paper, roughly how many issues you have read or looked at recently – it doesn't matter where. As you look at each card, will you tell me which of the statements applies.'

The interviewee is then asked to say which of a series of frequency statements printed on the page being shown – is applicable. Interviewees are also asked to say, when they 'last read' each publication, apart from today, and are included as readers if their answer fell within the 'publication interval' – (yesterday for a daily, within the last week for a weekly, etc.)

Subscribers to the NRS receive copies of the detailed figures of readers, sub-divided in a number of ways, including by:

(a) sex, age, six social grades (*see* Section 11.2.3)
(b) survey region and ITV region
(c) weight of ITV viewing and radio listening
(d) readership among special groups, such as housewives with children, possession of certain consumer durables, etc.

It is well-recognized that the NRS has certain limitations, in particular the sheer memory discrepancies of interviewees asked to say what they have read. The definition 'read or looked at' also leaves a wide area of uncertainty about how much a 'reader' actually reads – certainly there is no guarantee that they actually study each page of every issue and it is highly improbable that they avidly seek out advertisements and study them carefully. Nonetheless, the information is extremely valuable, especially as a way of comparing one publication against another with a particular target audience in mind.

11.2.3 Geodemographic classifications

Locality marketing
Geodemographics work on the well-proven principle that people who live in similar 'neighbourhoods' are likely to have similar behavioural, purchasing and lifestyle habits. By effectively codifying people by key characteristics, geodemographic classifications can offer great accuracy

in the targeting of customers on both a demographic and geographic basis

In Britain, most geodemographic information is derived from the Census. By linking the results of the Census with data from other sources it is possible to 'profile' consumers by geographical area. Other data sources used in geodemographic classifications include:

- market research data;
- Postcode Address File (PAF), the official Royal Mail file of all addresses in Great Britain;
- the Electoral Roll (ER);
- credit-related data (provided by credit referencing bureaux);
- other data (e.g. companies' own in-house customer data, industry specific data, etc.).

Of these, market research data and PAF are perhaps the most important. Market research data provides the bases from which geographic and demographic comparisons can be made, while PAF data allows for demographic classification to an average residential 'area' of 15 households. This compares to Census data, where the smallest recorded residential areas average approximately 150 households.

Uses of geodemographic classification
The principal uses of geodemographic classification include:

- Consumer profiling by geographical area – establishing how a product may sell in a certain area.
- Identification of product use across geographical areas – establishing who is buying a certain product.
- Defining the market potential of existing customer databases, mailing lists – targeting potential customers from consumers of other products.

As such, geodemographics provide a vital tool for many key marketing and site location operations which demand a close understanding of the consumer potential in a database or an area. They allow sellers/suppliers to *differentiate* between different groups of buyers/users, and establish which groups of people are key target users, which groups are potential users and which groups are non-users. This offers opportunities for specific targeting of likely customers and the potential for increasing return on investment.

ACORN
ACORN classification profiles customers in a trading area or on a database into six categories, 17 groups and 54 types (plus one unclassified), so that

marketers can understand more about their likely consumer characteristics. Table 11.1 shows the ACORN profile of population projection 1998 for Great Britain.

Table 11.1

ACORN category	Population projection 1998		ACORN groups	
	Category (%)	Group (%)		
A Thriving	19.9	15.2	Wealthy achievers, Suburban areas	1
		2.3	Affluent greys Rural communities	2
		2.4	Prosperous pensioners, Retirement areas	3
B Expanding	11.6	3.8	Affluent executives, Family areas	4
		7.8	Well-off workers, Family areas	5
C Rising	7.8	2.3	Affluent urbanites, Town & city areas	6
		2.1	Prosperous professionals, Metropolitan areas	7
		3.4	Better-off executives, Inner-city areas	8
D Settling	24.0	13.4	Comfortable middle agers, Mature home-owning areas	9
		10.6	Skilled workers, Home-owning areas	10
E Aspiring	13.7	9.7	New home owners, Mature communities	11
		4.0	White collar workers, Better-off multi-ethnic areas	12
F Striving	22.6	3.6	Older people, Less prosperous areas	13
		11.5	Council estate residents, Better-off homes	14
		2.7	Council estate residents, High unemployment	15
		2.7	Council estate residents, Greatest hardship	16
		2.1	People in multi-ethnic, Low-income areas	17
Unclassified	0.4			

Socio-economic gradings

The 'Social grade' breakdown included in NRS figures – and much other research data in the UK – is based on a classification agreed to and used by the majority of market research organizations. This has the advantage that, however imperfect it may be, a vast amount of research data is compatible and useful cross-links can be made. The classification is based on the occupation of the head of the household.

The population distribution by social grade of chief income earner in the UK – with the approximate proportion of the UK population they represent is shown in Table 11.2.

Table 11.2

| Social grade | All adults 15+ | |
	'000s	%
A	1,415	3.1
B	8,348	18.1
C1	12,837	27.8
C2	10,350	22.4
D	7,843	17.0
E	5,357	11.6
Total	46,150	100.0

Note: Figures are based on the social grade of the chief income earner.
Source: National Readership Survey (NRS Ltd), July 1996–June 1997

NRS social grade definitions* are shown in Table 11.3.

Table 11.3

Social grade	Social status	Occupation
A	Upper middle class	Higher managerial, administrative or professional
B	Middle class	Intermediate managerial, administrative or professional
C1	Lower middle class	Supervisory or clerical, and junior managerial, administrative or professional
C2	Skilled working class	Skilled manual workers
D	Working class	Semi and unskilled manual workers
E	Those at lowest level of subsistence	State pensioners or widows (no other earner), casual or lowest-grade workers

*Note: These are the standard social grade classifications using definitions agreed between Research Services Ltd and NRS.
Source: National Readership Survey (NRS Ltd), July 1996–June 1997

It is well recognized that this is a very crude classification and increasingly so, when definitives such as 'head of household' become blurred and when traditional class systems and values are changing rapidly. However, in spite of much effort and discussion, with some more complex systems to take its place this classification at least has the benefit of being relatively easy to operate.

The Sagacity life cycle groupings
The basic thesis of the Sagacity grouping is that people have different aspirations and behaviour patterns as they go through their life cycle. Four main stages of life cycle are defined, which are subdivided by income and occupation groups (Table 11.4).

Table 11.4

Life Cycle:	Dependent		Pre-Family		Family				Late			
Income:					Better off		Worse off		Better off		Worse off	
Occupation:	White	Blue	White	Blue	White	Blue	White	Blue	White	Blue	White	Blue
% of adults: 1996*	6.7	5.8	6.4	4.8	12.0	9.2	2.4	6.8	10.9	7.1	10.4	17.6
% of adults: 1997*	7.0	5.6	6.3	4.8	11.9	9.3	2.3	6.4	11.1	7.4	10.4	17.5

Definitions of life cycle stages

Dependent	Mainly under-24s, living at home or full-time student
Pre-family	Under-35s, who have established their own household but have no children
Family	Main shoppers and chief income earners, under 65, with one or more children in the household
Late	Includes all adults whose children have left home or who are over 35 and childless.

Definitions of occupation groups

White	Chief income earner is in the ABC1 occupation group
Blue	Chief income earner is in the C2DE occupation group.

*Year to June.
Source: Research Services Ltd

11.2.4 Target Group Index (TGI)

First published in 1969, this is a private-venture survey by the BMRB and therefore not governed by a Joint Industry Committee. It is available to anyone on a subscription basis. Unlike the National Audit Survey (NAS), TGI is mainly based on product usage, which can be cross-referenced against demographics and media.

It is based on a sample size of 40,000, representative of the population in total, and published yearly. The postal questionnaires are received from informants who have been previously contacted by random location methods in 200 areas of the United Kingdom.

TGI reports on the characteristics of users of over 3,400 brands across more than 200 consumer product fields and relates demographic characteristics to heavy, medium and light usage of the products and to readership, viewing and listening habits for the main media.

A full range of standard demographics as per the NAS are measured, along with 'lifestyle' statements. It can also be cross-referenced with ACORN, etc. social groups and against BARB.

Example runs could be made against, for example, all Guinness drinkers who play rugby league, or where the majority of heavy wine drinkers live (the highest concentrations are in Kensington, Hampstead and Brighton).

11.2.5 Other media surveys

The NRS and TGI data provide a vast array of detailed information as a basis for comparing and selecting the best media for reaching a defined target audience. The media data form (*see* Section 11.2.1) can be very helpful in selecting publications for some types of business-to-business advertising. In many cases, however, none of this information is relevant.

Media planners are then dependent on surveys, where they exist, carried out on behalf of publishers. Provided these are properly set up and professionally conducted they can be very valuable. However, they do need to be scrutinized very carefully and the basis of the figures clearly recognized. For example, some publications rely on postal questionnaires inserted in the magazine, with results based on a very low percentage of replies – which means the findings must be suspect. There is also the lurking suspicion that unfavourable results may be suppressed and only the favourable ones circulated.

With the vast expansion of new titles and greater diversity of printed media to choose from, it may be necessary for advertisers to commission their own research to establish what are the best channels for communicating with their particular special audiences.

Verified Free Distribution (VFD)
This is a self-financing subsidiary of the ABC, formed in 1981, to certify the distribution of the growing number of free publications. This is in effect a proper audit carried out by professional auditors. It is based on six- or

twelve-monthly circulation figures. Business publications are now audited by the Business Press Audit, which was established in the mid-1990s.

The Businessman Readership Survey
This survey, conducted since 1973, is much like the NRS but goes more in-depth into the habits of business people. Consequently, business-oriented magazines are included along with the mid and up-market newspapers/colour supplements.

Research for the 1992 survey was based on a sample of 2,332 business people and covers areas such as income, car ownership, credit cards, industry, financial investment and travel.

JICREG (Regional Press Bureau)
This was launched in 1990. It gives annual reporting on approximately 26 evening, 89 paid-for weekly and 163 free newspapers. Morning and free monthly newspapers are not included.

JICREG is supported by a number of organizations, including the IPA and the ISBA.

Readership figures are based on a 'model' from the regional newspapers who have conducted their own research.

11.3 Characteristics of the press as an advertising medium

Section 7.3 indicated very briefly that each of the advertising media have their own advantages and disadvantages. The main characteristics of the press are as follows:

Coverage
Various forms of press media offer a very wide selection of titles to choose from, yet none of them has universal coverage. The NRS published the following figures for the year to July 1997 by way of illustration (Table 11.5).

It is true that today virtually every conceivable taste is catered for by one or other magazine. Programme publications, both for commercial television and the BBC, are read by over 10 million. Over half of women read a woman's weekly magazine and, although the readerships of monthly magazines are lower, *Reader's Digest* is read by over 5 million adults and there are now 25 titles in the women's monthly field with women readerships of more than a million.

Available Information
Another characteristic of the press medium is how much we know about it, although in order to make the right decision on media selection we

Table 11.5

Newspapers	Av. period	%	Magazines	Av. period	%
Any national morning	weekday	57	Any general weekly	week	42(a)
Any national Sunday	week	64	Any general monthly	month	51
Any regional evening	weekday	23	Any women's weekly	week	42(b)
Any regional morning	weekday	9(c)	Any women's monthly	month	52(b)
Any regional weekly (paid)	week	39(c)			
Any regional weekly (free)	week	65(c)			

(a) Includes TV listings magazines.
(b) Readership by women only.
(c) Data from TGI.

always want to know more. Readership data in tremendous detail is available from the National Readership Survey on many of our major publications. In addition, we have audited circulation figures for most of these. We have circulation figures too for most of the publications not covered by the National Readership Survey, although this is an area in which further information can legitimately be demanded. Apart from other large-scale quasi-industry surveys, which cover press readership, the media owners themselves have commissioned a very large number of surveys into all aspects of their readerships, although, as said, the information is often somewhat circumspect.

Selectivity
One of the most important aspects of the press as a whole, for the media planner, is the ability to choose widely contrasting vehicles for the advertising message. It is important to realize that the message is affected by the media. For example, if you had been fortunate enough to receive some windfall shares from a building society and wish to re-invest the money, you might turn to the press for guidance. Now if you had read something in the *Sun* (a tabloid) and the same thing in the *Financial Times*, which would you tend to believe most?

Flexibility
The range of flexibility in the press medium is almost as great as the range in any other measurement of the medium. It is possible to place a classified advertisement by telephone in the morning and see it appear in the midday editions of the evening newspapers. For full colour reproduction in monthly magazines, however, copy is frequently required up to three months before the publication appears. Similarly with cancellation periods. A great deal of classified advertising may be officially cancelled at no more than two days' notice. Some publishers still ask for six months'

cancellation notice for colour. The general tendency is towards greater flexibility and it is often possible to effect considerable advances on the official
positions by special negotiation.

Production
Production costs can be kept to an extremely small portion of the budget.
A direct response advertiser for a pension plan has carried the same copy
unchanged for upwards of 20 years. At the other extreme, a fibre manufacturer illustrating a wide number of styles in a wide number of publications can easily run up to 25 per cent of the advertising budget in
production. Some remarkably effective advertisements have been prepared by the publication itself, and even more sophisticated advertisements may carry a low entrance fee into the medium.

The quality of colour printing in newspapers has improved considerably over the last few years, and even the most modest of local freesheets
is carrying full colour pages. However, given the speed of printing, the
quality can never be expected to match the quality of magazines.

Although colour does attract, there are many occasions when full
colour is not always justified. A full colour, full page advertising campaign
was suggested by an agency of a veterinary pharmaceutical company to
reposition an existing brand. After some focus groups were run it was
found that the same effect could be expected by small-space spot colour
advertising. While this could reduce the cost of the media to achieve the
same level of impact, the reduction in the cost of production alone would
more than compensate for the cost of the research. When the more modest
campaign was running, audience research showed that the awareness of
the brand's repositioning meant that some of the media space booked
could be re-allocated to other brands in the portfolio.

Sizes, shapes and colours
The basic unit of space in newspapers is the single column centimetre;
most other spaces are built up from this size. In magazines the basic unit is
the page and other spaces are either built up from or reduced from this
space. Shapes can vary widely, although most of them are rectangular.
Recent years have seen something of a return to the pre-war concern with
shapes other than rectangular.

Colour is playing an increasingly important role in the press, not only
in advertising but also in editorial matter. We have seen great developments
over the last decade and more are coming, as discussed in Chapter 15.

11.4 Summary

1   The printed media – newspapers and magazines – offer a wide range
     of very varied advertising opportunities.

2   Circulation figures are available for virtually all of the printed media and readership figures are available for the major publications.
3   The Audit Bureau of Circulation is the source of circulation figures and the National Readership Survey and Target Group Index form the basis of readership information.
4   Other readership information may be provided by research commissioned by publishers or advertisers.
5   The major special characteristics of the press as an advertising medium are their selectivity and flexibility.

11.5 References

1 *National Readership Survey*, June 1997.

11.6 Further reading

The Effective Use of Advertising Media by Martyn Davies (Business Books, 1981) contains a useful catalogue of media organizations and sources of information.

The MRG Guide to Advertising Media Research (Media Research Group, 1981) is an excellent review of the basis and usage of media research in the UK.

Baker, Michael J. (Ed), *The Marketing Book* (2nd Edition), Oxford: Butterworth-Heinemann, 1991.

Corstjens, Judith, *Strategic Advertising: A Practitioner's Handbook*, Oxford: Heinemann, 1990.

11.7 Questions for discussion

1   What implications do the increasing number of publications and the fragmentation of many markets have for advertisers?
2   Compare and contrast the various geodemographic classification systems.
3   What would you say to convince a colleague that press media was a better option for selling furniture than television?

Chapter 12

The broadcast media

'While changing technology has the potential to affect all our lives, it is the interaction of technology and social change that will really shape the advertising industry of twenty years' time.'

James Walker, Henley Centre

By the end of this chapter you will:

- Understand the impact of the rapid rise in the variety of broadcast media;
- Appreciate the changing share of television audiences;
- Have sampled the variety of European television management;
- Understand the impact of the 'new media', including digital, virtual reality and the Internet;
- Be aware of the on-going debate over on-line advertising to children;
- Appreciate how the effectiveness of TV advertising is evaluated;
- Have reviewed the recent developments in television;
- Appreciate how TV airtime is bought;
- Understand how broadcast media audiences are measured.

In the post-war period, the economic, political and lifestyle consensus of mass marketing and keeping up with the Joneses gave an era of mass media and branding. There were just three channels in the UK, only one with advertising, and that (ITV) frequently had a 50 per cent audience share. The collective consciousness of so many watching the same TV programmes at the same time built and reinforced the same consensus about social values. Advertisers built their brands (PG Tips; chimps, Esso; tigers) on these same values and left them embedded in popular culture.

The future looks different. These conspiring factors are unravelling. The growth of personal media (Walkmans, personal radios) at the expense of mass media, the resurgence of personal identity (keeping away from the Joneses, wanting to be different) and an on-going resentment of the value of brands (note the growth of own label) is expected to contribute to a decline in *conventional* advertising as the most powerful medium for marketing communication.

For example, if you are using a PC at home you cannot be watching television or reading a newspaper or magazine in the conventional sense. As consumers we are, therefore, already side-stepping advertising-financed media.

This chapter reviews the traditional broadcast media of terrestrial TV and radio and explores some of the newer technologies. However, with rapid advances in technology, the situation will be ever changing and the marketers of the future will need to invest heavily in their own education in order to stay in touch.

12.1 The development of 'terrestrial' technology

'Terrestrial' television is a term used to describe television broadcast from local TV stations and to distinguish such broadcasts from the 'satellite' stations that have expanded in the 1990s. However, with the advent of television broadcasts through cables running largely underground into people's homes, the term 'over-the-air' has begun to replace it.

While radio has been around for over 75 years and television effectively for 65, they have only carried advertising since 1955. This was because until then broadcasting was a government monopoly and no advertising was carried. Independent television was established on a separate basis, where the stations were funded by paid-for advertising, and the government-owned BBC (British Broadcasting Corporation) continued with its existing services funded by licence fees. Commercial radio was not permitted in the UK until 1973 when the first station was opened.

There have been instances where radio stations based in other parts of Europe which did accept advertising were receivable in most parts of the UK. Radio Luxembourg was one such popular example.

The changing share of television audiences from 1991 to 1996 in the UK is outlined in Table 12.1

The European picture is more complex. The 1996 *European Television Directory* lists over 130 television channels in over 30 countries, although this does include some cable and satellite channels. A selection of information illustrates the complexity of the situation.

12.1.1 Italian television

Telepiu is the holding company that controls the three over-the-air television channels: Tele+1, Tele+2 and Tele+3. It was established in Milan on 30 October 1990.

Table 12.1 *Share of televsion Audiences*[1]

	1991 (%)	1996 (%)	% change
BBC 1	34.1	33.3	−2.35
BBC 2	9.9	11.1	+12.12
All BBC	44.0	44.4	+0.91
ITV	42.1	36.1	−14.25
Channel 4	9.9	11.1	+12.12
Others	4.0	8.4	+110

Tele+1 is a pay channel completely dedicated to cinema and children's programming. It shows eleven films a day, a series of movies, tributes to individual directors or stars, news and information programmes. Programming is scrambled and is broadcast for 24 hours a day.

Tele+2 concentrates on sport and became a pay channel on 29 March 1992. While focusing on tennis, golf, motorcycling, boxing, volleyball and wrestling, since autumn 1993 it also broadcasts soccer games at the weekends. Again, it broadcasts for 24 hours a day.

Tele+3 began its new unscrambled programming in March 1993 with a schedule containing cultural and educational programmes, including music, cinema, opera, ballet and art. Broadcasting for 24 hours a day, it also offers thirteen hours of MTV Europe programmes every day.

12.1.2 Hungarian television

Experimental television broadcasting began in Hungary in 1955, with a main television department established in Hungarian radio a year later. In 1965, Hungarian Television, as part of Hungarian Television and Radio (MRTV), became a separate budgetary organ of the state. By 1974, Hungarian Television and Hungarian Radio became two separate entities.

In 1991, due to internal decentralization of MTV, TV-1 and TV-2 became self-contained organizational entities, and competing centres of production were set up. However, from June 1993, due again to reorganization, the two channels of MTV were reunited. The organization is funded mainly by licence fees and revenues from advertising, in addition to some government subsidies. Hungarian Television is not engaged in any cable or satellite broadcasting activities, nor is it involved with pay-TV.

12.2 Digital media

As the 1990s draw to a close, previously separate industries are trying to create a new world of digital communications. In 1996, DirecTV in the US, the digital satellite service offering 175 television channels across the continent, achieved more than 2 million subscribers. In Europe, digital multi-channel television is underway in France, Germany and Italy, and British Sky Broadcasting (BSkyB) plans to launch a service with up to 200 channels in the late 1990s after a number of delays. Digital services have already been launched in South America and Africa. Apart from just more channels of television, there is the opportunity to run pay-per-view movies services and pay-per-view exclusive sports events. It is sport that has introduced the new services to consumers and, with the English Premier League in particular, it is sport that has turned BSkyB into a business generating £1 billion revenues and pre-tax profits of £257 million[2].

The enormous data-carrying capacity of digital satellite means that they can be used for interactive services such as home shopping and home banking using the existing telephone line as the 'return path' to order the services you need. Broadcasters such as DirecTV and BSkyB are planning to broadcast the top Internet sites to consumers PCs so that regularly updated information can be interrogated in real time. Already it is possible to display such information on the television screen. Using digital satellites, the entire contents of a broadsheet newspaper such as the *Financial Times* can be downloaded onto a PC in a few minutes. DirecTV is planning to transmit electronic magazines in this way – such as *Sports Illustrated*, complete with moving pictures.

A study by Oliver and Ohlbaum[3] in 1997 suggested that the switch from analogue to digital cable and satellite may take until the year 2007, by which time pay-TV revenue (excluding interactive services like home shopping) will be generating £5.1 billion from over 12 million homes in the UK. However, the switch will put pressure on existing premium services, especially movie channels, which may explain why some operators – like BSkyB – may be slow to get fully into digital.

As we can see, the market is in its infancy and there will be many changes as it develops.

12.2.1 Virtual reality

It is predicted[4] that the global business Virtual Reality (VR) market will grow in value to close to £1 billion by 2001. (It was estimated to be worth £90 million in 1995.) This growth is fuelled by the fact that the expensive workstations initially used for VR are being caught up by faster PCs.

For many companies, the technology is fast becoming a standard technical problem-solving tool, beyond a simple plaything. Of the early adopters, most are using VR in multiple applications. The principal initial use of high-end VR is in the design visualization/simulation of buildings, products or processes before actual construction starts. Sainsbury's are using the technology to design supermarkets.

Two other areas are worthy of mention. The first is in training, where VR is already being used at McDonnell Douglas to simulate assembly, operation and maintenance of aircraft components. VR browsing of complex data is of potentially even wider application, particularly when used as a means of navigating the Internet.

It is early days yet, but the time will come when browsers will be able to walk through a virtual shopping mall on the Internet and do their shopping; the only vehicles left on the road will be the trucks distributing the goods to homes across the land.

12.2.2 The Internet

The Internet is the data equivalent of the international voice network – i.e. the linkage of computers and networks, worldwide, through the adoption of common standards. It had its origins in research institutions back in the 1960s at the US Defence Advanced Research Projects Agency. By the 1970s, their system was linked to counterparts in other countries, and by the late 1970s thousands of colleges, research companies and government agencies funded connections to the 'Net'. This network of networks became known as the Internet. By the 1990s the World Wide Web, or Superhighway, as it has become known, evolved through the development of graphical interfaces. These had the ability to allow individuals to browse for information, which led to an explosion in the user base and corporate presence.

The growth of the Internet has been put down to a number of factors:

- At its simplest level, one just needs a computer, a modem (which telephones another computer) and some software to get connected.
- It enables access to a wide range of global information and e-mail partners.
- It has a relatively low cost of access for colleges.
- The development of easy-to-use graphical interfaces and browsers ('the Web') which encouraged individuals to connect as the tariff model became acceptable.
- The growing user base encouraged corporates to offer services on the Net.
- The ever increasing services now on offer continue to attract subscribers.

For these reasons, the Internet has become a new medium to carry advertising and other information. However, a cautionary message comes from Bickerton, Bickerton and Pardesi writing in *Cybermarketing*[5]:

The main message of the book is that marketing on the cyberspace is not conceptually different from marketing in the real world. You need to have a deep understanding of your market, why people buy, what benefits you offer over and above your competitors and what marketing mix most suits your target audience. This information will prevent you from publishing a globally ignored corporate billboard. Basically, you need to have a clear marketing strategy in place before you consider using the Superhighway as a promotional mechanism.

Nonetheless, there is a rapid growth of organizations appearing and advertising on the Superhighway. According to New York-based Jupiter Research, overall spending on Web advertising was expected to reach well over $300 million by the end of 1996. Interestingly, the top ten publishers soak up two-thirds of these revenues and six of the top ten publishers – familiar names (to surfers) like Netscape and Yahoo – also rank in the top ten spenders on Web advertising.

Besides the 'dial-up' on-line systems, which users access by having their modem dial a special telephone number, there is a growing body of on-line versions of print titles, accessible through the graphics-based World Wide Web on the Internet. One of the most advanced is *Electronic Telegraph*, which is now taking its first paid advertising. A full-service package costs £25,000 for seven weeks. This consists of a week on each of six set sites plus one week on a site of your choice. The service also includes a weekly feedback on user profiles gleaned from registration details.

Among the first to take up the offer was United Airlines, who suggested that while it was just a test, it was their next step in advertising development and, if it proved successful, they would be moving more fully into the area. TSB's advertising on *Electronic Telegraph* has had an excellent response, and it is surprising how many users go into the advertisement and try out every section. People are curious. While it is still a small part of TSB's media and communications mix, it seems that it will increase.

It is perfectly possible for an advertiser to develop a 'site' of their own without paying anything to a media owner – the costs are in setting up the site and paying a relatively small sum for a connection to the Net. Among those who have already done so are: Pepsi (http://www.pepsi.co.uk), Coca-Cola (http://www.cocacola.com/), Sony (http://www.sonycom/) as well as The Bodyshop, which can be found at http://www.bodyshop.co.uk.

Creating the perfect website, however, is only half the battle: consumers need to be able to locate it – and that's where the new generation of on-line brands such as *The Guardian*, *The Telegraph* or *Time Out* score points.

Since users are not going to stumble across an advertisement on the World Wide Web, the address needs to be linked to other sites. Since consumers rarely seek advertising – on TV it is seen as something that is tolerated – for consumers to visit a WWW site, they must have already been persuaded that it is worth the effort: reaching them may well mean advertising within those branded on-line services where you know your customers are going to be.

At the moment, the Internet is something like a huge shopping mall, but you do not know where any of the shops are or even what shops are there. However, there are likely to be many changes in the next few years, so that accessing information will not be such a problem as it is now. Microsoft Network makes accessing the World Wide Web as easy as clicking an icon on your computer screen – early signs are that this is attracting a whole new group of customers onto the Net.

12.2.3 On-line advertising to children

There is currently an ongoing debate regarding the use of on-line advertising targeted specifically at children.

On one side are media watchdog groups, who have lobbied the Federal Trade Commission (FTC) in the USA to impose standards on on-line advertising which is geared towards children because they argue that the ads as they are currently structured:

1   Are an invasion of privacy; and
2   Are unfair and deceptive because they interweave advertising and content.

On the other side are the advertisers, who predictably do not feel that their websites are exploiting children.

In this section we aim first, to provide awareness of both the information available on the World Wide Web and sources regarding this issue and some of the exemplary sites themselves; and secondly, to provide a framework for an analysis of these issues. The issue of explicit material of a sexual or pornographic nature is not covered here.

There are a number of factors which have made targeting children on the Internet both compelling and practical:

1   Children comprise a significant and powerful consumer group. In 1995, children under the age of 12 spent $14 billion; teenagers spent another $67 billion; and together they influenced $160 billion of their parents' spending. (See:
    http://www.scils.rutgers.edu/~jakeman/advkids.html)
2   More and more children are going on-line and becoming 'digital kids'. According to Jupiter Publications, publisher of *Digital Kids Report*, today almost 1 million children are using the Web and at least 3.8 million have access to it. These figures are projected to quadruple by the year 2000. This has caught the attention of almost every children-oriented company, according to the 1996 *On-line Kids Report*.

3   Unlike television, radio and print mediums, the Internet is completely free of government regulation and advertisers have a free hand. The Computer Decency Act, part of the Telecommunications Act (1996), was an attempt to regulate the content of the Internet. However, it was recently declared unconstitutional and violative of freedom of speech by a United States District Court. In its opinion, the Court hailed the Internet as the greatest example of free speech that the world has ever known.

4   Unlike television, radio and print, the Internet is an interactive medium and allows advertisers to have one-on-one communication with children and thereby establish a special relationship. The interactivity appeals to children's imagination and fantasy.

5   The computer age, with all its new technology, has created a generation gap, with the result being that many children are allowed to explore the World Wide Web without the supervision and monitoring of parents and teachers. Due to the fact that children have a better aptitude and temperament for new technology, companies are using children in product development. An example of this is in the area of computer games.

6   Children are very trusting and vulnerable by nature and are capable of being psychologically manipulated.

7   The Internet, as an advertising medium, is relatively cheap compared to television, radio and print. Two sites which will give you some idea of the costs of advertising on the Internet are:
http://www.cadco.com/costs.html; and
http://cyberbound.com/rates.html

Together, all of these factors present children-oriented companies with an affordable, practical, unregulated medium possessing technologies enabling them to communicate and interact one-on-one with a very significant, trusting and vulnerable consumer group. This presents an atmosphere ripe for abuse, exploitation and manipulation. Many feel there is genuine cause for concern and fear.

In its news report released on 28 March 1996, the Centre for Media Education (CME), a non-profit research and advocacy organization founded in 1991 to educate the public and policy makers about critical media policy issues, documented several practices which children-oriented companies have resorted to in their efforts to reach out to young consumers on-line. The report was issued as part of CME's 'Action for Children in Cyberspace' project. Excerpts of the report, entitled 'Web of Deception: Threats to Children from On-line Marketing', are available on-line.

Specific practices which were deemed objectionable and harmful to children are:

1   Using surveys and the lure of prizes and games to elicit personal information from children.

2   Monitoring children's on-line activities and compiling detailed personal profiles which are then sold to market research firms.
3   Using this information to design personalized ads aimed at individual children.
4   Designing advertising environments to capture children's attention for extended periods of time.
5   Integrating advertising and content.
6   Creating product 'spokescharacters' to develop special interactive relationships with children.

CME recommended that the FTC create a specific set of policies designed to protect children from these practices by adopting the following principles:
1   Personal information should not be collected from children, nor should personal profiles of children be sold to third parties.
2   Advertising and promotions should be clearly labelled and separated from content.
3   Children's content areas should not be directly linked to advertising sites.
4   There should be no direct interaction between children and product 'spokescharacters'.
5   There should be no on-line microtargeting of children and no direct-response marketing.

As stated earlier, the recent attempt by the US government to regulate content on the Internet was declared unconstitutional. This raises severe doubts as to whether the government could successfully impose any restrictions on the content of the Internet, including imposing regulations on advertising. Nevertheless, an associated press article pointed out that the FTC's jurisdiction over deceptive marketplace practices extends to the Internet. Therefore, the FTC is the most appropriate government agency to develop rules and guidelines for on-line advertising. Other on-line articles which discuss CME's news report can be found at *San Diego Daily Transcript* and the *Salt Lake Tribune*. If, as suspected, any US government regulation of the content of the Internet would fail to pass constitutional muster, then one alternative would be voluntary self-regulation.

The Children's Advisory Review Unit (CARU) of the Council of Better Business Bureau (CBBB) has established Self-Regulatory Guidelines for Children's Advertising. The goals of CARU are to provide a mechanism to safeguard responsible advertising to children; to support voluntary self-regulation within the children's advertising industry; and to promote truthful, accurate advertising to our nation's youngest consumers.

The self-regulatory guidelines apply to children under 12 years of age and do not specifically mention the Internet or on-line advertising. However, several of the principles and guidelines, especially those which deal with exploiting a child's imagination or fantasy, are very close to CME's principles. Therefore, CARU's self-regulatory guidelines and principles can be used in conjunction with CME's news report and extended to the Internet. Then CARU and CME could seek voluntary change through the co-operation of advertisers and inform the public (parents, teachers, etc.) of any ads which violate their principles and guidelines. CARU's screening policies could prove to be a very effective mechanism for change.

If change does not come through government regulation or voluntary co-operation, another possibility is through the implementation of filtering software technology. There are many types of software currently available which offer parental control of the Internet. Unfortunately, as CME concludes in its news report, all of these filtering or screening software services were designed specifically to filter out sexually explicit images and text and will not help solve the problem of protecting children from manipulative, deceptive and intrusive advertising practices.

However, the Internet does have a way of creating markets for new software technologies, and hope lies in a new software developed by PrivNet called Internet Fast Forward (IFF). IFF was developed after CME issued its news report, and a Beta version is available for free on PrivNet's website. IFF has at least two noteworthy features that could protect children from the practices documented by CME. The first is that since ads (graphics) take longer to download than text, IFF has the ability to filter out all ads in their entirety. The second is the 'cookie' feature, which could protect children from having their on-line activities monitored. Since IFF is still in its development stage, no one knows for sure how or if it would work, but a review of the news features on PrivNet's website shows that IFF has advertisers worried, angry and anxious. This is a step in the right direction.

Thus far, we have proceeded on the premise that 'digital kids' need protection from the commercial world and don't possess the maturity, wisdom, intelligence or capabilities to protect themselves. Only one side of the coin has been presented, that of CME and CARU. However, a brand new book by Douglas Rushkoff (1997), entitled *Playing the Future: How Kids' Culture Can Teach us to Thrive in an Age of Chaos*, presents the other side of the coin.

Basically, Rushkoff argues that by playing video games and surfing the Internet, children are mastering the skills that will enable them to compete successfully and thrive in tomorrow's workplace and society. Therefore, no limitations such as v-chips or filtering software should be placed on them. Parents and teachers have nothing to worry about. He believes that 'Cybersmart Kids' possess five important skills:

1 An understanding of both the positive and potentially villainous effects of technology.
2 A broad attention range, enabling them to scan for pertinent information.

3   The ability to resist media hypnosis.
4   The ability to distinguish fact from opinion.
5   Superb hand–eye co-ordination.

The viewpoint embodied by Douglas Rushkoff and expressed in his book is evidence that there is a legitimate debate as to whether a problem exists at all and whether children need protection from on-line advertisers. At the very least, his position has validity with respect to teenagers. Children under the age of 12 may not be as 'media savvy' as Rushkoff believes.

A calm, dispassionate analysis of the issues leads to at least three conclusions.

The first, and most important, is that digital kids, despite the fact that they possess the aptitude and abilities to use the new technologies more effectively than adults, are still children and need the maturity, wisdom and guidance of adults. They need to be taught right from wrong and protected from those who would like to exploit, manipulate and use them. They also need to be shielded from commercialism and greed so that they can have a childhood and not be rushed into the adult world.

Second, on-line advertisers are currently getting away with practices that they would not be able to get away with on television, print or radio. This is due to the fact that the Internet is unregulated and interactive. This is enough to send up 50 red flags and panic warnings.

Finally, there are no safeguards available right now to ensure that children will be protected from these advertising practices. It is doubtful that voluntary self-regulation is the answer. Software technology such as IFF is the best hope. CME goes so far as to say that software technology is not the answer because of its costs, and the necessary time it would take to install, maintain, learn how to use, and regularly update.

Perhaps the parents and schools which can afford to install and maintain the Internet in the first place would have the financial resources, time and abilities to purchase, install, use and maintain the software. After all, in the wake of the recent US court opinion, pursuing government regulations does not make much sense.

12.2.4 Interactive media

Early 1995 saw the introduction of one of the first interactive television services on the cable network. A box plays a selection of videos which can be changed by dialling a number; while a fairly basic interactivity, it did mark the transition from passive TV to active.

Interactivity in marketing has been here since the beginning of time: after all, what were smoke signals, if not interactive? A letter to Australia will evoke a response measured in weeks. What has changed, however, is the speed and scope of interactive communication. We can all chatter away on the Internet as if we were all in the same room. However, most people agree that by 2005 interactive media will still be a long way down the list of marketing communication options.

It will be important not to ignore it. Just like video recorders, mobile phones and home computers, everyone will be at it. The interesting thing about the three big technologies (telecommunications, computing and television) coming together is that almost anything will be possible.

12.3 Advertising on television

TV advertising is a very effective medium through which to communicate. First, it is a very regional medium, as advertisers can choose a particular area in which to launch a product and then widen it as sales develop. Secondly, TV commercials are very real – they present life-like situations with which people can readily identify. Finally, TV is unique in being able to offer the viewer, in the comfort of his own home, a professionally produced image, combining vision, movement, sound, timing and colour. However, it is also very transient, being on the screen for only a few seconds, and it is difficult for the viewer to respond directly because there is inevitably going to be a time lapse before any action can be taken. The TV advertisements have to get the message across precisely without becoming boring or persistent because of too much repetition.

12.3.1 TV advertising's effectiveness

Although it is hard to prove any immediate consequences or effects of advertising in a numerical sense, it is possible to measure the effectiveness of single messages.

In some respects the effectiveness or influence of advertising can be attributed to recent technical improvements and developments, changing the significance of the image and visual representations of reality. Over the past 30 years new, sophisticated equipment has begun to produce spectacular and persuasive imagery on screen that now organizes our experiences and understanding. The word 'image' nowadays refers to a fabricated or shaped public impression created with the help of visual techniques.

One can see that images have become more interesting than the original – the shadow becomes the substance. Advertisements seem to encourage extravagant expectations because they are more dramatic and vivid than the reality – they present us with images and then make them seem true. As a result, they confuse our experiences and perceptions of the real world by offering spectacular illusions. They form part of the continual whirling mass of sense impressions which bombard the eye – we can't stop to evaluate all the pieces of sensory input that we receive and can't make all our decisions in rational steps.

However, imagery is still generally considered to be the most effective means of communicating in TV advertising. It is suggested[6] that only 15 per cent of communication in this area is directly verbal; the remaining 85 per cent occurs through non-verbal mechanisms, such as movement, colour, mood, etc. Imagery such as this provides the means for encoding all experiences, the process of which involves all senses.

Many TV commercials consist simply of a spoken announcement with an accompanying picture and caption, and therefore rely less on imagery and more on verbal means of communication. These so-called *simple* advertisements are generally unobjectionable – they contain only core information in a neutral setting. However, some contain more emphasis on visual and aural styles and images and are generally more successful.

In *compound* advertisements, what is mild encouragement in simple ones becomes subtle association and persuasion. Information is still given, but there is more use of imagery and visual communication to do the persuading. The emotions aroused by the general atmosphere should be subtly transferred to the product.

Complex advertisements usually concentrate on the presentation of the background into which the product should merge. The visual and verbal imagery evoke the intended product image, and it is this that is the selling point, not the actual physical product.

Sophisticated advertisements are extensions of the complex. They usually explore hidden or subconscious feelings, and subtle associations are made between product and situation. The visual imagery might be blurred to suggest a dream-like state, and colours or lighting are used to emphasize this.

12.3.2 What do TV advertisements mean?

Analysing the content of advertisements involves looking at both verbal and non-verbal (i.e. visual) aspects of communication and examining the techniques employed in this process, known as the Rhetoric of Advertising. Pictures and images are easier to understand, and generally have more impact and opportunity to communicate mood. Although we usually think of pictures and images as life-like and real, we should be aware that their meaning is constructed and manipulated by the advertiser.

One way of analysing advertisements is, therefore, to classify them according to their themes, or the attitudes they are meant to appeal to. Emotions can be aroused by associating a product with, for example, happy families, rich lifestyles, dreams and fantasy, romance and love, success, beauty, comedy and humour, celebrities or nature. Some advertisements are based on appeals to emotions, made on scientific fact, or on the technique of 'before and after' using the product. Another powerful technique of persuasion is to play on guilt feelings and worry or the fear of being socially ostracized.

When trying to understand the meaning of an advertisement, we must consider not only the elements of which it is made up but also the overall impression that it creates, and the techniques used to create it.

We need to concentrate first on the visual, illustrative material, and then try to perceive links with other elements of the picture, and the verbal means of communication.

Visual communication of meaning

The art critic, Panofsky, studied the imagery and symbols of paintings, and proposed a model for the analysis of the subject matter of visual communication. He suggested that there are three levels of meaning in a visual image:

- The first level is that of *primary subject matter* – light, shape, colour and movement – and the understanding of representation.
- The second level is that of *secondary subject matter* relating to the wider culture, at which all images are linked to themes and concepts.
- The third level involves the *intrinsic meaning* which is arrived at by unpeeling the first and second levels.

This approach is valuable in breaking down the meaning of advertisements and identifying the constituents of each scene and relating them to the concepts of a wider cultural meaning.

An important element in Panofsky's model is the process of *visual perception*. We actively explore, select and organize sensory stimuli in the visual field, and this process affects the recognition and understanding of what we see before us. In order to interpret the meaning, the non-verbal, visual communication patterns have to be perceived.

Verbal communication of meaning: the language of advertising

Advertising language is a manipulative, distorted and loaded language, and its primary aims are to attract our attention, catch our imagination and then dispose us favourably towards the product or service on offer.

The words used in advertising communicate feelings and associations, bring ideas to our mind and describe things in an appropriate manner. We have already seen the importance of brand images, and it is brand names themselves that use words to communicate connotatively.

Sheer repetition of words (or images) is also a powerful instrument of persuasion, as are devices such as slogans, catch-phrases or jingles (e.g. Kellogg's Fruit 'n' Fibre' – 'It's tasty, tasty, very, very tasty'). They are all mechanisms of conveying imagery through language, attracting viewers' attention and also influence the memorability of advertisements and particular brands.

It is not only words that act as verbal communication, the voice of a speaker, seen or heard, is also relevant. This 'tone of voice' of the advertisement generally will sometimes try to recreate the experience of enjoying the product, and should match the image of the product.

Language, being the primary system in normal communication, must not therefore be overlooked in visually dependent TV advertising. Normally, a single commercial uses a combination of communicating mediums, visual and verbal, and both areas should convey the same unique message and connotative meaning to build a complete communication image.

The rhetoric of advertising

Rhetoric is an important part of any analysis of advertising, since it refers to those techniques, visual or verbal, that are designed and employed to persuade and impress people. One can consider that there are four fundamental operations within which all rhetorical figures can be classified, and all of which help gain viewers' attention.

1 *Addition*. This involves operations such as repetition; similarity of images; accumulation of elements within a single image; the opposition of elements within an image; and ambiguity, whereby images play on the opposition between appearance and reality.
2 *Suppression*. Much less common than addition because advertisers rarely wish to suppress their case. However, any absence in advertisements requires the viewer to 'fill in' along the lines suggested by the particular advertisement. Similarly understatement, humour and jokes involve an absent element that needs deciphering. This element therefore requires a deeper level of processing or thought in the perception and encoding process, hence increasing memorability.
3 *Substitution*. The use of images in place of reality, or the slight distortion of reality, is an attention-getting mechanism. Ideas can be transformed into images, or images may be used where there is a continued interplay of two optional or alternative meanings.
4 *Exchange*. This involves two reciprocal substitutions of images or elements, to give a double ambiguous meaning.

We can therefore see the applicability of rhetoric to TV advertisements, and an examination of this is useful in that it draws attention to the constructed nature of them. One can argue that they can all be seen to be based on a number of rhetorical figures, and these formal rhetorical devices should help us to understand how advertising works internally, according to its own specific representational imagery.

In general conclusion, it seems that the 'success' of an advertisement will depend not on its logical propositions but on the kinds of fantasies it offers, and the methods by which they are communicated. The world of advertising is a dream world in which the people and objects are taken out of their material contexts, given new, symbolic meanings and placed on the screen, where they become images.

Advertising appropriates things from the real world and mystifies it, thus depriving us of any understanding of it. The more we are isolated from this reality by the media, the more we seek images from them to give us a sense of social reality, and thus the more we are influenced by their portrayal.

Few people, however, believe, or take seriously the slogans of advertisements: 'Daz with the blue whitener washes cleanest'; 'Heineken reaches the parts other beers can't reach', even though they are effective methods of maintaining brand imagery and brand recall. It is the signifiers of the images of these advertisements – those seen using the product – that are effective. Advertisements offering chances to obtain luxury, happiness and perfection provide the images that we remember, rather than the claims made on behalf of the product. We don't use a product for what it is; we identify with the result, and it is ultimately the images that we are left with, and the images of the slogans, not the products or slogans themselves, that make advertisements so successful.

This is why we must be aware of the structure and content of the advertisements, the way meanings are communicated and the way we are called upon to create this meaning. Only in this way can we understand the way ideology works and how advertising shapes society's values, habits and direction.

12.3.3 Television ratings (TVR)

A 'rating' is the percentage of sets in homes that *can* receive commercial TV (which means virtually all homes in effect) which *are* in fact switched on to a commercial channel at any given time. So a spot which went out at a time when 20 per cent of sets were switched on would achieve 20 TVRs. These are added up to give a cumulative total, so that 400 TVRs would mean that *on average* each household had received the commercial four times. The snag lies in the words 'average' and 'household'. Some households will have received the commercial more than four times, others not at all, and the fact that a *household* received the transmission does not necessarily mean that everyone within that household has seen it.

12.4 Current developments in television[7]

12.4.1 Independent Television Commission (ITC)

Since 1 January 1991 the ITC has been responsible for controlling all aspects of independent commercial TV in the UK, taking over the previous responsibilities of the IBA and the Cable Authority. The ITC is located at 33 Foley Street, London W1P 7LB (0171-255 3000).

12.4.2 Terrestrial television

Channel 3 (ITV)
Channel 3 is split into 14 regions, in each of which one contractor has the sole right to broadcast TV programmes and sell advertising between 9.25 am and 5.59 am the following day. The exception to this is London, where Carlton take the weekday (Monday–Friday) contract and LWT the weekend (Friday evening–Sunday).

Each contractor holds his licence for around ten years. The last re-allocation was in 1991, when licences were awarded on a tender basis to the highest bidder, subject to a quality threshold. Twelve licences remained with their existing contractors, and four changed hands: those for the south and south-east (from TVS to Meridian), the south-west (from TSW to Westcountry TV), the London weekday service (from Thames to Carlton), and the national breakfast service (from TV-am to GMTV).

During the last few years there has been considerable consolidation of advertising sales within ITV, mainly as a result of changes in ownership of the ITV franchises. Carlton, Laser and TSMS have been responsible for selling the various regions.

Programme schedules on Channel 3 stations are broadly similar, with about 70 per cent of programming being the same for all stations at the same time, particularly during peak time. Since 1993 this situation has been consolidated, with the appointment of a network scheduler.

Advertising minutage is an average of seven minutes an hour, with a maximum of seven and a half minutes in peak time.

Channel 4
Channel 4 is a statutory corporation operating under licence from the ITC with a remit to be complementary to (and different from) Channel 3. It is responsible for commissioning its own programming (it has no production facilities) and (since January 1993) for selling its own advertising. If advertising revenue is below 14 per cent of total terrestrial advertising, Channel 3 is responsible for contributing up to 2 per cent more. If it rises above 14 per cent, Channel 4 must pay 50 per cent of the surplus to

Channel 3. In 1995 Channel 4 took 19.6 per cent of total advertising revenue.

Channel 4 is a national channel, but does offer macro-region airtime opportunities for advertisers, which are generally larger than those available to Channel 3.

S4C

The Welsh language channel, S4C, is broadcast on the Channel 4 frequency in Wales (part of the Wales and West area). It started at the same time as Channel 4 and carries a high proportion of Welsh language programming. Programmes carried by both Channel 4 and S4C are often broadcast at different times.

Breakfast TV

The licence for the national breakfast TV service on Channel 3 was awarded to GMTV in 1991 and started in January 1993. Since then, Channel 4 has also been responsible for its own breakfast-time service and advertising sales. Again, the channel can be bought nationally or on a regional basis.

Channel 5

Jointly owned by United News Media, Pearson Television, Warbourg, Pincus & Co and CLT UK, Channel 5 began broadcasting as the fifth terrestrial TV channel in the UK on 30 March 1997.

Initial predictions of an 8 per cent share of viewing have not been realized; C5 now represents just under 5 per cent of commercial impacts. C5 performs best against younger mid-market audiences, and sees its best audiences for one-off sports events (the England versus Poland match had a 20 per cent share of audience nationally), or its flagship 9.00 pm films. At present C5 can only be bought on a national basis and can only be received in 75 per cent of households

Digital Television

In June 1997 the ITC awarded the three Digital Terrestrial TV (DTT) licences to British Digital Broadcasting (BDB), owned by Carlton Communications and the Granada Group. These three DTT multiplexes will be run by the BBC, ITV/C4 and C5/S4C. Here the offering will be 'simulcasts' of the analogue channel, along with wide-screen specialist channels, e.g. BBC 24-hour news. The aim for DTT subscription in the UK by 2006 is a conservative 13 per cent. The BBC's digital broadcasting channel came on air in October 1998.

Teletext

Teletext UK Ltd was awarded the franchise for Teletext services on ITV in 1991. The service took over from Oracle Teletext on 1 January 1993.

12.4.3 Cable television

Cable penetration in the UK is still relatively low. In July 1996, 6.5 per cent of all homes were connected to cable systems (21 per cent of homes passed). There are 114 operational franchises in the UK, almost 20 per cent of which have become active over the past year. The largest operators are shown in Table 12.2.

Table 12.2

| Operator | Homes | | Penetration (%) |
	Passed	Connected	
Telewest	2,012,532	423,959	21.1
NYNEX	1,156,658	226,849	19.6
Comcast	818,997	214,521	26.2
Bell Cablemedia	680,930	138,466	20.3
Videotron	635,062	130,923	20.6
CableTel UK	382,024	100,567	26.3
Telecential	415,644	91,016	21.9
General Cable	440,231	86,003	19.5
Diamond Cable	190,549	44,317	23.3

Advertising and sponsorship
Advertising and sponsorship on all TV channels in the UK are controlled by the ITC, under codes of Advertising Standards, Programme Sponsorship and Rules on Advertising Breaks published in January 1991. These codes apply to both ITV and satellite broadcasters, and incorporate elements of previous rules established by the International Broadcasting Authority (IBA) and the Cable Authority, as well as the European Directive on Television Broadcasting. Sponsorship income for 1995 was £48 million, twice that of 1994.

12.4.4 Direct broadcasting by satellite (DBS)

DBS is the name which is given to television transmissions via medium-to high-powered satellites which can be received on dishes of less than 1 metre diameter, suitable for private homes. It has been available in the UK since February 1989, when Sky TV started as part of the Sky multi-channel package, including the Disney Channel and Paramount TV (Table 12.3).

Subscription income, from both individual subscribers and cable operators (who pay programme licensees for the right to broadcast their programme services), is the main source of income for non-terrestrial licences.

Table 12.3 *English language channels on Astra, Autumn 1996*

Premium channels	Sky multi-channels	Others
Sky Movies	TCC	OVC
The Movie Channel	UK Gold	NBC Superchannel
Sky Movies Gold	UK Living	Eurosport
The Disney Channel	Challenge TV (Fam. Ch.)	CNN
Sky Sports	MTV Europe	TNT/Cartoons
Sky Sports 2	VH-1	Adult Channel
Sky Sports 3	Learning Channel	Playboy TV
Sky One	Nickelodeon	Television X
Sky Two/Nat Geo.	Paramount	Granada Plus
Sky News	History Channel	Granada Good Life
Sky Travel	EBN	Granada Talk TV
Sky Soap	Sci-Fi	Fox Kids
Discovery	CMT Europe	WBN
Bravo/Trouble		

12.5 Buying television time

In some ways media buying is much simpler with television than with the press, since there are only a handful of channels to deal with as distinct from many hundreds of publications. However, it does have complexities of its own and requires great skill on the part of media buyers. One factor in this of course is that although there is intense competition with other media, a TV contractor in the UK has a relative monopoly of TV advertising for their area – if you want to buy TV time to reach homes in that area, you have to buy it from them, although Channel 4, satellite and cable are providing real alternatives.

In addition, the range of choice is much more limited. As we saw earlier, the IBA strictly controls the length, timing and type of advertising. Programme sponsorship was once frowned upon, although Virgin Vodka did sponsor the Friday Night horror film weekend back in 1995. There tends to be stricter control also on the content of advertising – what it says and how it says it: the Independent Television Companies Association (ITCA) have a role to play (*see* Section 15.6.2).

There is, however, considerable choice in how a particular sum of money is spent on TV, and much skill lies in getting the maximum value for money – quite apart from the very important negotiating skills that determine how good a 'buy' can be achieved through sheer buyer pressure and bargaining power.

The basic choices that have to be made in television media planning and buying are:

(a) Length of 'spot', ranging from 7 to 60 seconds (although mainly in 15-second multiples, 15, 30, 45 or 60 seconds; you cannot buy a 17-second or 33-second spot for example). The contractors are becoming much more flexible of late, however.
(b) Time of day. This usually operates on a time segment basis, with 'peak' time being the part of the day with the highest viewing figures; then 'pre-peak', 'post-peak', 'daytime', etc.
(c) Fixed time spots (which usually carry a price premium) or leaving the contractor some degree of flexibility as to when he can run the advertisement.

The complications start to set in when we realize that not only do advertising rates vary by length of spot and time of day, but that 'packages' are available. 'Run of week' means that the contractor decides on which days to screen the commercials even though the time segment may be agreed and this will cost less than insistence on specific days of showing.

Many packages are based on 'Guaranteed Home Impressions', where the contractors can run the commercial when they like and as many times as they like as long as the eventual cumulative audience reaches an agreed figure. There are clearly disadvantages here in that the time-scale and 'bunching' of the transmissions may not be ideal. Moreover, the total audience may have a less than ideal composition (for example because most of the transmissions were in the afternoon period when the 'women and children' component of audiences tends to be higher than average and this was not the main target audience).

12.6 Buying radio time

If we look at the growth in popularity of this medium over the 1990s, we can see that while the total advertising expenditure has grown as a percentage of the total advertising spend on all media, radio has taken a larger share (Table 12.4).

Table 12.4 *Radio expenditure, including production costs*

	1991	1992	1993	1994	1995	1996
£ million expenditure	149	157	194	243	296	344
Percentage of total ad spend	2.0	2.0	2.4	2.7	3.0	3.2

With an increasing number of independent radio stations (some 150) and four national independents, there is plenty of scope for advertising.

Most radio time, except for the four nationals who sell direct, is sold to major advertisers and agencies through one of the eight sales companies. This eases the complexity of buying time rather than buying direct. Scottish Independent Radio Stations (SIRS) handles most of Scotland's radio sales while the others have less of a regional bias. A few stations still sell direct but they tend to be London-based. Alpha 103.2 FM, Coast FM in North Wales, Sabras Sound in the East Midlands and Channel Islands radio are notable exceptions.

While there are plenty of local radio stations carrying local advertising, radio has ceased to be just a local choice. Classic FM announced in February 1998 that it had just become the world's most popular radio station with 5 million regulars, giving a weekly audience of 8 million listeners.

Time is sold on a somewhat similar basis to television, either as specified spots or as packages. The standard type of package is the Total Audience Package (TAP) of 49, 35 or 16 spots, rotated evenly through the day and night-time during the course of the week. There is a growing tendency, especially for the more sophisticated advertisers, to purchase more concisely to catch specific times and audiences, for example peak morning and evening rush-hour times when there is a high level of 'in-car' listening with a predominantly male audience.

12.7 Audience measurement

12.7.1 Television

Introduction
The Broadcasters' Audience Research Board Ltd (BARB) was set up in August 1980 by the BBC and ITCA (now the ITV Association) and started operating in August 1981 to provide a single system for TV audience research in the UK. The BARB television audience measurement contract is held jointly by Audits of Great Britain (AGB) and RSMB and was updated in 1991 to cope with the changes in the market. RSMB have responsibility for the Establishment Survey and for panel recruitment, AGB have the data supply and data processing contracts. The measurement of audience appreciation of television programmes is carried out for the BBC, the ITV companies and Channel 4 by RSL (Research Services Ltd) under contract to BARB.

Establishment survey: sample and methodology
Forty thousand people selected by multi-stage probability sampling, stratified by defined geographic broadcasting boundaries, taking into account differences between overlap and non-overlap areas and incorporating the

Pinpoint classification system. Data are collected continuously throughout the year.

Establishment survey: information collected
The Establishment Survey is used to measure the size and characteristics of the television audience, providing the basis for projections of the universe data to be used in the calculation of results.

Continuous audience measurement: sample and methodology
Four thousand four hundred and thirty-five households selected from the Establishment Survey. Sampled using a 24-cell demographic matrix taking into account average weight of viewing within each cell. There is reduced sampling of C2DE early school leavers and inactive, no longer working groups. There are also regional controls (both ITV and BBC) on the panel. Data are collected by means of 'peoplemeters', with a remote detection unit (RDU) attached to the TV sets and video recorders in use. The RDU monitors TV channel and VCR usage for every second it is switched on. A remote handset is used by viewers (either household members or guests) to record every time they enter or leave a room where the television is on. All information is fed into the meter and stored until it is collected via an automatic telephone link between 2 and 6 am.

Continuous audience measurement: information collected
Viewing data collected from the panel households are merged with data from post-transmission logs of TV programmes (for all terrestrial and satellite channels) and TV commercials (for channels concerned). Data are provided electronically or in hard copy reports.

BARB is currently located at Glenthome House, Hammersmith Grove, London W6 0ND (0181-741 9110).

12.7.2 Radio research

The Joint Industry Committee on Radio Research (JICRAR) was set up in 1974 and comprises representatives from AIRC (Association of Independent Radio Contractors), the IPA, AMCO and the ISBA. Research in independent local radio (ILR) is carried out by RSGB.

Sample sizes are based on population within each area, with the maximum size on which a station is able to publish results being 500 adults. Apart from the station-specific listening information, the sample are also asked about non-ILR stations, TV viewing and local and national press.

Age, sex and class breakdowns are similar to the National Readership Surveys. There is also an on-line system called RATS (Radio Analysis Terminal System). It enables a buyer to run listening for non-standard demographics, schedule duplication between two services and reach and frequency analysis for any service to be extracted.

12.8 Direct response television (DRTV)

According to research by British Telecommunications and Channel 4, the number of advertisements carrying telephone numbers rose from 12 per cent in 1993 to 19 per cent in 1995, and this growth was found to be due to a wider mix of sectors using DRTV. The need to demonstrate clearly the return on investment in marketing, combined with the investment in database technologies, has led inexorably to the use of responsive media. TV has become central, as it yields high volumes of data very quickly.

While lead generation remains an important function of DRTV, there is an emerging distinction between two types of responsive commercials – leaving aside one-stage direct selling, which has been priced out of all but the satellite marketplace. On the one hand there is the more mature market of DRTV, and on the other is brand response.

For DRTV one is looking for as large a response as possible, but for brand response one is more discerning. For example, Orange wanted ABC1 males aged 34. This audience would not be watching late afternoon game shows like *Countdown*. Orange wanted different airtime, a change to the product offer, different programmes and end breaks. So, by looking at the lifetime value of the customer, rather than just the response rates, the cost can be justified.

This is a long way from the traditional approach favoured by financial products or charities; yet even they are willing to consider spending £75,000 on airtime if it ultimately produces £500,000 worth of legacies or covenants.

The infrastructure for handling calls is unable, in many cases, to handle the responses generated from peak-time TV slots. It is estimated that as many as 30 per cent of calls are being lost, so adopting a low-key approach may be the only way to avoid alienating so many customers who cannot get through. For this reason, many of the direct response advertisements appearing on TV are aired during off-peak periods and this has an impact on the media planning and buying (*see* Chapter 14).

12.9 Summary

1 Technology has driven changes in the way people live their lives in a way not foreseen a decade ago. This has important implications for advertising-financed media and, therefore, advertisers.
2 Terrestrial television has seen many changes in recent years and digital technology is poised to make the next big change.

3   The Internet has grown tremendously in the past decade and its use as
     an advertising vehicle will grow.
4   The on-line advertising to children has fuelled lively debate.
5   What advertising does and how it does it still interests many.
6   A variety of measurement methodologies track the viewer.

12.10 References

1 BARB/Young & Rubicam.
2 *Financial Times*, 11 December 1996.
3 Reported in *Marketing Week*, 8 January 1998.
4 Reported in *connected@telegraph.co.uk*, a weekly supplement to the newspaper in June 1995.
5 Bickerton, P., Bickerton, M. and Pardesi, U., *Cybermarketing*, Butterworth-
   Heinemann, 1996.
6 Bailey, A., *An Evaluation of the Use of Imagery as Means of Communication
   in TV Advertising*, Durham Business School, Occasional Paper 9203, 1992.
7 *The Marketing Pocket Book*, NTC Publications, 1998.

12.11 Further reading

Aaker, David A., *Managing Brand Equity*, New York: Free Press, 1991.
Ries, Al and Trout, Jack, Positioning: *The Battle for Your Mind*, New York:
Warner Books, 1982.

12.12 Questions for discussion

1   If you build a better 'webpage', then the world will beat a path to your
     door. Discuss.
2   How would you ensure that the policies recommended to the Federal
     Trade Commission were adopted in your home market?
3   Based on your recent experience of television advertising, which were,
     in your opinion, the most effective, and why?
4   What are the implications for the television advertiser of the advances
     of digital technologies?
5   Discuss the limitations of the various television audience measure-
     ment systems.

Chapter 13

Other media and media terms

By the end of this chapter you will:

- Understand the range and creative characteristics of outdoor media;
- Understand how poster sites are booked in the UK;
- Have explored the variety of transport advertising and its audience reach;
- Understand the profile of cinema audiences;
- Have reviewed the costs of a wide range of alternative media, from aerial banners being towed by aircraft to a scoreboard at Wembley Stadium;
- Understand a wide variety of everyday media terms.

13.1 Whose other media?

Chapters 11 and 12 reviewed 'the main media' of print (newspapers and magazines) and broadcasting (TV and radio). They are termed 'main media' because they take by far the biggest share of advertising expenditure, both in the UK (*see* Section 1.3.2) and also in most other countries. Thus for the majority of advertisers, they represent the most important media and the ones demanding most scrutiny to ensure cost-effective expenditure.

Section 1.3.3, however, pointed out that below-the-line expenditure is growing at a much faster rate than above-the-line expenditure. Sales promotion activity in particular (*see* Section 8.4) is a very important medium in some marketing programmes, as are some of the other forms of below-the-line activities reviewed in Chapter 8.

What lies beneath the overall figures showing the total allocation of expenditures is the important fact that the various media will have differing levels of importance to different advertisers. Thus, some companies rely entirely on direct mail as a means of communicating with their customers. To some the annual exhibition is vital. Many 'industrial' marketing companies (e.g. in specialized medical products such as contact lenses) rely heavily on seminars, conferences and papers in professional journals as their main method of communication.

In other words one company's 'main media' may be a complete waste of money to another and its 'other media' a vital link with its key customers.

Part of the problem here is that it is usually the big expenditures by large agencies on behalf of multinational clients that get written up and hit the headlines. Their campaigns are seen by millions and are of general interest. They may often too be the main ingredient in the marketing mix.

The 'lesser' media, however, are just as important within the specialized marketing mix of which they form part. So a broadly based knowledge of advertising must include some understanding of the role of all media. Two of them which frequently occupy a 'support' role to the press and broadcast media but which may sometimes stand alone are 'outdoor' – posters and transport advertising – and the cinema. So we look at those first before briefly reviewing a wide range of media not mentioned elsewhere in this book.

13.2 Outdoor advertising

This term embraces a very wide range of advertising and promotional activities. This form of advertising has an almost infinite variety, ranging from hand-painted signs gracing a roadside vegetable stand to the elaborate displays in Times Square. In recent years it has expanded to include such diverse forms as taxis (not strictly transport media like railways and underground), parking meters and petrol pump handles. There are essentially four main categories:

1   *Posters* (*see* Section 13.2.1).
2   *Painted bulletins* – similar to posters but usually larger and individually painted rather than printed in bulk.
3   *Signs* – on the outside of stores advertising what they sell and roadside signs for service stations, motels, etc.
4   *Spectaculars* – the large illuminated signs on large buildings in city centres.

In the UK, the term 'outdoor' usually also embraces advertising on trains, buses, stations, etc. – but can be categorized separately as 'transit' advertising although in the UK it is usually called transport advertising.

Outdoor advertising covers a variety of individual media in many different locations. The major section of the business consists of the conventional poster, but there are plenty of other possibilities; bus sides and interior panels, railway and underground sites and panels, illuminated signs, 'poster motors', balloons, sky-writing, etc. Even more exotic possibilities exist, of course, ranging from sandwich-men to suitably decorated cattle grazing beside railway lines. One company produced the 'Lamb-Mac', a specially designed plastic covering rather like a black bin-liner used to cover new-born lambs to protect them from the chilling effects of wind and rain. Printed on the side was an advertisement for 'CopperCaps' capsules, a copper product given to older lambs and calves to protect them from copper deficiencies – a prime site for neighbouring farmers!

In individual special circumstances any one of these techniques – and the many more implied – could be used creatively to great effect. In particular this whole area presents great opportunities for imaginative promotion in limited localities and with restricted budgets. However, the most frequent uses of outdoor advertising and the majority of the expenditure fall into the two main categories of posters and transport advertising.

13.2.1 Posters

The term 'posters' normally refers to pre-printed sheets which are 'posted' or pasted up onto boards on a variety of sites which can be hired. Sites are available in large numbers in most towns and there are around 200,000 poster sites in the UK of varying sizes and qualities, half of which are considered permanent and key sites.

One of the advantages of posters is that they can be used very selectively, to display messages in particular towns, types of locality and even near specific shops (where they can provide an invaluable timely reminder to people in the throes of a shopping expedition). A limitation to this flexibility is that many prime sites are booked on a Till Countermanded (TC) basis by advertisers using them as a long-term medium and so may not be available on a short-term basis.

Another advantage is that posters provide a large, colourful and dramatic reminder of the campaign theme. Usually (except on railway platforms, etc.) they are seen by a passing audience and so the copy has to be extremely short, which can be a limitation. On the other hand they may achieve a high level of repetition if placed on busy commuter routes.

Audience characteristics
Outdoor posters are a mass audience medium rather than a selective medium. A group of posters, located in high traffic areas and distributed throughout the market area, will reach a significant proportion of adults in the market (*see* Table 13.1).

Although outdoor is not highly selective, there are certain groups who are more likely to be exposed to it than others. People who drive automobiles are more often exposed to posters because posters are most often placed along roadsides. This also means that the audience is probably more heavily weighted with working people, adults, and men.

Outdoor can be a geographically selective medium. It can be purchased on a market-by-market basis so that coverage fits the advertiser's distribution area. In addition, the location of individual posters can sometimes be specified, permitting the advertiser to emphasize certain neighbourhoods in a market. For example, an outdoor advertiser particularly interested in reaching blue-collar workers might concentrate on poster locations near access roads to local factories, or an advertiser of a grocery product might attempt to rent posters located near shopping centres to give a last-minute reminder to shoppers.

Creative characteristics

It is important to remember that the audience is exposed to an outdoor advertisement for only a very brief span of time, so the message must be very short and very clear. Much of the communication in outdoor advertising is through use of symbols rather than words; outdoor is definitely not an appropriate medium for long or complex messages. Outdoor usually serves as a reminder and is frequently used to supplement another medium, such as magazines or television, that can provide a more detailed message.

Outdoor allows the use of colour, and, because of its size, also allows for some striking effects. In the Guinness 'Guinless' campaign a few years back, they used eight attractive female models standing behind real deckchairs copying a frequently used 48-sheet poster on the A4 at Earls Court. Their waving stopped the traffic!

Another unfavourable characteristic of outdoor is the environmental quality that the medium lends to the message. The outdoor medium does not lend prestige to the product as does, for example, a quality magazine. The association, in fact, may be a negative one among those people who feel that outdoor advertising clutters and obliterates the natural beauty of the environment. One result has been enactment of federal and state legislation that has forced removal and relocation of posters in many locations.

The advertiser should also recognize that outdoor is a non-intrusive medium. Despite the great frequency with which people pass by an outdoor bulletin, they may not perceive it. Unless the outdoor message is provocative and changed regularly, it has a tendency to become a part of the background. This is a particular problem for the more permanent forms of outdoor, such as painted bulletins and signs.

In a RSL Signpost research survey of 300 interviews with respondents within the M25 area around London in 1995, they were asked if they could remember a poster shown to them with the logo removed and then if they could recall the brand name. The wide variations in awareness and recognition were astonishing. The best remembered posters scored far more highly than the lowest within each of the product sectors, while the variations can be just as high when it comes to attributing a brand name to a poster. These variations occurred within each category, irrespective of product sector, weight of expenditure or any other classification. They refer purely to the impact in the consumer's mind and are due primarily to variations in creative context and form. Not surprisingly, those posters that were well branded scored highest in the recognition and attribution tables. It seems that branding has a greater impact on effectiveness than expenditure levels.

Posters in the UK are booked through four major contractors, AdRail, Maiden, Mills & Allen and TDI, who in turn deal with the very many contractors – often operating on a fairly local basis – who own other sites. Standard poster sizes are mainly based on the 4-sheet (60" × 40") with 12-, 16- and 48-sheet multiples. There is a tendency for more and more posters to fall into the 4-sheet or 48-sheet categories. This is mainly through town-planning constraints, together with the growth of 'Adshels' – 4-sheet posters on bus-stop shelters in major towns.

Posters are frequently bought on a package basis, often consisting of PSCs (pre-selected packages) each consisting of a certain number of selected-size (4 or 48, for example) sheet sites designed to provide a given coverage of all adults in one week. Campaigns are normally booked on a half-monthly basis. The Maiden 800, which is 800 × 48-sheet sites nationally, gives a coverage of 26.9 per cent of all adults who are estimated to see it (frequency) 8.1 times at a package cost of £220,000.

As in the United States, large, individually prepared 'bulletin boards' are available in some locations – typically on routes from airports into major towns for example, and a recent innovation is a set of three-dimensional panels that rotate from time to time to present a change of poster. On station platforms especially back-lit posters are sometimes available. But all of these are 'specials', not the norm.

13.2.2 Poster audience research (POSTAR)

This is the industry system for assessing the audience of the 100,000 stationary roadside panels. Controlled by POSTAR Ltd and funded by the Outdoor Advertising Association (OAA) and Council of Outdoor Specialists (COS), it offers:

- target audience demographics for 28 groups nationally, by ISBA TV overlap areas;
- based on net (visibility adjusted) likelihood to see data;
- available on CD-ROM disk for planning, buying and post-campaign evaluation;
- also includes physical proximity data on each panel, e.g. type/named retailer, station, etc.;
- data continuously updated through ongoing audit.

Table 13.1 *Sample data of monthly net coverage*

	All adults (%)	ABC1 (%)	Adults 15–34 (%)	Adults 35–54 (%)
1,200 average 48-sheet panels	28.2	30.0	31.2	29.5
3,000 average 6-sheet panels	38.3	40.3	41.9	39.8

Outdoor Site Classification Audience Research (OSCAR)
OSCAR can provide coverage and frequency calculations for 171 demographic groups on a national level and 21 demographic groups on a regional basis.

The research also delves into the exposure to other media so that multi-media campaigns can be evaluated.

13.2.3 Transport advertising

Poster sites are available on railway and Underground stations and because their audience is temporarily immobilized and able to concentrate for a few minutes, they are often used for detailed announcements, like concert programmes. In some areas a complete bus can be used as an advertising message: in Norwich, a provincial city 130 miles north-east of London, one red bus was painted by hand to look as if it was made from children's building bricks (Lego) for the promotion of a toy shop prior to Christmas.

The main part of transport advertising, however, consists of bus backs and sides (with tube cards – inside Underground trains – having some significance in London). There are two recent innovations worthy of mention.

Mega rears
These are vinyl-clad bus backs, including windows, which are regularly used by fast-moving consumer goods, motor, fashion and film advertisers. A national double-deck bus back would cost £650 per month for the site in 1998, with production extra at £2,000 per bus.

Wrapped buses
Here the whole bus, including bodywork and windows, is covered with computer-generated vinyl. This is reserved for training buses only in London. The vinyl graphics ensure that the artwork is displayed as one coherent message that delivers unparalleled visual impact. The roof is excluded. In 1998 the cost per bus was £15,000 per national double-deck bus for a whole year, with a further £17,000 for production.

Like posters (*see* Section 13.2.1) transport advertising can be used selectively and locally. It is in fact used much more frequently by local traders wanting to cover their own immediate area. In large conurbations like London, it is possible to buy bus sides on selected routes.

Bus research
According to some research provided by TDI Advertising Ltd, the agency that handles national bus and London Underground advertising, buses reach a wider audience than regional radio or newspapers (Table 13.2).

Table 13.2

Media	% of adults
Buses	69
Local weekly freesheet	68
Commercial radio	64
Local weekly, paid for	39
Any regional evening	25
Any regional morning	10

Source: BMRB/TGI, Rajar, TGI National BUSADS
- Buses: typical medium weight campaign
- Newspapers: maximum reach based on advertising in every regional/local paper
- Radio: maximum reach of all commercial radio stations combined

National BUSADS (Bus Audience Data System), only available since 1990, is a coverage and frequency system extended nationally from London BUSADS. The model calculates the audience for bus advertising not only at a national level but also by TV region, conurbation or district level. National BUSADS consists of regional variables such as population density, demographics, number of bussed roads, total number of buses, bus mileage and data from the National Travel Survey about people's travel habits.

Table 13.3 *Monthly coverage of adults in London TV region*

Panel type	Number of panels	All adults (%)	ABC1 (%)	Adults 15–24 (%)
Double deck side	750	79	82	81
T side	500	82	85	84
Lower rear	750	81	85	83
Upper rear	1,100	83	86	84

Source: BUSADS 1997

London Underground research

Introduced in 1989, Tube Research Audience Classification (TRAC) is a database of audience coverage and frequency on the London Underground. Five thousand Underground users recruited at 220 stations on both the London Underground and Docklands Light Railway completed 28-day travel diaries. Each year the sample is re-weighted to Target Group Index by age, sex, social class and normal frequency of travel. Apart from the normal demographic information, details are gathered on employment, shopping habits and visits to the cinema, theatres and museums.

Table 13.4 *Monthly coverage of adults in the London ITV region*

Panel size	Number of panels	All adults (%)	ABC1 (%)	All adults 15–24 (%)
48	50	23	29	32
16	300	30	36	39
12	125	27	33	36
4	450	31	38	41
6 sheets illuminated	100	28	34	36
Tubecar panels	8,000	31	38	42
Escalator panels	700	28	35	38

Source: TRAC 1996

By far the most expensive billboard in the world is the Formula One motor car. The car's main sponsor will get the prime advertising sites in return for funding the team for between £11 million and £15 million for a season. The engine supplier, which spends up to £30 million, gets next choice, followed by component and tyre suppliers – but sponsors will pay a minimum of £500,000. The cost of your logo on the nose fin will cost you that; the tail fin costs £1.6 million. Even so, these 200 mph billboards are still the greatest moving poster in the world, with upwards of 1 billion television viewers for each race.

13.3 Cinema

Expenditure on cinema advertising is a tiny proportion of the total in the UK (0.7 per cent in 1996, a rise from 0.5 per cent in 1991) and in most other countries – although in a few it rises to around 5 per cent. Fundamentally the availability of television has killed off the cinema as a main source of entertainment for the majority of people. Even in countries (India for example) where the ownership of television sets is very low, there is often a large number of communal sets available to large audiences.

The appeal of the cinema is the films themselves, and with films such as *Goldeneye* taking £3.6 million at the box office in its first weekend there are some blockbusters around. For the advertiser, the appeal is the audience these films attract. In the UK, cinema audiences are predominantly young adults, and affluent ones at that. With the audience completely dominated by the sheer scale and power of the environment, cinema can be a most impactful and memorable media choice.

Table 13.5 *Adult audience composition, January–December 1996, percentage population profile*

	Average audience	UK population		Average audience	UK population
Males	51	49	Class AB	33	21
Females	49	51	Class C1	35	28
Age 15–24	41	15	Class C2	16	22
Age 25–34	29	20	Class DE	16	29
Age 35+	30	65			

Moreover, the coverage and frequency through using all screens can, for the younger adult audience, be quite high (Table 13.6).

Table 13.6 *Coverage and frequency (using all screens), January–December 1996*

Target audience	8 weeks duration		16 weeks duration	
	% cover	Av. OTS	% cover	Av. OTS
15–24 adults	43.8	2.23	58.4	3.34
15–24 males	42.6	2.39	55.9	3.64
15–24 females	44.7	2.08	60.5	3.08
15–24 ABC1	53.8	2.35	69.8	3.62

The cinema, therefore, is mainly used as a selective means of advertising to these audiences the kind of products for which they are an important market – soft drinks and the snack foods eaten with them; jeans, motorcycles and banks (anxious to catch the attention of the new wage-earners who, having once chosen their bank, typically stay with it for life).

Provided this audience is suitable for the product, the cinema does have a great deal to offer as a medium. A 'captive' audience, with the large screen giving great opportunities for creative and dramatic presentation.

Another great advantage is that cinema advertising can be local and hence is available to local traders at reasonable cost (often using simple slides or pre-made films to which their name can be added in the 'voice-over'). For them the fact that relatively few adults attend may not be so important, since it could still be the cheapest way of reaching them dramatically in a small area – a TV area for example would be far bigger than the one or two towns a retailer or local restaurant might draw his business from. In 1997, the cost of a 30 second slot in central London would cost £139.00 per week against the rest of the UK at £87.00.

Cinema advertising is booked in the UK through a limited number of contractors and may be booked on a package basis, with many variants. The advertising can be bought by individual cinema, by region or nationally, and for any length of time from a week upwards. Each commercial will be shown once every performance. An increasingly popular method of buying cinema is in packages linked to major films such as *Titanic* that are guaranteed to get large audiences. Similar packages for children's products can be bought with Disney Films.

Cinema advertising commercials are shown within one reel which is screened at all performances (except children's matinees), with the house lights down, prior to the main feature film. You can buy screen time in this reel on the basis of standard time-lengths of 15, 30, 45 and 60 seconds. Longer time-lengths can usually be accommodated, subject to negotiation.

13.3.1 Cinema audience research

The Cinema Advertising Association represents the cinema advertising contractors in the UK and regularly publishes admission figures and audience composition. The admissions are based on Department of Industry figures and audience breakdowns, frequency of attendance, etc. on NRS and TGI sources (*see* Sections 11.2.2 and 11.2.4). The TGI information includes product usage data among heavy, light and medium cinema-goers and non-cinema-goers. Contractors will make actual admission figures achieved by specific campaigns available provided twenty or more cinemas have been used.

CAVIAR (Cinema Video Industry Audience Research)
The first CAVIAR study was conducted in 1983. The main CAVIAR survey is carried out annually, funded mainly by the CAA (Cinema Advertising Association) and researched by BMRB International from 1992.

It researches the entire film market, from cinema to video tapes, both rented and bought, and contains information on television, satellite and cable watching. It also covers the readership of newspapers and magazines.

CAVIAR is one of the only regular surveys to cover children, in that it researches the child audience right down to the age of 7 (and sometimes even younger). The research is based on a sample of 3,000 individuals aged 7+ spread throughout the UK.

13.4 Minor media

Outdoor advertising (*see* Section 13.2) covered a very wide range of activities. It can be extended indefinitely. Many companies buy poster sites on football grounds, athletics tracks, ice rinks, etc., especially when a major sporting event with TV coverage might get the name viewed in millions of homes – even across the world in some cases.

But the opportunities for advertising are limitless – book-matches, litterbins, bingo hall and theatre programmes, directories of all kinds and right down to church magazines. While many of these are of great importance to some advertisers (the village shop or the local undertaker might derive considerable business from their advertisement in the church magazine for example) they do not merit much attention as part of the total advertising scene.

- *Aerial (banner)*: banner construction charge from £60/towing charge from £270 per hour.
- *Airport lightbox*: London Heathrow from £200,000 per annum.
- *Airline in-flight television*: KLM TV programmes per two months per 30-second spot: news £13,529/magazine £11,863.
- *Balloon displays*: £800 per balloon per day.
- *Balloon releases*: from £850/printed helium balloons from £85 per 1,000.
- *Bus tickets*: colour advertisements from £1.50–£3.00 per 1,000, depending on volume.
- *Cloakroom*: above hand-basins/dryers £75 per A4 poster per 28 days.
- *Cricket*: Test grounds from £7,000 per board per season.
- *Football*: per board per match: BSkyB live games from £630/BBC highlights from £1,000.
- *Golf*: inside holes from £156 per month/tee signs from £250 per annum.
- *Hospitals*: waiting room posters (A1 size) £888 per poster per year.
- *Motor*: poster 48-sheet advertising van from £255 per day.
- *Post Office*: DRTV (continuous video tape) £9,000 30-second advertising (five weeks) DRTV and leaflet dispensing as DRTV plus £7,500 (five weeks).
- *Rugby Union*: 5 Nations grounds from £5,000 per board per season.
- *Taxi cabs*: per month: interior panel from £7 per month/dispenser units from £12/exteriors from £30; liveried taxis £5,000 per annum excluding production.

- *Video tapes*: cover, front and back £128,000 for three-month period (Blockbuster Express 595 stores, 9 million rentals).
- *Wembley Stadium*: scoreboard from £250 per 10 × 15-second slots.
- *Teletext*: full page per week: national ITV £4,800/Channel 4 £3,850.

Sources: BRAD, August 1997; Organizations concerned, 1996, 1997

13.5 Some media terms

One of the problems for newcomers to or students of the advertising business is the mass of jargon that exists and which those in the business tend to use very freely. In the media area it is particularly rife. It will be useful to introduce some of it before going on in Chapter 14 to deal with media planning and buying, where some of the terms explained here will be extensively used.

Advanced (early) booking discount rate
A reduced rate for advertising booked in advance, either by a specified number of weeks or by a given date in the month preceding transmission. Usually given as a fixed percentage off the rate card but occasionally separate advanced booking rates are offered.

Air date
The broadcast date of a TV or radio commercial.

Airtime
The time available for transmission of programmes and commercials in a contractor's area. Thus, an agency buys airtime comprising individual spots for an advertising campaign.

Attention factors
Research-based factors applied to the BARB-reported audience to allow for distractions or breaks in viewing.

Audience composition
The profile or number of different population sub-groups that comprise the audience to a given medium/media group.

Audit
Normally used in one of three contexts: (a) audited circulations, (b) in-home audit – counting the household's stock or consumption of goods, (c)

retail audit – check on display, stock-holdings or purchase at retail outlets.

Average issue readership
Number of people who claim to have seen or looked at a publication within the last relevant issue period, i.e. the last 24 hours in the case of a daily newspaper, seven days for weeklies, a month for monthlies, etc.

Basic rates
The price for spots bought according to day and time of transmission.

Bonus spot/airtime
A free spot given when a TV contractor makes a mistake in a previous transmission. Sometimes allowed for in rate cards at times of low demand to supplement a booked campaign.

Broad (segment) spot
A spot booked in a given time segment. The contractor usually negotiates in which particular commercial break the spot is transmitted.

Cancellation
Cancellation of bookings, which is normally permitted without penalty up to six or eight weeks in advance of transmission. Thereafter different sliding scales of penalties apply.

Card rates
Quoted rates for advertising. The negotiated cost of a commercial spot may be subject to one or more discounts.

Circulation
Number of copies of each issue of a publication distributed either by sale or free – *see* 'Controlled Circulation'.

Commercial break
A break in a television or radio transmission (theoretically natural) during which advertisements are transmitted.

Commission
A 15 per cent deduction from quoted rates allowed to recognized advertising agencies by commercial TV stations. The advertiser may negotiate partial repayment of commission or pay additional fees to the agency.

Controlled circulation
The distribution free of charge of a publication to a member of a professional association, or to people who are selected because of their position, job-function or profession. A publication that is not available to the public at large.

CPI – cost per inquiry
Total cost of mailing or advertisement divided by the number of inquiries received.

CPT – cost per thousand
Cost of reaching a thousand readers/viewers/listeners with a given advertisement.

Coverage
The proportion (expressed in percentage terms) of a target audience having an opportunity to see/hear the advertising.

Cumulative audience
Net – has the same meaning as coverage. Gross – the sum of the audience to all the individual advertisements in the campaign.

Date-plan
Plan showing when and where the advertisements in a campaign will appear. Largely replaced by 'Schedule'.

Demographics
A description of a population or a market in terms of age, sex, socio-economic class, location, etc. The characteristics of a market or audience.

Duplication
The extent to which the audience/readership of one medium overlaps with that of another. For example, between programmes on television, or readers of publication A with those of publication B, or between TV and press.

Exposure (advertisement)
The actual exposure of the advertisement to the member of the target audience. The conversion of an 'opportunity-to-see' into an impact. Not currently measured by our standard media surveys. (*See* 'Exposure Value' and 'Impacts'.)

Exposure value
A value given to a medium to allow for those with a specific chance of seeing the advertisement, e.g. 'present in room during commercial break' or 'opening the spread of the publication in which the advertisement appears'.

Frequency
The number of times the target audience has an opportunity to see the campaign, expressed over a period of time.

Frequency distribution
Target audience broken down by number of advertisement exposures, e.g. 10 per cent had 5 opportunities to see the advertisement, 15 per cent – 4, 25 per cent – 3, etc., often shown as follows:

Saw	0	1	2	3	4	5	
%	20	10	20	25	15	10	= 100%

Impact(s)
The actual exposure of the advertisement to a member of the target audience. When an 'opportunity-to-see' is deemed to have been taken. After the qualifying factor has been applied to a media vehicle's total audience, e.g. the publication in which the advertisement appears has an average issue readership of 500,000 and average spread traffic of 85 per cent, therefore the number of advertisement 'impacts' will be $500{,}000 \times 0.85 = 425{,}000$ (impacts).

Impressions
Once misleadingly interchangeable with either 'impacts' or OTS, but now falling into disuse except in the buying and selling of TV airtime as in 'guaranteed home impressions' (GHI).

Intensity (of reading)
Degree of thoroughness with which a publication is read. Can be estimated via page traffic or a picture scale illustrating the proportion claimed to have been read. The latter has in the past been used experimentally in the NRS, but is no longer in use.

Market weight
Value given to a section of the population based on actual or probable product consumption/purchase, when assessing media vehicles.

Media weight
A value, applied to the readership of a publication, to express its worth in

terms of any or all of: (a) reader traffic, (b) reproduction, (c) editorial environment, (d) circulation trends.

Narrow cast
All uses of a TV other than receiving a signal through an aerial (broadcast), e.g. local cable programmes, video games, etc.

Net Coverage
Proportion of target audience having the opportunity to see at least one advertisement in a campaign.

OTS (H)
Opportunity to see (hear) (OTS (H)) an advertisement. The media vehicle audience. As an example, the issue readership of a magazine would be considered to have had an 'opportunity-to-see' an advertisement appearing in that particular issue.

Normally shown as an average OTS among the audience reached, such as '80 per cent coverage with an average OTS of 4' . Not interchangeable with the term 'impact(s)', which is a more precise definition of actual advertisement exposure.

Overlap area
An area where two or more ITV stations can be received.

Penetration
Once synonymous with 'coverage' or 'reach', but now falling out of use as a media term. It is, however, used widely in other marketing contexts, such as the proportion of housewives purchasing a product, i.e. 'Product A has a market penetration of 30 per cent'.

Pre-empt structure
The theory of the pre-empt system for buyers is that the final cost will be governed by demand. If a buyer books a spot at a low rate but another is prepared to pay a higher rate for it, the former can be pre-empted and he loses the spot.

Profile
The composition of the readership or audience, which sum to 100 per cent. For instance '20 per cent of the readers are aged 16–24 years, as opposed to 5 per cent of the 16–24 years age group who are readers'. The latter percentage is the 'coverage', 'reach' or 'penetration' figure.

Programme schedule
A schedule of programme plans usually issued four times a year by the TV contractor, which the TV buyer can use to estimate audiences when deciding which spots to book.

Ratings (rating points)
Normally television – the percentage of the potential TV audience who are viewing at a given time, or the percentage of ITV homes with sets switched on at a given time.

Reach
See 'Coverage'.

Response function
The numerical relationship expressing the value of successive advertising exposures. Normally shown as a curve relating advertisement frequency to sales. Response functions seek to place numerical values on the effect of 1, 2, 3, 4, etc. impacts.

Schedule
A media schedule – a list of media vehicles, usually with accompanying data, such as insertion dates, rates, etc. (*See* also 'Date Plan'.)

Selectivity
A media vehicle's ability to select particular audience categories, i.e. regional selectivity, age selectivity, etc.

TVR
Television Rating (*see* 'Ratings').

Target (universe audience)
The people or market that the campaign is designed to reach.

Target ratings
The total number of ratings a time buyer aims to achieve by area in a given time.

Viewdata
Any system that links TV screens to central computers by means of telephone lines. The user can call up different computers, select pages of data and send messages back to the computer.

13.6 Summary

1 Although most expenditure goes on the press and the broadcast media, other media may be far more important to particular advertisers in specific circumstances.
2 Posters and transport advertising can be used on their own but are mainly used as support media because of the high level of repetition and hence reinforcement of the main message which they can provide.
3 Cinema audiences in the UK are predominantly young adults and it is therefore used for the kind of products for which they are a prime target audience. It is also used on a restricted basis by local traders.
4 Both outdoor advertising and cinema can be used selectively to provide local cover where it is required.
5 There is an infinite variety of additional 'minor media' which may have a role to play in specific situations but which are not a significant part of the total advertising scene.
6 Section 13.5 provides a glossary of some key terms which are used in media selection and buying (*see* Chapter 14).

13.7 Further reading

Nylen, David W., *Advertising: Planning, Implementation and Control*, South Western Publishing Co., Cincinnati, 1975.
Nylen's book provides a very good analysis of the various media and although it is American based, the main insights are universally relevant.
Davis, Martyn, *The Effective Use of Advertising Media*, Business Books, 1981.
Davis again provides a useful list of sources of information.
Ogilvy, David, *Ogilvy on Advertising*, London: Pan Books, 1983.
Doyle, Peter, *Marketing Management & Strategy*, Hemel Hempstead: Prentice Hall International (UK) Limited, 1994.

13.8 Questions for discussion

1 Describe the relative advantages and disadvantages of four of the following media groups:
   (a) independent television;
   (b) IBA radio;
   (c) women's magazines;
   (d) popular newspapers;
   (e) cinema;
   (f) posters.

Answers must include some indication of the coverage possible and broad costs which apply in each situation.

2 Select any of the 'minor media' referred to in Section 13.4 and consider in what circumstance it could be a valuable advertising medium.

3 Discuss the ways in which:
   (a) the national press;
   (b) commercial television;
   (c) the poster industry;
   provide evidence and facilities to help the media buyer make his commercial decision from these media.

4 Comment on the use of 'outdoor media' by any current advertiser of your choice. In particular consider why this particular medium appears to have been included and its likely role within the total media schedule.

Chapter 14

Media buying, planning and scheduling

'There is, in my opinion, no distinction at all between a sales person and a buyer. They are both the same. Buyers have to sell themselves, their media department, their client to the media salesperson. The media salesperson has to be a buyer to listen to the rationale as to why he should accept the argument from the so called buyer.'

Martin Lester, ISBA Workshop on Media Buying, 1997

By the end of this chapter you will:

- Recognize the role of the media department;
- Understand the advantages of using media independents;
- Know how to brief media people;
- Understand the value of sound research in media planning;
- Understand both sides of the second media debate;
- Be able to evaluate media schedules on the basis of frequency and duration;
- Gain an insight into the qualities of a good media buyer;
- Understand the nuances of buying the main media of TV and press and the cinema.

14.1 The media department

The media department is responsible for selecting the media in which the advertisements will appear, and for negotiating the best possible deal with the media owner. This function – sometimes known as the 'space-buying' department – was a relatively neglected one until about 15 years ago, but in recent years, as media costs have escalated and as the media world has become more complex (with new forms of television, more specialized publications and so on), clients have realized that enormous sums of money can be saved by better negotiation of space and airtime. In many countries this has led to the rise of specialist media buying companies, acting on behalf of advertisers.

The media department, headed by the media director, consists of media planners, who select the media to be used, and media buyers, who do the negotiations. This is another area of agency organization where there is some debate as to what is the most effective structure. Some agencies like to employ media staff as both planners and buyers, with each person planning the media schedule to be used, and then buying the newspaper or TV spot. The argument here is that the planner knows the overall objectives of the campaign and so can buy more effectively. Others separate the two functions, with the planner handing the schedule to the buyers, who then do the negotiating. The arguments here are that people who are good at planning a media schedule are not necessarily the best negotiators, and that space and time can be bought more cheaply by people who are negotiating in the market full-time, day in and day out. This is particularly the case with TV advertising in those countries where every spot is negotiable, and the price paid can fluctuate dramatically.

Some agencies employ specialist media researchers. These are market researchers who can analyse the data about the audiences for each medium and their comparative costs, and provide back-up to the planners and buyers. In agencies without such full-time researchers, this job is done by the media planners.

Some agencies might have an in-house specialist outdoor manager. The press and TV manager would then have media planners or a combination of planner-buyers reporting to him. And last but not least, there are the media assistants and trainees.

14.1.1 Who decides on the media?

All considerations – such as cost, audience and the characteristics of the various media – will be taken into account before the media decision is taken. But who actually takes the media decision? Is it left simply to the media department of the agency to work out the numbers and decide which is the most cost-effective way of reaching the target audience? Presumably not, since the characteristics of each medium can be as important as the cost and the audience. How much say does the creative department have, since its people will actually be producing the advertisements? Are the media the creative people like to use given preference over less fashionable media? How much influence does the account team have in reconciling possibly conflicting views? Does the account director simply tell the creative and media departments to get on with it? And what about the advertiser who will actually be footing the bill?

Naturally there are elements of all these influences on the final outcome, but there are also two levels of media decision to be taken, and the influence of the parties varies in each. By and large, the media department has more influence over the second stage – the intra-media decision as to which titles or stations should be used – than it does over the inter-media decision between TV and the press, or radio and posters.

The advertiser, the account group and the creative department are all likely to have strong views on the inter-media decision, and while they will take advice from the media department on the overall cost and audience considerations of their decision, the media specialists' views will carry no greater weight than anyone else's, and often considerably less. The creative department, for example, has an indirect power of veto, since it can suggest that no creative solution can be found for a medium its people are not keen on. This can be a dangerous tactic, however, for if the client is determined to use that medium it may well decide to find an agency that can find a creative solution.

Once the overall inter-media decision has been taken, it is generally left up to the media department to work out the detailed schedule, to decide which publications to use and when the commercials should be transmitted. The advertiser, account group or creative department may have views on the particular editorial environment of certain programmes, but after that it is the media department's job to plan and book the campaign.

14.1.2 The sales department

None of these decisions gets taken in a vacuum. Every media company has an advertisement sales department, whose job it is to pull in as much ad revenue as possible. In some cases, such as that of most commercial television and radio companies, advertising may account for the firm's entire income; for newspapers and magazines the proportion may be anything between 30 and virtually 100 per cent for freesheets; but whatever the proportion, advertising is vital to each company's commercial success.

Media companies cannot simply sit back and hope that advertisers will decide to put money into their magazine or newspaper, and so there is as much competition between the media owners to sell advertising as there is in any of their customers' markets. The size and structure of advertisement sales departments varies considerably depending on the size and nature of the company – a small publisher may have only one or two sales staff while a large newspaper or TV station might employ 100 or more. In general, however, the department will be headed by an advertisement director or manager, and will be divided into groups of people, each with specific responsibilities. These groups may be divided by advertising agency, with each group responsible for the clients of a number of agencies, or by advertiser, but whichever way they are organized their job is to get to know the people responsible for the media decision, and to ensure that they in turn know everything they need to know about the medium.

At a typical media owner there would be a large research department able to supply media evaluation and media runs showing how an ad campaign would benefit from the particular medium. There may also be a client manager and an agency manager. The function of the media sales department (other than selling the airtime) is to ensure that no media department buys at a 'better' rate than the other media departments buying for brands belonging to the same client, e.g. a Kellogg's brand based at one agency versus another agency also buying a Kellogg's brand could be very interesting!

14.1.3 Media independents

Sixty years ago the media had sales agents, who went to clients and persuaded them to buy space. The media sales agents produced the creative ideas and the media gave them a 15 per cent commission for selling the space. These media sales agents became the advertising agents of today, and in 1971 the first media-only agency started trading with K-Tel Records. At first it was television-only clients who flocked to the new companies, but within five years press and then other media clients went the same way.

Today, clients from government to financial, consumer goods to retail now use the services of media independents. There are over 80 such organizations in London alone, most offering to plan and buy across all media. Some are off-shoots of full service agencies, such as Zenith out of Saatchi & Saatchi. Some offer international planning/buying as well.

The advantages of using a media independent are as follows:

1 Concentration of media expertise.
2 Media-only specialists.
3 Closer links to the client (no account director looking for agency profits).
4 Media planning and buying plus research facilities.
5 Lower commission than a full service agency.

Today, around 35 per cent of all above-the-line goes through media independents without accounting for the full service agency derivatives, and the trend is that more is yet to follow.

The major disadvantage is that in many cases the client is more exposed to media issues, and this can take up more time of what may be an already busy schedule. However, when one takes into account that the media is generally the largest part of the advertising mix, perhaps this is not such a bad thing.

14.1.4 Booking direct

There are, in certain circumstances, reasons for an advertiser to book media direct. If you have a massive media spend you may be able to afford to set up your own media department and buy in the creative work where it does make some sense. At the other end of the spectrum, a small advertiser using direct mail and local trade press may possibly be able to justify not using a media department, but beware – media sales people can be very persuasive.

What do the media offer by booking direct? To the advertiser, this can so often look at first glance as being a highly desirable offer. The media are today taking an increasing number of clients on a direct basis, yet there are a number of flaws for advertisers taking this route. There are enormous risks if you are a small to medium advertiser.

(a) How good is the offer? Can you be given guarantees that the offer is at least better than average?
(b) The costs are high not just in staffing but also media/marketing research.
(c) What are you likely to gain? Perhaps a saving of 2–3 per cent media commission compared to a media-only agency deal.

Martin Lester summarized the buyer/seller relationship at the ISBA workshop:

At the end of the dialogue an agreement or compromise is reached ... and the deal is done. A 'good' deal is one where both parties walk away believing that they have a 'good deal'. If one party feels that they have been taken for a ride they will be very wary of any future negotiations and memories can on some occasions last for eternity.

There is an enormous amount of hype on both sides ... the sales team extolling the virtues of their medium, the buyer suggesting that the client is the biggest thing since sliced bread. At the end of the day, when the dust has settled down, it is the relationship between two individuals that comes to the fore. If the relationship is one of trust and sticking to the ground rules, then there is a future. If not, then the relationship breaks down. There are in most media departments regular discussions on the performance and trustworthiness of the media reps. Very often media directors will be asked to change the respective sales team handling the agency if it is felt that they are not performing well. This does not mean that they are not offering the 'best' rates but equally important the servicing of the account is vital.

14.2 Briefing media people

A well-thought through media brief is vital. Whoever is to carry out the buying, the planning and the scheduling, a key factor in getting the media aspect 'right' is the briefing given to the media people. 'Rubbish in, rubbish out', as the saying goes.

The following checklist serves as a general guide:

- Always make sure you write the brief down. The process of writing is a very good discipline, as it helps you formulate your ideas clearly and saves so much time in the long run. It will give you a clear basis upon which to evaluate media proposals, too.
- Be clear, give plenty of time for questions by the media people.
- Be available, i.e. if they require further information let them have access to you and to your team.
- Do not change the brief one day before the media people come back to make their presentation, it leads to a very fraught atmosphere and, so far as the media planner is concerned, it means that you don't know where you are going (which may well be the case, but you don't want them to know!).
- It is vital to be honest. Include as much information as possible. Do not leave out the 'sacred cows', and equally do not leave out the negatives. The brief must reflect the latest agreed targets and plans that the advertiser wishes to implement.
- Ensure that methods of evaluation are in place, so that the media plans can be changed if necessary.
- Ensure that contact meetings are set aside in advance and that regular meetings for de-briefing are also arranged.
- Get as much information as possible on competitive activity and ensure that this information is kept flowing between yourself and the agency.
- No media plan is cast in tablets of stone – they can be changed, but normally at some financial or positioning penalty. Make sure that you are aware of the costs involved if a campaign has to be cancelled, delayed or shortened. Make sure that the media buyers are aware in advance if this is likely to happen – it will help you enormously in reducing any financial penalties, and this is particularly true in a flat or depressed market.
- Ensure that the media brief is given with some information about creative work. The last thing you want is for the media department to be surprised to see that the advertisement contained a coupon which had to appear on the outside right-hand edge and left-hand pages had been bought. (This can so easily happen!)

14.2.1 The media brief

The content of the media brief will vary, depending on your relationship with the media buyers. If they have not worked with you before or they are new to the brand, then they will need a more comprehensive brief. If they are familiar with your business and you are just giving them an update for a new period of advertising, you will probably only need to give them an update on sales performance and revised campaign objectives. The following list is comprehensive and identifies issues to cover in a new, full media brief. Your current situation will define what needs to be included in your next campaign brief:

- Campaign objectives (why are we advertising and what do we hope to achieve?)
- The market, including own market, competitor activity, historical information
- Market intelligence / research
- Awareness, attitudinal research
- Type of product or service. Price (relative to competition)
- Distribution (where is the product to be found, what influences distribution?)
- Target audience (specific details, i.e. age, socio class, male / female, sagacity)
- Who makes the buying decisions?
- Creative requirements (demonstration, colour). Creative size of ad. Length of commercial. Production lead times. Length of campaign(s)
- Coverage (cover, frequency, impact, share of voice)
- Regionality (where, what gaps?)
- Seasonality (when? Key times?)
- Budget (what's for media, don't forget production)
- Other activities (timed plans for all marketing communications)
- Retail, direct sale, target audience
- Previous campaigns
- Benchmark measurements
- Budget and balance: no matter how big the budget, no media plan can deliver complete satisfaction in terms of coverage (penetration of target audience (reach) and frequency) nor in terms of impact (size, length, time, use of colour, etc.)
- New product launch: test rates applicable
- Media test

Almost certainly something will have to be sacrificed and the brief may have to indicate whether (for example) it is more important to reach the whole target audience (at low frequency or impact) or to achieve high impact and / or high frequency even if that means reaching only part of the target audience (in which case, which is the most important part?)

14.3 Media Planning

Good media planning is based upon research and then upon the most important and diffi-
cult ingredient obtainable i.e. expertise and knowledge to fine tune the research findings.
Martin Lester at the ISBA workshop

Media and market research is such an important subject, and is always an area where a client can so easily be blinded with science. This is the part of the media planning exercise where the target market comes together with the precise candidate media.

Research is a necessary evil of the advertising world but ensures that the detail of the facts and figures neither clouds nor loses the original concept. For example, always look at the sample size and take a view as to whether or not the interpretation of the figures may carry less weight than possibly first thought because the sample is so small.

It would be so much easier if all research for all media were based upon one sample only, i.e. single-source data. We could then access the sample, specify the target group and find out what they read, watch and listen to. Unfortunately, this is not the case in the UK market at present, in part due to cost and part due to history. In Australia single-source data is used, and very successfully, too.

So the media planning process, has to commence with a reasoned evaluation of the media available. At each stage of this checklist the medium is compared with the requirements of the brief. The objects of the evaluation are:

1 To see which media are feasible.
2 To pick the main medium.
3 To prepare for the decision on how it should be used.
4 To see whether there are suitable supporting media if required.

In deciding 'which media are feasible' a number of aspects have to be considered, the main ones being:

(a) *Creative suitability.* Which media allow scope for putting the message across effectively – colour may be vital or the ability to include a coupon may be very desirable. You may wish to demonstrate a product in use or focus on a particular sound.
(b) *Experience.* Knowledge that a particular medium has proved effective in the past or in current similar situations will count in its favour.
(c) *Availability and lead time.* If a campaign is necessary at short notice, colour magazines with long copy dates (i.e. needing artwork, etc. a long time in advance of publication date) are not feasible; some products, such as cigarettes, are prohibited on some media, some publications may be fully booked at the desired period.

(d) *Regionality*. The brief may call for advertising in some areas and not others or heavier weight in some than others. This is possible with some media (television, some magazines, local newspapers, outdoor) but not with others (most national newspapers, and magazines).

(e) *Competition*. While it does not always follow that we should advertise where the competition is, it can be an important factor, especially for example when the purpose of the campaign is to hold market share against competitive attack.

(f) *Effect on 'the trade' and sales force*. It was once very much the case, and may still be so to some extent, that dealers and retailers were much more impressed with TV advertising support than by any other media. Sometimes it is important that the media used carries a high 'visibility' with the trade and the advertiser's own sales force, especially if an important objective is to improve their morale and stimulate them to greater commitment and selling activity.

(g) *Coverage of the target audience and cost per thousand*. Clearly the most important factor of all. But note 'cost per thousand who?' Low cost is irrelevant unless the measurement is made against a specific target audience profile.

Good planning often means finding an angle that could, for example, use a different medium where you gain a greater share of voice and therefore advertising impact. (London Weekend Television (LWT) used posters for the first time in the early 1980s rather than, for example, national press, although it may be argued that since they sell their medium against the press by using them, they would suggest that newspapers do indeed work.)

14.3.1 Media weight

A refinement of the 'cost per thousand' element in media assessment can be achieved by attaching 'weights' to various components of the total target audience. This can get very complicated indeed (Broadbent covers it in some detail in *Spending Advertising Money*) but the essence of it is expressed by the following simple example.

In a particular case, all housewives might be included in the target audience. However, housewives with children are particularly interesting to us. They might therefore be given a weight of 100, whereas housewives without children could be weighted 60. The housewives with no children element in the coverage of a particular medium would then contribute less value to cost per thousand calculations than those with children.

Broadbent talks in terms of 'Valued Impressions per Pound' (VIPs) arrived at by the formula:

$$\text{VIP} = \frac{\text{readers (or viewers) in target} \times \text{media weight}}{\text{cost}}$$

Various computerized models take this approach into far greater complexity and detail in order to provide increasingly accurate methods of measuring the value of one medium against another.

14.3.2 The intra-media and inter-media decisions

Section 7.6 outlined these two important stages in arriving at a final recommendation on the most appropriate media.

14.3.3 One medium or several

Once the main medium has been selected, it will often be necessary to consider whether this is to be the *only* medium or whether one or more others need to be added.

There are arguments both for and against using a second medium:

Arguments against a second medium
(a) *Loss of domination.* Only if there is a satisfactory campaign in the first medium should a second be considered. Concentration in the preferred medium gives the best chance of beating the competition and building up a large number of repeated, effective exposures. There are also arguments against the need for repeated exposures (*see* Section 14.4.1).

Any other medium which might be used will by definition have lower cost effectiveness than the first. Only in the case of seriously decreasing returns in the first medium is there a case for switching money out of it. The planner should ask questions like: 'Would you prefer that someone should see their tenth repeat of your TV commercial – or would you prefer that someone else, who would otherwise not see the TV advertising, could see their first press advertisement of yours?'
(b) *Additional production costs.* To use a second medium requires the time, creative thought and cost of preparing additional advertisements.

Arguments for a second medium
(a) *Wider cover.* Usually a single medium does not give everyone in the target an adequate exposure to advertising. There is heavy repetition on some people, while many of the others are at best lightly exposed though they could be reached adequately with the second medium. Consideration of the second medium could therefore involve a new

target definition: those not yet properly exposed to our advertising, or those not sufficiently reached by a competitor. Consider a campaign aimed at all adults under 65. TV would be first choice for such a wide audience, but what about the influential 15–24-year-old adults? They are notorious light viewers of television. So, where a normal TV campaign seldom reaches light viewers (30 per cent) and of course does not reach non-viewers of the campaign (10 per cent) at all, if these people account for more than 40 per cent of purchases of your product group, you may be wise to consider cinema. Remember, 41 per cent of the average audience at the cinema is composed of adults 15–24 years old.

(b) *Greater effect from two media.* In some cases the effect of two media reaching the consumer has creative benefits neither can give alone. For example, a TV commercial may demonstrate a product and tell the viewer to study the details and perhaps fill in the coupon in a press advertisement. Or a cheap poster may trigger off recall of the main point of a more expensive TV commercial. The use of two media may convey an impression of size and domination: 'They're everywhere: they must be important'. This effect could be particularly important when influencing the trade.

(c) *Wider media experience.* Using several media gives the opportunity to learn more about advertising for the product. The tests carried out with a second medium may lead to a case for a media switch being made next year. Media owners become more anxious to give service when they see other media being used, or their own being given a chance.

14.4 Media schedules

At some stage the broad media plan, indicating how much money is to be spent in which media and how that money is to be allocated (size, frequency, etc.) has to be developed into a detailed schedule. This indicates precisely how and when the advertisements appear (often indicating even which advertisements in a series will appear on which dates, which time segments, positions, etc.).

Sometimes, however, dates, in the case of press advertisements, may be only approximate. In the case of broadcasting media, especially when packages are bought (*see* Section 12.4), the schedule may only indicate the week and time segment or even 'peak-equivalents', i.e. the number of spots which would be bought if only peak-time segments were used.

14.4.1 The problem of frequency

Clearly one decision that has to be made is how often is it necessary to 'hit' people with an advertisement over what period of time to have the desired effect. As with so many aspects of advertising there are no hard and fast rules.

In printed media there are conventionally two considerations. The first is the frequency of publication, and the second the frequency of purchase of the product. Most planners would consider nine insertions in successive issues of a monthly magazine to be a fairly high frequency over the year, but would not consider nine insertions in either a daily or a Sunday newspaper to be adequate for a 12-month campaign.

Planners frequently time insertions in sympathy with the buying frequency of the product. That is to say they will seek, if they can afford it, weekly insertions of a product which is bought weekly and will be content with monthly insertions for a product which is bought monthly.

When considering television the principle of a threshold may apply: 'unless advertising for a brand reaches a certain level it may be wasted'. Thus, the logical conclusion is to concentrate. Some suggest that one exposure a week is the threshold, though others would say two a week. In research language this means achieving 100 or 200 TV ratings a week (*see* Section 12.3.3). Since hardly any brand can afford this rate throughout the year it is normal for them to work in bursts of three, four (very common) or six weeks.

If most of the impact of an advertisement in a seven-day period is generated by just one opportunity-to-see, an awful lot of advertising money is probably wasted. That is effectively the conclusion of a book called *When Ads Work* written by John Philip Jones. Discoveries made by him from his analysis of Nielsen single-source data have continued to excite wide interest. Since the publication of this book in 1995 there has been a lot of debate about its implications and the validity of Jones's research (*see* 'The effect of advertising on sales', *Admap*, June 1995).

One of the best ways of testing new hypotheses is, of course, to subject them to further testing, and this is just what Colin McDonald has been doing in 1996, using the long dormant but still highly relevant Adlab data, courtesy of the current owner, Carlton Television.

The Adlab panel is a data source which, some have long felt, ought to be able to contribute to our learning in this area. It consisted of 1,000 housewives in the Central TV area of the UK who provided 'pure' single-source information: daily purchases in 23 product categories with brand, volume, price and promotion information, TV viewing and newspaper and magazine readership. The panel was run by Taylor Nelson, and lasted from September 1985 to March 1990.

While the McDonald analysis uses an entirely different database, it does appear to provide some support to Jones's argument, although some brands seem to benefit from higher frequencies. There are also new insights into how the advertising works (by reinforcement or attraction) and the importance of timing: *when* you advertise may sometimes be as important as *how often*.

New evidence from Germany[1] is now showing how the Short-Term Advertising Strength (STAS) measure can be deployed to help evaluate the effectiveness or otherwise of particular campaigns.

So, is once enough?

One of the main controversies raised by Jones's findings has been the frequency question. Jones has claimed that most of the effect of advertising, as measured by STAS in a seven-day 'window', is accounted for by just one Opportunity To See (OTS): two or more add little extra. If we look at all brands together, we find the results shown in Table 14.1.

Table 14.1 STAS (7 days) at different frequencies showing that most of the effect of advertising comes from one OTS

	I+OTS	2+OTS	3+OTS	4+OTS
Cereals	133	138	142	143
%	+33	+4	+3	+1
Automatic washing powders	128	133	137	139
%	+28	+4	+3	+1
Shampoos	144	151	161	150
%	+44	+5	+7	−7
Non-automatic washing powders	97	96	−	−
%	−3	−1	−	−
Chocolate bars	+148	154	164	165
%	+48	+4	+6	+1

Source: Admap

The Adlab data confirms Jones's findings on the crucial question of frequency: most of the short-term effect comes from just one OTS. A STAS index figure of over 100 is positive, i.e. the brand took a greater share of purchases when it was advertised than when it was not. So, for example, from Table 14.1, when a cereal brand is advertised the purchases in the following seven days are 33 per cent greater than when it is not advertised. The second opportunity to see the advertisement only adds a further 4 per cent increase. The question is then, is this incremental increase in sales worth the extra media cost?

STAS can be seen as an indication that advertising is working to stimulate the next purchase in the short term: if positive, it does not imply an overall rise in sales share, merely that when advertising has been seen there is a greater likelihood that a purchase will follow. It can be seen that most individual brands show a positive STAS, i.e. a positive creative effect of advertising, but there is a wide variation. Of 67 individual brands studied, 18 (27 per cent) have a negative STAS, which means that their advertising was too weak to stand against that for the competition. This is consistent with Jones's finding that 30 per cent of brands have a negative STAS.

Some brands, however, do benefit from a higher frequency – see Table 14.2.

Table 14.2 *STAS (7 days) at different frequencies showing that some brands benefit from higher frequencies*

	1+OTS	2+OTS	3+OTS	4+OTS
Kellogg's Cornflakes	106	109	109	110
Weetabix	107	108	112	115
Rice Krispies	110	115	129	130
Bran Flakes	107	109	113	121
Special K	116	123	132	116
Persil Auto	100	103	105	108
Bold 3	126	137	142	151
Daz Auto	108	107	112	119
Ariel Liquid	108	111	117	122
Mars Bars	105	108	118	125
Palmolive	114	145	228	248
Silvikrin	104	133	142	120

Source: Admap

14.4.2 Burst or drip?

In certain cases, rather than concentrate the expenditure in a series of 'bursts' it may be preferable to spread it evenly in 'drips' throughout the year. Knowing which is best in a particular situation is the problem. Much research and discussion has led to the firm belief that there is no one pattern that suits *all* situations. So what is needed is a method of determining the best answer for any particular situation.

One of the bases for deciding is the concept of *'response functions' (see* Section 13.5 for a definition). It specifies what sort of schedule is thought best. Is it one with high cover and additional impressions not very useful? Or are repeated impressions very important and cover matters relatively little?'

In other words response function is a measure of the *additional* effect on an individual of receiving two, three . . . etc. additional impressions of a particular advertisement. In some cases the near-maximum effect is achieved very rapidly and further impressions add little (a convex response function). In others (S-shaped response function) the effect is slow to build and *then* flattens after a number of impressions.

Some notes by Ogilvy and Mather 'What is an effective frequency of advertising', having analysed the available research and reviewed some case histories, conclude:

(a) The typical relationship between advertising frequency and sales effect is that of a convex curve.

(b) But in the case of new products an S-curve will apply.

(c) For most products a minimum threshold of frequency probably does not exist in consumer terms.

(d) Low frequency of OTS over time is likely to be more sales effective than high frequency of OTS, for repeat purchase products at least.

The notes go on to say that the precise relationship depends on many factors and that 'in the end decisions will still be made on judgement'. However, ' judgement can be aided by study of past data on sales and advertising frequency'.

14.4.3 The 2/3/4+ OTS rule for television

This is the basis for so many television media plans. It means that the ideal number of OTS should be four. In other words, the first three exposures to the messages are building up to a full understanding of the message by the audience. This was researched many years ago in the USA and is still the basis of TV planning models.

It does really depend upon the complexity of the message, the response mechanism and the target group as to whether or not this should be the correct number of exposures or not. For example, in the record market experience shows that only one OTS is required in this specific market.

14.5 Buying media

There is one consideration which is vital to buying media, and this is the very quality of the media person. The qualities of a good time buyer are[2]:

- *Controlled aggression and persistence*. Getting what you want sometimes means being intimidating and annoying.
- *Control under stress*. The ability to handle up to 20–30 individual campaigns, all in an incomplete state and changing on a daily basis, without flapping.
- *Numeracy*. Prospective buyers without a grasp of mental arithmetic give up now. Mistakes cost thousands of pounds (an account query could cost more than £300,000 per spot on TV).
- *Willingness to compromise*. There is no point fighting to the death over a principle or minor detail, there should always be an escape route.
- *Social attitude*. Most good TV buyers are good at handling people as well as money. Be a team player.

And from the same source, some media buying don'ts:

(a) Don't tell them how big your budget is.
(b) Don't forget what you said in your last conversation. You mustn't forget the made-up target audiences you use.
(c) Don't tell the media that they come top of the cost rank.
(d) Don't pitch at the rate you want to pay, always pitch lower.
(e) Don't tell the media that your response levels were high the last time you advertised.
(f) Don't get bogged down with too many volume and share deals.

14.5.1 Buying TV airtime

TV negotiation differs primarily from other media negotiation in that the airtime is not secure until transmission (unless you pay the top-of-the-range price) and that essentially we are in a monopolistic marketplace. The only rule is that there are no rules! To book a national ITV campaign each transmission has to be handled individually or through the sales houses. However, GMTV and Channel 4 can be negotiated on a national basis. Channel 4 can also be negotiated on a macro-regional basis.

Planning a campaign is best done by buyers who know the current market conditions. When this is totally separated the results are almost certain to be unsatisfactory. There are four key problems that need to be addressed.

(a) In order to secure good media values on any particular campaign, it is essential to secure 'deals' with the majority of areas being used for the campaign.
(b) In order to obtain a good 'deal', you have to guarantee to commit, over the campaign period or the calendar year, a proportion of your total budget (share) or a guaranteed volume.
(c) Invariably, the share a contractor requires for a good deal is greater than both the contractor's net homes share (its 'Net Homes') and its aggregate network revenue share (its NAR). This means that if you deal with everyone you have to commit about 120 per cent of your budget – a little difficult!
(d) Each contractor has a different price for its airtime dependent upon demand – the greater the demand, the higher the price. London, for example, can cost up to 170 per cent more per thousand adults to reach than the network average. Small contractors cost proportionately less.

Towards a solution?

• Deal with most TV contractors (approaching 90) – this makes the media tail wag the marketing dog. It means that plans are made to satisfy the TV contractor rather than the client. It also places you at the mercy of the TV contractors who know that you have to spend money with them to reach contractual deals, and this leads to awful problems, particularly at the end of the year or campaign. This is the way that probably 80 per cent of agency deals are done.

- Tend to operate a system whereby you have clear-cut friends or enemies. Have favourite contractors, and do little business with the fringe contractors. The ones who know and trust you have been developed into a special relationship.
- Always repay 'favours' and do not take advantage of anyone's good nature.

By using this system you should never over-commit yourselves to share deals as most agencies tend to do. Some deals are on a handshake basis only and are not legally enforceable (controlled deals are audited). You will normally be left in the position of having most deals met at the end of the year, with money to spare. You have within your grasp the ultimate sanction of being able to 'de-plan' areas if they displease you. (Well, that's the theory!)

What factors influence the price of TV?
TV contractors can only sell a limited amount of airtime. This averages out to 7 minutes per hour of transmission. Even BSkyB operate within this standard. The maximum is 8 minutes per hour in peak time. Advertisers' demand for airtime will either push rates up or down.

The last variable factor is the viewing audience. The higher the audience, the cheaper the airtime (dependent upon the deal).

How does the buyer work out if the rate offered is good or bad?

- Is the airtime being bought for reasons beyond 'cost per thousand'? If so, the buyer can pick and choose airtime and make a judgement as to its value to them on behalf of the client through initiative and gut feel.
- If the buyer is buying against a plan, the calculation is almost the same as the contractor's: they will 'guesstimate' the revenue, the audience delivery (the 'ratings' or 'TVRs'), and the contractor's share of the market. Estimates of a 'station price' come from that. Obviously, the nearer to station price or below that the buyer can buy the better, since they are paying less for the same airtime. Competition is extremely fierce and often business moves on the basis of 'cheapness' alone.
- Quality airtime does not come cheaply, poor airtime does. Balancing the two into an acceptable value for money campaign is the art of the time buyer.

This has been over-simplified but demonstrates the point. Note:

- Peak airtime must always be sold at a premium (and demand means that it is).
- Off-peak airtime must be sold at a discount (and lack of demand means that it is).
- Obscure airtime (daytime C4 and between 0100 and 0529 hours) is almost given away, as demand is extremely weak.

However, if demand grows, with higher audiences or more money in the marketplace, this policy will change. Normally a 'station price' is set to maintain the rates. The contractor will restrict anyone buying or selling his airtime outside these parameters, typically by pre-emption.

There is a lot of airtime where the rules fall to pieces – let's say the centre break of *Coronation Street*, where the demand may force the rate into orbit.

Let us consider an example of media buying and selling. This is a question which has a different answer depending upon which side of the fence you sit. In reality, the buying is right if your product or service has a successful TV campaign which can be measured in increased volumes of sales or increased awareness of the service. Audience selectivity is therefore only a means to an end, not an end unto itself. The increased awareness in audience selectivity sophistication benefits the media owner in a very easy-to-follow way. The TV contractor will 'optimize' his airtime and sell the client, via an independent or media buyer, the most cost-efficient airtime according to them if they are allowed to do so.

Here is an exaggerated example: If you declare a sub-audience of 55+ adults, a media owner might slot your commercial in *Blockbusters* (a children's afternoon game show) because it 'converts' at 100 per cent better TVRs than adults (the norm). Therefore, according to the media owner, you 'must' go into *Blockbusters* because it's the best programme for your 55+ adult targets. Common sense now comes into play. Does a programme such as *Blockbusters* really fit into the buying brief of, let's say, retirement plans, when you could buy something like *Emmerdale* instead? After all, *Blockbusters* is aimed at school-age teenagers, not pre-retirement adults. The fact is, older people watch more TV more frequently than younger, more affluent viewers, so distorting the data on airtime such as this. It is vital to buy the correct environment for the target market. Although audience appreciation studies are being carried out, it is down to the buyer's experience and expertise to a very significant degree.

Needless to say, by keeping (in the current marketplace) audience categories as broad as possible, giving the media planner/buyer the flexibility to buy and negotiate outside the way contractors would like buyers to deal, gives buyers the competitive edge with their media plans. One must always be aware of sophistication in planning and buying, but only use it when it suits buyers and their clients, not for its own sake, and definitely not to make the media owners' optimization models work as they would wish them to.

Some further suggestions on how buyers can maximize their opportunities are as follows

- Look at the way an advertising campaign can be tested and rolled out into other regions without losing test market and other incentive rates.
- Examine the possibility of using an overlap situation, where one can transmit the commercial at different times in the hope that the audience will switch in the overlap to your advertisement.
- Look at the offers the contractor may make regarding other marketing tools, such as retail support, direct sales force, telegram mailing, dealer/trade commercial, TV production, studio visits/presentation.

Teletext
Jointly owned by Philips and Associated Newspapers. They are developing the medium more aggressively than their predecessors; penetration of the medium has increased from 18 per cent to 39 per cent since 1992. They have produced viewing figures of data to be 14.5 minutes per visit. Advertisers can buy a full page or a series of solus pages which are signposted on other high-traffic pages, e.g. ITV listings. Alternatively, they can take specific pages within an editorial carousel (i.e. that succession of pages under any given topic), or finally, any combination of the above.

It is an immediate advertising medium. One can be on-air within minutes of agreeing copy. It can be bought on a network basis, by region or by individual transmitter (25 in total). It lends itself to being an ideal direct response medium and for adding to the length of a TV commercial at a fraction of the ITV cost.

Against these advantages are the limited awareness of the medium, the confusion with BBC's services, the length of the message on the screen, the poor creativity of the medium and finally the very credibility of the medium.

14.5.2 Buying space in the press

The following represents some consensus of opinion of how things should be done.

First, it is common practice to think in terms of groups within press media as possible alternatives. For instance, one may have a newspaper schedule, or one may have a magazine schedule. It is usually possible to find an acceptable reason for not mixing the two. Some would go even further and propose a daily newspaper schedule, or a Sunday newspaper schedule; a weekly magazine schedule, or a monthly magazine schedule.

However, the use of the media model makes this difficult, unless one restricts the candidate list entirely to one particular type of vehicle.

There is some feeling that advertisements of a 'newsy' nature look best in newspapers, and clearly this is valid in so far as the combination of copy dates and reading times may mean that news in a magazine will be several months old.

Days of insertion are sometimes related to different classes of goods. In the case of newspapers, convenience goods, for example, are often advertised only in the daily newspapers, on the theory that the advertisement should appear close to the time of purchase. This has a strong bearing on the fatness of Thursday and Friday newspapers compared with the rest of the week. Mail order advertisements appear largely on Saturdays and Sundays, with the exception of the advertisements for department stores, particularly those concerned with fashion (usually seen on Mondays). On the other hand, Sunday is thought to be a particularly suitable day for selling consumer durables. The theory is that the purchase can then be discussed by spouses who are available to look at the advertisement together.

Newspapers' policies
Newspapers work in two ways. Some work towards a *yield* policy (*Daily Mail, Mail on Sunday, Independent*) and others work to a *volume* policy (Express Newspapers and the *Observer*). High-yield papers prefer a smaller newspaper with good-priced advertising, whilst volume papers aim for a big newspaper and thus drop on rate more easily. The best example is the comparison between the *Daily Mail* and the *Daily Express*, where circulation and profiles are similar but you will pay at least 25 per cent more for advertising in the *Daily Mail*.

Where one should use newspapers
Newspapers are excellent for new-product introductions. People read newspapers to find out what's new. Market-wise advertisers often make use of newspapers in new-product introductions to take advantage of this news aura. *Advertorials* (where information is written like an editorial) make good use of this situation.

Print advertising lends itself more readily to merchandising than broadcast advertising. Retailers and wholesalers are more likely to tie in with manufacturers newspaper promotions than with any other kind. Advertising support in the local newspaper indicates to these middlemen that they are truly being given local support.

Where one should use magazines
Magazine advertising is especially suited to new products and services that require educational campaigns. Longer copy can be used than in newspapers, because magazine readers spend much more time with their magazines than with their newspapers. In addition, magazines are often

kept for a long period of time, and advertisements can be read and re-read.

Coupon returns and write-in promotion offers perform well in magazines, since the reader is provided with the convenience of a coupon or entry form. When attending to broadcast media, a person must have a pencil and paper at hand at a specific time.

When an objective of advertising is to achieve packaged identification, magazines cannot be bettered. Full and faithful colour reproductions of the package can be achieved to match the exact appearance of the package on retail shelves.

A dozen smart buying techniques to try when buying press media[3]

1   Convince the media owners that you don't need them. (Ask questions that will make them come out with negative statements about their titles.)
2   Use a target audience that is realistic but least suits their title.
3   Salesmen are taught to make you talk! Put them on the back foot by asking them the questions they are going to ask you.
4   Humour them, particularly in heavy negotiation, because it softens them up.
5   If you've had a row, let them ring you first and then in negotiation tell them how sorry you are for putting the phone down on them the time before.
6   Flirt! If you're male, play 'little boy lost' who will lose his job if he doesn't get the rate. If you're female, play 'little girl lost' or offer to take the rep out to lunch if they give you the deal.
7   Lose your temper as seldom as possible! Temper is a sign of weakness!
8   Be economical with the truth! Tell the media owner what you are paying elsewhere if it helps your argument. If not, say nothing!
9   Traditional mechanical sales methods (AIDA [Attention, Intention, Desire, Action] DIPADA [Definition, Identification, Proof, Acceptance, Desire, Action]) can be used by buyers. Closing techniques are also similar.
    'I'll offer you £25 scc?' says salesman. *'All right, count that booked at £20,'* says buyer.
10 If your negotiation goes around in circles, change the subject! Talk about soap operas, crack a joke ! It puts the salesman into a false sense of security and makes them more vulnerable.
11 Tell the salesman that your client reads the rival title and really likes it.
12 Make the sales rep feel actively part of your client's business.

One other point, and that is that today more than ever the national press will offer other facilities, such as competitions and advertorial opportunities, to advertisers. They have recognized that they can no longer afford to be blinkered in their sales objectives and have to face up to the real world of marketing.

14.5.3 Buying space at the cinema

There are essentially three cinema buying routes available:

(a) Audience discount package: based on a fixed cost per thousand admissions

£ per 30 seconds	
London/Southern	42.20
All other ISBA regions	29.40
National average	34.15

(b) Screen by screen: Screens may be bought on an individual basis

	£ per 30 seconds	*Average rate per week*
Greater London:	Rest of UK:	National average:
139	87	95

(c) Film packages: Individual titles can be followed. School holiday (Disney) and art screen packages also available.

14.6 Evaluating media buying

One tends to measure a media department's performance purely in cost terms, and possible cost in relation to rate card. This is not always a very useful yardstick as to the real performance of the buyers. For example, positioning of the ad within the correct environment is imperative to most creative treatments. What is the point of running an ad at the back of a newspaper, for example promoting a new film, when it should appear in the entertainment section where reading and noting is much more important? Equally, on television there is little point for the majority of advertisers to end up in the last break of the evening with a very low-cost spot and a very small audience, even though the cost-per-thousand may be cheap.

There are systems whereby a commercial break within a programme can be evaluated for audience appreciation and a factor can be applied so that a break in a high-scoring programme is worth more than another with a lower score even though the ratings may be the same.

You need to use some form of audit or other technique to measure buying effectiveness. If you have friends in high places, you may be able to evaluate your own buying performance. However, if not, what do you do?

For example, say you are offered a 50 per cent discount. This may sound brilliant, but how would you feel if the going rate was in fact 60 per cent off rate card? It is the most contentious area of advertising. If your agency was briefed late and had to pay a premium for the media, another media department would not know this and could state that you have bought poorly.

When assessing the media buy, the only problem is that since much of the previous media planning work is theoretical you need to have some sort of yardstick as to how well you are doing compared to other similar sized companies. Every media director will claim that their media department 'buys best' and this, by implication, cannot be true. There is also the question as to whether or not the larger client and/or agency is offered the so-called 'best deals'.

Consider a totally hypothetical situation concerning TV. (This medium has been deliberately chosen since there is a fixed amount of airtime to sell, unlike the press, which theoretically can put in extra pages if advertising demand increases.)

Suppose the contractor needs to sell 10 minutes of airtime at £2,000 per minute to cover his costs and to make a profit = £20,000. Now Universe Media, who represent 50 per cent of all advertising, are also acting as media brokers and offer to take 50 per cent of the airtime at a discount of 25 per cent. They then sell on to the clients at 15 per cent off the £2,000 per minute rate.

The television company 'Silly Tele' has now got to sell the remaining 50 per cent of airtime. Availability has to be sold at a premium of 25 per cent in order to achieve the required income from the airtime. They may not be able to sell it to other advertisers because the cost is too high. They could possibly switch to other media or perhaps use satellite television. The airtime could possibly be sold to Universe Media but they do not have enough advertisers to justify their booking activity, and anyway Silly Tele would lose revenue.

There is another problem associated with large buying points. If, for example, you have two airline accounts both wishing to appear in *News at Ten* breaks in June, how are these allocated by Universe Media without upsetting either client? At least by being with a media department with no competitive product or brand, there is no question that, if the media negotiations go well, then the airtime will be bought on behalf of one or other of them.

The deal can go sour in the real marketplace – there is an organization called Media Audits and other media evaluation organizations. Also, the contractor media department itself is attempting to ensure that for brands split between agencies each media department involved is buying on equal terms so as to avoid the slanging matches which result from the losing agency's media department. At the same time, the larger clients are running their own evaluation of media buying projected costs in order to take advantage of any short-term cost differences being offered.

Media Audits will cost around 1–2 per cent of your media billings value; one may consider this relatively expensive, considering that the information obtained is historical. Also, the data is based upon around 60 per cent of all advertising and tends not to be live data.

14.7 Summary

1 Media departments select the media and negotiate the best deals on behalf of clients, although the role of the media independents has come into sharp focus in recent years.
2 The media sales departments are very proactive in trying to attract advertising revenue, a task made ever more demanding by the growth of new media titles, channels and stations.
3 In order to get the best place for the advertisement, it is essential to provide a clear well-thought-out media brief.
4 While media research is often complex and expensive to attain, there is no substitute for individual expertise and knowledge to fine-tune the research.
5 For some products, there is strong evidence to suggest that repeated showings of the same advertisement may have diminishing returns for the advertiser.
6 There are a number of 'smart things' that one can do when buying press media.

14.8 References

1 'Advertising's short-term effects: findings from the German market', *Commercial Communications*, March 1996.
2 Taken from a presentation written by London Media Broadcast, 9 March 1992.
3 Martin Lester, *ISBA Workshop on Media Buying*, 1997.

14.9 Further reading

The monthly magazine *Admap* contains many excellent and topical articles and is probably the best way of keeping up-to-date both on areas such as the burst/drip discussion and media developments such as the many changes currently taking place in TV viewing patterns.

Ehrenberg, C., *Repeat Buying: Theory and Applications*, London: North Holland, 1992.

Jones, John Philip John, *What's in a Name: Advertising and the Concept of Brands*, Lexington, MA: Lexington Books, 1986.

An interesting collection of papers on branding by European contributors is in a special issue of the *International Journal of Research in Marketing*, March 1993, edited by Partick Barwise.

Leslie de Chernatony's paper 'Categorizing brands: Evolution processes underpinned by two key dimensions', *Journal of Marketing Management*, April 1993, pp. 173–88, provides an interesting perspective, again using European examples.

14.10 Questions for discussion

1   Compare and contrast the benefits of using an agency's media department and a media independent.
2   Describe how you would go about testing the hypothesis that 'more frequent advertising does not yield better sales'.
3   Discuss the advantages and disadvantages of buying direct from the media owner.

Chapter 15

The production of advertising material

By the end of this chapter you will:

- Recognize the importance of production;
- Understand the main printing methods;
- Have reviewed the digital imaging process;
- Gain an insight into the advantages and disadvantages of the main colour printing technologies;
- Understand how press advertisements are produced;
- Understand how TV commercials are produced;
- Understand how radio advertisements are produced;
- Understand how posters are produced.

15.1 The importance of production

In producing the final advertisement there is more than only agency staff involved. In fact, especially when it comes to below-the-line material (*see* Chapter 8), the responsibility for production is very likely to be carried by 'in-company' staff rather than through their agencies. Moreover, there is a growing importance of the very wide and ever-increasing range of audio-visual and electronic media. While the printing processes – many of them unchanged since the Middle Ages in the principles they use – still predominate for much of the printed media, there is the newer technology of digital imaging and print.

The small to medium-sized enterprises are also able to harness new print technologies for many forms of communication to both in-company and external audiences. The use of electronic media for so-called *e-commerce* has also created new opportunities in communication for businesses.

However, it is a fact that at the present time the vast majority of promotional messages are still transmitted in printed form. Not only advertisements in newspapers and magazines, but sales literature and catalogues; posters and point-of-sale material; coupons and packaging (which often carries a publicity message). The list is endless.

Important as are the copy and design aspects of this material (*see* Chapter 10) they can be efficiently carried through or ruined by the way they are finally produced. The transition from an idea, probably expressed in the form of a typescript and a fairly sketchy visual indication of how the finished job is intended to look (the 'layout'), to the final glossy brochure or TV film is the production process. In agencies this is the responsibility of the production department (*see* Section 6.2.4).

In the traditional printed methods of communication, the production stage was largely a mechanical one of ensuring that the writer's and designer's intentions lost as little as possible in the process of translation into print. Generally, the art director – a member of the creative team – would himself supervise photography or commission other illustrations. The choice of typeface and the size, style and layout of the type was also closely controlled by a typographer, who was also a member of the creative team. So the production department in an advertising agency (*see* Section 6.2.4) still works to precise instructions from the creative department and is charged with ensuring that as little as possible gets lost in the transition to the printed page.

In the case of radio and television, the creative process does not cease with the conception of an idea and the capturing of it in the form of a storyboard. The production of the film or the audio-tape is itself a creative process. The selection of actors, music, sound effects, scenery and so on all make a profound contribution to the finished result. It is no longer a question of straight conversion of the ideas from one form (copy, artwork, etc.) to another (printing plates and onto paper). The ideas and concepts continue to evolve. The creative team, therefore, stay close to the situation right the way through.

There is still, however, an important role for the production department in ensuring e.g. that audio or video-tapes are available in the right form, in the right number, delivered to the right address at the right time.

Let us first, however, take a very brief look at the mechanics of the more 'traditional' processes by which printed material is produced before looking at the newer print technologies within reach of many businesses for particular purposes.

15.2 The main printing methods

There are three main methods of printing commonly used, depending on whether ink is transferred to paper from a surface which is:

(a) Raised – relief or *letterpress* printing
(b) Level – planographic or *lithographic* printing
(c) Sunken – intaglio or *gravure* printing

In addition, *screen* printing is sometimes used – the technique where ink is forced through holes cut in a stencil.

Each of these methods has particular qualities and demands the appropriate preparation of the material to be printed.

15.2.1 Letterpress printing

This is the process invented by Gutenberg in about 1450. Raised letters were originally carved from blocks of wood. Illustrations similarly were handcarved from wood (woodcuts). Printing was carried out by applying ink to the raised surfaces of the wooden blocks and then pressing them onto sheets of paper. This meant that the material was turned round during the process and so the type and illustrations had to be a mirror image of what was required on the paper.

These days the printing surfaces are of metal and the unwanted surfaces not carved away by hand but etched off with acid (*see* Section 15.2.2). The basic principle, however, remains exactly the same.

15.2.2 Photo-engraving for letterpress printing

The raised printing surfaces which carry the ink for letterpress printing are exposed by etching away with acid the surrounding areas. The metal plate (copper, or more usually zinc) is coated with a light-sensitive chemical and then covered with a photographic negative of the material to be printed. When a strong light is shone through the negative onto the plate the chemical hardens on those areas not to be etched away. The chemical not so affected is then washed off and the plate immersed in acid until the non-printing areas have been etched away to a sufficient depth.

The process is as simple as that when only solid areas are to be printed, such as type or line drawings. If photographs or other illustrations with graded tones are to be reproduced, then a 'half-tone' plate is necessary. In this case the photographic negative used is photographed through a 'screen'. This is a sheet of glass with fine lines ruled on it at right angles to form a series of tiny squares. This breaks up the picture into a series of dots when light is shone through it. In the light areas of the picture the dots are very small, in the heavy areas they are much bigger and the spaces between them much smaller. These dots become the areas left on the plate when it is etched so that what is printed is the same series of dots in the form of ink on paper. With a magnifying glass, the individual dots can be seen, but they are usually invisible to the naked eye. The screen used can be very fine (i.e. many ruled lines close together) or coarse depending on the smoothness of the paper to be printed on. For example, cheap newsprint is usually fairly rough and cannot reproduce clearly the fine dots of a fine screen illustration, whereas this is possible on the paper used in high quality magazines (which use 'coated' paper in which china clay is added to the mix to fill in the gaps between the wood fibres which form the paper).

15.2.3 Photo-engraving for colour printing

The only difference in the plate-making process for printing in colour rather than in black and white is that several (normally four) plates have to be used and the same number of printings carried out, using different colour inks.

The fundamental principle used is that all colours are combinations of the three primary colours, red, yellow and blue. By using coloured filters a photographic process can extract the three elements from any coloured illustration and a printing plate can be made to reproduce that element of the total coloured picture. By superimposing these three printings on each other the original effect can be achieved.

In practice four plates are normally made, to print magenta (red), cyan (blue), yellow and black inks. (The black plate is used to give additional 'body' to dark areas and to produce neutral shades of grey, which are difficult to make with the three primary colours.)

If especially accurate reproduction of subtle colours is required (e.g. in fine art books or pattern books for fabrics, etc.) then a larger number of printings using special ink colours may be used, but normally the four-colour process is sufficiently accurate and aesthetically pleasing and permits colour reproduction at reasonable cost.

15.2.4 Offset lithography

In spite of the sophistication attained by the letterpress process, most colour printing is now carried out by the lithographic process. Literally this means printing from stones and it was originally just that (the process was developed in the late eighteenth century). Now, specially treated metal plates are used instead of stones (except occasionally for very special short runs of artist's prints). The basic principle involved is that grease and water tend not to mix, so those areas of the printing plates which are not required to print are treated chemically so that they accept water and reject ink. The printing areas will accept ink and reject water. It is by this means that printing from perfectly smooth plates is made possible. Because the plates – usually of aluminium – can be quite thin, they can easily be curved round a cylinder and can be much lighter than letterpress plates, which have to be thick to carry the depth of type and also have to be of a metal that can easily be cast. Such plates are relatively cheap and easy to produce – one of the attractions of the process and an important factor in its increasing use.

The process currently used is *offset* lithography (shortened to offset-litho), so called because the ink is transferred (offset) onto a rubber 'blanket' and thence onto paper, rather than printing directly onto the paper. Usually the paper is web rather than sheet-fed.

15.2.5 Gravure

The principle is the opposite of the one used in letterpress because here the areas to be printed are etched *into* the surface of the metal instead of standing above it. The etching process used is similar to that used for letterpress plates (*see* Section 15.2.2). The printing plate is cylindrical. Ink is applied to it so that the hollow areas are filled, the surplus scraped off by a 'doctor blade' so that the flat surface areas have no ink left on them. When paper passes over the printing cylinder it, as it were, sucks the ink out of the holes on the printing cylinder to carry it away on the paper.

15.2.6 Screen printing

The principle here is that of a child's stencil kit, where ink is pressed through the holes in the stencil. In the commercial use of the method, the stencil is supported by a 'screen' originally of silk (hence it was called the silk-screen process) but nowadays of a mesh of woven synthetic fibre or metal threads. The range of effects is very much wider than the basic toy 'stencil kit' and indeed can match those of the other printing methods. The main attraction of screen printing is that stencils can be produced very quickly and cheaply and the process can therefore be very economic for short runs of things like posters and show-cards with full colour illustrations. However, the stencils wear out quickly and on long runs it loses its advantage.

15.3 Typesetting (composition)

Sections 15.2.1 and 15.2.2 referred to printing from raised surfaces, which nowadays are prepared largely from plates. Originally letterpress printing (*see* Section 15.2.1) was from wooden blocks each carrying a raised letter.

Later, metal blocks replaced the wooden ones. Typesetting or composing was carried out by assembling these individual letters into the appropriate order to provide the text to be printed. The letters were available in an increasing range of different typefaces, consisting of alphabets and numerals in a variety of styles.

A second transition is now under way from mechanical to electronic typesetting (the first being from hand-setting to mechanical and increasingly automatic setting). The basis of this is usually photocomposition (photosetting) where instead of using metal, each required character (letter or numeral) is photographed directly without the need to go through metal composition and proofing. An enormous advantage is that type no longer has to be stored in a range of sizes because it can easily be enlarged or reduced as required.

Adding computer technology now means that: (a) a vast amount of copy can be stored and changed or up-dated at will, and (b) prepared programs can give instructions to the composing equipment to produce whatever is required.

At the other end of the scale, modern computers are becoming increasingly sophisticated (e.g. with desktop publishing packages featuring hundreds of typefaces) and, when linked to office printers, a whole new world of sophisticated print is available at modest investments.

These technical advances have impact on the whole way in which the printing industry will operate in the future. For example, it is possible with voice recognition for newspaper reporters and feature writers to dictate their material straight into their PC for it to be typed as they speak. The implications on employment, levels of remuneration, etc. are considerable and currently being fiercely fought over in many countries.

15.4 The digital imaging process

15.4.1 Capturing an image

Many graphic projects begin with 'analogue' images, such as 35 mm slides, transparencies or reflective art. To produce a 'digital' image, these elements are converted to digital files which can be manipulated on a computer system. This step is usually accomplished by scanning the analogue image. The scanner measures reflected or transmitted light from the analogue image, assigning numerical values to the colours or tones in the image to create a digital copy.

With the image 'translated' into a series of numbers, the information can be stored on a computer hard disk or other electronic media such as a removable drive, PhotoCD or magnetic tape. Once the image has been converted to numbers, it can be transferred from one computer to another or sent electronically.

Terms to know
- *Analogue* – data stored in a continuous form. Your holiday photos from last year's beach trip are analogue images.
- *Digital* – data processed using binary numbers (0 and 1) through on/off impulses. It is what a scanner will do to your holiday photographs.
- *Scanner* – an input device that digitizes images, creating bit-mapped (those 1s and 0s again) copies that can be manipulated electronically.

15.4.2 Design and layout – the digital way!

A wide range of software applications support digital imaging. There are applications for producing digital drawings, modifying digital photographic images, working with typography, as well as page design and combining elements into one composite image.

The graphics produced through the use of these applications can be divided into two primary groups or 'graphic types': object-oriented (*vector*) and bit-mapped (*raster*).

Object-oriented graphics are often used for line drawings, logos or any image that requires smooth, crisp edges. One of the benefits of object-oriented graphics is that they can be enlarged, reduced or distorted without loss of detail or sharpness.

Bit-mapped graphics are usually picture or photographic type images, such as those captured using a scanner. Bit-mapped images are made by 'mapping' the image to an imaginary grid created by the scanning software. Colour or tint is applied to each square of the grid, producing an overall image. Unlike object-oriented graphics, bit-mapped graphics cannot be enlarged without affecting image quality. As the image increases in size, the squares of the grid increase in size, reducing clarity. It is important to plan for the final output size when scanning a bit-map graphic in order to have enough information, or detail, to meet the output requirements. Your service provider can provide specifications for scanning requirements. Bit-mapped graphics are usually larger computer files than object-oriented graphic files, since more information is required to reproduce the image.

While graphics files are divided into two types – object-oriented (vector) and bit-mapped (raster) – there are many 'file formats' used to produce graphic images. Two widely used file formats are TIFF (Tagged Image File Format) and EPS (Encapsulated PostScript). TIFF files are usually bit-mapped while object-oriented files tend to be EPS files. Different types of images, such as photographs, logos and line drawings, can be imported into one assembly application for design and layout by using common file formats.

At the completion of the design and layout phase, all elements have been assembled into one file. This file may include both object-oriented and bit-mapped graphics saved in various file formats.

The file is now ready to be raster-imaged (bit-mapped) based on the requirements of the selected output device. A grid is established based on the resolution of the output device. All elements in the file, regardless of type or format, are bit-mapped, creating an image which can be reproduced by the output device.

Terms to know
- *Object-oriented image* (vector) – a scaleable image that can be enlarged or reduced without loss of detail.
- *Bit-mapped image* (raster) – a graphic image formed by a grid of pixels or dots.
- *Raster Image Processor* (RIP) – hardware/software which translates data into a series of dots for output.
- *Resolution* – the number of pixels (picture elements) per unit of linear measurement (inch) on a computer monitor or the number of dots per inch in output form.

15.4.3 Producing the image

Digital images can be produced from a wide range of output devices using various technologies. Liquid ink-jet, electrostatic, solid ink-jet, thermal-transfer and photographic are the primary technologies used today.

There follows a brief introduction to several of the technologies.

Colour printing technologies[1]: basics of computer colour printing
Like traditional offset presses and Impressionist painters, colour printers create images by building up patterns of tiny dots. Most colour printers work with 300 × 300 addressable dots per square inch (dpi), but advancing technologies are beginning to introduce higher resolution, such as 600 dpi and higher, in low and mid-range priced printers.

Colour printers use the subtractive primaries – cyan, magenta and yellow – to produce colour. The printer can overlay two subtractive primaries to produce red, green and blue, and can overlay all three to make black. Many printers include a separate black so that they can provide a very dense black for images. The printer's colour system is known as CMYK (cyan, magenta, yellow and black).

Solid ink
Solid ink technology uses solid, coloured ink sticks to generate exception-

ally vivid colour output. The wax-based solid inks melt at a specific temperature and the print head sprays drops of ink onto the page where they then re-solidify almost instantly. Because the ink cools so rapidly, it doesn't have time to bleed into the paper, so printed colours remain brilliant and well-defined and the dots consistent in size and shape. Solid ink technology is also capable of very fast print speeds, because the prints are completed in a single pass and the print head can be made to span the width of the page.

Advantages:

- Exceptionally vivid colour output
- Output on wide range of paper grades, weights and finishes
- Low copy cost
- Fast print speeds

Disadvantages:
- Needs a 15-minute warm-up period to melt the ink when first switched on

Thermal transfer
Thermal transfer uses a transfer roll of coloured wax that is segmented into consecutive, page-sized bands of coloured wax. Hundreds or thousands of individually controlled elements in the thermal print head are heated to melt pinpoint spots of colour onto paper or transparency film. The paper makes three or four passes under the print head – one for each primary colour, plus an optional pass for a separate black.

Advantages:

- Good to excellent colour quality on paper
- Excellent quality on transparencies
- Fast print speeds
- Reliable

Disadvantages:

- Constant print cost, regardless of image printed
- Generally requires special media for best print quality
- Standard page sizes only

Dye sublimation
Dye sublimation produces continuous-tone, photo-realistic output at significantly less cost than that of traditional photographic alternatives. For reproducing bit-mapped or scanned images, the print quality is particu-

larly outstanding. In dye sublimation printing, the colouring agents are in the transfer roll – a plastic film that contains consecutive panels of cyan, magenta, yellow and, optionally, black dye. The transfer roll passes across a print head, consisting of thousands of heating elements, and the dyes diffuse into the paper's surface once they are hot enough to vaporize. The process requires special paper which is designed to absorb the vaporous dye on contact. The paper is clamped to a drum and makes a separate pass across the transfer roll for each colour.

Advantages:

- Excellent continuous tone for photo-realistic output
- Maximum image detail

Disadvantages:

- Requires special media
- Relatively slow print speed
- Relatively high printer cost and cost per page
- Copy cost constant

Colour laser
The colour laser printing technology is based on principles similar to those used in photocopying machines, but with the added complexity of colour. A photo-receptive drum or belt is initially charged with an even charge across its surface. It is then exposed to a laser beam that discharges those areas that are to be printed. A dry toner is applied to the discharged areas, with a separate pass to apply each individual colour. An electrostatic charge then transfers the toner to the paper or transparency. The final step involves a fusion process, which uses heat and/or pressure to set the toner into the media.

Advantages:

- Fast print speeds – 5 ppm colour, 14 ppm black and white
- Plain paper
- Capable of excellent output quality
- Image durability

Disadvantages:

- Complex operation
- Relatively expensive maintenance

Liquid ink-jet
Liquid ink-jet printing is a low-cost colour printing alternative. It is capable of high quality text and good quality spot colour on plain paper at a reasonable cost. Liquid ink-jet printing propels fine droplets of ink towards the surface of the paper. When printing on plain paper, the inks tend to soak into the paper enough to mix with the ink from adjacent dots, thus producing muddy colours. However, with specially treated paper, liquid ink-jet can produce highly saturated colours.

There are various forms of inkjet printing:

(a) *Drop on demand.* Ink is released by applying pressure to force a drop of ink onto the media as needed to create the image.
(b) *Continuous.* Ink is continuously under pressure, forming a stream of droplets. The droplets required to form the image are channelled to the media, while the unused droplets are recycled.
(c) *Thermal.* A gas bubble is created in the nozzle, creating pressure to force a droplet of ink onto the media.

Advantages:

- Inexpensive purchase cost
- Reasonable plain paper capability
- Good colour quality on coated paper
- Excellent monochrome text quality
- Fast monochrome print speeds

Disadvantages:

- Print cost goes up with increased ink coverage
- Slower printing for colour or transparencies
- Requires special coated paper to achieve high print quality
- Drying and smudging issues

Selecting the right printer
Table 15.1 is designed to help you identify the right printer for your requirements.

Table 15.1

	Ink-jet	Thermal wax	Colour laser	Solid ink	Dye sublimation
Workgroup for the office					
Management reports (mixed colour and monochrome pages)	2	2	5	4	1
Management reports (colour on every page)	2	2	5	5	1
Presentations (text andgraphics)	1	5	3	4	2
Presentations (text and photos)	1	4	3	4	3
External communications	1	2	4	5	2
Internal communications	2	3	5	4	1
On-demand brochure printing	2	2	5	4	1
Price lists	3	2	5	4	1
Spreadsheet publishing	3	2	5	5	1
Graphic design for workgroups					
Detailed imaging/photography	1	2	4	3	5
Graphics design	2	3	3	5	4
Newsletters	2	2	5	5	1
Short-run posters	3	1	2	5	3
Proofing	2	3	3	3	5
Workgroup sharing					
Image quality	1	2	3	4	5
Colour correctness	2	3	3	4	5
Cost per page	5	2	4	5	1
Purchase cost (low price is good)	5	3	2	3	1
Print speed	2	3	5	4	1
Ease of use (user maintenance)	4	3	1	5	3
Adaptability	3	2	4	5	1
Range of media	3	2	4	5	1

Totals (Please total up the score for each technology)

How to score
Just highlight the rows that correspond to the applications that are important to your company. Then add up the highlighted numbers in each column to give a total score for each technology. The total scores then act as a guide to which technology is best for your application. The higher the number, the more suitable the technology

Scoring:
5 – Excellent
4 – Recommended
3 – Good

2 – Not Good
1 – Not Recommended

Application of digital images
Digital images can be applied to paper, vinyl, fabric, plastics and many other materials. Depending on your specific requirements, your service provider can help you select the best output device.

Finishing
Using special media, inks and/or laminates, images can be produced which withstand sunlight and most weather conditions. Also, adhesives are available which provide the opportunity to apply digital images to various surfaces. You'll find digital images on buses, planes, buildings, ceramic tiles, textiles – just about any surface imaginable.

Advantages of digital imaging
When it comes to visual communication, digital imaging has changed the rules. Cost, colour, size and turnaround time – for years, these were the 'Big Four' challenges facing purchasers of large format graphics. Digital technology has successfully addressed these concerns and made large format graphics more available and affordable than ever before.
Here's how digital imaging addresses the Big Four:

(a) *Cost.* Digital pre-press or pre-print costs are dramatically lower than for conventional printing methods, making it affordable to produce short runs or even a single copy of an image – in full colour!
(b) *Colour.* Digital imaging is a colour process, eliminating the expensive pre-press steps that make conventional colour too costly for many projects.
(c) *Size.* Digital images can be produced in virtually any size. Output devices range in size from a few inches wide to over 16 feet in width. For even larger graphics, images can be 'tiled' and assembled in pieces.
(d) *Turnaround time.* Digital imaging is an automated process, providing fast turnaround and the ability to change images late during production. With digital imaging you not only can have it when you want it, but you can modify your images or messages individually.

15.5 Producing a press advertisement

It is true that the overall process is much less complex than creating a TV commercial, so creating a press advertisement does seem a good deal simpler. However, creating a good press ad is at least as hard as creating a good TV commercial, and most people in the business feel that there are comparatively few really good press ads around these days.

Compared with the opportunities to use sound, movement and glossy production values as offered by television, the restrictions imposed by the printed page make great demands on the creative team. It is very easy to flick straight past a press ad, or to concentrate on the editorial matter next to it, so a press ad has to grab the reader's attention and then hold it for as long as it takes to get the message across.

However, there are compensations. In a press ad, it is possible to impart a great deal more information – and hence sales points – than on television or radio. One can also target an ad more specifically at one group of people and so, in many cases, press ads can operate at a more detailed and intellectual level than most TV commercials.

15.5.1 Writing the press copy

Writing copy for press is far more challenging than writing for TV. To start with, most copy written for television never communicates directly with the public, since it is describing what is to be seen in the commercial rather than what is to be said. Even those words that will be heard by the public will be heavily influenced by the way (body language) and by whom they are delivered. By contrast, no one gets between the press copy-writer and the audience. Every word will be displayed for the public to see – whether or not the public reads them depends on the skill of the writer and the art director.

As with television, the creative team can choose from a wide range of possible treatments – humour, demonstration, shock, emotion, celebrity – and the copy-writer will probably make the decision as to which of these is used. It will be the copy-writer who will pore over the product literature, reading the consumer research and looking for a creative concept that will meet the brief.

15.5.2 Design roughs

Whatever the final form of the ad, it will first appear in the form of a rough design – traditionally known as a 'rough' or a 'scamp' – prepared by the art director. This will almost certainly include the headline (though even this may be tidied up or reworked later), but not always the body-copy, which will be indicated by 'Latinese' – a series of non-words resembling Latin to give the feel of typefaces used. The main feature of the illustration will be apparent, as will its position on the page, so the rough should convey the eventual look of the ad, if not its detail and polish. It is in this form that it will be shown to the creative director and then the account group.

With the introduction of computer aided design on the 'Mac', clients expect roughs that are more finished than might have been the case ten or fifteen years ago. With in-house colour printing, the 'rough' may appear in quite a finished form. It is possible that an ad will go through several stages of roughs before being approved. Most press ads are researched at the rough stage, to ensure that they are on the right lines.

Most press ads do not have to be submitted for approval by the regulatory authorities, unlike TV ads. Press ads are occasionally turned down by a media owner because of objections to their content – and if there is any doubt the rough should be submitted for approval first – but this is comparatively rare. However, in some countries, a handful of categories do have to be approved in advance. For example, the UK's Advertising Standards Authority insists on pre-vetting cigarette ads.

15.5.3 Photography and illustration

Once the rough and the copy have been approved, the production of the ad can begin, and one of the key elements is the decision whether to use illustrations or photographs. This may well have been decided already when the ad was conceived, but often the decision cannot be made until various executions have been tested.

Two of the most important factors affecting choice are whether the ad is intended to be in colour or black and white, and whether it will appear in a magazine or a newspaper. Many newspapers are printed on such poor quality paper ('newsprint', as it is known) that a complex photograph, with lots of detail and varying degrees of light and shade, may not reproduce well. While there are ways around this, many art directors decide that the best answer is not to use a photograph at all, but a line drawing. This can also be the solution if an ad has to be produced very quickly, since a simple line drawing or cartoon is usually quicker than a photograph.

15.5.4 Typography

Not all press ads use a picture. Some rely totally on the layout of the type: the typeface itself and, occasionally, a technique such as 'reversing out' (white type on a black background) to attract the reader's attention. Whether or not there is a picture, typography will have a major impact on the look of an ad – through both the typeface chosen and the manner in which it is laid out. By maintaining a consistent 'look' in its advertising a company establishes a house style, and the typeface is one of the most important elements.

15.6 Producing television commercials

A 'commercial' (meaning a commercial film as distinct from the programme material which has an informational, educational or entertainment purpose) is the term commonly used to describe an advertising film
for transmission by television.

Whichever medium the ad is intended for, the process of creating the
concept and pre-testing the advertisement is largely the same. In fact,
many campaigns run in a selection of different media using the same basic
strategy. For example, the 'Stella Artois – reassuringly expensive' concept
was originally developed as a television campaign, but it had to be equally
applicable in posters if it was to be used (posters are a major medium for
beer advertisers in the United Kingdom). Later it was adapted for the press
and for radio. Incidentally, while it has been used below-the-line, the
phrase has not been used at point-of-sale.

However, some creative teams always work with one particular
medium. Writing a script for television requires different skills from those
needed for a press ad, and a radio script demands different techniques
again. A single clever copy-line may be equally appropriate for each
medium (and indeed, since it becomes part of the brand identity, it should
be transferable), but turning that line into an advertisement is a separate
process. While some copy-writers and art directors feel comfortable with
many media, most teams have their preferences. While TV is the most
glamorous medium, direct mail copy-writing is the fastest growing area –
and to do it well is by no means easy.

TV has wider creative scope than most other media (the obvious
exception is cinema, which is even more glamorous). This is in part due to
the combination of sound, movement and colour, but also because occasionally one has to film on location in exotic places, or with well-known
actors and actresses, or both. There may not be much glamour in creating
a hard-selling, home-based TV ad for a vacuum cleaner, but there is more
glamour involved in it than there is in creating a press ad for the same
product.

15.6.1 Writing the TV commercial script

The script is not just the words used in an ad – indeed, in some commercials there may be no words spoken at all. The script has to convey what is
to happen in vision as well as on sound, complete with music, sound
effects, cuts, close-ups and all the other elements that will affect the way
the commercial looks, sounds and is made. For this reason, the art director
is just as likely as the copy-writer to have a major hand in writing the television script. Most agencies pair their writers and art directors in creative
teams, who work in the same room and bounce ideas off each other.

However, some writers like to work alone, then hand their script to an art director who will then put his or her visual stamp on it. This draft script will subsequently be reviewed by a creative group head (in a larger agency), or the creative director and the agency TV director. They may well have ideas about how it should be done. Finally, after it has been approved by the creative director, it will be shown to the account team, who may well have suggestions to make on it before it is presented to the client.

The script is divided into two elements, visual (or vision) and audio (or sound), and they are written alongside each other so that it is clear how the two come together. More often than not, the art director will produce a rough story-board to go with the script. This is a sequence of sketches that represents stills from the ad – and by the time the script is presented to the client this will probably have been redrawn in more detail, to give a clearer impression of the look of the commercial.

15.6.2 Approval of scripts

The regulatory system for TV advertising varies from country to country, but it is wise to get the script approved by the regulatory body before going to the expense of making the commercial, to ensure that it does not infringe the rules.

In the United Kingdom, commercials have to be approved by the Independent Television Companies Association (ITCA). This is to ensure that they do not infringe either the Television Act or the Code of Advertising Practice (*see* Sections 9.4 and 9. 5). In practice a check is usually made with the ITCA at script or story-board stage.

The ITCA considers nearly 10,000 new television scripts each year, and has detailed discussions with the agencies on most of them. Many have to be amended, and a number are rejected altogether. Even if a script has been approved, it does not mean that the film itself will be – it may go further than the script indicated – but the ITCA will point out areas for concern at the filming stage. For example, no one associated with alcoholic drink in an advertisement 'should seem to be younger than about 25', according to the rules, and this is something that cannot be accounted for at the script stage.

15.6.3 Animatics

An 'animatic' is often made of the commercial by agencies to help persuade the client to accept the idea. It is also produced for research purposes. Making animatics is a unique skill, some artists make a very good living by producing the drawings. Animatics often require a great deal of detail in the locations and character in the faces if they are to carry the image of the finished commercial. Some animatics are very realistic, mimicking the final commercial itself.

Sometimes, however, an agency will not bother with an animatic, since it could not convey the impact of a particular commercial which lies in the production values.

15.6.4 Production companies

When the client and the regulatory bodies have approved the script, and the animatic has been given the all-clear, the commercial can move into the production stage. The agency will select a production company and director to make the commercial. If the agency does not already know who it wants, quotes may be taken from two or three companies. Factors that will be taken into account include the company's 'show reel', the agency's own experience of the firm and the cost – and any special skills required for the particular commercial.

Once the production company has been appointed, it will be given a highly detailed briefing covering both the creative and financial parameters of the production. This will cover the production techniques to be used, the casting, music, locations and so on. While the script and storyboard may convey much of this information, a lot of detail will have to be sorted out in discussions between the agency and the production company.

Once the full scope of the production has been clarified, the production company must produce its quote for the work. Commercials can be frighteningly expensive, even for a 30-second ad. The standard form often used in the UK for a production quotation, which runs to six pages, can illustrate why they are so expensive. The form is divided into 16 sections, including pre-production expenses, casting, production salaries, unit salaries, equipment costs, studio costs, location charges, recording and dubbing, film editing charges and videotape post-production charges. Each of these is also broken down into a great many separate elements.

15.6.5 Getting the actors right

While most rely on the TV producer or creative teams (often with the help of outside freelances) to select the actors, actresses and models for the commercial, a few large agencies have their own casting department. Either way, getting the actors right is of paramount importance for the commercial's success.

Some scripts are built totally around the personality of a well-known character – but it is often the less well-known faces that are hardest to select. Many commercials call for 'typical' families, while others require people who have particularly photogenic teeth, hands or legs, depending on the product. Voices, too, have to be chosen very carefully.

In a study on the role of women in advertising[2], it was found that females are portrayed quite differently from males in TV commercials in both France and the UK. Women are younger, more likely to be shown in a dependency role (spouse, parent or housewife) or to be a product user. They are rarely portrayed as authority figures, either as on-screen characters or as voice-overs.

15.6.6 Choosing locations

Can the commercial be shot in a studio, or is an outside location necessary?

With a labour force of 10, an average studio set can take two days to build and all the furniture and contents will have to be hired or purchased. To allow for the building and dismantling of the set, a studio may have to be hired for four days – all for one day's filming!

'Outside' does not always mean open-air – many ads are filmed inside real homes, partly because of the cost of building sets in a studio, and partly for greater realism. With the advent of lightweight and mobile filming and lighting equipment, this has become common practice.

Outdoor locations do not necessarily have to be in hot parts of the world, but they often are, simply because the weather is more predictable and, with an expensive film crew on hand, it is more likely that the film will be completed on schedule. Although sometimes the weather will win!

15.6.7 Music

Even more important to the final success of the commercial is a third element – music. Like casting, this can be built into the script stage if the creative team already know a piece of music that they would like to use – some commercials have been built round existing music, one of the earliest and best-known of which was the jingle 'The Esso sign means happy motoring', to a tune from *Carmen*.

However, it is more common for the music to be selected later, either from existing work or composed specifically for the commercial. The relationship between the music world and advertising works both ways, in that while advertising often borrows existing tunes, a number of songs created for commercials have themselves become hits. Getting an old song associated with a new advertisement is a sure way of giving it a startling new life as a re-release

In late 1997, BBC Radio 2 filled a two-hour John Dunn evening programme with music that had been used in advertising, there were so many of them.

15.6.8 Post-production

Depending on the medium, video or film, after each day's shooting the 'rushes' can be reviewed. Some rushes consist of many thousands of feet of film or several hours of video – and all this for a few seconds of final advertisement. There may be more film if the final version uses slow motion.

At this stage, the editor has to reduce the film to the required length, working closely with the agency's TV producer and the director. Meantime, sound-track work will be on-going. While any dialogue on the commercial will have been recorded at the filming stage, other sound material (whether music, voice-over or sound effects) will be added later. This process will be concurrent with the film editing, since the visual and sound elements of the commercial must match exactly. This is known as the 'double-head' stage, with the sound-track and film being run through in parallel and changed independently of each other. Eventually, the two parts are put together, along with any screen text and other special effects that may have to be added to the commercial. In video production this is 'rostrum' work produced by computer. Normally the client will be called into approve the film before it is sent back to the laboratory for this final stage to take place.

Special effects include any switches from one scene to another, such as 'dissolves', which are designed to soften the effect of a straight cut. They involve taking a duplicate of those frames that need altering, and then working on them frame by frame to produce the desired effect. (Videotape, which is becoming virtually universal in the production of commercials, can produce such effects almost instantaneously.) At this stage, the print also has to be 'graded' to ensure that the colour quality is correct all the way through. Eventually, all these elements come together in the final print, with sound and vision perfectly married.

The commercial now has to be put into a form in which it can be transmitted by the television stations, and there are several ways in which this can be done. One is to produce 'bulk prints' of the commercial, which are then sent to each of the TV stations who define their needs. Since each print costs a fair amount to produce, this method is becoming much less common, being replaced by videotape. However, it is still used for cinemas, and here the need is for many more bulk prints.

The popular alternative is to transfer the film onto videotape, and either put it onto a spool and physically send it to the TV station (which only needs one copy), or have it piped direct to each station by landline, through one of the video facilities companies.

15.6.9 Animation

Animation can be used either to produce commercials in the form of cartoons or to make models move, and many of the best-known and most effective commercials have used these techniques. Such commercials are produced by specialist animation companies.

Cartoons are often used for the creation of characters who can be strongly associated with the brand. The Spillers flour-graders, the Tetley tea-folk, the Frosties tiger Tony are a handful of the characters that have become famous in the United Kingdom, and every other country has its own cartoon favourites. Sometimes advertising takes cartoon characters who are already well-known, such as Rupert Bear, and uses them for its own purposes, e.g. promoting the issues associated with insulin-dependent diabetes to children. In recent years, however, cartoon animation has been used not merely for the creation of humorous characters, but also to create mood and emotion.

The other form of animation is *model animation*, in which puppets or other inanimate objects are made to move. Plasticine models – like Wallace and Gromit – came into their own in the late 1990s.

15.6.10 Film versus videotape

Animated commercials were traditionally shot on film (but with advances in television technology this has changed of late). However, commercials made for the cinema are usually shot on film. (The former because video does not lend itself easily to the hours of patient frame-by-frame work required, the latter because most cinemas still have no video projection facilities, and the picture quality is still not as good as that of film.) However, for most other commercials the question of whether to shoot on film or videotape can be a difficult one.

Videotape is simply the visual equivalent of magnetic recording tape – it does not require processing, as film does, but can instantly be played back. It is possible to shoot a commercial on video in the morning, and have it piped by landline to the TV stations for screening the same evening. This is how the newspapers produce TV commercials that incorporate material from the following day's paper (and it dents the argument that television is a medium that requires a long time for the ad production stage). It is generally slightly cheaper than film. However, the picture quality tends to be less good, though it is improving all the time.

Where video does score, however, apart from being quick and cheap to produce, is in the special effects it can generate. There is virtually no limit to the effects that video can achieve, from turning pictures upside down and revolving them, to changing their colour and halving their size, all thanks to computer technology. Optical effects that would take days to achieve on film can be generated very quickly on video. This in turn has led to the increasing use of computer animation – brilliant colours and futuristic digital effects in which letters and logos zoom towards the camera and away again, or technical drawings which are traced out on the screen.

15.6.11 Is there a simpler way?

The advertiser who wants to be on television but who does not want to go through this complex and usually expensive method of production has an alternative. At its most basic level, a TV commercial can consist simply of a slide, showing words and a picture, and a voice-over. Most television companies will produce such commercials for advertisers who do not want to go to the trouble of making their own ads.

The slide and voice-over route may be cheap and it will reach a large audience, but it does not take advantage of one of television's greatest strengths – movement – and it is unlikely to convey much atmosphere.

However, with some creativity, short ads can work. In 1983, 10 second commercials accounted for 14 per cent of the ads on TV. By 1995, the number had nearly doubled to 26 per cent.[3] In March 1995 there were TV advertisements for the magazine *Wired* which appeared as 2 second slots in commercial breaks – so-called 'blipverts' – that featured a blend of video graphics with computer technology to show a face mouthing a single phrase. Interestingly, the Broadcasting Authority Code of Conduct (BACC) still insisted on having half a second's silence at the beginning and end. This left exactly one second of sound to get something across. And they got noticed. The campaign was reinforced with posters.

Later that year, there was another new form of advertisements created that also raised some eyebrows. There were a series of 3-minute spots of the beer 'Miller' which began to blur the boundaries between advertising and programming. The mini-programmes – advertisements does not seem to be the right word for them – followed the format of a US-style chat show. They were aired in the same spot every week, had a name 'Miller Time', a host, Jonny Miller, and a series of real-life guests. The campaign included promotional posters and press ads featuring the Channel 4 logo.

15.7 Producing radio advertisements

This is similar to producing television commercials. Both rely on actors, composers and musicians, and both need to create images that will linger in the mind. Furthermore, both need to do this in very short periods of time – generally, although by no means always, 30 seconds. Indeed, the sound-tracks of some television commercials have made very effective radio commercials, as 'reminders' of the TV campaign.

However, the differences between creating ads for radio and television cannot be over-emphasized, as these are substantial. Many advertising people maintain that radio is the more problematical of the two. It is not too difficult to improve a poor television script by hiring a top director and adding glossy 'production values' which make the commercial look wonderful. On radio, no amount of production – except, perhaps, a very strong music track – can save a script that is no good. Moreover, radio is more difficult as the absence of any visual image means that everything the ad has to convey – name, price, stockists, functions, varieties (size, colour, flavour) or whatever – has to be on the sound-track; in television, much of this information can be given on the screen, without being spoken at all.

15.7.1 Writing the radio script

As with any medium, the first decision is deciding which sort of treatment should be used. In radio, it often comes down to a choice between humour and music. This is largely because these are the two most effective ways of stimulating a reaction from radio listeners, and of getting them involved in the commercial.

A radio script looks very similar to a television script, except that there is no column for the visual half of the commercial. However, the writer should still have a strong visual image of what is going on. The script is usually written by the agency creative team, but sometimes the agency – or occasionally the client – calls in a radio production company to create the commercial from start to finish. Many of the most successful radio commercials have been made in this way.

15.7.2 Producing the commercial

Having written the commercial and had it approved, the agency must appoint a production company (assuming one has not already been involved before this stage). It is possible for an agency creative team to cast its own actors, hire a studio and produce the ads itself, but this rarely happens since the results tend to be less good than when a specialist radio production company is involved. The casting is important and is generally seen as part of the production company's job, unless the agency script has been written specifically with someone in mind (or unless the agency has appointed a writer/performer, such as John Cleese or Mel Smith and Griff Rhys-Jones, to do both jobs).

It is at the production stage that the use of writer/performers comes into its own, since they can make the script sound natural and achieve the best possible timing. This can make all the difference between a very good commercial and a poor one.

15.7.3 How to write a great radio ad[4]

1   Do a storyboard. I'm not kidding. 'Pictures in sound' has become a tired cliché because people worry about the sound and forget the pictures. If you know what your commercial looks like, you'll find the sounds come a lot easier.

2   Write a two sentence description of the characters in the commercial, including the end voice-over. Give them names; flesh them out a bit. A dialogue featuring MVO1 talking to MVO2 doesn't give actors anything to hang a performance on, which means it won't give the listener much either.

3   Simple is always better. If you've got a good message, try not getting in its way; there's something really exciting about a beautifully-crafted and presented straight commercial. But if you do write a two-hander, ask yourself the next question:

4   Is it really dialogue? A monologue divided into two parts isn't. Make sure there's a relationship between your characters, and a reason for the conversation. This isn't as obvious as it looks.

5   Do your own people watching. Sitcoms are someone else's observations of real life so if you use television dialogue as a source, you're a generation removed from the original before you start. Well-executed pastiche is valid. Well-observed life is special.

6   Take your time. Here's a foolproof method for determining how long a commercial should be:
    (a)   Write it.
    (b)   Read it aloud.
    (c)   Number of seconds taken for step b equals length of commercial.
          Any media man, account exec. or client who tells you a radio spot must be any particular length is talking rubbish.

7   Write in a 'bumper' – a line or bit of atmosphere that helps the listener separate your ad from the rubbish that's likely to precede it. Do the same at the end.

8   Take your time (2). Good radio needs as much thinking time as good TV and press, more if you're not used to it. It's worth fighting for.

9   Talk to a specialist about production. (You didn't think you were going to get away without a pitch did you?) A good radio director can help even your simple commercials in the same way as a film, type, art or music director. The closer and earlier you involve him (or her) the better your chance of making it special.

There are maybe half a dozen decent radio production companies – listen to our reels, talk with the directors, go with whoever feels and sounds right.
There are a lot more hints and notes and not enough space, so I may do another ad like this. Frankly it depends on the reaction to this one ...

... Call Tony Hertz on ...

15.7.4 Post-production

Commercials can be put onto either cassette, cartridge tapes or even compact disc – although the first is more usual – for delivery to the radio stations, or they can be played to stations via landlines from a central studio. The station will transfer the commercial to their preferred medium – usually cartridge – where all the advertisements from other companies can be played at will at the touch of a button.

15.8 Cinema commercials and films for 'private' showing

These are produced in much the same way as TV commercials but since they are often longer, more material can be used and there is slightly less need for concentrating the message. The large screen makes possible the greater use of long shots (as opposed to close-ups), expansive landscapes, etc.

As well as being used as advertising in public cinemas, films are of course also produced for showing at exhibitions, in private cinemas, etc. These are produced in the same way but obviously give much more scope for a detailed portrayal of a company or its products. Furthermore, instead of being seen by those people who happen to be 'cinema-goers', such films can be produced for showing to selected target audiences. The key factor here is to be clear before making the film:

(a)   what is/are the intended audience(s)?
(b)   how will those audiences be assembled?

Many excellent films have been produced which were seen by very few people and so did not justify their cost.

15.9 Creating posters

In many ways, poster production is very similar to producing a press advertisement. Indeed, a number of advertisers use the same artwork for both print media. However, there are several important differences between the two, and these will affect the way the creative team treats posters.

Posters have been described as an art director's rather than a copywriter's medium. They are large, colourful and very public. In most cases, they have to be absorbed quickly and from a long way away, which means that they must be simple and easy to read. For once, a snappy headline can be all that is needed in the way of copy, because there simply is not time for the audience to take in anything more. A single headline and a picture will generally carry the most impact, and it often helps if the words are at the top of the poster, because they are less likely to be obscured by trees and buses.

15.9.1 Producing the poster

Such one-offs have to be produced in whatever way is appropriate for the site concerned. Most outdoor advertising is in the form of printed paper posters which have to be stuck onto each site by a bill poster, though on many new hoardings the poster is now held in position by glass or perspex.

Most posters are printed by the litho method, and the production process is exactly the same as that of a press ad. The difference comes at the printing stage, since this part of the process is the responsibility of the advertiser and the agency, unlike in press advertising, where it is done by the publication. The agency has to print sufficient copies of each poster to provide one for each site, together with spares in case of damage by weather or vandals. Large posters are printed in several sheets, which are put together by the staff of the poster contractor when the poster is being put up. It is the agency's job to make sure that the contractor has put up each poster correctly, but this is obviously a time-consuming and expensive job, and so in the United Kingdom the poster industry has set up a Poster Audit Bureau to oversee the whole operation.

15.10 Summary

1 Printing methods today reflect those used in the Middle Ages, although there are some new innovations that are changing the face of printing.
2 Computer technology has simplified the use of a wider range of typefaces for printed messages. With digital technology, images can be manipulated as never before.
3 Colour print technology has become affordable for the small business, opening up a whole new world of colour for the dissemination of messages.
4 The process of producing a television commercial is as involved as producing any other film designed to entertain and inform – and as expensive.
5 The production of radio commercials is a specialist art – but one where striking results can be obtained.

15.11 References

1 Information from Tektronics, Marlow, Buckinghamshire, manufacturers of colour printers.

2 Whitelock, J., *A Review of the Literature Relating to Women in Advertising*, Department of Business & Management Studies and the Northwest Centre for European Marketing, University of Salford, Working Paper 9601, March 1996.
3 *Marketing*, 23 March 1995.
4 Taken from an advertisement by The Radio Operators, a production company, and written by Tony Hertz.

15.12 Further reading

Printing Reproduction Pocket Pal (Advertising Agency Production Association) is an excellent short and simple review of printing processes, photo-engraving techniques and typesetting methods. There is unfortunately no equivalent for the other media, but the following book has a chapter which covers the topic rather superficially and mentions some other references: *The Practice of Advertising* by Hart and O'Connor (William Heinemann, 1978).

Majaro, Simon, *The Creative Process*, London: Allen & Unwin, 1991.

Rapp, Stan and Collins, Tom, *The Great Marketing Turnaround*, Englewood Cliffs, NJ: Prentice Hall, 1990.

15.13 Questions for discussion

1 Describe briefly (30 to 40 words) the main features of the following printing processes:
   (a) letterpress;
   (b) offset litho;
   (c) screen printing;
   (d) gravure.
2 Discuss the role and importance of the production department in a modern advertising agency.
3 Outline the main stages in the production of a TV film, from initial idea to first showing.
4 How does the role of the production department differ in arranging the production of a TV film as compared with an eight-page four-colour glossy brochure?
5 What effect do you expect the development of electronic methods of typesetting, etc. to have on the structure of the publishing industry?

Chapter 16

Measuring advertising effectiveness I: theories of how advertising works

'If advertising is to be effective and handled with the maximum efficiency it is necessary to know what it is intended to achieve.'
David Corkindale and Sherril Kennedy, *Managing Advertising Effectively*, MCB Books, 1975

By the end of this chapter you will:

- Understand the key ingredients in effective advertising;
- Be aware of the main theories of how advertising works and of their limitations;
- Understand what is meant by attitudes, beliefs and cognitive dissonance;
- Appreciate how advertising must be measured in terms of the task it is designed to carry out;
- Have an overview of the main methods of market research.

16.1 What makes for effective advertising?

Advertising is all about communication. So to be effective it must be based on:

1   A precise definition of *to whom* we are trying to communicate.

2   A clear understanding of *what* we need to communicate.
3   Some understanding of what effect we expect the communication to have.

and also (much more difficult):

4   An understanding of how the communication process works.

Given these four things, we can then define what we expect to happen as a result of the advertising and can set out to measure whether it has been achieved or not.

As we shall see in Chapter 17, there are research techniques available to help us measure whether advertising is achieving the desired results, or even whether the advertising we are planning is *likely* to work. However, they can only be applied successfully if we have a clear idea of what the desired results are (points 3 and 4 above). This can be extremely difficult to arrive at and involves some familiarity with some of the theories about what advertising does and how it does it.

16.2 Advertising's role in the 'total selling' process

Sometimes of course it is absolutely clear what advertising's role is. An advertisement in a newspaper or a magazine inviting people to send money or use their credit card to buy a CD or a handbag through the post is an example. The advertisement is designed to bring in orders and can be seen to have succeeded or failed to the extent to which it does so within a time-scale of a few days.

As we saw in Chapter 2, however, much advertising is not of this character. The effect of a TV advertisement for BP talking of the benefits the company's investment will bring the nation, or for Orange mobile phones stating that 'The future is orange', cannot be measured in the same simple way. Somewhere along the line advertising such as this is expected to contribute to profitability but measuring this contribution has to be a much more complex and sophisticated business.

Even when advertising is much more directly aimed at increasing sales, it is clearly not the only factor at work. Prices, availability of alternatives, level of distribution, competitive advertising all play a part. For many products, such as beer and soft drinks, the weather plays a crucial role. Derek Bloom[1] refers to a number of factors influencing the Beecham product Lucozade (*see* Section 4.3.1) and concludes: 'Possibly the most important of these and obviously outside the control of marketing management, was the influence of influenza epidemics.' Advertising will frequently be only one influence among many on how consumers behave and what products they buy.

It was the recognition that advertising was only one factor in the total process of selling that led to the development of a series of models based on the idea that advertising can help move consumers through a series of steps which gradually built up the necessary conditions for a sale – the so-called 'Hierarchy of Effects' approach (such as DAGMAR – *see* Section 16.3.2).

16.3 'Hierarchy of effects' theories of advertising

Scientifically, this approach is related to what is often referred to as learning theory. The classic well-known experiment was that of Pavlov's dog, which he trained to associate the idea of food with the ringing of a bell – to the extent that the dog eventually salivated when the bell rang, even if no food was presented.

Advertising was thus seen, as a stimulus (like the bell) giving rise to a 'conditioned response' (salivating). A further development of learning theory gives rise to the so-called 'linear sequential' or, as in the section heading, 'hierarchy of effects' theories of advertising. The suggestion in all of them is that, to be effective (i.e. to result in the desired behaviour) any piece of persuasive communication must carry its audience through a series of stages, each stage being dependent on success in the previous stage. People must climb a ladder rung by rung as it were and the task of the advertising or other piece of promotional activity is to encourage them to do so.

16.3.1 The Starch model and AIDA

Daniel Starch in the early 1920s put forward the idea that in order to be effective, any advertising:

1   Must be *seen.*
2   Must be *read.*
3   Must be *believed.*
4   Must be *remembered.*
5   Must be *acted upon.*

This is a very useful rule of thumb or check-list against which to measure whether an advertisement seems likely to include the necessary ingredients. It runs into difficulty, however, when we try to pin down precisely what each of the 'steps' actually entails. For example, does 'read' mean scanned quickly or studied in great detail? Does remembered mean remembered for a long time? How long? In how much detail?

An alternative, which is still often used as a quick check on whether an advertisment 'looks right' is the AIDA model, which suggests that an effective advertisement is one which:

1   Commands *Attention*
2   Leading to *Interest* in the product
3   And thence to *Desire to* own or use the product
4   And finally to *Action* (normally purchase or at least a step towards it e.g. completing an enquiry coupon).

16.3.2 The DAGMAR model

In 1961 Russell Colley published a book titled *Defining Advertising Goals for Measured Advertising Results* (DAGMAR for short). The main conclusions were expressed in the following quotation:

> All commercial communications that weigh on the ultimate objective of a sale, must carry a prospect through four levels of understanding.
>
> The prospect must first be aware of the existence of a brand or company.
> He must have a comprehension of what the product is and what it will do for him.
> He must arrive at a mental suspicion or conviction to buy the product.
> Finally, he must stir himself to action.

This is an improvement on the earlier models because it recognizes the need to take account of the recipients' reactions and does not deal purely with the message as such yielding an automatic response. However, it still has some problems e.g. is it always *necessary* to have a clear comprehension of what the product is before having a conviction to buy? The main objection is the underlying assumption that it is advertising that brings all this about and that the effects on advertising can be observed in isolation from the many other influences (*see* Section 16.8).

Nonetheless the DAGMAR model has one enormous value. It enables the main purpose of a particular advertising campaign to be defined as, for example, to increase awareness or to improve comprehension of the product. This lends itself to 'before and after' surveys which can measure what changes have taken place. Where sales may result at some distant time this can in some circumstances give a much more immediate measure of whether the advertising has been effective.

In relation to the *action* part of the DAGMAR hierarchy it has been pointed out that a great deal of advertising is intended *not* to generate new users and thus calling for action, but rather to persuade existing users not to change. However, it can be argued that this apparent *inaction* is still in a sense creating a sale. But this kind of consideration does highlight the fact that the model, whilst a useful one, is nowhere near as precise as it at first appears.

16.4 What acts on whom?

A number of people have pointed out that all of these models tend to assume a passive audience being influenced by advertising messages aimed at it. They argue that often the reverse viewpoint is relevant – an audience actively seeking advertising messages because they are looking for the best answer to a well defined problem such as 'which is the most economic car in my price range?' or 'which camera will give me the instant pictures I need?' e.g. Colin MacDonald of BMRB[2] refers to 'this picture of random forces batting the poor purchaser about like a tennis ball' and would prefer an alternative model which 'would recognize the purchaser as an active principal'. The suggestion here is that people deliberately and purposefully select the messages that are of interest to them and 'filter out' those that are not.

Similarly Barnard[3] says, 'It has been insufficiently recognized that consumers are purposeful beings with goals of their own and adapt to the restrictions imposed by their environment'.

In his 1992 book *How Advertising Works*, Colin McDonald[4] reviews in depth the arguments for and against the hierarchy of effects models such as DAGMAR and concludes that they are not so much theories of how advertising works, but rather *necessary conditions*. It is, for example, self-evident that people are unlikely to respond to advertising that has not caught their attention. It is this apparently obvious inherent truth in these models which accounts for their continuing to be strongly held by many. This is particularly the case since in some circumstances, such as direct response advertising, the hierarchy of effects approach may still have relevance.

However, in most cases we have to look at the alternative approaches discussed in the next Section.

16.5 Alternative views of advertising

The realization that many factors are involved has led to the relegation of the hierarchy of effects models to a far less dominant position than they once held, even though they persist strongly in some quarters and may still have relevance in a few circumstances.

Alan Hedges points out[5], 'To the consumer advertising is mainly just part of the background scene. Advertisements form part of the continual whirling mass of sense impressions which bombard the eye . . . Just as we cannot take all our consuming decisions in discrete rational steps, so we cannot stop to evaluate and classify all the pieces of sensory input we receive. This too, has to be relegated to very low levels of consciousness for the most part.'

Hedges suggests that advertising can operate at a number of different levels:

1   Simply by creating a sense of familiarity, an awareness that the brand is 'around'. People are more likely to buy a brand that they recognize, although that recognition may not consciously be associated with remembering the advertising.
2   Advertising may 'surround the brand with particular associations, with moods, feelings, emotional colours and so on'.
3   Advertising may convey information e.g. about price, functions, etc.
4   Sometimes rational arguments may be put forward. It is probably only at this level that the customers' conscious attention is likely to be engaged.

Advertising of everyday consumer products normally works over a period of time. Its effect is cumulative rather than instantaneous and may often be concerned with helping consumers to identify with a particular brand. Cases where advertising contributes to a 'once and for all' acceptance of a reasoned argument are likely to relate to occasionally purchased consumer durables, industrial capital goods, etc. (*see* Section 4.5).

The 'brand switching' situation referred to in Section 4.5 means that as Joyce[6] puts it, 'much of the work of advertising consists of *preventing a decline in sales*'. He goes on to suggest that 'much advertising must be judged largely on its performance among present users, i.e. those who are already favourably disposed to the brand'.

Both Hedges and Joyce highlight the fact that much purchasing must of necessity be a matter of routine. As Joyce says '. . . a powerful determinant of consumer choice is habit or inertia. It suits the customer to treat much of her activity as a matter of routine. To indulge in a process of conscious deliberation at every purchase would take an enormous amount of time and mental effort which, not unnaturally, there is a strong drive to avoid'.

By 'her' Joyce was presumably referring to 'the housewife' – a stereotype which was always questionable and has now been almost entirely discarded. However, much the same inertia will be found in any regular purchaser of any type of commodity. Even industrial buyers are reluctant to make the effort and take the risk of changing suppliers without strong reasons.

All of this comes down to the fact that a strong factor is the customers' relationship with and attitude towards products. A key function of advertising is to shape or reinforce those attitudes.

16.6 What do people do with advertising?

This is the question posed in a paper by Judie Lannon and Peter Cooper[7]. They explore, like MacDonald and Barnard (*see* Section 16.4) the probability that the mechanistic theories of advertising such as DAGMAR concentrate too much on what the advertising does and pay too little attention 'to what has become known as the sophisticated consumer'. They suggest that we need to recognize 'the consumer as *active* participator in communication'. Lannon and Cooper go on to suggest that 'consumers endow the brands they buy and use with meanings, over and above their sheer functional value. It is the creative task to communicate these meanings in ways which motivate and reinforce; research is to unlock them and make them available to the creative process. We are then making a clear distinction between the *ostensive* or face-value aspects of brands and their *latent* or symbolic values.'

The authors suggest that it is the product as such and the symbolism associated with it that gives rise to a strong brand. The two aspects are illustrated in Figure 16.1.

Neurological research has given rise to the belief that we all have two types of consciousness residing in the two hemispheres of the brain. The left hemisphere (which controls the right side of the body) is the practical

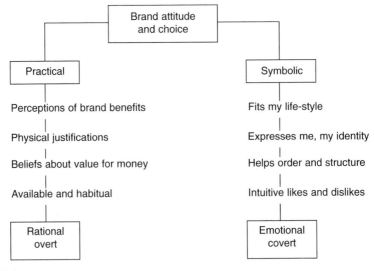

Figure 16.1

side, the right hemisphere (controlling the left side of the body) is the symbolic side. Lannon and Cooper suggest that 'much advertising is essentially and increasingly "right hemisphere" communication, dealing in symbolic communication'. They picture the concerns of the left and right hemispheres as shown in Figure 16.2.

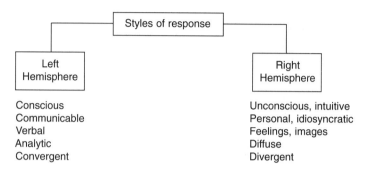

Figure 16.2

Examples of symbolism frequently used in advertising are class (e.g. in After Eight chocolate mints advertising with its 'upper-class' overtones, and Hovis bread with its 'working class' ones), youth, sex, indulgence, freedom.

The idea of the 'active consumer' is summarized by Lannon and Cooper in the following paragraphs:

Expectations of advertising
Advertising is capable of entering language, daydreams and intuition because of its independent existence. It does not simply do things to people in the sense of treating consumers as objects to manipulate, nor does it merely do things to products, like creating USPs, brand personalities. Rather, people do things to advertising, interact with it, and produce surprising outcomes. As we suggested earlier, in the UK:

1 Advertising is expected to exaggerate, sing praises, transform products. It has psychic energy.
2 It fascinates, compels, we know we are being sold to (conscious self); it 'should' be suppressed, but we need to project, get involved, be surprised, be attracted, confront our irrational selves.
3 It is living, childish, dramatic, contentious, foolish, magical, glossy.
4 It reaches into the depths of personal motivations and collective feelings, using symbols to portray, tricks to release.
5 Its rituals and repetitions communicate with the deeper self. Successful advertisements enter public vocabulary and become part of ourselves.

How we react to advertising has changed. It has lost its manipulative reputation stimulated by The Hidden Persuaders – and become part of culture. As we saw earlier, *there is less suspicion nowadays and more enjoyment of, and involvement in, advertising. There is a feeling of greater trust, greater marketing literacy, along with a willingness to participate, enjoy and respond, accepting exaggerations and brand praise, and making allowances for these.*

16.7 The active consumer

The Lannon and Cooper idea of an active, participating consumer, rather than a passive one that advertising 'does things to' is explored further by McDonald. He states 'those who receive advertising are *actively in control and pick and choose what they will attend to'*.

In other words, nobody is forced to pay attention to or respond to any advertising.

This approach has the following ingredients:

1 Habitual purchases for everyday use cannot be explained in terms of a sequence of (hierarchical) steps.
2 People can and do screen out advertising which has no relevance to them – most advertising is of no interest to most people most of the time.

We can distinguish between *passive* (non-intrusive) advertising which is 'there' for us to refer to when we need it (jobs and other 'classifieds') and *active* (intrusive) advertising which tries to command our attention for items we would not go searching for.

Taking this view, suggests McDonald, puts a premium on the need to *target* advertising so that it is likely to 'find the right way to speak to those who are prone to be interested in what it has to say'.

In *How to Plan Advertising*,[8] Jeremy Elliott suggests that 'The way advertising affects consumer choices, in totality, is not a neat, sequential and mechanistic system, but a largely muddled, often irrational and essentially *human* process. He suggests that Joyce's model of 1967 (*see* Figure 16.3) is still valid. He concludes: 'Different advertising campaigns, fulfilling different roles, will produce different kinds of effect' (along the lines suggested in Section 16.10).

16.8 Attitudes and beliefs

The Concise Oxford Dictionary defines an attitude as '... a settled mode of thinking' and belief as '... acceptance (of things, fact, statement, etc.) as true or existing'.

Psychologists define attitudes as 'a learned predisposition to respond in a consistently favourable or unfavourable direction towards a given attitude object', whereas a belief is 'any statement of any kind which connects the attitude object with some other object goal or value' (see *How do we choose?*) for further discussion of these ideas[9].

Psychologists arrive at a clear picture of attitudes by getting people to 'agree or disagree' with a series of statements. Sometimes this is modified by asking people to rate a statement on a scale e.g.

'Whisky is a strong drink'
    Strongly agree
    Slightly agree
    Neither agree nor disagree
    Slightly disagree
    Strongly disagree

By getting a number of people to respond in this way to a series of statements a picture of prevailing attitudes can be built up.

The idea, embraced in the psychologists' definition given above, that attitudes are *learned,* suggests that they can be modified and much advertising attempts to do this e.g. government advertising attempts to change people's attitudes to smoking, drinking and other behaviour which is seen as unhealthy or socially undesirable; a company seen as old-fashioned, conservative or antisocial may wish to encourage a different series of attitudes; a product seen as 'not for people like me' may need to be represented so as to become acceptable to 'people like me'.

Attitudes can be changed by the following means:

1   Reasoned argument leading the audience to judge the suggested conclusion as 'true' or 'false' (an example is the use of accident statistics to attempt to change people's attitude to the wearing of seat belts).
2   Positive emotional appeals e.g. 'Stop smoking and you will feel fitter and food will taste better'.
3   Negative emotional appeals e.g. 'Don't stop smoking and your lungs may end up looking like this'.

Some recent theories on customer behaviour have developed out of market research work on brand choice and related matters. A theory which has gained much support and certainly offering an elegant approach is that of Fishbein, encapsulated in the equation:

$$BI = \underset{w1}{A\ act} + \underset{w2}{SN}$$

where BI is the Behavioural Intention, 'A act' the Attitude to the Act and SN the Subjective Norm; w1 and w2 are the weightings to be attached to the components 'A act' and SN.

Stated in words, the theory postulates that the way people intend to behave is influenced by two main factors, as follows:

1   Their attitude to the proposed act or behaviour (in terms of 'Do I like/dislike, approve/disapprove of this act').
2   The 'subjective norm' i.e. the way they believe other people expect them to behave.

The first component 'A act' is in turn the summation of a set of beliefs about the act i.e. the connection a person perceives between the act and its possible/probable consequences. The beliefs included in the summation are those Fishbein calls 'salient beliefs' i.e. those which have the most influence. In practice these are usually taken as being the first seven 'beliefs' the respondent lists in answer to an open-ended question such as 'Tell me what you think (about the act in question').

A problem of the whole attitudes and beliefs approach to influencing behaviour (including purchasing habits) is that the causal link between attitudes and behaviour is not proven e.g. studies on racial attitudes in the USA have shown that people's stated beliefs can be strongly at variance with their actual behaviour.

Favourable attitudes to products can often be shown to follow rather than precede purchase (a serious defect in the 'Hierarchy of Effects' models).

16.9 Cognitive dissonance

It is a well-known fact that the way people see something depends on what they expect to see. Supporters of opposing football teams or political parties will react to a particular incident on the field or in a TV interview quite differently.

L. Festinger[10] has developed these findings into a body of theory labelled *cognitive dissonance*. It argues that humans seek to maintain a state of mental 'consonance' or equilibrium. Anything that disturbs this causes 'dissonance' because it upsets the patterns of knowledge (cognitions) that the person has learned to find acceptable. In order to avoid dissonance, information which is inconsistent with the existing pattern will be rejected, whilst anything reinforcing it will be welcomed.

Gerald de Groot in *The Persuaders Exposed*[11] suggests that this works along the following lines in a marketing situation:

> Assume that somebody uses brand A and a marketing effort is made to convince him that brand B is 'best'. This information would be inconsistent with the existing mental set and would, therefore, set up dissonance, which is intolerable and must be resolved. Because of

this there will be a tendency to ignore the message; it will not form part of the psychological environment of brand A purchasers. Something very much like this would appear to happen to a great deal of advertising in the real world. But if the message is too powerful to be ignored, it can be distorted. The recipient can convince himself that what is being said is not 'brand B is **best**' but that 'brand B is a good brand', which is acceptable information and would not cause dissonance. If, however, the message is so powerful that it can be neither ignored nor distorted, then dissonance results. The obvious way to resolve it is to buy brand B. There are then two possibilities. Brand B may be found not to be 'best' and, therefore, the purchaser goes back to buying brand A, convinced that brand B's advertising and marketing is making false claims. Therefore, the purchaser does not experience dissonance. Or brand B may indeed be found to be 'best', in which case a change of purchasing behaviour will result and as a consequence so will a change of attitudes and beliefs.

16.10 Towards a synthesis

All of the above theories and statements represent varying ways of looking at how advertising seems to work. None of them has really yet reached the status of a truly scientific approach. That is to say it is rarely possible to use them as a means of *predicting* exactly what will happen as a result of a particular advertising approach. Some do not even stand up to Karl Popper's criterion of a scientific statement – is it capable of being disproved if it is untrue?

What does seem to be the case is that the whole process of which advertising forms a part (*see* Sections 16.2 and 16.5) is a complex one. People's attitudes, social norms, existing purchasing and usage behaviour, as well as their reasoning power all have a part to play – as do other factors such as competition, the availability of alternatives, economic circumstances and many other things. Joyce[6] has attempted to illustrate this diagrammatically (*see* Figure 16.3).

Hedges[5] emphasises the importance of making it easy for people to identify easily with products. This means first that brands must have a clear identity which is a function not merely of advertising, but of all forms of promotion and also of the product itself, its name, packaging and so on. The identity of the product has three parts, suggests Hedges:

1　The prominence or salience of the brand (the extent to which it springs readily to mind).
2　The clarity or distinctiveness of its identity (the extent to which it is seen to have clear and pronounced characteristics and properties).
3　The nature of its identity (the kinds of feeling, thought and belief which people have about it).

All of this adds up to the fact that what matters (and therefore what needs to be 'measured' – *see* Chapter 17) is not just what people know about the product but how they feel about it and how they are able to relate

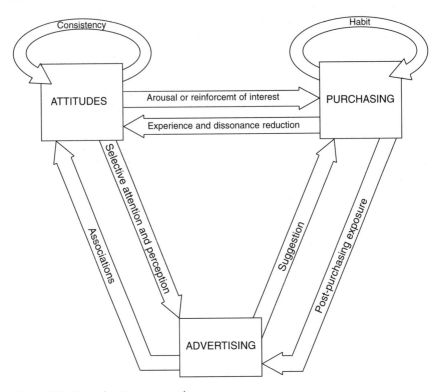

Figure 16.3 *How advertising may work.*

it to their own personalities and life-styles. The effect of advertising then becomes much more part of a continuing relationship than a step-by-step sequential activity as envisaged in the earlier hierarchy of effects models (*see* Section 16.3). The right or creative/intuitive side of the brain will probably be more involved in purchasing decisions than the left or rational/logical side. Research and measurement techniques need to reflect this emphasis.

16.11 A Scale of Immediacy

Stephen King[12] has drawn attention to the discrepancy between the various theories of advertising and the largely pragmatic ways of measuring effectiveness. He suggests, 'I don't think we should try to produce advertisements or evaluate their effect without having *some* theory of how they are meant to work. At the same time I don't think we will ever solve the "how advertising works" problem. But there is surely a middle course'.

King's middle course is to suggest that advertising operates in a number of different ways according to his 'scale of immediacy'. (*See* Figure 16.4.)

'So far', says King, 'I have been encouraged by the way this helps to bring together many of the results of JWT's basic research programme over the last ten years. It does not seem to require all those disclaimers that we all write at the beginning of pieces on advertising theory ("only fast-moving grocery goods need apply"). It does seem to be able to cope with today's changing circumstances, changing consumer attitudes, different product types, different types of advertising, different media values. The attractive thing about a scale is that it is a nice simple entity, yet it does not suggest that one single mechanism can explain everything.'

He goes on to relate the scale to the following kinds of advertising:

1 *Direct* ('selling off the page').
2 *Seek Information* (or 'tell me more' advertising).
3 *Relate to own needs, wants, desires* (the 'what a good idea' response).
4 *Recall satisfactions; reinforce/re-order short list* (the 'that reminds me' response).
5 *Modify attitudes.*
6 *Reinforce attitudes* (common with established brand leader products such as Persil, Heinz soup, Kellogg's cornflakes).

The methods used to determine advertising effectiveness will then clearly depend on the part of the 'scale of immediacy' in which we believe a particular piece of advertising is operating.

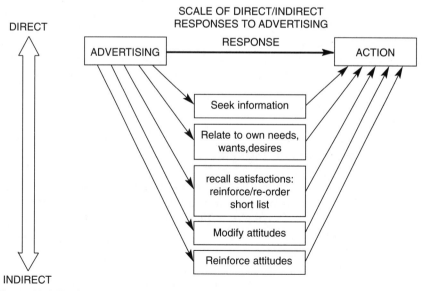

Figure 16.4 *King's scale of immediacy*

16.12 Basic market research methods

The following chapter considers some of the research techniques used specifically to measure advertising effectiveness. Most of them employ methodology which is used much more widely in all kinds of research into many aspects of marketing. It will be useful therefore at this stage to summarize briefly some of the methods and terminology which are employed.

16.12.1 Sampling

The use of sampling is based on the concept that, if a small number of items or parts (the sample) are selected at random from a larger number of parts of a whole (the universe), then the sample will tend to have the same characteristics in approximately the same proportion as the universe. The 'universe' is sometimes called the 'population'.

'Random' has a special meaning in this context. It does not mean, as in everyday usage, aimless or haphazard. A random sample is one selected in such a way that every single individual unit in the universe from which it was chosen had a full and equal chance of being included in the sample. Its implications are perhaps best understood by looking at examples of sample selection that are *not* random:

1   A sample of householders obtained by selecting numbers from the telephone directory cannot be random, since householders not on the telephone have no chance of being selected.
2   A sample of marketing men selected from the membership list of the Institute of Marketing cannot be *random*, since it excludes those who are not members.
3   Questionnaires inserted in a motoring magazine for completion and return by readers cannot provide a random sample of all car owners because:
    (a) it excludes non-readers
    (b) it excludes readers who did not see that particular issue
    (c) it excludes those who are too busy or disinclined to fill in the questionnaire and return it.

So far we have been talking of sampling in terms of random sampling of the entire universe. But we have also referred to the need for marketing research to operate within cost limitations. This latter point means that in practice other approaches to sampling are frequently used. The main division is between the following:

1   *Random sampling* – where each unit in the universe has the same chance of being included in the sample.

2   *Quota sampling* – where the interviewer selects the individuals to be interviewed, but is given detailed instructions on the characteristics (age, sex, class, occupation, etc.) of the people to be interviewed, numbers of each category to be interviewed, conditions of interview (at home, at work, etc.).

Random sampling needs a 'sampling frame' i.e. a complete and up-to-date list of all members of the universe, such as that provided by the electoral roll, for example (although it, like any sampling frame, is never totally accurate). The units to be included in the sample are then selected along the lines of the following example.

On any given section of the electoral roll randomly select (by means of a more sophisticated version of the 'drawing lots' principle) a starting point, such as the 10th household. The interviewer is instructed to interview the head of that 10th household, then the 25th, 40th, 55th and so on, or the 30th, 50th, 70th and so – on the interval depending on the total sample size required. The interviewer must interview the person specified and must, if necessary, call back repeatedly until he or she finds the interviewee at home. Strict rules are laid down to cover such contingencies as death or permanent absence, and the interviewer can only include someone else in the sample instead if he is so instructed.

In the case of a quota sample, the interviewer selects the people to be interviewed, although strict criteria are laid down to ensure as far as possible that the final sample, when all the individuals interviewed by the different interviewers are put together, does represent the universe.

16.12.2 Questionnaires

In most surveys the interviewer is provided with a questionnaire. The purpose is the following:

1   To list the questions the interviewer is to ask, in the precise words to be used and in the right sequence.
2   To provide space for recording the answers, usually in such a way that they can be readily analysed. Frequently a 'magnetic' pencil is used, so that an electronic device can read off the marks and transfer them directly to disk ready for computer analysis.
3   To record details of the respondent – age, sex, occupation, etc., and sometimes such other factors as whether he is a car-owner or not, or a householder or not, depending on the needs of the particular survey.

Questions asked in interviewing are of three main types, as follows:

1   *Dichotomous* i.e. answered by a simple yes or no (usually with a 'don't know' column as well).

2   *Multiple choice* – where a number of possible answers are listed and the interviewer indicates which are selected (sometimes more than one).
3   *Open-ended* – where no particular kind of answer is presupposed and the interviewer has to write in the respondent's answer.

Open-ended questions have the disadvantage of being slow, difficult to analyse, and yielding answers which are perhaps irrelevant or incoherent. On the other hand, they allow the possibility of much fuller answers, with shades of meaning, they reduce the possibility of bias from answers suggested by the researchers, and they may overcome the reluctance of some respondents to answer direct questions. The selection of types of question will depend on the kind of information being sought and the depth required, the type of respondent, and the cost limitations imposed on the research.

In order to reduce bias, care has to be taken in working out the sequence and wording of questions. Some of the 'rules' are as follows (but judgement and experience play a large part):

1   Questions on matters of a private or emotional nature should come at the end of an interview, as should complicated questions and those requiring thought, so that the respondent's interest is engaged.
2   Conversely, easy questions and those most likely to capture a respondent's interest are placed at the beginning.
3   Questions should be short, easy to understand, and phrased in colloquial language.
4   There should be no ambiguity and, 'double-barrelled' questions should be avoided ('Did you drink coffee with lunch and dinner yesterday?' comprises two questions).
5   Leading questions (i.e. where it appears obvious what answer is expected) must be avoided.
6   Questions that rely heavily on the respondent's memory ('Which magazines have you read during the past six months?') must be avoided.
7   Questions must be as precise as possible. For example, in the previous point what do we mean by 'reading' a magazine? From cover to cover? A quick glance? Editorial or advertisements, or both?
8   There are severe limits to the length of questionnaire that will hold a respondent's interest. To go beyond them increases the risk of ill-considered or flippant answers.

16.12.3 Analysis

The results of the fact-gathering part of a marketing research operation will be a large pile of completed questionnaires in the case of a survey, or masses of figures gathered as secondary data from various sources. The way this material is analysed and presented is a crucial factor in how valuable the research will be.

Questionnaires must frequently be edited as a first stage in processing: that is, they must be carefully scrutinized by an experienced person who will reject obviously unreliable questionnaires, and correct or complete any answers not clearly written in by the interviewer (but where it is obvious what is meant). In appropriate cases the editor will check that the various answers in the questionnaire are consistent with each other, that the answers are not merely frivolous and so on.

The questionnaires screened in this way will then be processed to extract the data in tabular form. This may be done manually (in the case of a small sample or a complex questionnaire with many 'open-ended' questions), or by computer. Computers are invariably used for continuing surveys such as audits, but it may well not be worth setting up a program for a 'one-off' survey.

Once the information is available in the form of tables of figures, their significance must be examined and interpreted. This interpretation will emerge finally as a report, which will draw attention to the similarities, discrepancies, changes and other important features the analysis has uncovered.

16.12.4 Ad hoc and continuous research

A great deal of marketing research is carried out on a continuous basis. Many government statistics are gathered quarterly, annually, or at some other regular interval. Many commercial studies are carried out on a 'panel' or 'audit' basis. The great value of this is that we can plot trends and see whether a particular factor is increasing or decreasing, whether any of the elements being plotted are departing from what the trends were indicating, and so on. Any departures from the 'expected' trends may point to new factors of importance in the marketplace.

On the other hand, this is costly, and not every aspect of every market justifies the expense. Many marketing investigations, therefore, are carried out on an irregular, infrequent or even a once-for-all basis. The term usually applied to these cases is *ad hoc* research.

16.12.5 Panels and audits

Panels consist of permanent samples of the universe concerned. Members of these panels agree to give regular interviews and/or regularly record information in special 'diaries'. They are usually paid a small fee. This has obvious advantages in that sampling is itself costly, and using the same

sample over and over represents a saving. But the main reasons for the use
of panels are the following:

1   Comparison is easier and more reliable, since we are comparing over
     time the behaviour and/or attitudes not just of similar people but of
     the same people. It is even possible, if desired, to study individual
     behaviour over a period of time.
2   Because they are specially recruited and instructed, panel members
     are usually more 'forthcoming' than people interviewed 'out of the
     blue' and can be asked to carry out more complicated and extensive
     procedures.

Disadvantages of panels are that members may become self-conscious
and no longer truly representative. Indeed, it may be that willingness to
participate is in itself a non-characteristic response. Another problem is
matching the succession when, for one reason or another, people leave the
panel.

However, panels are used to gain regular information on such matters
as the following:

1   Household purchasing patterns.
2   TV viewing and radio listening habits.
3   Current stock patterns – an example of this is the 'pantry check',
     where a regular call is made by interviewers on a panel of households
     to check what products they are using (providing valuable informa-
     tion on such matters as changing preferences for pack size, quantities
     bought at a time, etc.).

Since the panel type of research often necessitates regular visits to
households by interviewers, other information can be gained at the same
time by adding *ad hoc* questions to the regular questionnaire.

The retail audit technique uses panels of shops to establish brand
shares and volume of sales from retail outlets to customers (which, because
of changing stock levels, may be quite different from the volume of deliv-
eries from factory to retailers). This looks likely in the near future to be
replaced by electronic checkout (EPOS) information (which, incidentally,
will put this most valuable information firmly under the control of the
major retail chains).

A. C. Nielsen & Co. Ltd, operating in twenty-one countries, are leaders
in this kind of research. Starting with their *Food Index* then moving on to a
Drug Index (based on audits of grocery and chemist shops), they now regularly publish indexes for confectionery, liquor stores and cash-and-carry
wholesalers.

16.13 Summary

1   In order to measure whether advertising is effective we have to know what it is trying to achieve.

2   Whilst this may sometimes be as simple as 'achieving the projected level of sales', more often advertising has to be seen as merely contributing to the conditions that ultimately lead to a sale.

3   Recognition of the limited role of advertising led to step-by-step or 'hierarchy of effects' models which saw advertising as helping people along a rather logical path towards ultimately purchasing the product.

4   More recent thinking suggests that attitudes, feelings and existing beliefs are likely to have more importance than a rational approach. People will react to products because of what they symbolize as well as what they do.

5   Social norms and existing habits of purchase and usage will also be strong influences.

6   Advertising is then viewed as one of many factors, along with the product itself, its name, packaging, etc. that help people to feel comfortable with the product.

7   People are likely to interact with, and only with, advertising that is relevant to them and largely screen out the rest.

8   Section 16.9 briefly outlines some key aspects of similar research techniques.

16.14 References

1 Bloom, Derek, *The Business of Advertising,* ESOMAR Seminar, June 1978.
2 MacDonald, Colin, 'How different advertising stimuli might work together', *Admap,* August, 1980.
3 Barnard, Neil, 'On advertising effectiveness measurement. An idiosyncratic view', *Admap,* July 1978.
4 McDonald, Colin, *How Advertising Works,* Advertising Association, 1992.
5 Hedges, Alan, *Testing to Destruction,* IPA, 1974.
6 Joyce, Timothy, *What do we know about how advertising works?,* ESOMAR, 1967.
7 Lannon, Judie and Cooper, Peter, 'Humanistic advertising', *International Journal of Advertising,* July-September 1983.
8 Cowell, Don (Ed), *How to Plan Advertising,* Cassell, 1989.
9 Tuck, Mary, *How do we choose?,* Methuen, 1976.
10 Festinger, L., *A Theory of Cognitive Dissonance,* Row, Peterson, 1957
11 de Groot, Gerald, *The Persuaders Exposed.*
12 King, Stephen, *'Practical progress from a theory of advertisements',* *Admap,* October 1975.

16.15 Further reading

Alan Hedges' monograph and the ESOMAR paper by Timothy Joyce both give a very wide-ranging and excellent review of the whole area.

For wider insight into theories of consumer behaviour generally Gordon Foxall's *Consumer Behaviour – a Practical Guide* is a good introductory text, as is *Behavioural Aspects of Marketing* by K. Williams (Heinemann, 1980).

16.16 Questions for discussion

1   Discuss the current value of the 'hierarchy of effects' models of advertising.
2   To what extent do you consider that consumers have an active role rather than a passive one in relation to advertising?
3   What are attitudes? Can they be changed? What is the relevance of attitudes to communications, advertising and marketing?
4   Identify current advertising campaigns that appear to fit into the various levels of Stephen King's 'scale of immediacy'.

Chapter 17

Measuring advertising effectiveness II: a review of research methods

'... a hard look at the numbers does not preclude judgement.'
Simon Broadbent, *Accountable Advertising*, Admap Publications 1997

By the end of this chapter you will:

- Be aware of how research can be used at various stages to improve advertising effectiveness;
- Understand the difference between qualitative and quantitative research;
- Have a basic understanding of what econometrics is and how it is used.

17.1 Planning for measurement

At the beginning of Chapter 16 it is stressed that in order to measure the effectiveness of advertising, we must be clear what effect we intend it to have. The rest of that chapter examines some approaches to determining what advertising might be expected to achieve.

Alan Hedges[1] considers that there are three main ways in which research can help to make advertising more effective.

1   *At the stage of strategy planning* research can help us to understand how our particular market really works (*see* Chapter 4 and Chapter 16).

2   *At the stage of advertising development* research on experimental advertising can provide a vital feed-back mechanism.

3   *When the campaign has finally been exposed* research can study what happens in the market place.

This chapter is concerned with the second and third of these stages, and here research takes several forms:

1   Research to ensure that creative work is based on a true understanding of the target audiences involved – Hedges calls it creative development research.

2   Testing the effect of advertising *before* it is exposed in the media.

3   Measuring the effect of advertising campaigns *after* they have run.

17.2 Creative development research

It can be important very early on in the creative process to check that the imaginative ideas being developed are such that consumers can understand them and relate to them. David Ogilvy was quoted in Section 10.3.2 as saying that the creative imagination can express half-truths vividly. Expressing vividly the half that our chosen audience cannot grasp or do not feel to be important would be useless. So there is often a need to check that the creative approach being developed is one that consumers can relate to.

17.2.1 Qualitative research

Often this is done through some form of qualitative research. That is, interviewing in some depth a (usually, though not necessarily) very small sample of the target audience to establish how they think and talk and feel about the product in question and what it means to them. The most commonly used technique is group discussions. Small groups (typically eight) of people are encouraged to exchange views with each other in a relaxed atmosphere and the 'interviewer' has the task of encouraging the discussion to take place, rather than asking formal questions. An alternative is to talk to individuals in depth rather than to groups.

The problems of the qualitative approach to research are fairly obvious.

1   The samples are usually small (even if, as normally happens, three or

four discussion groups are held) and so may not be typical of the 'universe' (the whole of the target group). By contrast 'quantitative' research normally interviews far more people (often hundreds, sometimes thousands) and the results can far more reliably be projected and 'number-crunching' – manipulation of the resulting percentages etc. – can be done with confidence.

2   Control of the discussions (e.g. to ensure that the outcome is not swayed by one or two strong personalities) is difficult and calls for skill and experience.

3   The biggest problem of all is the interpretation of the results, since they will be in the form of, often rambling, snatches of conversation and ill-considered comment rather than the structured and easily tabulated questions and answers of quantitative research.

There will often be room for differing views on the precise meaning of what people have said in this rather contrived situation and over how much importance should be attached to it.

However, there are also strong advantages in the use of qualitative research in general and group discussions in particular:

1   They are normally very inexpensive compared with quantitative research (mainly because of the cost of setting up and conducting large numbers of interviews).

2   They can be arranged very quickly.

3   They uncover information that more formal approaches might well not do. The group situation encourages a similar kind of interaction to that which psychiatrists look for from group therapy sessions. Members of the group 'spark each other off' through verbal and emotional associations and are able to express things they would find it more difficult to get out by themselves.

These attributes make qualitative research ideal for getting:

(a) some idea of how people think and feel and react to the kind of product under consideration

(b) their reactions to particular approaches, statements, words, pictures, etc. which could be used in advertising the product

As Alan Hedges[1] puts it, 'Putting advertising (and particularly creative) people in touch with real live consumers is perhaps one of the most important functions that direct research into creative material can have.'

Potter and Lovell[2] similarly point out that, 'Another problem with specialists is that their cultural and social life is completely different from any of those who will be exposed to their advertising.'

So qualitative research can often be valuable simply in providing information on which creative people can base their thinking and with which they can direct their imaginative processes into the right channels. But it can also be used to check at an early stage that their work is proceeding along useful lines.

17.3 Pre-testing advertising

This is the second type of research listed in Section 17.1. Its purpose is to check whether the advertising is likely to work *before* large sums of money are spent on it. There is a crucial and unavoidable problem here. The earlier in the process we can get a reaction from the target audience the better. To take a television campaign as an example, the cost of screening it may well be enormous and to find out after screening that it was ineffective is interesting (and valuable from the point of view of developing the next campaign) but frustrating. It would be much better to know *before* money is spent on air-time whether or not the advertisements will work. Since even producing the commercial is also a rather expensive business, to know at the creative stage whether the commercial is effective or not would be even more valuable.

Unfortunately, the earlier in the proceedings testing is carried out, the less realistic the situation is, compared to how consumers will ultimately be reacting to it, both in terms of what they see and of the conditions under which they see it. Thus viewing a finished commercial completely unselfconsciously in one's own home as part of an evening's entertainment or as an adjunct to watching news of the latest political developments or sporting events is one thing. Seeing a 'mock-up' of how the advertising might look, in a test theatre, and then being asked questions about it is quite a different matter.

Where large expenditures are involved, testing at various stages is frequently carried out, both:

pre-production – checking the reactions of members of the target audience to creative ideas and concepts, using various kinds of prototype before incurring the cost of producing the advertisement and
post-production – testing reactions to the finished press advertisement, TV film, etc. after it is made but before it is transmitted

Often it will be possible to make changes even at the post-production stage without incurring unacceptable costs (for example, changing the sound track at double-head stage – *see* Section 15.6.8 – or modifying the headline of a press advertisement at artwork stage).

17.3.1 What pre-testing can measure

Alan Hedges[1] questions whether research at the creative development stage is strictly testing at all and prefers to regard it as a (very important and necessary) way of 'studying consumers in order to gain some better understanding of the way they are likely to react to stimuli of different kinds, the stimuli being advertisements or advertising ideas'. He takes this view in order to emphasize that 'there is no kind of reliable advertising quality control procedures to which proposed advertisements can be submitted with a view to filtering out the duds and passing only the winners'.

However, most people deeply involved in producing advertising which plays an important role in a successful marketing programme would be very unhappy to go ahead with an advertising campaign which had been subjected to no kind of reaction by any members of the target audience. Potter and Lovell[2] suggest that pre-testing can obtain reactions against the following criteria:

1 *Impact.* Does the advertisement attract attention or merge into the back-ground of other material with which it appears.
2 *Involvement.* Is the reader/viewer able to relate personally to the advertisement ('that looks nice, it would fit beautifully in our kitchen').
3 *Recall.* An advertisement which has impact at the time it is seen, may or may not be remembered. Many campaigns are well known but people find it difficult to say which brand they feature. So what people can remember (recall) from an advertisement may be significant.
4 *Communication.* What did the reader/viewer think that the advertisement was about? ('it seemed to suggest that X Brand soup was more tasty and easy to prepare') (Remembering that advertising can often convey attributes of a product by the way it is pictured, without necessarily spelling them out in words.)
5 *Image.* What *kind* of product do they think the product is (good or average quality, exclusive or for everybody)? Potter and Lovell warn here that for an established brand, people will already have an image and seeing a new advertisement once is unlikely to change it. So an indirect approach such as asking questions about the people shown using the product may be more meaningful.
6 *Credibility.* Do people find they can easily believe the claims being made for the product?
7 *Like/Dislike.* Potter and Lovell warn that whilst liking or disliking the advertisement can be checked, it is also necessary to consider whether it matters (consumers will sometimes buy more of a product which is advertised in an abrasive – and therefore noticeable way – than if the advertising is 'warm and comfortable' but bland).
8 *New Learning.* Has the advertising told people something they didn't

know before (and is that something significant to them)?

9   *Intelligibility.* Did people find the advertising easy or difficult to understand?

10   *Distinctiveness.* Does the ad seem new, original, out of the ordinary?

Other criteria which have been used, but about which Potter and Lovell tend to be somewhat guarded are:

11   *Propensity to Buy.*
12   *Persuasion.*
13   *Emotional Arousal.*
14   *Simulated Sales.*
15   *Absence of Negatives.*

Clearly which of these various criteria *need* to be measured and which are more valuable and relevant will vary from one situation to another. They need to be selected in the light of an understanding of how the particular market works and how this particular advertising campaign is intended to influence people's behaviour in it.

17.3.2 Pre-testing methods

Methods of carrying out pre-testing advertising usually involve giving the selected test group of people an opportunity to compare the advertisement(s) being tested against others. In the case of press advertising a *folder test* is commonly used. The advertisement under test is placed with others in a folder or perhaps pasted or bound into a dummy magazine or newspaper. It is important that it is not too obvious which is the advertisement under test and this may mean – if the advertisement is still at an early stage (e.g. photography is simulated by a sketch) 'doctoring' the other advertisements so that they are in a comparable state of finish. The respondents are then asked to leaf through the various advertisements or pages and comment on what they see.

Potter and Lovell[2] suggest that 'Advertisers believe . . . that they can get at least an inkling of what is going on in the mind of the informant when he first sees a test ad. They also believe that they can usually, on the basis of their experience, tease this out from attitudes that are subsequently assumed and later rationalizations of first comments'.

Reactions to test folders may be obtained through group discussions (*see* Section 17.2.1), mini-groups (about four people in each), individual depth interviews or semi-structured interviews. The latter means that although there is not a formal question and response type of questionnaire, the interviewer does none the less lead the interviewee through a series of set topics, whilst still allowing the comment to be free and 'unstructured'.

This approach is likely to be used if quantitative results are required.

TV advertising is similarly tested by showing people a simulation of the finished result along with other commercials and getting people's reactions and comments. Here, what is meant by a simulation can vary quite considerably, ranging from a static story-board showing scenes from the commercial with the script in written form, through to video-taped commercials using non-professional actors and fairly simple visual devices. In between comes the commonly used 'animatic' film which is made by shooting a series of pictures from a specially drawn storyboard. This can produce an almost moving picture with a varying length of focus and adding a sound track produces a fairly convincing 'commercial'.

There are various ways of getting people's reactions:

1   *Theatre tests.* Informants are invited to a studio or cinema ostensibly (to quote from Potter and Lovell) 'to give their opinions of pre-release films'. Interspersed in the programme are TV commercials and these are assessed by questionnaires. The programme may last for two or three hours, so that to some extent it is possible to measure 'attitude shifts' as a result of seeing the commercials. Since many people's reactions can be tested to several commercials in one sitting, this can be a very economic way of obtaining quantitative reactions. However, getting the right sample of people to attend can be difficult and it can be argued that viewing commercials on a large screen with many other people is an artificial situation.

2   *Hall Tests.* Here the commercials are screened (typically with video-tape on TV screens) to smaller numbers of people who are invited in from the street into, for example, a church hall or a room in an hotel at short notice. Sampling is easier and interviewing more easily controlled (because there are fewer people at a time) but the duration is normally only 20 minutes or so, which is the maximum people can be persuaded to 'take off' from their shopping etc.

Both theatre tests and hall tests give quantitative results. Showings can also be given on a group discussion basis in order to get qualitative reactions.

17.4 Testing campaign results

Tests can clearly also be carried out after the advertising campaign has started running and at various stages while it is running. Typically, Alan Hedges urges caution, pointing out that it is generally 'difficult to find out what effect is due to a particular media campaign rather than to other causes'. He points out also that, 'The whole market is in a state of flux. In order to see what our advertising is doing we must be prepared to make assumptions about what would otherwise have been happening. For example, sales might have fallen anyway, in which case in measuring the effect of advertising we should need to look not for positive change but a reduction in the negative effect.'

The outcome of this caution is that:

1   We need to analyse rather carefully (*see* Chapter 16) how we think advertising is likely to be functioning and what contribution it might make before deciding to measure attitudes, image perception or what-ever.

2   Measurement is likely to have to be:
     (a) looking at various aspects not just one
     (b) carried out on a continuing, rather than a once and for all basis – since measuring *change is* likely to be more important than estab-lishing absolutes
     (c) wherever possible controlled tests – where changes in advertising can be isolated from the other factors – should be used

In a key passage, Hedges sums up as follows:

What can usefully be done is to monitor the overall progress of the brand in the market place without necessarily trying to pin down the precise contribution of different spheres of marketing activity. This should be done by taking quantitative surveys fairly frequently and continuously if it is to be of any real use. Checks need to be taken once a quarter or more often. Each check does not necessarily have to be large enough to provide highly precise estimates on its own, and adjacent time periods can be grouped for more sophisticated analysis. But frequent checks allow continuous trend lines to be built up so that changes over a period of one or two years can be examined. If monitoring is carried out only on an annual basis several years are necessary to establish any sort of trend data. Of course the desirable frequency should depend on the speed with which the particular market is expected to change and the period over which results are expected. Nothing is more frustrating than looking at a long series of checks which imply that nothing is happening simply because they are too frequent relative to the reaction time of the market. Indeed I have known companies to be panicked into changing course long before they might rea-sonably have expected their advertising to bite simply because they were making very frequent measurements all registering no change.

On the other hand more companies make the opposite mistake and monitor too infrequently. They can tell whether things are better or worse than three or four years ago, but they have no idea whether their position is currently improving or deteriorating.

The subject matter of these checks must depend in detail on the market and on the general campaign strategy. They will usually need to include measures of brand awareness, general disposition towards the brand, brand and product images on relevant dimensions and purchasing and usage behaviour, with suitable demographic or other analysis meas-ures. It will normally be important to cover the brand and its principal competition in the immediate product field, but it may often be useful to include brands or products from neighbouring product fields where there is likely to be fairly direct competition with them –

even though at first sight they may appear to be physically dissimilar and members of different product categories. For example, anyone monitoring a campaign for (say) potato crisps may well (in certain phases of the market development) need to monitor confectionery consumption, which might at first not appear to be very closely related.

The monitoring questionnaire should certainly include questions which will enable the advertising target group to be taken out for separate analysis, and there will be occasions when the monitoring research can be confined to the target group alone.

It will also obviously need to include measures which relate directly to the intended effects of the advertising (or indeed to any feared and undesirable side-effects).

Where the job of the advertising is to change the identity of the brand, for example, we shall need to have image measures covering the areas of change; and probably others covering some of the areas which may change unintentionally as a side-effect of the campaign.

One of the problems of measuring image changes is that our images are composed of subtle nuances and shades of meaning which may elude the gross measures we try to apply. Careful piloting research is called for, and also a willingness to tolerate a high level of apparent redundancy in our scales and question batteries. Meaning is elusive and language is clumsy and imprecise. We must be ready to have a number of scales covering very similar topics if we are to disentangle the difference between a brand being; inexpensive; a bargain; cheap and nasty; less expensive than expected; cheap in capital outlay, cheap in running costs, etc.

Something which is often measured with arguably more harmful than beneficial effects is advertising awareness or advertising recall. Unless there is some very good and specific reason for wanting to know this it is probably better not to do so. To begin with it takes up questionnaire space which can certainly be better devoted to something more profitable (anyone who finds he has spare space on a monitoring questionnaire has very probably not really thought out what he needs to measure).

Secondly, really reliable measures of advertising awareness are very difficult, since people's general notions about which campaigns they have seen bear little relation to any kind of reality. There is a good deal of confusion between campaigns, a general tendency to imagine that one has seen advertising for well-known brands, and so on. It is possible to try to 'prove' recall, but this is difficult and expensive if done properly, and in any case only removes a small proportion of the uncertainty.

Thirdly, it is very difficult to know what to do with advertising awareness measures when you have them. How high would you expect them to be? Does it matter much whether they are high or low? Are you trying to get people to remember your advertising, or to buy your product? To devise advertising which people will remember is child's play. To devise advertising which will help to sell products is more difficult. Are we not interested in the latter rather than the former? In practice measures of advertising awareness are either ignored or give rise to quite irrelevant worries which are prone to divert attention from the real problems.

Much the same applies to shorter-term advertising recall or 'impact' measures – 24 hour or 7-day studies of supposed advertising impact. Again these should only be used if there is a real problem which their use can help with, and not in a general attempt to 'take the temperature' of the advertising.

One outcome of the recognition (see the beginning of this section) that advertising is only one factor in the market situation is that ideally *all* the

relevant factors need monitoring. Section 16.2 highlighted the importance
of influenza epidemics on Lucozade sales. It is well known that summer
temperatures have a tremendous effect on sales of beer, soft drinks and ice-
cream. Such things need to be monitored and related to sales figures. Brand
share trends (obtainable in many instances from retail audits) and competitive marketing activities need also to form part of the information system.

Analysis of the mass of data that becomes involved in this kind of situation demands very sophisticated techniques of statistical analysis.

17.4.1 Econometrics

A central idea of statistics is that of *correlation*. A correlation exists when
two factors in a given situation are related to each other e.g. the taller a
person is the heavier they tend to be (all other things being equal). The
term *regression* is connected with this. If we plot the height and weight of a
series of individuals we get a series of points on a graph. Through these we
can draw a line of 'best fit'. This is called the 'regression line' and is an indication of the way in which any particular increase in height is accompanied
on average by a related increase in weight – the steeper the slope of the
line, the greater the regression.

Multiple regression is the technique of assigning relative significance
(based on statistical analysis) to a series of interrelated factors e.g. a
person's weight is due not only to height but also to other factors such as
age, occupation, life-style, eating habits, etc.

The availability of computers to handle the vast amount of data
involved has enabled a series of factors to be analysed together even when
the inter-relationships become complex. The various factors are first
analysed statistically (regression analysis), then a mathematical model is
constructed which expresses these inter-relationships. Computers can then
be programmed to carry out the necessary calculations which enable us to
predict what effect a change in one of the related factors will have on the
others e.g. how will a change in the weather or an increase in advertising
expenditure affect sales.

This description makes the process sound extremely precise. In fact
there are problems. Statistics normally predict probabilities, not certainties.
Because of the many factors that go to produce the end result of sales, not
all of them can be disentangled precisely, however much sophisticated
regression analysis is carried out – hence judgements have to be made and
the end result is a function of these judgements (another way of saying
informed guesses) as well as of precise measurement and calculation.

'Modelling', as it is called, has, however, come a long way since this
book was first written and is now in common use by many large advertisers. Broadbent, in *Accountable Advertising* (Admap Publications,1997)[3],
gives an extensive and understandable review of the techniques and their

value. He accepts that because of the complexities that affect responses to advertising, measurement is unlikely to be always precise and the models will often be approximate. He suggests that we should

> ... *use the results of regression analysis with caution, but still use them. I do not claim that marketers enjoy the certainties, such as they are, of the laboratory. If you have better data (from an experiment with individual stores, for example), use that in preference. If the suggested results of a regression offend common sense, reject them. But if you have no better guidance and the findings look sensible − it is foolish not to make them part of your decision-making.*

The Broadbent book is an invaluable review of the current approach to the whole field of advertising measurement. Further valuable insight can be gained by studying the case histories in the annual volumes of *Advertising Works*[4] (often referred to affectionately as *Adworks*) published annually by the IPA.

17.5 Advertising research and the scale of immediacy

Section 16.11 referred to Stephen King's 'scale of immediacy'. In the same article there referred to, King briefly relates methods of research to the types of advertising according to the scale. It is a valuable pragmatic approach to what kind of research is worth doing. As King puts it:

> *It seems distinctly easier to discuss which advertising research measures are best, if one can work out which is the most important role for advertising. To look at it very simply indeed:*

> *Direct. Post-exposure, the old familiar direct response measures of keyed advertisements. Pre-exposure, small-scale simulations, in time working out weighting (or aiming-off) factors.*

> *Seek information. Same as Direct.*

> *Relate to own needs, etc. We need some way of measuring 'impact' here, to get a hint of whether there is a what a good idea or an I must try that response. I think it might have to be qualitative research, but it could be more purposively directed than usual.*

> *Recall satisfactions. We know that diary studies work here but they could be impossibly expensive. There is some evidence that first brand coming to mind or brand choice from constant sum scales may be measuring the mind-jogging effect.*

> *Modify attitudes. The changes here are likely to be so sensitive that it is hard to see anything other than qualitative, diagnostic research helping pre-exposure decisions. Post-exposure, continuous attitude research.*

Reinforce attitudes. At this level, I think the most one could hope to do pre-exposure is eliminate elements from advertising that are dissonant with the existing brand personality, through sensitive qualitative research. Post-exposure, it seems unlikely that any research will ever positively link individual advertisements with reinforcing attitudes. It can only be done, with great leaps in interpretation, for whole campaigns over long periods. And the measures will have to be of the intrinsic worth of a brand as a totality – maybe through blind versus named product tests.

17.6 The simpler situations

The complexities we have been considering arise from the need to disentangle the effect of advertising from all the other things impacting on the customers – from competitors' activities and price differentials to social change and the weather. Sometimes, however sales can *only* be due to advertising. Direct mail calling for an immediate telephone or postal purchase is an example. Led by Direct Line, it became increasingly common during the 1990s to sell insurance and other financial products through responding by telephone to television advertising.

With the development of the Internet this is likely to develop much further. In the March 1998 issue of the magazine *Revolution*, the magazine for new-media marketing, there was an article headed 'Internet advertising shows its mettle'. The article quoted research indicating that '41 per cent [of Internet users] said they had considered buying on the high street after seeing an Internet ad while 24 per cent said they actually did buy something on the high street after seeing it on the web. Significantly the article goes on to say that this is three times the number who bought something on the Net after seeing the ad: *'Part of the reason for this is that it is not that easy to buy on the Net'*. Only 35 per cent of web sites '… were set up to do business …'. Once more of them are, it should be easy to relate sales to advertising expenditure on what promises to be an increasingly important way of doing business.

17.7 Summary

1   Measuring advertising effectiveness must be a planned and continuous activity.
2   It should be carried out:
     (a) at the stage of strategy planning
     (b) at the stage of advertising development
     (c) when the campaign has been exposed
3   Research, especially at the second stage, will often be of a qualitative nature.

4   A wide range of attributes can be measured (impact, image, recall, etc.) and it is important to be clear which are the key factors.
5   In order to get an accurate picture of the effect of advertising on the final market situation many other factors must be monitored.
6   This leads ultimately to the statistical analysis of all relevant factors and to the econometrics approach.
7   Stephen King's 'scale of immediacy' is a useful pragmatic approach to the kind of advertising research that is valuable in practice.

17.8 References

1 Hedges, Alan, *Testing to Destruction*, IPA, 1982.
2 Potter, Jack and Lovell, Mark, *Assessing the Effectiveness of Advertising*, Business Books, 1975.
3 Broadbent, S., Accountable Advertising, Admap Publications, 1997.
4 Broadbent, S., (Ed) *Advertising Works 1 and 2*, IPA 1981 and 1983.

17.9 Further reading

The last two books above between them give a very comprehensive overview of the considerations and techniques involved in testing advertising.

The papers of The European Society for Opinion and Marketing Research (ESOMAR) seminars and the *Journal of the Market Research Society* provide excellent sources of current examples.

Advertising Works. These biennial IPA publications contain a number of advertising campaigns where details of research methods are given.

Grant, Sunny and Housden, Matthew, *Marketing Research for Managers* (Butterworth-Heinemann), gives an excellent overview of all aspects of marketing research.

17.10 Questions for discussion

1   Discuss the value of discussion groups as a technique useful in developing effective advertising campaigns.
2   What research methods are available to enable a marketing manager to evaluate the effectiveness of his advertising programmes?
3   For any consumer product of your choice outline briefly the various types of testing you might use to ensure that the most effective advertising was developed.
4   Write notes on the following kinds of market research, emphasizing

the differences between them in terms of cost, likely accuracy and timing in relation to a given campaign:

(a) usage and attitude study;
(b) corporate image study;
(c) advertisement testing.

5   Argue the case for continuous assessment of all advertising right through the life of a product.

Part 4

Advertising internationally

Chapter 18

Media and other services around the world

'The basic principles of media planning and purchasing are generally the same whether the planner is operating in New York or New Delhi ...However, the application of these principles will vary from one market to the next.'

Barbara Mueller, *International Advertising*, Wadsworth Publishing Co, 1995

By the end of this chapter you will:

* Appreciate how the practice of advertising varies around the world.

18.1 The UK is not the world

In the Preface to this book it was clearly established that mainly UK figures and examples would be used. This was because it is very difficult to make any sense of advertising in the abstract. Facts and figures have to be used. It seemed sensible to make them consistent with each other and UK sources were the obvious choice because

1   The book is being written in the UK.
2   Ample facts and figures about the UK are available.
3   It is not too untypical of the major areas of the world where advertising is well developed.
4   In some aspects (the voluntary control system and education for example) UK practice has set standards which other countries follow.

However, it is perfectly clear that many readers and students in other countries will find themselves in a situation which has quite considerable differences from the UK. Equally those operating from the UK will encounter those differences as soon as they get involved in advertising to other countries. This chapter attempts to indicate some of the main areas in which the differences will be encountered. Chapter 19 deals with the management and control of advertising on an international basis.

18.1.1　Some obvious media differences

An extract from a 'Marketing in Europe' supplement to the journal *Marketing* in October 1980 makes the point dramatically:

> Television is of far greater importance in the UK advertising scene than in any other major European country, where the press is generally predominant. In only one major European country – the UK with 34% – and five minor countries – Greece 48%, Portugal 41%, Austria 36%, Eire 34% and Spain 27% – does television account for more than 20% of advertising expenditure. The comparable figure for West Germany is 15% and for France 16%. There is no TV advertising in Sweden, Norway or Denmark. In Belgium there is officially none, but RTL (Radio-Television-Luxembourg) has a cable service into the country.

(An ISBA International Newsletter in March 1983 referred to a 30 per cent tax on all TV advertising in Greece 'in an effort to channel more advertising money into the stricken Greek press'.)

The reason for this difference has little to do with the number of homes that have TV sets or the effectiveness of TV as a medium. It is much more a function of the way that TV advertising is allowed (or not allowed) to operate. The *Marketing* article continues:

> In West Germany TV advertising is in four blocks of between three and eleven minutes in length ... and appearing only between 5.30 p.m. and 7.30 p.m. on one channel and between 6 p.m. and 8 p.m. on the other. Advertising needs to be booked for the following year by the end of September and demand is roughly twice supply.

In France and Italy similarly demand for TV advertising time exceeds supply.

By contrast in Central America TV advertising is around 50 per cent of expenditure with radio another 15.9 per cent in 1980. Here the main reason is that a low literacy rate means that TV is the only mass medium (it has close on 90 per cent coverage in urban areas).

These situations of course are not static. In 1998, the *International Journal of Advertising* was saying: 'Since 1980, television spending has increased by 200% in real terms while newspapers and magazines have grown by only 53% and 21% respectively ... In 1980 the press accounted for nearly three-quarters of the money spent on advertising in the European Union and television's share was just 16.3%.' In 1996, television accounted for 321.2 per cent of the total, newspapers' share had fallen from

46.4 per cent to 39.3 per cent and magazines from 27.1 per cent to 18.8 per cent.

It is not difficult to see how these changes may well continue with, for example, the development of cable and satellite TV and of the Internet.

Similar developments are taking place in other parts of the world – often even more dramatically. As China takes its rapid march into a new economic future, the number of newspapers has grown from 188 in 1980 to 2,335 in 1996. Similar increased availability of other media has facilitated a corresponding growth in advertising expenditure.

Hong Kong has often led the way in the region and may continue to do so now that it has become a Special Administrative Region of China. It was reported in *Media International* in October 1997 that a cable TV provider started service in June and that Hong Kong Telecom is set to mount the world's first full-scale video on demand service.

18.2 Advertising services around the world

Whether or not the same media are available, other things will almost certainly vary.

First of all the quality of the media will vary. Newspapers and magazines will be superbly produced in some countries but in others badly written and poorly printed on low-quality paper. Television, in some African countries for example, may look like a rather bad amateur video production.

Similarly the support services may vary in quality or not be available at all. Good quality printing may be expensive and/or difficult to find. Film-making facilities may not exist or be of very low quality. Statistical information is often in short supply and of dubious accuracy. Even population figures may be available as estimates only in countries with a large and backward rural population and poor communications. In Brazil, a country with highly developed industrial and commercial cities like Rio de Janeiro and Sao Paulo, new Indian tribes are still being discovered in the Amazon jungle and a visitor to Sao Paulo in the late 1970s was given population figures for the city ranging from 10 to 14 million. The latter discrepancy is partly because the 'concrete jungle' city of high-rise apartment blocks is surrounded by 'Favellas' (shanty towns) full of people from the rural states to the north of Sao Paulo State who have come to seek work. Not only are these people hard to count but their numbers change on a day-by-day basis, and furthermore government officials and business executives are reluctant to admit their existence, at any rate to foreigners. Yet in the same city highly sophisticated research teams can provide the same kind of service as would be available in the UK or the USA (concept testing, for example, is used as a planning tool as a matter of course).

Table 18.1 *Five multinational advertising agencies in Beijing*

Agency	1995 world rank	Year of establishment	Foreign investment	Major accounts
BBDO	5	–*	joint-venture (51%)	Apple Computer, Bayer, Sara Lee, Volvo
Leo Burnett	6	1995	representative office (100%)	Philip Morris, McDonald's, United Airlines, Carlsberg
DDB Needham	7	–*	joint-venture (61%)	Henkle, Volkswagen Audi
Grey	8	1992	joint-venture (70%)	Smithkline Beecham, Nokia, Goldstar, Procter & Gamble
DMB&B	17	1991	representative office (100%)	Mars, GM, Bausch & Lomb

Note: *Although I did not obtain the exact years of their establishment, both BBDO and DDB Needham were set up in 1991.
Source: Interviews with advertising executives in Beijing, spring 1996. For 1995 world rank, see *Advertising Age*, 15 April 1996, p. s15.
This table is taken from the following article: Jian Wang, The foreign ad industry in China, *The International Journal of Advertising*, 1997.

The differences and difficulties are made easier to handle because in most major centres of population and commerce there are advertising agencies of a very high standard. Many of these are offshoots of (most frequently) American or (sometimes) UK agencies. As multinational companies have opened up markets in various countries, they have sought help in producing advertising which combines the best of international know-how with a high degree of local knowledge. American companies in particular have looked to their home-based agency to provide such service and this they have done, either by starting an office from scratch or by purchasing a local agency already in existence.

In China, for example, the number of advertising agencies grew from four in 1990 to 180 in 1993 and now includes many of the large international agencies (*see* Table 18.1).

However, this is not universally the case. A feature in *Media International* of October 1997 lists the leading agency networks operating in Africa (*see* Table 18.2), but also comments:

> ... across a continent of 58 nations, ad agencies are still thinly spread. Most markets are too small and undeveloped to support a full-service agency, so many networks adopt a 'hub and spoke' strategy, setting up a full agency in regional centres such as Nairobi, Harare, Abidjan or Lagos and satellite offices in surrounding countries.

Table 18.2 *Leading African networks*

Billings	Total billings 1994 (US$m)	Number of countries	Number of of staff
Ogilvy & Mather	190	16	960
Lindsay Smithers–FCB	125	7	448
McCann-Erickson	100	19	620
Young & Rubicam	95	5	481
Ammirati Puris Lintas	75	9	450
Saatchi & Saatchi	65	16	400
Grey Advertising	50	8	39
J. Walter Thompson	45	8	488

Source: Media International, October 1997

Table 18.3 (the World's top 50 ad agencies) indicates how world-wide agency activity is concentrated, with the once-dominant American agency chains being challenged from London, Tokyo, Paris and elsewhere

Advertising Age International published in September 1997 a table under the heading 'World Brands' with the comment: 'This year the top 23 advertising agency networks are handling more than 500 clients in five or more countries as advertisers continue to align their business with fewer agencies world-wide.' This trend does not seem likely to end yet.

Largely because of this trend involving large multinational companies and their agencies, support services are also catching up rapidly in some regions. *Admap* of February 1997, for example, published an article by Andrew Green of Zenith Media on media research in the Asia Pacific region. Table 18.4 summarizes part of the discussion.

In spite of rapid development, Green comments that in terms of analytical software '... Asia is behind countries like the UK.'

18.3 Summary

1   In many other countries the advertising scene will be quite different from that in the UK where this book was written.
2   The relative importance of the various media shows considerable variation between one country and another.
3   The quality of media (e.g. printing standards) of available services (such as research) will also vary enormously.
4   However, there are quite strong trends towards equalizing standards, as multinational advertisers and agencies strive to achieve the same standards as they are used to 'at home'.

Table 18.3 World's top 50 advertising organizations

Rank 1996	Rank 1995	Ad organization	Headquarters	Worldwide gross income 1996	Worldwide gross income 1995	% chg	Capitalized volume 1996	Capitalized volume 1995
1	1	WPP Group	London	$3,419.9	$3,125.5	9.4	$24,740.5	$22,688.4
2	2	Omnicom Group	New York	3,035.5	2,708.5	12.1	23,385.1	20,805.4
3	3	Interpublic Group of Cos.	New York	2,751.2	2,465.8	11.5	20,045.1	17,621.1
4	4	Dentsu	Tokyo	1,929.9	1,999.1	-3.5	14,047.9	14,597.2
5	6	Young & Rubicam	New York	1,356.4	1,197.5	13.3	11,981.0	9,857.6
6	5	Cordiant	London	1,169.3	1,203.1	-2.8	9,739.9	10,021.9
7	9	Gray Advertising	New York	987.8	896.6	10.2	6,629.4	6,005.5
8	8	Havas Advertising	Levallois-Perret, France	974.3	924.4	5.4	7,295.1	6,931.4
9	7	Harkuhodo	Tokyo	897.7	958.6	-6.3	6,677.0	6,909.3
10	10	True North Communications	Chicago	889.5	805.9	10.4	7,040.9	6,358.1
11	11	Leo Burnett Co	Chicago	866.3	805.9	7.5	5,821.1	5,386.7
12	12	MacManus Group	New York	754.2	713.9	5.6	6,830.3	6,247.1
13	13	Publicis Communication	Paris	676.8	624.8	8.3	4,617.7	4,270.5
14	14	Bozell, Jacobs, Kenyon & Eckhardt	New York	473.1	404.5	17.0	3,675.0	3,050.0
15	15	GGT/BDDP Group	London	398.1	380.6	4.6	3,149.1	2,977.5
16	16	Dalko Advertising	Osaka, Japan	256.7	263.6	-2.6	1,853.4	1,998.3
17	17	Asatsu Inc	Tokyo	242.0	254.2	-4.8	1,904.8	1,958.8
18	19	Carison Marketing Group	Minneapolis	222.0	189.0	17.5	1,880.8	1,574.5
19	18	Tokyu Agency	Tokyo	214.0	231.1	-7.4	1,844.6	1,926.1
20	20	TMP Worldwide	New York	194.6	177.4	9.7	1,297.0	1,182.8
21	21	Dai-ichi, Kikaku	Tokyo	164.5	168.4	-2.3	1,249.0	1,291.0
22	22	Dentsu, Young & Rubicam Partnerships	Tokyo/Singapore	164.2	161.6	1.6	1,245.5	1,201.8
23	24	Chell Communications	Seoul	152.0	124.9	21.7	1,005.1	869.8
24	28	Abbott Mead Vickers	London	137.1	106.5	28.7	1,079.0	926.0
25	23	Yomiko Advertising	Tokyo	125.9	133.0	-5.3	1,106.3	1,149.5

26	25	I&S Corp.	Tokyo	124.7	124.9	-0.2	969.1	1,038.6
27	27	Gage Marketing Group	Minneapolis	122.5	108.5	12.9	816.8	723.8
28	26	Asahi Advertising	Tokyo	106.7	114.7	-7.0	692.8	757.1
29	36	Campbell Michun Esty	Minneapolis	94.2	79.2	19.0	785.2	633.2
30	31	Wilkens International	London	94.1	89.1	5.6	631.1	597.7
31	29	Man Nen Sha	Osaka, Japan	94.1	97.4	-3.4	608.8	630.9
32	35	DIMAC Direct	Bridgeton, Mo	88.8	80.7	9.9	452.0	396.3
33	53	CKS Group	Cupertino, Calif	86.4	49.1	76.0	548.1	364.8
34	33	Daehong Communications	Seoul	86.0	84.0	2.4	330.0	320.0
35	38	Oricom Inc	Seoul	85.0	76.6	11.0	280.0	249.6
36	34	Clemenger/BBDO Group	Melbourne	84.3	81.6	3.3	503.0	487.0
37	40	Bronner Slosberg Humphrey	Boston	83.2	67.5	23.3	554.9	450.2
38	30	Oricom Co	Tokyo	81.7	89.2	-8.4	547.9	599.8
39	51	Nelson Communications	New York	77.2	51.8	48.9	635.5	418.4
40	44	Wieden & Kennedy	Portland, Ore	75.0	59.4	26.3	625.0	475.0
41	37	Nikkelsha	Tokyo	74.9	77.3	-3.2	454.5	483.8
42	39	Hal Riney & Partners	San Francisco	74.6	68.8	8.6	622.0	550.0
43	47	Arnold Communications	Boston	73.1	57.7	26.7	551.2	425.5
44	32	Sogel	Tokyo	70.4	85.3	-17.5	458.1	563.4
45	43	LG Ad	Seoul	67.6	60.4	11.9	619.0	552.2
46	50	Hill, Holliday, Connors, Cosmopulos	Boston	66.5	52.6	26.4	443.6	351.0
47	52	Barry Blau Partners	Wilton, Conn	63.7	49.9	27.8	425.0	332.7
48	46	Duallibi, Petit, Zeragoza Propaganda	Sao Paulo, Brazil	63.0	58.1	8.4	269.9	251.2
49	55	Frankel & Co	Chicago	62.9	47.5	32.3	459.6	348.8
50	42	W.B. Doner & Co	Southfield, Mich	62.6	60.5	3.4	569.1	504.2

Source: Advertising Age

Table 18.4 *TV audience measurement: an overview*

Country	Operator	Coverage	Panel homes	Data collection	Start date
Australia	Nielsen	Metro + regional	1900/1750	Peoplemeters	1991/94
China	CSM	52 cities	11500	Diary	1996
	Nielsen SRG	Shanghai	300	Peoplemeter	1996
	SCMR	4 cities	1200	Diary	1992
Hong Kong	Nielsen SRG	National	300	Peoplemeter	1991
India	IMRB-MRAS	Mumbai/Delhi/Madras	720	Peoplemeter	1995
	IMRB	9 cities	1800	Diary	1986
	ORG-MARG	5 cities*	750	Peoplemeter	1995
	DART	33 cities	7300	Diary	1990
Indonesia	Nielsen SRG	5 cities	850	Diary	1991
Japan	Video Research	23 cities	5200	Set meter/diary	1962
Malaysia	Nielsen SRG	Peninsular Malaysia	660	Peoplemeter	1995
New Zealand	Nielsen	National	440	Peoplemeter	1990
Philippines	Nielsen SRG	Metro Manila	300	Peoplemeter	1994
	Various	10 provincial cities	7000 (2 sweeps)	FTF interview	1995
Singapore	Nielsen SRG	National	340	Peoplemeter	1994
South Korea	Nielsen SRG	Greater Seoul	275	Peoplemeter	1991
Taiwan	Nielsen SRG	National	500	Peoplemeter	1993
	Red Wood (plan)	National	1000	Peoplemeter	1997
	Red Wood	National	1000	Diary	1985
	Red Wood	Greater Taipei	350/day	Telephone	1983
	Rainmaker	National	850	Diary	1986
	Rainmaker	Greater Taipei	350/day	Telephone	1982
Thailand	Nielsen SRG	Bangkok/C. Thailand	340	Peoplemeter	1985
Vietnam	Nielsen SRG	4 cities	8000	FTF interview	1993

* ABC cable and satellite households only.
Source: Zenith media

18.4 Further reading

An earlier issue of the *International Journal of Advertising* (Vol. 1, No. 1, January–March 1982) reviews 'Trends in total advertising expenditure in Twenty-nine countries 1970–80'.

The IPA booklet is one of a number on *Advertising Conditions in ... –* mostly European countries. They provide a useful preliminary view although they will of course rapidly become out of date.

Much detailed information on media and services, sources of market research data, etc. is provided by the *Concise Guide to International Markets* published by Leslie Stinton and Partners in conjunction with the UK Chapter of the International Advertising Association.

The IAA itself provides valuable information to members on a regular basis, as does ISBA with its *ISBA International News.*

The magazine *Media International* is also an excellent way of keeping up-to-date on the international scene; changing rapidly as it does.

18.5 Questions for discussion

1   For any country of your choice highlight the differences in the relative importance of the main media as compared with the UK.
2   Obtain a recent copy of any of the 'international media' (such as *Time* or *The Economist*). Analyse the types of advertiser using the media and explore the probable reasons for their choice.
3   Nominate *two* countries and describe *five* major differences in marketing facilities available. Show the effect of these differences upon the marketing policies open to the manufacturer of a product of your choice.

Chapter 19

Advertising messages around the world

'Campaigns with some international application are estimated to make up 50% of today's advertising business.'

Rita Clayton, in 'Planning to go Global', *Admap*, October 1997

By the end of this chapter you will;

- Be aware of the development of global advertising, its strengths, and its problems;
- Understand how cultures and attitudes vary around the world and how we have to respond to those differences;
- Appreciate the factors involved in managing advertising on a global scale and the options that are available.

19.1 Global advertising – how far has it developed?

Rita Clifton started off the article quoted above: 'In the mid-1980s "globalisation" was still something of an experimental science ... But the situation in the late 1990s is far different.'

Representing the multi-national agency Saatchi and Saatchi, she is understandably up-beat. And there is no doubt that global advertising campaigns and global brands are developing rapidly. The establishment of McDonalds in Moscow and Beijing is simply part of a broader cultural trend where increasingly TV programmes like *Baywatch* or *Coronation Street* are watched avidly in many different countries and CNN news is establishing itself as a leading communication channel for most of the world.

The tables at the end of the previous chapter indicated a growing presence throughout the world of global advertisers and global agencies. What does this much used term 'global' signify? When a producer first decides to develop business outside its country of origin, it 'exports' its goods or services to reach customers in other countries. Eventually it may start to produce in some of those countries and becomes a 'multinational'. The ultimate is when it is producing and delivering throughout a large proportion of the world. It has then become a 'global' company.

Movement in this direction has developed at an increasing pace throughout the twentieth century and many people were seeing the trend strongly established as early as the 1960s. An important element in this was the increasing amount of travel as air transport developed, alongside the even faster development of communication through telephones, Teletext, facsimile (fax) transmission, radio and television, and, more recently the Internet and video-conferencing.

When people are trading with each other across national and language barriers, the question arises: to what extent can the message be the same and be expressed in the same way?

Business to business communication has always found this easier to achieve. An aeronautical engineer or CAD/CAM user is likely to be looking for much the same benefits and to have much the same attitudes wherever they are in the world. But with consumers of everyday household and personal products it may be more difficult. The increase in travel and communication, however, is changing this.

An ISBA booklet *International Marketing Communications*, published in 1991, assumed the need to keep a common message as far as possible but asked; '… is there some degree of flexibility? As much as to permit the creation of an individual campaign for each market?'

The disadvantages of creating an individual campaign for each market are clear: greater cost of creation and development and the strong possibility of the same customers receiving different messages as they travel the world or watch programmes generated elsewhere but beamed into their homes by satellite or via the Internet.

To quote Rita Clayton again: 'The most visible issue in globalising brands is still how far the packaging and advertising actually looks and feels the same. The key questions are **should** it be the same, **could** it be the same from the perspective of real people and how are they changing?'

19.2 The world customer

This was the title of an article in the *Harvard Business Review* in 1962 by Ernest Dichter[1], world-famous at the time as the guru of motivational research. 'The World is opening up', said Dichter. 'The Common Market will broaden into an Atlantic Market and finally into a World Market. In order to participate effectively in this progressive development of mankind, it is essential to have a creative awareness of human desire and its strategy throughout the world – to understand and prepare to serve the new World Customer'.

It makes interesting speculation and discussion to consider how far we have moved towards Dichter's vision of the world customer. Certainly there are signs of it. The author has in the past few years visited California, Brazil, East and West Africa and South East Asia, as well as various parts of Europe. Sitting in a practically indistinguishable hotel room watching a TV screen of similar make transmitting almost identical commercials for many of the same products it is often possible to wonder if there are any differences between one country and another apart from language – and not even always that. Yet move not very far from that hotel room and things may be very different indeed. How far different will vary enormously from one country to another.

In 1962 Dichter talked of many countries of the world progressively becoming potential markets for US goods 'as human desires break the barricades of centuries in South America, Africa and Asia'. He saw a 'revolution of the middle class' taking place and decided that, 'It is the degree of development of a large middle class which makes the difference between a backward and a modern country both economically and psychologically.' He went on to list six groups of countries based on this kind of analysis, using different attitudes to automobiles to illustrate his point:

Group 1 *The Almost Classless Society – Contented Countries,* mainly Scandinavia with almost everyone 'middle class', few really poor, few really rich. The car is strictly utilitarian and showing off with one's auto is not considered correct.

Group 2 *The Affluent Countries,* including the USA, West Germany, Switzerland, Holland and Canada, all tending towards the US situation. Thus 'whilst the German still uses his car for prestige purposes, in the United States the status value of cars has substantially diminished and has been shifted to other products and services such as swimming pools, travel and education . . . Cars are not pampered; they are expected to do their job.' In these countries, says Dichter, 'Few people starve and there is still room at the top'.

Group 3 *Countries in Transition* such as England, France, Italy, Australia, South Africa and Japan. 'These countries still have a working class in the nineteenth century sense. But this class is trying to break out of its bondage and join the comfortable middle class . . . Prestige still plays an important role . . . Cars are pampered in these countries. They are an extension of one's personality.'

Group 4 *Revolutionary Countries* include Venezuela, Mexico, Argentina, Brazil, Spain, India, China and the Philippines. 'In these areas large groups of people are just emerging from near-starvation and are discovering industrialization. Relatively speaking, there are more extremely rich people, a small but expanding middle class, and a very large body of depressed economic groups that are beginning to discover the possibilities of enjoying life through the revolution in industry. Automobiles are available only to a relatively small group. They are expensive and considered a luxury ... People want to show off.'

Group 5 *Primitive Countries*. 'The newly liberated countries of Africa and the remaining colonies ... only a very small group of wealthy indigenous and foreign businessmen, new political leaders and foreign advisers ... There is no real car market as yet'.

Group 6 *The New Class Society*. 'In Russia and its satellite countries there is emerging a class of bureaucrats who represent a new form of aristocracy, while everybody else represents a slowly improving, low middle class. There is an interest in prestige cars. All the bourgeois symbols of capitalist countries are being copied ... particularly those of the United States'.

Whilst some aspects of this approach creak a little 20 years on, and were not universally accepted even when written, one can to some extent accept the basic analysis. However, this approach assumes that countries are homogeneous and this may be very far from the case. In Brazil, for example, the highly industrialized state of Sao Paulo is very different in its level of development from some of the more agricultural states and especially from the largely undeveloped Amazon basin in the North. Even in the USA, California, and Southern California in particular, is very different from parts of the Mid-West or New England.

In some respects Dichter's predictions can be seen as strongly substantiated, e.g. in the new economic development of China. He could not have foreseen (who did?) the break-up of 'Russia and its satellite countries' but many of them are now eagerly entering the world of global brands and global products.

Another, slightly later, interview categorized similar markets not in terms of countries but by types of people.

19.3 Consumer categories

This term was used by J. K. Ryans Jr[2] who suggested 'at least three broad categories of consumers based solely on their potential receptivity to the common advertising approach.'

1   *International Sophisticate*. Says Ryans ... 'there are at least a few people that might be termed 'world citizens' in most countries and

particularly in the Western World ... Such individuals, regardless of home base, would probably be as responsive to a universal campaign as would anyone with their same economic background and interests in the advertiser's own country. ' This smaller group of world citizens he sees being expanded by a larger group of middle- or high-income consumers 'who have a genuine interest and awareness for products, fashions and cultural activities other than their own.' This interest will have been developed by travel, access to international media, etc.

2   *Semi-sophisticates.* This much larger group 'includes many of the burgeoning number of middle- and high-income individuals found in the United States, Western Europe, Japan, Canada and South America. Through limited travel, television or documentary programmes, reading or a variety of other ways, these people have begun to become interested in other lands and cultures.'

3   *Provincial.* These people 'have one characteristic in common; a lack of interest, appreciation or "feel" for the non-domestic'.

This recognition that there are different types of people within a given country is almost certainly a more realistic and useful one than the kind of sweeping categorization of countries as 'developed' or 'industrialized' on one hand and 'undeveloped' or 'less developed' on the other. What advertisers then have to do is decide what kind of people they are addressing in each country.

Even this is in some respects too broad a categorization. The desire to own international fashion brands like trainer shoes and other designer clothing can be an aspiration for many people who are not necessarily sophisticated in other ways. But perhaps it depends on your definition of sophistication.

19.4 The hazards of advertising internationally

Ryans, in the article quoted in Section 19.3, is concerned with the problem of how far it is possible to use one advertising theme internationally with little or no change. He concludes '... a simple one-world customer does not exist at this time. Firms must exercise caution in adopting the same or similar advertising in multiple markets, especially if they are seeking a mass market.' He continues '... advances in communications, educations, etc. will ultimately create an atmosphere where the common advertising approach will be the rule rather than the exception. However, adoption of such an approach today is premature and advertisers should make use of it with caution.'

From an advertising point of view it can be a big difference. If we are concerned with advertising the same products in different countries, how similar are the people we are addressing and how similar will their responses be?

The ISBA booklet has a section headed 'Creative Opportunities and Constraints' which includes:

> The difference in complexity of advertising in various countries certainly imposes limitations of many kinds, but often the very fact that, for instance, it is inappropriate to feature people of one colour in commercials to be shown to audiences largely of another can prompt a creative switch into animation or non-human figures ...
>
> Restrictions exist on the use of children in commercials in most countries. The portrayal of women is increasingly under discussion, with moves in many countries for women no longer to monopolize domestic scenes or to exclude men from them.
>
> Cultural differences can very easily be overlooked. Cars are driven on different sides of the road. Understated English humour rarely finds an appreciative American audience. Year-end festivities are enjoyed in different ways on various dates. Local idiosyncrasies may not be obvious from head office.

An earlier version of the ISBA booklet quoted more detailed examples of some of these differences, e.g.:

- In certain Arab markets exposure of the female form is limited to the face.
- In certain European countries wedding rings are worn on the right hand.
- A Muslim will not consume pork and a Hindu beef.
- To the Chinese, white is connected with mourning.
- A brand name which is completely inoffensive to the English mind may either be extremely offensive or be otherwise quite inappropriate to speakers of another language.

19.5 Differences between markets

When considering the appropriate advertising approach for different countries, and in particular when deciding whether to use a common theme or a number of different ones, various facets of each market need to be considered in detail. Wilmshurst[3] suggests:

> First comes the obvious differences of language, culture pattern, distribution methods, advertising media and the like. Second, there is a difference that is not so obvious and therefore much more important to come to terms with – what James A. Lee has called the 'self-reference criteria'. Unconsciously we all see things from a particular viewpoint, according to our own cultural background. Carrying out an unbiased analysis and coming to clear-headed decisions about markets necessitates stepping outside this frame of self-reference.

These two things together (really they are the same thing viewed from two different levels) mean that the collection and analysis of facts about markets becomes overwhelmingly important. Although, if we are living in a particular country, we can always make use of more knowledge, there is much we already know. Just as we acquire our native language almost unconsciously, so, and in similar ways, we learn to sense how people react to certain things, and how best to present things to them. Similarly, we develop an awareness, at least in broad principle, of how advertising media function, what the distributive system is, how people shop. Take us outside the country we are most familiar with, and many of these assumptions will no longer apply. And the danger is we may not even realize that we are making assumptions.

So in considering advertising plans for countries we are not familiar with, a detailed and cold-blooded analysis is necessary.

19.6 Differences in the advertising 'climate'

As we go from one country to another a number of differences will appear, which may impinge on the kind of advertising which is:

(a) possible
(b) most effective

Attitudes to advertising
Some countries are much more receptive to advertising and relaxed as to the form it takes than others. In Section 9.2 we saw that the extent and type of legal and voluntary constraint of advertising varies considerably from one country to another.

Language and culture
Advertising must speak not only in the language of each country (sometimes of particular regions of the country) but also in the idiom and thought-patterns within which the nationals of that country express themselves. For example, Australia, Nigeria and India all use the English language extensively but Nigerian 'English' can be very hard for an Englishman to understand clearly because although the words and grammar are mainly identical, they are used with different nuances and to express different attitudes. Brash Australian everyday speech would be totally inappropriate in the *Straits Times,* the main English language newspaper of Malaysia. Similarly Spanish is not used in precisely the same way in neighbouring South American countries (and certainly you must remember that Brazilians speak Portuguese). Advertising addressed to women in some countries (for household durables for example) would have to talk to men in others.

Imagery

Design standards and the use of visual symbols can vary considerably. Distillers Co. used the theme 'You Can Take a White Horse Anywhere' for its White Horse Whisky. The illustrations had, for example, a white horse peering through a bathroom window – a pleasant and memorable whimsicality in some countries, a rather baffling juxtaposition of ideas in others. Even the classic Esso 'tiger', probably the most famous of all international themes, had to be modified in some countries, so as to be more appealing (more friendly, less fierce). Some countries are used to very basic visual treatments, others expect something highly sophisticated.

Media

As we saw in Chapter 18 the availability and relative importance of the various media alter considerably from one country to another and may force a change in the approach (e.g. because a campaign devised with TV in mind may not work in the press in countries where TV does not reach a wide enough audience).

Services

The standard of advertising agencies, market research, etc. can vary widely and may inhibit what would otherwise be possible.

Acceptability of the 'foreign'

Some countries have a highly antagonistic approach to imported goods – at least in certain categories. In other cases a foreign brand name may be regarded as prestigious, chic or simply reassuring. In Brazil there are locally produced whiskies which are perfectly acceptable to the palate of a moderately discerning English drinker of Scotch whisky. But no self-regarding senior Brazilian executive would buy anything but vastly more expensive imported Scotch.

However, Lipson and Lamont[4] report that 'In Africa, when English or French language descriptions were given up in favour of local languages, many Africans refused to buy the products with the new labels for fear that they were getting inferior products. This problem is particularly acute for marketers in the food and beverage industries'.

19.7 Advertising ideas that travel

When the situation is suitable, some ideas travel. This is when both theme and presentation do not need to be changed and remain acceptable in a number of different countries. There are some famous campaigns that fall into this category:

Avis Rent-a-Car for example transferred its successful 'We try harder' theme from the United States (in translation) throughout Europe and found it equally successful.

Esso's 'Put a Tiger in Your Tank' was successfully used even more extensively, indeed virtually world-wide. Minor modifications such as in France 'Mettez un Tigre dans votre Moteur' enabled the basic idea to travel, although it was apparently not totally successful in Sweden where the whimsical humanized tiger was treated rather sceptically. (Section 19.6 referred to the minor 'cosmetic' changes that were made in the way the tiger was drawn.)

Coca Cola was able to use the same theme based on the song 'I want to teach the world to sing ...' by combining it with film of people of obviously different nationalities all enjoying a happy life-style in which 'Coke' played a part. The same transmission of American culture, very appealing to hordes of aspiring young people throughout the world, accounts for the similar widespread use of advertising themes for Levi jeans and Marlborough cigarettes.

The McDonald's Golden Arches are recognized throughout the world.

An IAA Newsletter (May 1983) 'Report on International Advertising' referred to a number of Unilever products. Lux toilet soap is 'advertised in well over a hundred countries using the international film star creative positioning'. Impulse perfumed deodorant 'is now advertised in over 60 countries with a common creative strategy'. Said Don Staddon of Unilever's Marketing Division which made the presentation 'Good ideas have legs and can move'.

What these examples have in common is:

1   A very simple theme containing an idea which is easily grasped.
2   A product (or products in Philips' case) used by similar people in similar ways to satisfy the same needs.

It is for the second reason that industrial – business-to-business advertising normally crosses frontiers quite readily. Electronics design engineers or paper mill managers work on the same principles and have the same problems wherever they are and therefore welcome the same benefits presented to them in the same way.

Things get much more difficult when people in different countries perceive the same product in different ways. Thus toothpaste may be purchased for cosmetic reasons (shiny white teeth or breath control) or for health reasons. One person's everyday item is a luxury item for someone at a different level of economic development: or operating in a different culture pattern. A sewing machine might have to be presented as a basic piece of household equipment in some cases, as an aid to creative leisure activity in others.

A very highly regarded campaign in the UK is; the 'Singapore Girl' TV commercials for Singapore Airlines, which suggests the pleasant welcoming cabin service for which the airline is justly famous. However, in its South East Asia home territories, the airline's main competitors (Garuda of Indonesia, MAS of Malaysia, Cathay Pacific of Hongkong) all provide similar standards of cabin service, so this is no longer a 'plus point' and the theme is not used in advertising.

British Airways on the other hand (perhaps because it *has* to) uses the same basic themes throughout the world, although it has recently diluted its 'Britishness' to a more international look through the way its tail fins are decorated with a series of ethnically based designs.

19.8 Is standardization possible?

Walsh[5] maintains that 'Complete standardization of all aspects of a campaign over several countries is rarely practicable – language difficulties alone would often make such an approach impossible.' Indeed, many of the campaigns held up as the ultimate in the international approach – Coca Cola and Esso's 'Tiger in your tank' for example – themselves involve language changes. We saw (*see* Section 19.7) how in the Esso case at any rate this involved a noticeable change of idiom from 'Put a Tiger in Your *Tank*' to 'Mettez un Tigre dans votre *Moteur*'. The tiger campaign also involved actually modifying the tiger itself in certain cases. So, as Walsh goes on to elaborate, 'Standardization' will probably mean *not* identical campaigns, but rather 'usually implies a common advertising strategy, a common creative idea and message, and, as far as possible, similar media.'

Since we have already established that media may well not be very similar and that cultural differences may well enforce creative changes, we are likely to be dealing with some form of compromise. It is not really a question of *either* totally standard campaigns *or* totally non-standard campaigns, but of where we need to be along a continuum between identical advertising at one extreme and absolutely different advertising at the other extreme. Those recommending balance are right and people arguing for one extreme or the other are usually doing 'special pleading' probably based on a few (sometimes one) untypical cases.

After examining 30 case studies S. Watson Dunn[6] concluded that the most successful were those where a balance was attempted between complete internationalization and complete localization.

19.8.1 The options

The advertising approach in a particular country of course does not stand alone, but derives from the overall marketing strategy. The basic choices of marketing strategy have not been better put than by W. J. Keegan[7] who suggests five possible strategies:

Strategy One: Same Product – Same Message World-wide

As a company begins to move into foreign markets, there are good arguments for pursuing a uniform strategy of international marketing. This approach involves offering exactly the same product with the same advertising appeals to each national market. The uniform approach has a number of advantages. Firstly, and by no means the least, is its simplicity. Its demands upon executive and marketing time are minimal. It requires no original analysis or data generation, only execution or implementation. Since the product itself is unchanged, engineering and manufacturing costs that would be incurred by product changes are reduced to zero. In sum, it is the lowest cost international product strategy ...

Strategy Two: Same Product-Different Communications

When a product fills a different need or is used differently under conditions similar to those in the domestic market, the only adjustment required is in marketing communications. Bicycles and motorscooters are illustrations of products which often fit this approach. They satisfy needs for recreation in the United States and for basic transportation in many parts of the world. Outboard motors are sold mainly to a recreation market in the United States and some other countries, while the same motors in many countries are sold mainly to fishing and transportation fleets ...

Strategy Three: Different Product – Same Communications

A third approach to international product planning is to extend without change the basic communications strategy developed for the home market, but to adapt the home product to local conditions. The different product–same communications strategy assumes that the product will serve the same function in foreign markets under different use conditions.

Esso followed this approach when it adapted its gasoline formulations to meet the weather conditions prevailing in market areas but used without change its basic message, 'Put a Tiger in Your Tank'. Since the tiger is an almost universal symbol of power, Esso was able to use its campaign in Europe, America and Asia ...

Strategy Four: Dual Adaptation

Certain market conditions indicate a strategy of adapting both product and communications. As a result of different market conditions and the product's serving different functions, this combines strategies two and three.

US greeting card manufacturers have faced this in Europe, where a greeting card provides space for the sender to write his own message in contrast to the US card, which contains a prepared message, or what is known in the greeting card industry as 'sentiment'. The conditions under which greeting cards are purchased in Europe are also different from those in the United States. In Europe, cards are handled frequently by customers, which makes it necessary to package the greeting card in cellophane ...

Strategy Five: Product Invention

The adaptation and adjustment strategies are effective approaches to international marketing when customer needs and the conditions under which products are used are similar to those in the home market. Unfortunately, this is not always the case, particularly in the less developed countries which contain three-quarters of the world's population. For these markets, the strategy should be invention or the development of an entirely new product designed to satisfy customer needs at a price within reach of the potential customer. This is a demanding, but – if product development costs are not excessive – a potentially rewarding product strategy for the mass markets in the middle and less developed countries of the world.

The Keegan article which gives many more examples, is the classic statement on this issue and concludes:

The choice of product and communications strategy in international marketing depends on three key factors:

1   *The product or service itself, defined in terms of the function or need it serves.*
2   *The market; defined in terms of the conditions under which the product is used, the preferences and ability to buy of potential customers.*
3   *The costs of adaptation and manufacture of these product-communications approaches.*

Only after analysis of the product–market fit and of company capabilities and costs can executives choose the most profitable international strategy.

It is point 3 that makes the international approach so appealing and generates so much argument in its favour. Not only does it cost hard cash to develop different advertising in different countries, but the cost in executive time can be enormous. There is the additional problem that really outstanding creative ideas are scarce and having found one, it is natural to want to exploit it to the full.

Don Staddon of Unilever argued that:

The task for the advertising person – whether client or agency – is to have the wit and wisdom to recognise the idea when it emerges. It is a gift given to few. Unilever achieves it after years of experience and does so by adhering to four simple principles:

1   *Organisation – open communication between the centre's coordinating units and the operating companies – training of staff involved with advertising and marketing.*
2   *Trust – a total trust between the centre and the operating companies. Each knows the other well and although the operating companies have final responsibility for profitability, on marketing matters the centre has been known to state 'This is only a suggestion but don't forget who's making it'.*
3   *Flexibility – the subtle relationship between the centre, the operating companies and its agencies.*
4   *Ideas cross national and cultural boundaries. There is no room for the well known cliché 'not invented here', beloved by so many international subsidiaries and their local agencies.*

19.8.2 The special case of business-to-business

Much of the discussion of this 'International' or 'Local' argument turn on consumer marketing examples, such as the oft-quoted Coca Cola and Esso. However, a rather different situation applies in the case of industrial or 'business-to-business' marketing. Here a number of the factors which may bedevil attempts to talk 'across borders' to consumers, no longer apply. In particular the cultural differences are very slight or non-applicable. A business man in New York or Jakarta may clean their teeth differently or have a different attitude to their car. But the benefits they derive from a machine tool or a word processor are likely to be much the same (although even here caution is necessary – saving labour for example may be highly desirable in some countries because of high wages, but far less so in others).

But, in general, as Trebus[8] points out, the similarities among business people in various countries far outweigh the differences. Because of the emphasis on detailed sales literature, operating manuals, etc., the problems in this field are the much more detailed practical ones, for example, of so designing brochures that illustrations can be printed in one 'run' for a number of countries, leaving space for overprinting the text in different languages which come out at widely differing lengths, although the content is the same.

19.8.3 The basis for the standardization decision

It will be clear from the above that each situation needs to be considered individually before deciding where to come down between 'international' and 'local'. Walsh[5] suggests the following factors should be taken into account:

(a) the general similarity or otherwise of the markets to be covered by the campaign, e.g. where cultural differences are limited, and income, education, etc. are similar, buying motives are likely to be the same;

(b) the nature of the product, e.g. industrial goods, for instance, are purchased more on objective criteria, and are therefore particularly suitable to a standardised approach, as are 'tourist' products such as films and petrol;

(c) local advertising agency standards, especially in terms of creativity, the importance of which has already been stressed, and which in some countries are of a low standard;

(d) government and other restrictions, which may prohibit certain copy themes or the use of certain media;

(e) the non-availability of media, e.g. television, in certain countries;

(f) media spillover possibilities;

(g) the availability of suitable international media.

19.9 Organization for international advertising

Answering the questions raised by Walsh (*see* Section 19.8) is related to another series of questions about how to organize and manage the programme which is decided upon. Majaro[9] indicates the following as being particularly important and suggests that answers must be found for all of them 'unless the firm is prepared to muddle its way through the maze of international communication problems in a haphazard way'.

> How far should Head Office concern itself with the communication activities of foreign subsidiaries?
> Should there be a centrally-formulated policy regarding corporate image, colouring, logotype, etc.?
> Who should determine communication budgets?
> In the event that budgets are determined centrally how should priorities be decided upon?
> Should the firm employ one international agency or allow each subsidiary abroad to make its own arrangements?
> Who should determine the communication mix?
> Where a number of languages are involved who is responsible for executing and controlling the translation work?
> Who should be responsible for measuring communication effectiveness?
> Where policy and objectives are centrally planned how does one cope with the variations in media availability?

The options and the associated-problems of implementing control are elaborated by Majaro[9] as follows:

> A firm that has opted for a radically centralised approach will probably find a strong planning team at the centre a fairly simple solution. Managers at the various local outposts will have to comply with requests for data emanating from the central planning personnel and will have to fill in all the forms that will be transmitted to them from time to time. Technically such an approach can work quite well, but it is seldom easy in such circumstances to attain maximum commitment to the planning task among distantly located personnel. At best they will co-operate with the whole process; at worst they will fill in the forms in a spirit of suppressed-distaste. Inevitably the quality of the 'inputs' in such circumstances cannot be of the highest!
>
> In a decentralised structure the position is very much more complex. By definition a decentralised firm allows freedom to the various operating units. Freedom means that each unit wishes to plan its own future. At the same time some central control of the planning process must exist unless the firm is prepared to allow each branch to grow wild. Referring back to the tree analogy, even a wood needs a keeper to ensure that the various trees in the wood do not interfere with each other's growth. Moreover somebody must collate the various sub-plans. Where should this be done and by whom?
>
> Different solutions have been developed for this problem by various companies. The success of these solutions seems to hinge around the personality the people selected for

the task of co-ordinating this vast input from all over the world. They cannot order or direct, they can only advise, persuade and communicate ideas. To be able to cope with such an ill-defined task one must possess personal attributes which virtually make such an individual capable of walking on water! Choosing the right person as a focal point is much more important than his location. In fact a few creative firms have decided to rotate the responsibility for collating and interpreting data in the process of preparing international marketing plans from one main market to another. The pay-off can be substantial: first it helps to develop promising managers in the art of planning in various parts of the world; secondly it helps to generate a better understanding of the planning philosophy in remote offshoots. Knowing that for the next two years the person responsible for planning the marketing effort is one of 'our boys' has a tremendous morale boosting value in a complex decentralised international situation.

It is very difficult to offer an easy formula which will enable every firm to decide how it should organise its corporate and marketing planning activities on an international basis. Every firm must evolve its own solution ...

19.9.1 Some practical problems

It must not be overlooked that, quite apart from the organizational aspects, there are some purely practical problems involved in international advertising. In particular timing and the translation problem.

1 *Timing.* If activities in a wide range of countries are to be tightly controlled, directed and co-ordinated then time must be built into the programme to allow for the sheer complexity of communicating what is required and for checking that instructions are correctly understood and implemented.
2 *Translation.* It is quite obvious that translating into a number of different languages may cause problems but the difficulties are all too commonly underestimated – as reading the instruction leaflets for a few important domestic appliances will quickly demonstrate.

  The instruction for an Italian portable toilet (for use by campers and caravanners in the UK) suggests, for example, 'Do not fill eccessively (sic) the upper tank ... ' and goes on 'When the rubbish has flown down, it is necessary to act on the piston-pump to wash-up the toilet'. (There is a legend in the advertising business that the original Japanese name for the new baby car from Toyota was Toyolet.)
  Two safeguards are necessary if this kind of hilarity is to be avoided:

1 Have the foreign-language version checked by sales staff in the country concerned (or better still by some of the customers!)
2 Have it translated back into the original language to ensure that it still says what was intended. (*See* Section 19.4.)

Dealing with translation in this way – desirable as it is – does of course add still more to the time problem and this is one of the reasons it is frequently not dealt with properly.

The ISBA booklet suggests the useful picture of a 'quadrilateral' arrangement. *See* Figure 19.1.

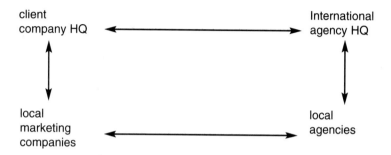

client
company HQ ⟷ International
agency HQ

local
marketing
companies ⟷ local
agencies

Figure 19.1 *The 'quadrilateral' relationship*

19.10 Summary

1   It is possible to see the various countries of the world as having reached different stages of development.
2   An alternative, perhaps more useful approach, is to recognize different types of people – at different levels of sophistication – existing in varying numbers throughout all countries.
3   Advertising in a number of countries demands taking careful note of these differences.
4   The differences may be categorized under the headings of:
   (a)   attitudes to advertising
   (b)   language and culture
   (c)   imagery
   (d)   media availability
   (e)   standard of services
   (f)   acceptability of the 'foreign'

19.11 References

1 Dichter, Ernest, 'The World Customer', *Harvard Business Review,* July–August 1962.
2 Ryans, J. K., Jr, 'Is it too soon to put a tiger in every tank?' *Columbia Journal of World Business,* March–April 1969. Included in *International Marketing Strategy,* [Ed] H. B. Thorelli (Penguin, 1973).

3 Wilmshurst, John, _The Fundamentals and Practice of Marketing_, William Heinemann, Second Edition, 1984.
4 Lipson, H. A. and Lamont, D. F., 'Marketing decisions facing international marketers in the LDCs', _Journal of Marketing_, Vol. 33, 1969. Included in _International Marketing Strategy_ – see reference 2.
5 Walsh, L. S., _International Marketing_, M & E Handbooks, 1978.
6 Watson Dunn, S., 'Case study approach in cross-cultural research, _Journal of Marketing Research_, February 1966.
7 Keegan, W. J., 'Five strategies for international marketing', _European Business_, January 1976. Included in _International Marketing Strategy_, [Ed] H. B. Thorelli (Penguin, 1973).
8 Trebus, Robert S., 'Reaching overseas business markets', _Industrial Marketing_, July 1978.
9 Majoro, Simon, _International Marketing_, George Allen & Unwinn, 1977.

19.12 Further reading

For a general review of international marketing, including communications, see _International Marketing_ by Paliwoda and Thomas (Butterworth-Heinemann, 1998).

Integrated Marketing Communications by Tony Yeshin (Butterworth-Heinemann, 1998) has an excellent chapter on the international aspects.

Principles of Marketing (European Edition) by Philip Kotler _et al._ (Prentice-Hall, 1996) has many illuminating case histories.

19.13 Questions for discussion

1 For any country of your choice, highlight the main cultural differences between it and the UK.

2 You have been asked by your client, a well-established multinational company, to prepare an advertising campaign for use in fourteen European countries from the Mediterranean to Scandinavia. Write a letter describing how you plan to proceed so that as much material as possible can be centrally produced.

3 Comment on Dichter's ideas on 'The World Customer'. These were developed in 1962. To what extent do you believe things are developing as Dichter predicted. If there are differences, what are they?

4 What advice would you give to a manufacturer of a range of men's toiletries contemplating international advertising for the first time (having just set up distribution facilities throughout North America, the EEC and the Middle East).

5 Select any advertising campaign which appears to be successful in a wide range of different countries and say what you believe to be the reasons for this success.

Index